Young v. Old

TRANSFORMING AMERICAN POLITICS
Lawrence C. Dodd, Series Editor

Dramatic changes in political institutions and behavior over the past three decades have underscored the dynamic nature of American politics, confronting political scientists with a new and pressing intellectual agenda. The pioneering work of early postwar scholars, while laying a firm empirical foundation for contemporary scholarship, failed to consider how American politics might change or to recognize the forces that would make fundamental change inevitable. In reassessing the static interpretations fostered by these classic studies, political scientists are now examining the underlying dynamics that generate transformational change.

Transforming American Politics brings together texts and monographs that address four closely related aspects of change. A first concern is documenting and explaining recent changes in American politics—in institutions, processes, behavior, and policymaking. A second is reinterpreting classic studies and theories to provide a more accurate perspective on postwar politics. The series looks at historical change to identify recurring patterns of political transformation within and across the distinctive eras of American politics. Last and perhaps most importantly, the series presents new theories and interpretations that explain the dynamic processes at work and thus clarify the direction of contemporary politics. All of the books focus on the central theme of transformation—transformation in both the conduct of American politics and in the way we study and understand its many aspects.

FORTHCOMING TITLES

Revolving Gridlock, David Brady and Craig Volden

Broken Contract? Changing Relationships Between Americans and Their Government, edited by Stephen C. Craig

Congress and the Administrative State, Second Edition, Lawrence C. Dodd and Richard L. Schott

Governing Partners: State-Local Relations in the United States, Russell L. Hanson

Midterm: The Elections of 1994 in Context, Philip A. Klinkner

The Divided Democrats: Ideological Unity, Party Reform, and Presidential Elections, William G. Mayer

Seeing Red: How the Cold War Shaped American Politics, John Kenneth White

New Media in American Politics, Richard Davis and Diana Owen

Extraordinary Politics: Dissent and Collective Action in the American System, Charles C. Euchner

The Irony of Reform: Roots of American Political Disenchantment, G. Calvin Mackenzie

The Tragic Presidency, Robert L. Lineberry

Young v. Old

Generational Combat in the 21st Century

Susan A. MacManus

WITH

Patricia A. Turner

WestviewPress

A Division of HarperCollinsPublishers

To Mrs. Leila K. Cofield
and Dr. Daisy Parker Flory

Their dedication to a democratic society
inspires the young and the old

Transforming American Politics

Copyright © 1996 by Westview Press, Inc., A Division of HarperCollins Publishers, Inc.

Published in 1996 in the United States of America by Westview Press, Inc., 5500 Central Avenue,
Boulder, Colorado 80301-2877, and in the United Kingdom by Westview Press, 12 Hid's Copse Road,
Cumnor Hill, Oxford OX2 9JJ

Library of Congress Cataloging-in-Publication Data
MacManus, Susan A.
    Young v. old : generational combat in the 21st century/Susan A.
MacManus.
        p.   cm.—(Transforming American politics series)
    Includes bibliographical references and index.
    ISBN 0-8133-1758-4—ISBN 0-8133-1759-2
(pbk.)
        1. Young adults—United States—Political activity.   2. Aged—
United States—Political activity.   3. Intergenerational relations—
United States.   I. Title.   II. Series.
HQ799.7.M23   1996
305.23'5—dc20   95-4950
                                                                                               CIP

The paper used in this publication meets the requirements of the American National Standard for
Permanence of Paper for Printed Library Materials Z39.48-1984.

10   9   8   7   6   5   4   3   2   1

Contents

PART THREE
DIFFERENCES IN PUBLIC POLICY PREFERENCES
AND PRIORITIES

PART FOUR
PROJECTIONS FOR THE FUTURE

Tables and Figures

Figures are located near their callouts within the chapters. Tables are positioned at the ends of chapters.

Tables

Figures

Acknowledgments

Thanks are due to a great many people for their assistance and encouragement. I am particularly indebted to the Times Mirror Center for The People & The Press and its director, Andrew Kohut, for making its national survey data accessible to researchers. Carol Bowman, research director, was never too busy to help me access key data and materials.

I am also greatly appreciative of the Florida data provided by the Survey Research Laboratory in the Policy Sciences Program at Florida State University. Suzanne L. Parker, director, and her assistant, Lisette Kelly, and graduate assistant, Chris Stream, spent many hours generating tables and data from the Florida Annual Policy Surveys and expediting data collection from other survey organizations. Suzanne's insights into the topic of intergenerational politics were extremely valuable.

I am also indebted to Warren J. Mitofsky of Mitofsky International for sharing his insights and data on the 1994 midterm elections and to the Roper Center for Public Opinion Research for helping me obtain some of its data broken down by age. Helpful materials were also supplied by the Lead . . . or Leave and the Third Millennium organizations, *St. Petersburg Times, The Miami Herald, The Tampa Tribune,* and the Associated Press.

I am deeply appreciative of the assistance of Patricia A. Turner, who spent untold hours preparing and editing the tabular and graphical materials included in this volume, developing survey instruments and taking charge of the data entry, gathering numerous other materials, and offering important recommendations on the book's content.

The University of South Florida's strong support of faculty sabbaticals created the opportunity for me to engage in this research. I am grateful to the Department of Government and International Affairs and the College of Arts and Sciences for endorsing my plan of study. Graduate assistant Lesa Chihak was very helpful in tracking down key materials and coordinating the distribution and receipt of a survey of Florida's legislators. Delores Bryant, office manager, made sure that persons with important information were able to locate me in Washington, D.C., where I spent a great deal of time working on this project.

A number of professional associations and institutions helped me acquire data for this endeavor. Thanks are due to the International City/County Management Association and its survey director, Woody Talcove, for providing age data on city council members across the United States. The Legislative Reference Bureau in Tallahassee helped me access information on the age profile of Florida legislators. The National Association of School Boards provided materials highlighting the changing age profiles of school board members throughout the United States. Paul Honig, demographic consultant, was very helpful in gathering U.S. Census Bureau socioeconomic and political data broken down by age. Dr. Lynn Casper of the U.S. Census Bureau provided the 1994 registration and voter turnout data.

Many professional colleagues spent a great deal of time and energy providing data and publications. My thanks go to professors Charles Hadley, the University of New Orleans; Harold Stanley, the University of Rochester; Charles S. Bullock III, the University of Georgia; Christine Day, the University of New Orleans; Anne Kelley and William Hulbary of the University of South Florida; and James Anderson, Texas A&M University.

Lynn Vavreck, graduate student at the University of Rochester, provided the cohort breakdowns of data from the University of Michigan National Election Studies in a timely, professional manner. It was a real pleasure to work with her.

The excellent editorial work of Barbara Langham, professional writer and editor, Austin, Texas, was invaluable. She has an extraordinary ability to make recommendations that make a book exciting to a wide range of readers. I am also extremely grateful to have benefited from excellent editorial assistance from Larry Dodd, editor of the Transforming American Politics series, and Westview's senior editor of political science, Jennifer Knerr. The recommendations and suggestions made by the book's reviewers, Robert Huckshorn and William Alonso, were excellent.

No book can be completed without strong support from friends and family. Marilyn Byram, neighbor, friend, and assistant, was always there when I needed books or materials shipped from Florida to Washington. Brigitta Keitgen assisted Patricia Turner in working on the graphics and tables. My dear friend Kim Strunz gave me a place to stay in Washington and made sure I took some time to enjoy the nation's capital. My cousins, their spouses, and kids were the source of constant encouragement upon my periodic returns home, as were my aunts and uncles, who often gave me ideas to pursue.

The special love of my parents, Cameron and Elizabeth; my sister, Lou; and my brother, Cameron; their spouses, Warren and Julia; and my nephew and nieces, Cameron, Allison, Susan, and Genelle, was the biggest inspiration for writing a book with an intergenerational theme. The intergenerational love and respect I have seen within my own family give me hope for our nation's future as our age profile changes drastically.

Susan A. MacManus

Acronyms

AARP	American Association for Retired Persons
ACIR	Advisory Commission on Intergovernmental Relations
AGE	Americans for Generational Equity
AIDS	acquired immunodeficiency syndrome
COLA	cost-of-living adjustment
CPS	Current Population Survey
FAPS	Florida Annual Policy Survey
HMO	health maintenance organization
NAFTA	North American Free Trade Agreement
NATO	North Atlantic Treaty Organization
NES	National Election Survey
NORC	National Opinion Research Center
PAC	political action committee
VAP	voting-age population

PART I

An Overview of the Changing Age Profile

1

The Nation's Changing Age Profile: What Does It Mean?

No amount of Grecian Formula can hide the fact that the population of the United States is rapidly graying. For decades, the United States was described as a nation of the young because the number of persons under the age of 20 greatly outnumbered those older than 65. But this is no longer true. Declining birthrates and longer life expectancies have aged our population. Suddenly, everyone from car makers, soft-drink manufacturers, and TV producers to political pollsters, pundits, and candidates have become aware of the country's changing age profile, and they are working fast to target their messages to distinct age-groups.

A simple flip through the TV channels affirms that age targeting has arrived. Whether it's *Sesame Street* or *Thirtysomething* or *The Golden Girls,* a program for virtually every generation flashes before the eyes of Americans on a daily basis. Age targeting is just as evident in the public sector. From city hall to the county courthouse, the local school board to the state legislature, and onto the floor of Congress, different age-groups and their advocates wield their clout to influence the taxing, spending, and regulatory decisions made by governing entities at every level. Although most of the attention has been focused on the competition between the age extremes—that is, the young versus the old—the real strain in the future may be in relations between the middle-aged, or working-aged, population and the dependent segments, which are both the young and the old.

Ours is now an age-conscious nation in which perceptions of a widening generation gap and even outright generational conflict prevail. Stereotypes abound and undoubtedly influence individual opinions and the actions of public policy makers. But just how true is the notion of generational differences? Do older Americans really participate more actively in politics than their younger counterparts? Do the generations differ sharply in their opinions about government, public officials, taxing, and spending? Do the generations substantially disagree on most public issues and policies? Or do some issues tend to bring them together? If so, what are they? And will all this change over the next few decades?

These are questions *Young v. Old* addresses in what I believe to be the first extensive look at the impact of age on the U.S. political landscape as it has been painted in the past and will be designed in the future. I will test a host of age stereotypes through a longitudinal look at what's happening in the nation, coupled with a close inspection of generational differences over the past decade in Florida, a state widely accepted as the bellwether for the rest of the country. I will use national and Florida data as the basis of my forecast of what to expect in the political arena in the decades ahead.

I begin with a look at the demographic trends, past and projected, that have created this new fixation on age as a major determinant of political participation and public policy.

DEMOGRAPHIC TRENDS IN THE UNITED STATES

Most of those living in colonial times never survived to reach what we now commonly define as old age—65 and older. (Sixty-five is the age at which a person gains full eligibility for Social Security benefits.) During George Washington's day, half the U.S. population was younger than 16. But things were altered drastically over the succeeding two centuries as fertility, life expectancy, and immigration patterns changed. By 1990, fewer than one in four individuals (23 percent) was younger than 16, and 12.5 percent of all Americans were 65 or older.

The nation's age profile will continue to change. The Census Bureau predicts that by 2030, persons 65 and older will outnumber the young (see Figure 1.1). By 2050, more than one-fifth of the U.S. population will be 65 or older. Moreover,

FIGURE 1.1 Old to Outnumber the Young by 2030

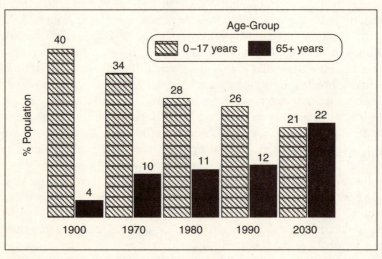

Source: U.S. Bureau of the Census. As reported in *The Tampa Tribune*, January 15, 1992, p. 3A.

nearly 5 percent will be the "oldest-old," 85 years or more.[1] The median age will continue to rise well into the next century.[2]

Changes in the Median Age

In 1790, the median age of the population was roughly 16, meaning that half the population was younger than 16 and half was older. By 1990, the median age had jumped to 33. It is expected to rise to 39 by 2010 and reach 43 by 2050. It could even rise to 50 in 2050 if levels of fertility, mortality, and net migration are lower than currently projected by the Census Bureau.[3]

The Changing Age Pyramid

The nation's rapidly changing age profile can be visualized by looking at age-gender pyramids from 1905 to 2050, taken from the Census Bureau's *Sixty-Five Plus in America* report (see Figure 1.2).[4] Age pyramids graphically display the relative size of successive generations, with the younger positioned beneath the older. The distribution of the population by age and gender in 1905 is often described as the classic age-sex pyramid—considerably wider at the bottom than at the top. In other words, the number of young persons greatly exceeded the number of old.

By 1945, the pyramid had begun to take on a different shape. The smaller-than-usual youth population reflected the lower birthrate of the 1920s, the Depression, and the World War II years.[5] By 1990, the age pyramid was even less steep than in 1945, and it had a middle-aged spread; the bulge represented the widely touted baby boomers, those born between 1946 and 1964. By 2050, the nation's age distribution will only slightly resemble a pyramid. All but the oldest-old age-cohorts will be nearly equal in size. (A cohort is a group of individuals born within the same time interval, usually five or ten years.)[6]

Shifting Societal Support Ratios

The nation's changing age profile has sparked concern among those representing the middle-aged portion of the population. The major source of anxiety becomes clear when we look at societal support ratios. These are the ratios of the number of youth (younger than 20) and elderly (65 and older) to every 100 persons aged 20 through 64, the principal ages for participation in the workforce. Such ratios, according to *Sixty-Five Plus in America,* are regarded as useful "indicators of potential change in the levels of economic and physical support needed" and as predictors "of the periods when we can expect the particular age distribution of the country to affect the need for distinct types of social services, housing, and consumer products."[7]

Working-aged individuals fear that they will be forced to increase their financial support of the dependent populations—the young and old—in the not too distant future. In 1990, the total support ratio (youth plus elderly in relation to the working-aged population) was about 70:100. Experts project that by 2050, the

FIGURE 1.2 The Changing Shape of America's Age Profile: 1905–2050

Population, by Sex and Age: 1905

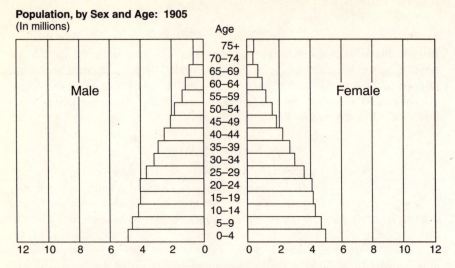

Source: U.S. Bureau of the Census, *Estimates of the Population of the United States, by Single Years of Age, Color, and Sex: 1900 to 1959*, Current Population Reports, Series P-25, No. 311. U.S. Government Printing Office, Washington, D.C., 1965.

Population, by Sex and Age: 2050

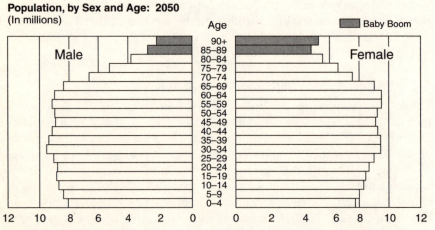

Source: Gregory Spencer, U.S. Bureau of the Census, *Projections of the Population of the United States, by Age, Sex, and Race: 1988 to 2080,* Current Population Reports, Series P-25, No. 1018, U.S. Government Printing Office, Washington, D.C., 1989 (middle series projections).

total support ratio will be 82:100.[8] This phenomenon is expected to occur across most racial and ethnic groups.

A big worry of today's younger workers is not just the projected increase in persons 65 and older but also the proportion of that increase that will be made up of those 80 years and older. This proportion will jump from 22 percent in 1990 to 36 percent by 2050. Because the oldest-old are the most likely to have health and disability problems and fewer economic resources, younger workers worry that the fast growth of this resource-shy but needy group will mean they will pay considerably higher taxes than their predecessors, leaving them less disposable income to support themselves and their families.

Younger workers, recognizing that they will be in their "golden years" in the coming decades, also worry about the shrinking size of the workforce relative to older individuals. Their primary concern is that the workforce will not be large enough to sustain the fiscal viability of the nation's Social Security system. By the beginning of the 1990s, there were only 3.4 workers for every retiree, down considerably from 40 in 1935.[9] There will be even fewer by the middle of the next century (see Figure 1.3).

Whether the focus is on median age, the shape of the age pyramid, societal support ratios, or shifts in the relative percentages of the youth and elderly populations, it is easy to see why so many prognosticators are forecasting dramatic changes in the relationships between young and old over the coming decades. From home to work to play, life will be different as these age changes, in turn, affect the relationships between men and women, racial and ethnic groups, different income and educational levels, rural and urban areas, and even one state and another.

Age Trends Create New Socioeconomic (and Ultimately Political) Realities

Aging does not affect everyone in the same way. For example, women tend to outlive men by an average of seven years. Life expectancy rates of whites exceed those of nonwhites, primarily because whites have higher incomes and better access to good medical care. The expected life spans of the more educated and affluent are longer than their poorer, less-educated counterparts. Rural areas have fewer numbers but higher proportions of older residents than metropolitan areas (as the young leave to find jobs in the cities). And the young elderly, those 65 to 74 years of age, in the Sunbelt states are younger, healthier, and wealthier than those left behind in the Snowbelt states of the Midwest and Northeast.

Even the concept of *old* is changing. "Twenty years ago, when somebody reached the age of 65, we thought they were old," says one Florida official who deals with concerns of the elderly. "Now we don't say that until they're over 80." Consider Flora Eskenazi, a 62-year-old New Yorker who divorced seventeen years ago, raised her children, enjoyed a career developing a chain of restaurants and selling real estate, and now is trying to figure out what to do for the next twenty or thirty years. "I feel like my life is just beginning," she says. One thing is sure, she

FIGURE 1.3 Why the Young Have Their Doubts About Social Security

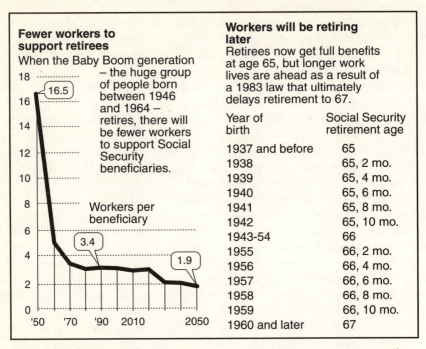

Fewer workers to support retirees

When the Baby Boom generation – the huge group of people born between 1946 and 1964 – retires, there will be fewer workers to support Social Security beneficiaries.

Workers per beneficiary

16.5

3.4

1.9

'50   '70   '90   2010   2050

Workers will be retiring later

Retirees now get full benefits at age 65, but longer work lives are ahead as a result of a 1983 law that ultimately delays retirement to 67.

Year of birth	Social Security retirement age
1937 and before	65
1938	65, 2 mo.
1939	65, 4 mo.
1940	65, 6 mo.
1941	65, 8 mo.
1942	65, 10 mo.
1943-54	66
1955	66, 2 mo.
1956	66, 4 mo.
1957	66, 6 mo.
1958	66, 8 mo.
1959	66, 10 mo.
1960 and later	67

Source: Social Society Administration, House Ways and Means Committee. Reported in Gregory Spears, "Boomer Wave May Force Up Quitting Time,"*The Tampa Tribune,* November 8, 1993. Reprinted with permission from *The Tampa Tribune.*

adds, reflecting on her 87-year-old mother who lives alone in Miami Beach, "I don't want to live like that."[10]

At the other end of the spectrum, the young as a group are much more racially and culturally diverse than the nation's older population. This greater diversity can be traced to higher birthrates among minorities of childbearing age and the large number of youth in recent waves of immigrants, especially Hispanics and Asians. Today's teenaged females are much more likely to be single heads of households than were females from older generations. And children born in the 1980s and 1990s are more likely to be poor and experience more health problems than those born earlier. In fact, more than one-fifth of the children in the United States live in poverty. The long-term implications could be severe. As Lee Smith wrote in *Fortune* magazine: "A work force cheated of protein when it is young won't have the muscle required when it matures to keep the economy rolling."[11]

As youth become more racially and culturally diverse, so do the nation's elderly. From 1990 to 2050, the black elderly population will quadruple, and the number of Hispanic elderly will increase seven times. The combined Native American, Asian, Pacific Islander, Eskimo, and Aleut elderly group will more than triple. Unlike whites, minority elderly tend to rely more on family and neighbors for support. But because many minority households are already stretched beyond their fiscal limits, social programs in the community will become increasingly important.

Those who study the nation's changing age profile have identified many past and future consequences of the uneven aging of the nation's population.[12] Some of the most significant are discussed under the categories of home, work, and lifestyle that follow. I will look at others in later chapters where I focus on varying public support for specific public policy areas, such as health, education, and the environment.

Aging Differences and Home Life. Our traditional way of organizing ourselves into living arrangements continues to change (some would say decline). In 1940, nine in ten U.S. households were composed of married-couple families, but in 1992, only slightly more than half fit that description. This change reflects not only an increase in divorces in the postwar years but also a difference in life expectancy between men and women. At ages 65 to 69, elderly women outnumbered men five to four in 1990, but for those 85 years and older, women outnumbered men five to two. Interestingly, however, the life expectancy gap is narrowing. During the 1980s, the greatest improvements in life expectancy at age 65 were among white men.

With improved life expectancies for both men and women, middle-aged persons will increasingly find themselves "sandwiched" between their children and their aging parents. Indeed, the average American woman can expect to spend more years caring for her parents than she did caring for her children. At the same time, her own children may be slower to leave the nest than she might expect. Among never-married adults aged 18 to 24, for example, 58 percent were living with their parents in 1990, up from 48 percent in 1980. As a result, more Americans can expect to live in a three-, four-, or even five-generation household, creating real financial pressures on workers and delaying the accumulation of savings for their own retirement. Multigeneration households will also cause emotional and social stress, as Junior's rock music vies with Gramps's plea for quiet.

Given the potential for day-to-day living conflicts and their own need for independence, most elderly parents prefer not to live with their grown children. Healthier, relatively affluent elderly people are more likely to move to the Sunbelt soon after retirement, but most older citizens tend to stay where they have spent most of their adult lives. The least likely to move are the frail, the poor, and the oldest-old. If members of these groups move, it is usually to nursing homes or to be near their children. Actually, three-quarters of elderly parents live within twenty-five miles of their adult children. The vast majority—85 percent—have at least weekly contact with their grown children, and 58 percent say they see their grandchildren quite often.

Among the elderly, women generally fare worse than men. Most elderly men have a spouse to assist them, especially when their health fails, but the majority of elderly women do not. Among elderly Americans who live alone, four of five are women, and many are poor. Elderly women's poverty stems from many factors: low wages, a history of part-time jobs, lack of benefits, time taken out from the labor force to rear children or care for aging parents, age discrimination, and inequities in the Social Security system. This means that each day throughout the nation, millions of older women are asking questions such as: "If I pay the doctor, can I pay the rent?" and "Where will I go when I can't afford to stay here?" Out of necessity, older women will begin pooling resources and rooming together, not unlike the television characters in *The Golden Girls,* to live more safely and inexpensively.

The vast majority of older homeowners plan to stay in their homes until the end of their lives. To do so, many will have to modify those homes to accommodate the disabilities that often come with increasing age. Only 5 to 6 percent of the elderly are in nursing homes at any given time, and most of these nursing home residents are the oldest-old (85 and older) women. Although the elderly can expect to live alone or with their families for most of their twilight years, more than half of all elderly women and one-third of all elderly men will spend time in a nursing home before they die.

Aging Differences: Work Life and Economic Status. For decades, the path to financial security in life was straightforward: go to college, get a good job, buy a house, retire with a pension. This path, which until recently applied primarily to white, middle-class males, may soon recede into history.

Although it's true that those with more education are more likely to earn higher incomes at each stage of their lives, a college diploma is no longer a one-shot proposition. Advancing technology and global market shifts demand that workers return to school periodically to update their knowledge or change their careers altogether. In addition, people who never attended college or dropped out to raise families are enrolling in classes to earn degrees or satisfy personal interests. Given these factors, it's not surprising that by 1990, 41 percent of all college students were older than 25, up from 25 percent in 1976.

But a college degree does not necessarily guarantee a good job. According to the Bureau of Labor Statistics, a fifth of those graduating from college in the 1980s ended up unemployed or working in jobs that did not require degrees. For graduates in the 1990s, that proportion may rise to 30 percent. The dismal job prospects prompted one popular Austin, Texas, restaurant, whose outdoor sign offers passing motorists a running satire of current events, to announce: "Attention 1994 graduates. Now you too can make less than our waiters." As mentioned earlier, younger workers can also expect the segment of dependent elderly to grow in the years ahead. Nearly a century ago, in 1900, there were about 7 elderly people for every 100 people of working age. As of 1990, the ratio had climbed to 20 for every 100, and by 2030, the ratio will rise to 38 per 100. As a result, some experts predict that workers will have to stay in the labor force longer, not retiring until they reach 70 or 75.

For older workers to stay on the job longer, age stereotypes will have to change. Currently, workers in their 50s and 60s often detect negative attitudes from employers about their health, productivity, and ability to learn new technology. In fact, increasing numbers of older Americans are filing age-discrimination charges with the Equal Employment Opportunity Commission. Moreover, when older workers lose their jobs, they stay unemployed longer than younger workers, suffer greater earnings losses in subsequent jobs, and are more likely to give up looking for work. And older minority workers have higher rates of unemployment and discouragement and lower earnings than do older whites.

For those who enjoy secure jobs and management positions, the 50s and early 60s can epitomize the prime of life. People in this group, born before the postwar baby boom, often have paid off their home mortgages and sent their children away to college or jobs, and they still feel fit enough to play tennis or jog three times a week. Flush with cash, they have become a key market for advertisers, who have labeled them "well-off older people," or "woopies." Indeed, Americans 50 and older control 70 percent of the country's wealth, yet comprise only 25 percent of the population.

For many people, the decision to retire usually means adjusting one's buying habits to fit a fixed income. But with good health and grandchildren who delight in receiving gifts, retirees often choose to continue working in some capacity. A 1987 study found that 22 percent of older women and 24 percent of older men continued to work in retirement, in the sense that they were employed up to two years after first receiving Social Security retired-worker benefits. In fact, according to a 1981 nationwide poll by Louis Harris, about three-quarters of the labor force preferred to perform some kind of paid work after retirement. Among workers 55 and older, 70 to 80 percent indicated an interest in part-time work, a job that would allow a day or two a week at home, and job sharing. These figures will grow as the population ages and technology permits more in-home work.

For the present, however, most elderly families live on lower annual incomes than younger families. In 1989, the median income of families with household heads 65 and older was $22,806, which is about two-thirds the median income of families headed by persons 25 to 54 years old ($36,058). Actually, 45 percent of elderly households had a 1989 annual income below $15,000, and many householders 75 or older are women without substantial survivor or retirement benefits. Elderly income varies significantly not only by gender but also by geographic region, marital status, and race. Rural elderly in the southern states have the lowest median incomes, for example. Elderly married couples are the most affluent. Minority elderly have significantly lower incomes than white elderly.

Of all income sources for the elderly, Social Security is the most important, representing 79 percent of total income for poor elderly households and approximately 36 percent for nonpoor households. Some experts suggest that during the next thirty years, the income of Americans 65 and older may increase because of growth in pension coverage, increases in real earnings, and higher rates of labor force participation by women. Realistically, however, many older individuals will see few improvements in their economic status.

Though median income is lower for the elderly, their assets are greater. Gramps and Gram may own their home or other real estate, such as a farm, and may have accumulated substantial savings. The median net worth of household heads 65 and older was $73,471 in 1988, compared with a median net worth for all households (including elderly households) of $35,752. Of all age-groups, those 65 to 69 had the largest median net worth ($83,478). But even though the elderly as a whole have more assets than the nonelderly, many elderly households have little or nothing. In 1988, one in four elderly households had a net worth of less than $25,000, and one-seventh had a net worth below $5,000.

For the elderly, living alone carries a significant threat of lowered economic status. To wit: 24 percent of elderly people living alone are poor, compared with 14 percent of those who live with others. Those living alone in rural areas have the highest rates of poverty and near-poverty (defined as between 100 and 125 percent of the poverty threshold) compared to those in central cities and the suburbs. Furthermore, more than half of older blacks and two-fifths of older Hispanics who live alone are poor, in contrast to less than one-fifth of older whites who live alone. Despite the overall anticipated improvement in the economic status of older people, experts project that by 2020, more than two in five elderly people living alone will continue to be economically vulnerable—that is, they will have incomes below 200 percent of the poverty threshold.

Will women as a group face a rosier retirement than they do now? Certainly, they will have spent more of their adult years in the workforce. The average number of years women have served in the labor force has already risen from six years in 1900 to twenty-nine years today (or, put another way, from 13 percent of their life span to 38 percent). Additionally, more women will have worked in higher-income occupations once dominated by males, which means larger retirement incomes and better benefits.

Age Differences and Lifestyle. Never before in history have the vast majority of Americans been able to expect a third stage of life, a relatively long period of retirement after youth and working adulthood. Retirement can take various forms, but for many, it consists mainly of leisurely pursuits. As columnist William March wrote in *The Tampa Tribune:* "You pay for it with money you made while you were younger, and you try to do things you wanted to do then—travel, see your family, enjoy recreation, and have romance. Meanwhile, you hope your money and health hold out, and you hope society, still made up mostly of younger people, doesn't consider you irrelevant."[13]

Although often portrayed as sipping mint juleps at the country club after a round of golf, people 65 and older generally consume fewer goods and services than the nonelderly and spend slightly higher proportions of their budgets on essentials. For example, the elderly spent 59 percent of their 1989 consumption dollars on housing, food, and medical care, compared with only 50 percent spent by younger households on those items. The one commodity that the elderly spend more on (in actual dollars and as a percentage of total expenditures) than the nonelderly is health care and health insurance.

Quite simply, the elderly spend more on health care because they use it more. On average, an older person visits a physician eight times a year, compared with five visits annually by the general population. They are hospitalized more than three times as often, stay 50 percent longer, and use twice as many prescription drugs. Medicare pays less than half the average elderly person's total health care bill, and Medicare coverage terms require the elderly to pay part of their expenses, including a monthly premium for outpatient and physician services, a deductible for hospitalization, and the cost of all drugs.

At the same time, the elderly take better care of their health than the nonelderly. People 65 and older are less likely to smoke, be overweight, drink, or report that stress has adversely affected their health. (Their primary failing is a tendency to slack off on regular exercise.) Their moderate lifestyle no doubt reflects an effort to stave off heart disease, cancer, and stroke, the principal causes of death for three of four elderly people. Youth, by contrast, are more likely to die from accidents, violence (homicides), and cancer. Acquired immunodeficiency syndrome (AIDS) and suicide rates are also higher among the young.

Despite the fact that they spend more on health care, the elderly experience far fewer physical and mental limitations than is commonly believed. The 1990 census found than 62 percent of noninstitutionalized elderly Americans have no limitations that interfere with their daily lives. This means they manage their own homes, do paid or volunteer work, visit friends and grandchildren, and travel, among other pursuits. Of the remainder, 16 percent have a mobility limitation (they have trouble walking or moving about), and 12 percent have a self-care limitation (they cannot feed or dress themselves); only 7 percent have both.

A 1989 survey found that nearly 71 percent of elderly people living in an area with which they are quite familiar described their health, in comparison with others of their age, as excellent, very good, or good. Importantly, the perception of one's own health is directly related to income. About 26 percent of older people with incomes higher than $35,000 described their health as excellent, but only 10 percent of those with incomes below $10,000 did.[14]

Given this sense of well-being, many older persons make active and valuable contributions to their communities. A recent survey found that 4.9 million people who were 65 and older did some volunteer work for community organizations during one year.[15] "It's so satisfying to see some of these children develop," says one 73-year-old woman in El Paso, Texas, who worked with developmentally delayed preschoolers to prepare them for kindergarten. "Some come in not able to communicate at all and when they make progress, it's such a reward." More than two of every five older volunteers performed most of their work for churches and other religious organizations. On average, older volunteers worked more hours per week than did younger volunteers, and they also performed volunteer work during a greater number of weeks per year.

Activity sometimes slows down as the elderly enter the ranks of the oldest-old, those 85 and older. With increasing age, they may experience one or more of a long list of chronic ailments and debilitating conditions, such as deafness, blindness, osteoporosis, diabetes, hypertension, arthritis, incontinence, and the aftereffects of stroke. The growing numbers of frail but not acutely ill elderly will give rise to new types of housing, including assisted-living centers. (Medicare does not cover chronic conditions, nor does it pay for long-term nursing care.) These numbers, plus the preference for staying in one's own community, will drive up expenditures for home health care—from $7.9 million in 1990 to an estimated $19.8 billion by the year 2020.

Gains in life expectancy have produced an unprecedented number of the oldest-old. In 1990, the Census Bureau counted more than 35,800 centenarians (people 100 and older), and four out of five of them were women. An informal measure of this group's growth comes from NBC's *Today* show, which has been airing birthday greetings to centenarians since the mid-1980s. The show now gets fifty requests a day, double the number received five years earlier. An assistant on the show who verifies the person's age before airtime notes, "We've had people who crossed the country in covered wagons."[16]

The degree to which these age-related differentials might be expected to affect public opinion and public policy varies, quite predictably, according to the relative size of various age-groups and subgroups within a particular political entity.

AGE CONCENTRATION PATTERNS:
STATES, REGIONS, COUNTIES, AND CITIES

Tremendous differences in age concentrations exist across the nation's states, regions, counties, and cities. These concentrations changed significantly during the 1980s, when the U.S. population was highly mobile.

Concentrations of Older Persons

Every state experienced an increase in the number of elderly residents in the 1980s, primarily as a result of the general aging trend. However, the older populations in some states grew at a much faster pace than those in others. This variation in growth occurred for a variety of reasons, ranging from in-migration of the elderly (in the Sunbelt states), out-migration of the young (in the Farmbelt and Rustbelt states), low fertility rates, to some combination of these factors.

In an extensive look at the causes and consequences of elderly migration patterns, published in *American Demographics* magazine, Diane Crispell and William

H. Frey observed that "America's elderly populations are growing in different places for different reasons."[17] The young-old (65- to 74-year-olds)—most of whom live with a spouse, are in good health, and are financially comfortable—are more likely to move than the old elderly (75 and older). During the 1980s, they moved to counties in the Sunbelt (coastal regions), the Southwest, and the Rocky Mountains. These regions were attractive not only "because of their low crime rates, unhurried and friendly atmospheres, temperate climates, and other amenities" but also because moving there often permitted retirees to be closer to their children and grandchildren. Generally, retiree movers prefer to relocate to small retirement communities, to the suburbs, and to rural areas rather than to large, densely populated cities or metropolitan areas. "We moved here because the water was pristine and the deer eat the roses in my yard every morning," says one 65-year-old who retired from a telephone company job in Houston to the Texas Hill Country town of Llano. Demographers forecast that these young-old movers of the 1980s will be more likely to stay put (or to "age in place") at their new residences for the rest of their lives. Their relative affluence makes them highly desirable residents because their spending in the local economy creates jobs and expands the tax base.

Other parts of the United States have not experienced such sharp increases in their older populations. States in the nation's heartland—those in the Farmbelt, Rustbelt, and oil patch—experienced either slow growth or a decline in their older populations during the 1980s. Crispell and Frey attributed this to the fact that "these places had struggling economies that could do little to attract or retain people," regardless of their ages.[18] In these states, the exodus of younger persons exceeded that of the elderly, leaving behind a disproportionate number of less-well-off older persons than in other states. The youth exodus explains why many midwestern states had relatively high percentages of older residents by 1990.

In that year, nine states had more than 1 million elderly residents: California, Florida, New York, Pennsylvania, Texas, Illinois, Ohio, Michigan, and New Jersey. The Census Bureau forecasts that by 2010, more than half (56 percent) of the nation's 39 million elderly will live in these same nine states plus North Carolina. From a political standpoint, the more interesting statistic is the percent of a state's population that is 65 or older. In 1990, Florida (18 percent) topped this list, followed by Pennsylvania (15 percent), Iowa (15 percent), Rhode Island (15 percent), West Virginia (15 percent), Arkansas (15 percent), South Dakota (15 percent), North Dakota (14 percent), Nebraska (14 percent), and Missouri (14 percent).

Concentrations of Younger Persons

The proportion of the U.S. population younger than 18 shrank between 1980 and 1990, from 28 percent to 26 percent, and is expected to fall to 21 percent by 2030. The states with the largest percentages of residents 17 or younger in 1991 were Utah (36 percent), Alaska (32 percent), Idaho (31 percent), New Mexico (30 percent), Wyoming (30 percent), Louisiana (29 percent), Mississippi (29 percent), Texas (29 percent), and South Dakota (28 percent).

Both the teenaged and young adult populations fell between 1980 and 1990. The number of 14- to 17-year-olds dropped 18 percent, and the number of those 18 to 24 fell 11 percent. These declines were not spread uniformly across the nation. In *American Demographics* magazine, demographer William Dunn reported that the drop was most marked in the Northeast and Midwest as families and young adults moved south in search of jobs and cheaper living costs.[19] In some areas of the South and West, the teenaged and young adult populations actually increased, not just because of in-migration from one state to another but also because of international immigration. (As previously noted, newly arrived immigrants are younger and have higher birthrates than resident Americans.)

Dunn's analysis of the 1990 census found that young adult Americans 18 to 24 years old (the youngest group of voting age) are clustered in college towns, military towns, and towns near the U.S.-Mexican border. These are places with more racially and culturally diverse populations. (Hispanic and black fertility rates exceed those of Anglos.)

The young teen population (14 to 17) is concentrated in rural and low-income areas, such as the Deep South, and there are high proportions of minorities in such areas. The largest proportion of teenagers occurs in Utah, where a high birth rate is consistent with the religious tenets of the large Mormon population. Importantly, however, Mormon teens are less likely to be poor than black and or Hispanic teens. The young teen population is smallest in high-cost tourist havens, job-poor areas of the agricultural Midwest, and urbanized and eastern states characterized by high living costs and small families.

Florida: A Bellwether State in Which to Observe Age Trends and Impacts

By 2010, California will still have the largest number of residents 65 or older, but Florida will have the largest percentage—20 percent, up from 18 percent in 1990. Three percent of Florida's population will be 85 or older by 2010, in contrast to 2 percent nationally. At the same time, Florida has a larger than average younger constituency. In recent years, the rate of in-migration among younger working-aged adults has exceeded that among persons 65 and over.[20]

Since the publication of John Naisbitt's *Megatrends* in 1982, Florida has been viewed as a "bellwether state"—a state in which social and political invention is common. By 1980, the author of *Megatrends* had already observed "growing tension between the state's older and younger residents" due to Florida's demographics. He predicted then that by about the year 1995, the entire U.S. population would soon have an age-to-youth ratio similar to Florida's. Naisbitt and other futurists have continued to argue that "by carefully watching what is happening now in Florida, we stand to learn a wealth of information about the problems and opportunities the entire nation will face in the future."[21] This is why many political and public policy analysts regard Florida as one of the best places in which to test various age-based theories about politics and public opinion, although the state's older population is somewhat younger, healthier, and wealthier than the elderly population at large.[22]

For many political analysts, Florida's older resident profile (younger, healthier, and wealthier) is seen as more of a pro than a con when studying generational political differences. Its profile is similar to that of several other Sunbelt states with fast-growing in-migrant retiree populations: Texas, California, Arizona, North Carolina, and Georgia.[23] Together, these six states contribute almost one-fourth of the total vote for president. They also have younger populations that are more racially and ethnically diverse than the nation as a whole, often as a consequence of immigration. Thus, although Florida's young and old populations are seen as slightly atypical, they are also seen as highly relevant and important politically—and a signal of what is to come in a growing number of states as the nation's population grows, ages, and diversifies.

Florida is also a good place to study generational political differences because of its cosmopolitan population and its highly competitive party makeup. It does not display the traits of its Deep South neighbor states. Nearly two-thirds (65 percent) of its 1990 residents were born in other states. Once dominated by Democrats, Florida has blossomed into a highly competitive two-party state.[24] By 1990, Democrats made up 52 percent of all registrants, Republicans 41 percent, and independents/third-party members 7 percent. The registration gap between Democrats and Republicans had narrowed even more by 1994: Democrats 49.8 percent, Republicans 41.6 percent, and independents/third-party members 8.6 percent. This party breakdown makes it possible to contrast the party affiliation trends of younger and older Floridians much more effectively than would be possible in a one-party state.

In Florida, as in most states, the youngest and oldest residents are unevenly concentrated in certain geographic areas. Historically, older residents, especially retirees moving to the state from other parts of the country, have tended to choose coastal counties in central and south Florida, which are warmer than those in the northern panhandle. The largest concentrations of younger persons, by contrast, are in the state's rural panhandle counties (which also have poorer populations and higher concentrations of minorities), in the predominantly agricultural counties in central and south Florida (which have higher concentrations of migrant workers), in the college towns (18- to 24-year-olds), and in the large and more racially and ethnically diverse urban areas (Jacksonville in Duval County, Miami in Dade County, and Tampa in Hillsborough County).

Florida's geographical age imbalances occasionally give rise to regionally based political conflict. State legislators representing districts with different age profiles tend to disagree on legislation perceived to have specific age-cohort impacts. The common belief is that Florida's older voters, like those in other states, are much more antitax and antigovernment than its younger ballot-casters. (I will test this proposition later in the book.)

Part of the difficulty in testing such propositions is that social scientists often disagree about precise time lines used to define a generation, cohort, or life cycle. They even differ about which of these age groupings is more useful in understanding how age determines an individual's political behavior.

GENERATIONAL LABELS: AN INEXACT "SCIENCE"

Demographers, sociologists, psychologists, economists, historians, and political scientists rarely see eye to eye when it comes to defining and labeling a generation. When one considers that each of these disciplines emphasizes a different part of the human experience, one can more readily understand the inconsistency in labeling.

How Long Is a Generation?

No one agrees precisely on how many years compose a generation, primarily because birthrates, mortality rates, and social mores change. From a purely chronological perspective, a generation is defined as the average period of time from an individual's birth until the birth of that person's first child. Naturally, changing fertility and mortality rates, as well as shifts in social mores and lifestyle patterns, can alter this average period. Typically, however, time estimates of a generation have ranged from fifteen to thirty years.

Generation Has More Than Just a Temporal Meaning

In the words of one scholar, "Generations constitute an analytic entity not only because their members share a chronological coexistence but also because they are subject to common intellectual, social and political circumstances and influences."[25]

Like snowflakes, generational classifications are rarely identical (see Table 1.1). The purposes for which they are created and the criteria and data used to create them differ, based upon the creator's academic training.

A Historical Approach. One of the most popular recent studies, *Generations,* by William Strauss and Neil Howe, defined a generation as "a special *cohort-group* whose length approximately matches that of a basic *phase of life* (or about twenty-two years over the last three centuries) and whose boundaries are fixed by *peer personality*" (italics added).[26]

In Strauss and Howe's scheme, each cohort-group is truly unique because "all its members—from birth on—always encounter the same national events, moods, and trends at similar ages." But all groups go through a four-phase life cycle. At each phase, a person takes on a different social role:

Youth (age 0–21)—Central role: dependence (growing, learning, accepting protection and nurture, avoiding harm, acquiring values)

Rising adulthood (age 22–43)—Central role: activity (working, starting families and livelihoods, serving institutions, testing values)

Midlife (age 44–65)—Central role: leadership (parenting, teaching, directing institutions, using values)

Elderhood (age 66–87)—Central role: stewardship (supervising, mentoring, channeling endowments, passing on values)

Any major event, such as social upheaval, war, or economic crisis, affects each age-group differently according to its central role in society at the time of the event.

In *Generations,* Strauss and Howe defined peer personality as "a common generational persona recognized and determined by: (1) common age location; (2) common beliefs and behavior; and (3) perceived membership in a common generation."[27] Furthermore, each generation has "collective attitudes about family life, sex roles, institutions, politics, religion, lifestyle, and the future." Though Strauss and Howe saw each U.S. generation as unique, they also offered a theory that generations themselves are cyclical. In their scheme, one cycle takes about ninety years, or four generations.

1. A dominant, inner-fixated Idealist Generation. This generation grows up as increasingly indulged youths after a secular crisis; comes of age inspiring a spiritual awakening; fragments into narcissistic rising adults; cultivates principle as moralistic mid-lifers; and emerges as visionary elders guiding the next secular crisis. (A secular crisis occurs when society focuses on reordering the outer world of institutions and public behavior. A spiritual awakening occurs when society focuses on changing the inner world of values and private behavior.)

2. A recessive Reactive Generation. This generation grows up as underprotected and criticized youths during a spiritual awakening; matures into risk-taking, alienated, rising adults; mellows into pragmatic mid-life leaders during a secular crisis; and maintains respect, but less influence, as reclusive elders.

3. A dominant, outer-fixated Civic Generation. This generation grows up as increasingly protected youths after a spiritual awakening; comes of age overcoming a secular crisis; unites into a heroic and achieving cadre of rising adults; sustains that image while building institutions as powerful mid-lifers; and emerges as busy elders attacked by the next spiritual awakening.

4. A recessive Adaptive Generation. This generation grows up as overprotected and suffocated youths during a secular crisis; matures into risk-averse, conformist, rising adults; produces indecisive mid-life arbitrator-leaders during a spiritual awakening; and maintains influence, but less respect, as sensitive elders.[28]

The authors argued that each generation acts to correct its predecessor's excesses. In Strauss and Howe's classification scheme, the baby boomer generation (those born between 1946 and 1964) represents the idealist phase of one generational cycle; the baby boomlet generation (those born in 1980 and thereafter) is the reactive phase of the same cycle; the generation born between 1900 and the early 1920s represents the civic phase of the previous generational cycle; and the generation born between the mid-1920s and mid-1940s is the adaptive phase of a previous cycle.

The widely cited Strauss-Howe generational classification was historically based. It tracked eighteen generations through four centuries of U.S. history, beginning with the first New World colonists and ending with the "Thirteeners" born between 1966 and 1981. Relying heavily on historical archives, the authors attempted to define a generational life-cycle pattern that could be used to project the characteristics of future generations.

A Demographic Approach. Another widely cited generational classification was devised by demographer Fernando Torres-Gil in *The New Aging: Politics and Change in America.*[29] His time boundaries differed somewhat from those of Strauss and Howe. Focusing exclusively on the twentieth century, he identified five generations: (1) the "Swing" generation, born between 1900 and 1926; (2) the "Silent" generation, born between 1927 and 1945; (3) the baby boomers, born between 1946 and 1964; (4) the "Baby Bust," or "Boomerang," generation, born between 1965 and 1979; and (5) the "Baby Boomlet," or "Baby Echo," generation, born between 1980 and the present. The Baby Echo generation consists of children of the baby boomers. Torres-Gil's classifications, largely generated from demographic or growth cycles, were devised to analyze, explain, and better understand age-group differences in terms of support for public policies affecting the elderly—now and in the future.

Torres-Gil, like Strauss and Howe, highlighted what he regarded as the major events—social, economic, political, and cultural—influencing the political outlook and behavior of three of the twentieth-century generations. For the Swing generation, the major events occurred in the 1930s and 1940s (the Depression and World War II). "This group," he said, "exhibits unique values and attitudes about government and the political process." They hold "traditional and conservative values of individualism, self-reliance, family, and patriotism, coupled with a belief that, in times of crisis, government has a responsibility to respond."[30]

The Silent generation, born in the 1930s and early 1940s but socialized throughout the 1940s and 1950s, grew up in a period of relative prosperity as the children of parents who vowed to make life easier for their kids than it was for them. Torres-Gil described this generation as "the group that is changing the definition of being old from poor and needy, to well-off and productive."[31] He also speculated that members of this generation will most likely bear the brunt of animosity from the younger generations because they are perceived to have achieved their prosperity at the expense of others. According to Torres-Gil, they are not as politically powerful and adept as their parents, those in the Swing generation. (Others disagree with this assessment.)

The boomer generation has been heavily influenced by the civil rights movement of the 1950s and 1960s, which, said Torres-Gil, "affected their view of individuals and government, making them more tolerant of differences." Watergate, Vietnam, and the Iran contra scandal "deepened their mistrust of government, public authority, and bureaucracies (e.g., business, labor unions)." Contrary to popular opinion, they are "far from being the liberal and radical generation painted in the '60s." According to Torres-Gil, "As a group, they share the values of their parents; they are generally patriotic and relatively moderate in their social views. . . . They tend to be more flexible politically and are more likely to act on issues and personalities rather than political parties or partisan politics."[32]

Pop Culture Classifications. In addition to the classifications assigned to them by scholars, generations sometimes pick up informal titles coined by the media or other elements in popular culture. Perhaps the most recent example is "Generation X," a label that comes from a novel of the same name by Douglas Coupland, who, in turn, borrowed the name from a British punk rock group.[33] Generation X refers to young Americans born between 1961 and 1975. These are the restless, disaffected "twentysomethings" who are trying to reconcile themselves to a United States of seemingly shrinking potential. They may express their dissent with the political system, for example, by simply not voting.[34] Whether Coupland's thesis is, in fact, true is something I investigate in *Young v. Old*.

A Political Approach. Analysts looking at variations in the political participation and policy preferences of different age-groups across time must focus on data gathered from those of voting age at the time of their analysis. Consequently, the youngest generation (not yet of voting age) is typically excluded from politically focused generational classifications. This approach was developed, defended, and popularized by political scientists Warren E. Miller, Arthur H. Miller, and Edward J. Schneider in their widely cited *American National Election Studies Data Sourcebook.*[35]

Political scientists' generational classification schemes are often different from those devised by other social scientists. Political scientists give much more weight to political events occurring at the time an age-group is politically socialized. Political socialization theories generally posit that the major events influencing a person's political being and behavior typically occur in the teens and early 20s (young adulthood).[36]

Where possible, the data presented in *Young v. Old* focus on the five age-groups (generations) of voting age in 1991, who were, in turn, eligible to vote in the 1992 presidential election. The labels given to each generation reflect what I believe to be the key political event(s) that occurred during their teens and early adulthood:

- World War I generation (born between 1899 and 1910); 81 and older in 1991
- Depression/World War II generation (born between 1911 and 1926); 65 to 80 in 1991
- Cold War/Sputnik generation (born between 1927 and 1942); 49 to 64 in 1991

- Civil Rights/Vietnam/Watergate generation (born between 1943 and 1958); 33 to 48 in 1991
- Reagan generation (born between 1959 and 1973); 18 to 32 in 1991

Although other political analysts studying age differences in political participation and policy preferences may not use these exact labels, the age breaks many use are quite similar because many of the national survey firms focusing on the opinions of the voting-age public use similar age-break categories.

Decades as Age Definers

Age-difference analyses are not limited to generational contrasts. Books, films, and pop culture today all focus on the intellectual, social, and political uniqueness of different decades—from the 1920s to the 1990s. Even an individual's passage from one decade to another is treated as a major event. A bunch of black helium balloons stuffed into the back seat of a car, for example, is a sure sign that someone is feting a person turning 40. Greeting card manufacturers, taking advantage of these perceived landmarks, target birthday cards to persons turning 21, 30, 40, 50, and 60, thus signifying that their lives will be forever different. The first example—associating a particular decade with events that permanently affect all who live through it—is a "period effect." The second example—being 21, 40, or 65, for instance—suggests that passing each milestone means one's interests and abilities change as one ages—a "maturational effect."

Different Ways to Look at Generational or Age Differences

One common thesis is that a person's opinions and political participation rates change as he or she ages. To test such a proposition, a researcher must track the same individuals over their lifetimes—in what is known as a *longitudinal approach*. This approach, also referred to as a panel study, is used to determine whether differences across age-groups reflect an aging, or maturational, effect. It is an expensive way to test age-based hypotheses because many Americans change addresses several times in their lives. The most extensive political panel study is part of the National Election Studies, conducted every two years by the Center for Political Studies at the University of Michigan.

Another common thesis suggests that today's young (or old) differ in important ways from yesterday's young (or old). This hypothesis is a little easier to test because one needs only the data from several points in time for the same age-group (or cohort), obtained by asking questions in an identical fashion. For example, to determine if today's 20-year-olds are more likely to be Democrats than were 20-year-olds in 1960, one would simply compare the percentage of 20-year-olds in 1990 who labeled themselves as Democrats with a similar figure for 1960. This is known as a *time-lag approach* to measuring age differences. If such differences emerge, they are attributed to a "period effect." A period effect usually means that some important political, cultural, social, or economic happening yielded diverse political outlooks and behaviors for same-aged persons at different points in time. Data from major public opinion polling firms, such as Gallup, Roper, CBS/New York Times, CNN, the University of Michigan's National Election Survey (NES), and the Florida Annual Policy Survey (FAPS), lend themselves to such an approach.

Most data reported in popular public opinion polls are also analyzed using a *cross-sectional approach*. One calculates political differences between young and old simply by comparing the views and participation rates of the younger voters with those of older voters at a particular point in time. Any differences between the groups that emerge are regarded as "cohort effects."

It is often quite difficult to separate out maturational, or life-cycle, effects from period and cohort effects because many participatory acts and opinions reflect a little of each.[37] In *Young v. Old,* I rely heavily on data collected in time-lag and cross-sectional modes since longitudinal panel data are rarely available. As previously noted, most public opinion firms collect data on questions of interest at a particular moment in time and rarely track the same individuals over time. Nonetheless, I often give life-cycle, or maturational, explanations for generational or age group differences that appear in cross-sectional or time-lag data because previous research has shown that certain behaviors and policy preferences change as one ages.

AGE TO BECOME A MORE WEIGHTY FACTOR

Regardless of the approach used to gauge age-group differences, it is almost impossible to state unequivocally that age alone explains political behavior. As Torres-Gil observed:

> Belonging to an age cohort and identifying with a particular generation does not necessarily determine one's vote or political behavior toward another group. Taken alone, generational identity is an incomplete predictor of political view and participation. Other influences can carry greater weight, including level of education, racial and ethnic makeup, income and class status, and parents and families.[38]

However, as already noted, differences in the aging rate of groups defined by race, ethnicity, income, family status, and education certainly increase the likelihood that age will take on an equal or even greater weight in the not too distant future. I, like Torres-Gil, agree that age consciousness and age identification will intensify in the coming decades and that "the interaction of generations between and within themselves and with the political system will profoundly impact social, economic, political, and cultural institutions."

In Part 2, I will focus on the political participation rates of various age groups. In Part 3, I will contrast the public policy preferences of these age groups. *Young v. Old* ends with a forecast of what I anticipate will be the impact of this new emphasis on age in the political arena.

TABLE 1.1 Three Classifications of Generations Born in the Twentieth Century

Strauss and Howe, Generations[a]		Torres-Gil, The New Aging[a]		MacManus, Young v. Old[b]	
Generation label	Birth years	Generation label	Birth years	Generation label	Birth years
G.I.	1901–1924	Swing	1900–1926	World War I	1899–1910
Silent	1925–1942	Silent	1927–1945	Depression/World War II	1911–1926
Boom	1943–1960	Baby Boomers	1946–1964	Cold War/Sputnik	1927–1942
Thirteenth	1961–1981	Baby Bust (Boomerang)	1965–1979	Civil Rights/Vietnam/Watergate	1943–1958
Millennial	1982–2003	Baby Boomlet (Echo)	1980–	Reagan	1959–1973

Notes: [a]The Strauss and Howe and Torres-Gil classifications include the nation's youngest generation (the under 18 nonvoters).
[b]The MacManus classification focuses exclusively on those of voting age (18 and over) as of 1991.

Sources: William Strauss and Neil Howe, *Generations: The History of America's Future, 1584–2069*, New York: Quill, William Morrow, 1991; Fernando Torres-Gil, *The New Aging: Politics and Change in America*, New York: Auburn House, 1992.

PART II

Political Participation Differences

2

Using the Ballot Box: Registering and Voting

"Senior citizens register and vote. Young Americans don't." This, in a nutshell, is one of the most common perceptions of how younger and older citizens differ in their political participation rates. Another widely held belief is that the older one grows, the more responsible one becomes in terms of "doing your civic duty" and voting—at least until one reaches his or her 70s. Conventional wisdom holds that at this age, a person is a little less likely to vote, primarily because of illness or mobility difficulties.[1] But are these stereotypes myth or reality? Are there other equally plausible age-based explanations for differences in voter registration and turnout rates among the twentieth-century generations? And are there signs the participation rate gap may be shrinking?

REGISTRATION: THE FIRST STEP TO VOTING

The U.S. Bureau of the Census, which conducts registration and voting surveys, has defined registration as "the act of qualifying to vote by formally enrolling on a list of voters." The eligibility criteria for registering today are minimal compared with what they were in earlier periods of U.S. history. In most states, a person needs only to be a U.S. citizen, have reached voting age (18), and have lived in the state for a specified time. Some states, including Florida, also require registrants to sign a loyalty oath affirming that they meet their state's eligibility requirements and will protect and defend the constitutions of the United States and the state.

Ineligibles

Convicted felons and persons committed to penal institutions are usually ineligible to vote. However, some states permit convicted felons to petition to have their voting rights reinstated after a certain time.[2] Most states also prohibit the mentally impaired from registering and voting. According to the *Handbook of United States Election Laws and Practices,* it is not uncommon for states to disqualify "persons who are under guardianship, who have been adjudicated incompetent, or who have been committed to mental institutions."[3]

Determining Voter Qualifications: Primarily a State Responsibility

Historically, the establishment of voter qualifications has been left to each state. The U.S. Constitution, ratified in 1789, only briefly mentioned voter eligibility requirements because those drafting the Constitution could not agree on who could vote. Article I, section 2, clause 2 of the Constitution merely states: "The electors in each state shall have the qualifications requisite for electors for the most numerous Branch of the state legislature." In other words, the U.S. Constitution left to the states the major responsibility for determining who could register and vote. Some states have better track records than others in terms of being inclusive.

An Expanded Electorate

Initially, many states limited eligibility to white males 21 years of age and older who owned property or paid taxes. One electoral law history scholar reported that "as the country proceeded into the 1800s, property and taxpayer qualifications gradually disappeared [and] were replaced by other laws preventing certain persons from voting in some states: literacy tests, eliminating those who could not read and/or write, and poll taxes, eliminating those who were too poor to pay that tax."[4] In the South, these requirements, along with white primaries and grandfather clauses, disproportionately limited the political participation of blacks.[5]

But one by one, most of these restrictions disappeared. U.S. constitutional amendments, congressional acts, and federal court rulings have expanded the electorate to include racial minorities (the Fifteenth Amendment, passed in 1870), female voters (the Nineteenth Amendment, passed in 1920), residents of the District of Columbia in presidential elections (the Twenty-third Amendment, passed in 1961), and 18- to 20-year-old voters (the Twenty-sixth Amendment, passed in 1971).[6] Other eligibility criteria such as owning property, paying a poll tax (eliminated by passage of the Twenty-fourth Amendment in 1964), or passing a literacy test (in the South) have also been deleted, as have the white primary and grandfather clauses, which both were struck down as unconstitutional by the U.S. Supreme Court.

Residency requirements are still a prerequisite to registering and voting in most state and local elections, although the length of required residency has been shortened considerably.[7] Historically, states have defended residency requirements on the grounds that they "provide some assurance that the new voter has become a member of the community and that as such has a common interest in all matters pertaining to its government and is therefore likely to exercise this right more intelligently."[8] However, various federal laws—namely, the Federal Voting Assistance Act of 1955, the Overseas Voting Rights Act of 1975, and the 1970 amendments to the Federal Voting Rights Act—prohibit making residency requirements a prerequisite to voting in *federal* elections.

Closing the Registration Books

States differ in how far ahead of election day they close the registration books. Closing dates give election administrators time to prepare official voter registration lists for use by poll workers at each voting precinct on election day. These lists are often matched against voters' identification cards and signatures to reduce the likelihood of election fraud. In federal elections (presidential, congressional), no state is permitted to halt registration more than thirty days before the election.

States are allowed to establish different closing-date time frames for state and local elections. One state—North Dakota—has no registration requirement for voting. Four other states—Minnesota, Wisconsin, Oregon, and Maine—permit registration on election day. In these states, voters merely present themselves at their polling places with proof that they are citizens of voting age who meet the state's residency requirement. The fact that these five states are among those with the highest voter turnout suggests that closing the books too far ahead of an election may depress registration rates and turnout, especially in a mobile society such as ours. A 1987 study estimated that voter turnout would increase by 9 percent if voters didn't have to go through the hassle of reregistering every time they move.[9] But those worried about controlling election fraud still have concerns about the dangers of removing all preregistration requirements.

Making Registration Easier

State laws govern the time, place, and procedures for registering voters. Many states have made the registration process easier in one or more of the following ways:

- permitting registration by mail, usually with just a postcard
- increasing the number of voter registration sites to include schools, shopping plazas, and motor vehicle license bureaus—often called the "motor voter" method
- extending the hours (evenings) and days (weekends) of registration, especially immediately prior to an election
- preparing informational materials not only in English but also in other languages
- deputizing more registrars

Deputy registrars are ordinary citizens (rather than government election-office employees) who are given the right to register other citizens. Approximately three-fourths of the states allow such deputization. Where deputy registrars are legal, it is a common practice for political parties and interest groups to conduct voter registration drives, especially just before the registration books close for an upcoming election.

Catchy, media-based infomercials—that is, paid commercials in a news or information format—admonishing targeted groups to register and vote are also quite popular. Young voters were the object of such an approach during the 1992 presidential election campaign. MTV Network's "Choose or Lose" campaign and its acceptance of "Rock the Vote" ads sponsored by a California music association are credited with increasing the youth registration and turnout rates for the first time since 1972, when 18- to 20-year-olds were first eligible to vote.[10]

Do Registration Laws and Procedures Make a Difference?

Many studies of why people don't vote more often have laid a major portion of the blame on registration laws and procedures.[11] In *Who Votes?* (1980), one of the earliest studies to focus on registration, Raymond E. Wolfinger and Steven J. Rosenstone argued that registering to vote often requires more effort than the actual act of voting itself: "Citizens must first perform a separate task that lacks the immediate gratification characterizing other forms of political expression (such as voting). Registration is usually more difficult than voting, often involving more obscure information and a longer journey at a less convenient time, to complete a more complicated procedure. Moreover, it must usually be done before interest in the campaign has reached its peak."[12]

At the time their book was published, Wolfinger and Rosenstone predicted that registration and turnout in presidential elections would go up about 9 percent if all states had same-day registration provisions and enacted other reforms such as extending days and hours of operation for registration offices; permitting absentee (mail) registration for the sick and disabled and those who will be out of the district on election day; and less-frequent purging of registration lists for failure to vote in any election within a certain time frame. (Purging is the removal of registrant names from the voter registration list because of death, relocation, or, in some cases, voter inactivity—failure to vote within a prescribed time.) A later study came to basically the same conclusion.

Ruy A. Texeira, in *The Disappearing American Voter* (which was based on 1972, 1980, and 1984 data), estimated that registration would increase by nearly 11 percent if all states had election-day registration, evening and Saturday registration, consistent and regular registration office hours, and no purging. Texeira projected that by far the most effective reform would be to eliminate closing dates, thereby adopting an election-day registration requirement. More recent research has supported his claim. A study of the major voter registration outreach programs found that election-day registration was more effective in raising registration rates than the motor voter bill, deputy registrars, agency registration, or mail registration.[13]

In another widely cited study, *Why Americans Don't Vote* (1988), Frances Fox Piven and Richard A. Cloward argued vehemently for more federally enacted laws permitting expansive agency-based registration systems. Voter registration and turnout rates would jump dramatically, they asserted, if a wide array of agencies serving the public could register their users (e.g., unemployment and public assistance agencies, driver's license bureaus, hospitals, public health centers, day care centers, family planning clinics, senior citizen centers, family service agencies, public housing projects, libraries, parks and recreation centers, and agricultural extension offices). Their work laid the foundation for passage of the National Voter Registration Act, popularly known as the motor voter bill, in May 1993.

The federal legislation, effective January 1995, requires all states "to establish a system enabling citizens to apply for voter registration while applying for or renewing their driver's licenses, through uniform mail applications or by applying in person at designated government agencies, including public assistance bureaus and offices serving Americans with disabilities."[14] A wide range of groups, including those representing both ends of the age spectrum, supported this move to make it more convenient to register.

By the time the federal agency registration statute was passed, nearly half the states had already adopted legislation permitting people to register to vote in the same office where they apply for their driver's licenses or register their vehicles. Where adopted, registration rates had jumped by 3 to 8 percent.[15] But most of these states did not permit registration at social service agencies, which the new federal statute would later authorize.

AGE AND REGISTRATION: EXPECTATIONS AND REALITIES

Age, along with a host of other personal attributes such as education, income, race, ethnicity, and gender, can be used to predict fairly accurately whether someone will spend the time and energy to register (or reregister) to vote. Maturational theories assert that the older one grows, the more interested in politics and public policy a person becomes. A broader range of political and public policy issues become more relevant as a person matures, takes on more responsibility at home and at work, and becomes more active in community, civic, professional, service, and religious organizations.

Consistent with the notion of community activism, the biggest difference in interest level between the youngest and oldest cohorts shows up with regard to local, not national, politics. According to a survey by the Times Mirror Center for The People & The Press, a high percentage of young and old alike acknowledge they are "interested in keeping up with national affairs" (84 percent of the 18- to 24-year-olds and 88 percent of those 75 and older). But when asked about local politics, a much higher proportion of older persons answered in the affirmative (59 percent of those 18 to 24 but 75 percent of those 75 and older). Those most interested in both national *and* local politics were individuals in the prime of their working years (50- to 64-year-olds), who also tend to be the most active in community and professional organizations.[16]

Many still believe that after reaching 75, a person is more likely to begin to withdraw from societal attachments because of physical and mental infirmities; some refer to this as "societal disengagement." Naturally, once infirmities set in, a person is less likely to participate in politics at the same pace as before. That person will be less inclined to keep his or her registration active, especially in states that regularly purge voter lists, or reregister if forced to move to another voting precinct or jurisdiction (e.g., to a nursing home, to a congregate living facility, or to the home of a grown child or other relative).[17]

Another age-based registration theory asserts that older women are less politically active than older men, for several reasons: marital status, the nature of their infirmities, and the time period in which they became politically socialized. First, as seen in Chapter 1, fewer older women live with their spouses (women generally outlive men and, as widows, tend to live alone), and previous studies have found that older women remain more politically active when living with their spouses.[18] Second, older women have a higher incidence of infirmities that limit mobility. Finally, many of today's older women grew up in a time when politics was regarded as a male domain—when sexual stereotypes prevailed.

Such sharp declines in voter registration among those 75 and older or contrasts between the registration rates of older men and women will probably not be seen in the coming decades, especially if election laws quickly catch up with technology. Interactive networks in virtually every household, following completion of the information superhighway, will make it technically possible for every person to register (and vote) at home. And as the gaps between male and female educational and income levels narrow and sexual stereotypes fade, so, too, will participation rate differentials. The latter phenomenon is already happening: The difference in male and female registration rates for those 65 and older declined from 11 percent in 1968 to 5 percent in 1992.

Another common maturational theory links civic duty with registering and voting. The older one grows, according to this theory, the more he or she views registering and voting as a civic duty—again, up to the point at which one begins to disengage from society and politics. A survey conducted by the Times Mirror Center for The People & The Press during the 1992 presidential election campaign asked Americans whether it was their duty as citizens to always vote and whether they felt guilty when they didn't get a chance to vote. In each instance, older voters, even those 75 and older, were more prone to say yes wholeheartedly than younger voters.[19]

With age, some say, comes the ability to beat the system—or at least to know how to play the game. According to this thinking, older persons are more likely to register to vote because they are more familiar with how to maneuver through governmental bureaucratic mazes, including voter registration offices. Recent surveys have confirmed this theory, to a point. Persons at each end of the age spectrum are the most likely to identify "complicated registration procedures" as one reason they don't always vote. Among 18- to 24-year-olds, 14 percent gave this response in the surveys; among those 65 or older 19 percent. For age-groups in between, the percentages ranged from 9 to 12 percent.[20]

Another theory is that more informed persons are more likely to register and vote.[21] And the older one grows, the more likely one is to be informed about politics—paying more attention to the news and relying more on a broader combination of news sources (newspapers, news magazines, television) than younger persons. Studies of Americans' media habits by the Times Mirror Center for The People & The Press have confirmed both of these age-based notions about media use. Older persons are more likely to pay attention to the news and to rely upon a wider array of news sources to follow public affairs (see Table 2.1). This pattern may change as new computer-based, interactive, news-distribution mechanisms become more popular with the young.

Older persons are generally more knowledgeable about politics than younger persons.[22] At the height of the 1992 presidential campaign, less than half (45 percent) of 18- to 24-year-olds could identify which political party held a majority of the seats in the U.S. Senate, compared with 60 percent of those 65 and older. The same knowledge gap applied to which party controlled the House of Representatives. This was true in spite of a campaign theme that focused on whether a president could get more accomplished if he or she belonged to the political party that controlled a majority of seats in both houses of Congress! Generational knowledge gaps show up whether questions are asked about parties, candidates, or just the details of news stories in general. However, the interest levels of young and old differ far less than knowledge levels, and, of the two, interest is linked more strongly to acts of participation, including registration.

Although increasing age brings more interest in and more knowledge about politics, it also brings somewhat more cynicism about government and elected officials, especially those at the national level. (In fairness, it should be pointed out that cynicism has intensified across all age-groups in recent years—a point to be discussed in more detail in Chapter 6.) Older persons are more prone to say that "most issues discussed in Washington don't affect me personally" and to admit that they are "generally bored with what goes on in Washington." They are also more likely to say that "government is not really run for the benefit of the people." Surprisingly, this cynicism does not seem to cause fewer older persons to register or vote. It seems they think, "Even if things aren't going to change, come hell or high water *I'm* still going to tell them [the government and politicians] what *I* think!" Or it may be that even though older citizens have less confidence or trust in the federal government, they are more positively inclined toward state and local governments. This, in turn, motivates them to keep their voter registrations active. But many voting analysts attribute older citizens' higher registration rates to their strong belief that registering and voting are civic duties. (I will return to this point later in the chapter.)

Less clear is whether rising cynicism among the younger cohorts, which has developed much more rapidly in this group than among their predecessor generations, will translate into nonparticipation or merely serve as an incentive to become more active—as a way of rebelling against the system. The 1992 presidential election gives us some hints about this question.

The Young: Always Low Registration Rates?

Youth are often portrayed as less likely to register and vote for a number of reasons, primarily related to their unsettled life situations—single, in college, in the military, or in training or apprenticeship positions. But authorities offer other generation-based theories to explain why the young are not as politically active as their elders. Surveys of members of Generation X (ages 18 to 29) and the Reagan generation (ages 21 to 35) have concluded that during their politically formative years, there was less of an emphasis on "things politic" at home and at school than in the past. Historically, the family and schools have been two of the most powerful political socializing agents for Americans. But among these younger generations, politics was rarely discussed at home or at school, so they have grown up with little knowledge of—or interest in—politics and without a strong sense that registering and voting are civic duties. These patterns have many supporters of democracy worried about its future in America.[23]

Some uncertainty exists about whether younger Americans even comprehend the essential ingredients and benefits of democracy. The young are somewhat less inclined today to describe themselves as "very patriotic" than their elders, although the gap has closed to some degree in recent years. Some also fear that today's youth may be more alienated from politics and less likely to believe that politics can make any difference in their lives than youth from previous generations.

A more optimistic view is that the nation has finally turned the corner and is headed in a more positive direction, reaching out to youth at an earlier age through hands-on efforts like KidsVote and FirstVote and stimulating their interest and involvement in politics through less conventional media—music, television, computer networks. MTV Network's chair Tom Freston, reflecting on the youth turnout resulting from the "Choose or Lose" effort, said, "We've known all along that they're concerned, worried and politically independent."[24] Thus far, these new media socialization agents appear to be most effective on college campuses. (In fact, for the young and old, registration levels are much higher among the college educated.) In campus settings, media-disseminated messages are reinforced through the young person's peer group. But these unconventional methods of encouraging participation have also been effective in reaching youth who are not college students simply because younger people tend to use high tech more than their elders.

According to another optimistic theory, the historically low registration and voting rates of the young are only temporary and may be reversed quickly when things on the political horizon hit home—that is, when issues become more personally relevant.[25] Proponents of this theory cite as their primary evidence an increase in the registration rate of young persons in the 1992 presidential election, as compared to that in 1988. They attribute the rise to a more adverse economic climate and a greater awareness of economic pressures among young voters. Public opinion surveys throughout the campaign showed that a much higher proportion of the young felt less optimistic about their economic future than in the past.

Signs also indicated that these young voters had intergenerational conflicts on their minds—a situation likely to intensify in the future. Surveys showed that the young believe they will have to spend an increasingly larger portion of their paychecks to support the upcoming elderly, today's baby boomers. Consequently, the young fear they will have little left to support themselves and their families. "Many of us feel that we don't have a whole lot to look forward to," says one 22-year-old graduate of Northwestern University. "We're looking at each other and starting to say: What's going to happen to us? Will I ever be able to own a home? Will I be able to make enough money to raise children the way my parents raised me?" (see Table 2.2). Many young people are also convinced that by the time they reach retirement age the Social Security system will have gone bust and that they will get little or no return on the contributions they make during their working years. "Social Security is headed toward insolvency," notes one 26-year-old University of Texas graduate. "It will collapse on the backs of my generation."

Socioeconomic Explanations

Other explanations for the gaps between the registration rates of the young and old emphasize differences in the socioeconomic compositions of the two age-groups. To understand this perspective, we need to highlight what we know about the relationship between various socioeconomic attributes and political participation—in this case, registering to vote. Past research has shown that those most likely to be politically active: (1) have stronger roots within society as a whole and in their community (married, working people, churchgoers), (2) are better educated, (3) are more affluent, (4) usually have higher-status occupations, and (5) own their own homes. Whites are more likely to be politically active than racial and language minorities, although this is changing. And women now register at higher rates than men (a recent development).[26] Obviously, a greater proportion of older citizens fall into each of these categories—which will only increase if current population trends, outlined in Chapter 1, continue.

Are Registration Rates Inflated or Depressed?

Registration rates are calculated by determining the percent of the total voting age population registered to vote. (The optimal denominator would be the total eligible population, but that figure is not reported by the U.S. Census Bureau.) The most common sources of registration information for national elections (presidential, congressional) are the Current Population Survey (CPS) conducted by the Bureau of the Census after presidential and congressional elections, and the National Election Survey conducted by the Inter-Consortium for Political Research at the University of Michigan during the same periods. The registration figures reported in these studies are recognized as being somewhat inflated because they rely on self-reporting by the individuals surveyed. For example, estimates suggest that the inflation rate in the CPS is from 5 to 12 percent in presidential elections.[27] State-by-state registration rates are regularly reported in election compendiums like *America Votes* and *The Election Data Book.* These resources rely upon actual registration figures supplied by state election supervisors rather than survey-generated, self-supplied information.

The denominator in each calculation—the voting-age population (VAP), or the number of persons 18 or older—is generated by the U.S. Bureau of the Census. In some reports, census VAP figures do not include institutionalized people, but they still include other "ineligibles" such as noncitizens. (In general, one should take care when using or analyzing VAP data.) Because VAP figures generally include ineligibles, some believe that registration rates are not really *that* inflated.

From an age perspective, the youth registration rate may be even less inflated than the elderly registration rate, even though younger persons are more inclined to say they registered when they did not. This is because greater proportions of younger persons are noncitizens; moreover, younger persons are also more mobile, meaning that higher proportions may not meet the state and local residency requirements necessary for registration.

Registration Rates by Age-Group: 1968 to 1994 (Across the Nation)

The Census Bureau's CPS series reporting registration rates in U.S. presidential elections by age (see Table 2.3) confirms several age-based theories. First, voters 65 years and older register at a much higher rate than voters in the 18- to 24-year-old category. On average, older voters register at a 23 percent higher rate, although the figure for the younger cohort may be somewhat conservative for the reasons cited earlier. The gap is even wider in years when there is no presidential election.

Second, the registration rate of the 18- to 24-year-olds increased between 1988 and 1992 (presidential election years) and between 1990 and 1994 (mid-term election years). But it still had not returned to the level of 1972, the year of the first presidential election in which 18- to 20-year-olds could vote. This seems to support the arguments that youth are just temporarily disinterested in politics and that their interest can be stimulated when they perceive that issues are relevant to them. Clearly, the socioeconomic gap between young and old did *not* lessen between 1988 and 1994, thereby weakening purely socioeconomic-based registration theories.

Third, the registration gap between the 65-and-older group and 18- to 24-year-olds shrank between 1988 and 1992 (presidential years) and between 1990 and 1994 (mid-term years), primarily because of higher youth registration rates. It is not clear whether the gap will continue to shrink, but I suspect that it will, although it probably will never close completely. Undoubtedly, the greater relevancy of politics as perceived by younger voters in 1992 will likely also apply to the younger voters in future presidential elections as intergenerational economic and social issues become more prominent. (Florida data reveal the same patterns in state and local elections.) In addition, youth-oriented political groups like Lead . . . or Leave and the Third Millennium are pushing hard for changes that would make it easier for younger persons to register and vote, especially on college campuses.[28]

The registration rates of those 65 and older have remained much higher and more stable than those of the young, and this is not likely to change significantly. However, with longer life expectancies, it *is* possible that greater proportions of the oldest-old may not participate because of physical or mental impairments, thereby creating a drop in the registration rate of older Americans. But my guess is that as more states move to electronic or mail registration systems, the mobility problems of these "senior-seniors" may be minimized, keeping registration rates fairly stable.

Registration Rates by Generations: 1981 to 1993 (Floridians)

The Florida Annual Policy Survey is based on a sample of Florida's adult population 18 and older. Like the CPS and NES, it asks respondents whether they are registered. Although the self-reporting nature of the data suggests inflated registration rates, the high incidence of ineligible voters in the state actually makes these figures less inflated than the national census-based average. In 1990 alone, 8.2 percent of Florida's residents of voting age were noncitizens, compared to 5.4 percent nationally.

The registration rate patterns observed in the national data (census, NES) are even sharper in Florida. First, across each generation, an increase in registration rates occurred between 1981 and 1993—a maturational effect showing that the older one grows, the more likely one is to register. Second, strong cohort differences emerged. The older generations (World War I, Depression/World War II, Cold War/Sputnik) registered at much higher rates than the younger generations (Civil Rights/Vietnam/Watergate, Reagan). However, the gap between the cohorts was slightly narrower than that observed nationally. To me, this phenomenon suggests that the pace at which the gap is closing may pick up nationally as the nation's age profile approaches Florida's and as intergenerational economic issues take center stage.

Floridians, like Americans elsewhere, have grown more concerned and pessimistic about the nation's economic future, but the convergence of opinion between the generations has happened much more quickly in Florida than in the country as a whole. This fact supports my thesis that economic issues prompt the young to register and vote in greater numbers than normally expected, particularly when they see economics in "us-against-them" or young-versus-old terms.

My Florida data also showed a slight narrowing of the gap in the level of interest in politics between the youngest (Reagan) and the oldest (World War I) generations between 1981 and 1993. This is just one more piece of evidence supporting my thesis that the pace of convergence in participation rates is occurring faster in

Florida than nationally, and it gives an indication of what will soon happen at the national level.

VOTING: FACTORS AFFECTING TURNOUT

Voting is often seen as the most direct link between a citizen and his or her government—the essence of democracy. Not surprisingly, then, students of politics have always been curious about why some people vote and others do not, especially since a large number of Americans frequently do not. One prominent scholar has said that "about 38 percent of American citizens are 'core' or regular voters for major national and state offices; another 17 percent or so are marginals who come to the polls only when stimulated by the dramas of presidential campaign politics; and 45 percent are more or less habitual nonvoters."[29]

Theories about why people do or don't vote abound. They vary depending upon the historical time frame, the type of election (national versus state or local, primary versus general), data sources (individual versus aggregate), and how turnout is measured. But regardless of the theory or the approach, age has always been a good predictor of a person's likelihood of voting. Naturally, age is itself related to a number of other factors regularly included in voter turnout models: (1) legal, (2) socioeconomic, (3) social-psychological, (4) economic, and (5) political mobilization.[30]

Legal Factors

Since registration is generally a prerequisite to voting, the ease or difficulty of registering to vote certainly affects whether a person actually casts a ballot. Short closing dates, less-frequent purging of voter lists, mail (versus in-person) registration, voter registration drives by deputized registrars, and more accessible registration locations and hours enhance registration and, ultimately, turnout rates, although authorities disagree considerably about precisely how much.[31]

According to one of the most recent studies, closing dates affect voter turnout (especially by African Americans, Mexican Americans, and Puerto Ricans) more than residency requirements but far less than other factors. In *Mobilization, Participation, and Democracy in America*, Steven J. Rosenstone and John Mark Hansen reported that citizens who live in states with thirty-day closing dates are 3 percent less likely to vote than citizens who live in states that permit registration right up to election day. Those living in states with sixty-day closing dates were 6 percent less likely to vote.[32]

Turnout rates on election day are affected by other legalities, such as polling place hours and locations, election dates, frequency of elections, voting method (mail versus in-person), and ease of absentee voting. Turnout is higher when voting is more convenient—that is, when polling hours and locations suit workforce patterns, when absentee voting is easier,[33] and when voting by mail is permissible.[34]

When national, state, and local elections are held at different times (i.e., there are more frequent elections), the turnout rate tends to go down for all the elections but especially for the local contests.[35] Some refer to this as the "election overload" problem. Turnout rates also vary depending upon the type of election—presidential, congressional, gubernatorial, legislative, city, county, school board, or on an issue or bond referendum—and whether the election is a party primary or general election. Normally, presidential and general elections evoke the highest turnout. However, it is not uncommon for highly competitive or controversial state and local elections or referenda to yield higher turnouts.

Typically, states that hold their state or local elections at the same time as presidential contests have higher turnout in those races than states that hold them separately. However, even if multiple elections are on the same ballot, voters are less likely to vote in races or issues near the end of that ballot, especially if the ballot is a long one with many offices, issues, and candidates. Authorities refer to this as "voter roll-off" or "drop-off."[36]

The Link Between Age, Legal Factors, and Voter Turnout

Observers have discovered links between age and various legal factors assumed to affect turnout. For example, older voters are more consistent in their voting—that is, they are less affected by the frequency of elections than younger voters. They also are more likely to complete their ballots (i.e., they are less likely to "roll off"): Ballot length and complexity do not deter or intimidate them as much.

Age-groups also differ in what time of day they vote.[37] Older persons tend to vote in the morning; younger voters in the late afternoon. This means that a greater proportion of young voters, especially in the West, may be negatively affected by early network calls of presidential winners based on results in the East and Midwest. Hearing the winner, they may simply choose not to vote, thereby affecting the age profile of the turnout both in the presidential race and in any other state or local contests held at the same time.

States are often more lenient with older voters in establishing the conditions for absentee voting. Thus, it is not surprising that older voters exercise their voting right more vigorously than younger voters, although the difference in the proportions of each age-cohort casting absentee ballots is not as great as commonly perceived. In recent years, parties and interest groups promoting get-out-the-vote efforts among the young have made sure they make it as easy as possible for them to cast absentee ballots—providing detailed instructions on how to do it and, where permitted, even giving them the actual blank absentee ballot.[38] In the 1992 presidential election, Census Bureau surveys found that the oldest and youngest were actually the most prone to vote as absentees: 10 percent of the 18- to 24-year-olds and 13 percent of those 65 and over, compared to 5 percent of those 24 to 44 and 6 percent of those between 45 and 64.[39]

In summary, legalities related to election-day mechanics, most notably residency requirements, are generally thought to slightly depress turnout among younger voters relative to older voters.[40]

Socioeconomic Factors

A plethora of individual socioeconomic factors, including age, education, income or social class, occupation, race and ethnicity, gender, marital status, family status (children), and church attendance have been linked to voter turnout in numerous studies (see Table 2.4).[41] High-turnout individuals are older, more educated, more affluent, in professional and white-collar occupations, and active in their communities (homeowners, churchgoers). Among the middle-aged, those with school-age children are more likely to vote than those without.[42]

Whites turn out at higher rates than African Americans, Hispanics, or Asians, although new evidence has shown that in big cities, black turnout frequently equals or exceeds white turnout.[43] Hispanics and Asians are the least likely to vote, often because they are not citizens, lack language skills, or have immigrated from cultures where voting is not emphasized or voting rights are restricted.[44]

In the past, male turnout rates exceeded female rates, but in most parts of the country today, the reverse is now true. Changing educational patterns and the gradual erosion of sexual stereotypes have contributed to this reversal.

The Link Between Age, Socioeconomics, and Voter Turnout

As with legal factors, there is a relationship between turnout, previously mentioned socioeconomic indicators, and age, at least up to the point at which the elderly begin to disengage from social and political activities. Older voters are more likely to be white, better-off economically, homeowners, living with a spouse, and more active in the community and the church than their younger counterparts. A greater proportion of older voters are women. However, older voters are not as well educated as younger voters—the one factor that is not consistent with most high-turnout models.

The link between age and each of these socioeconomic factors has changed as the nation has matured because the makeup of the population itself has changed, as have social mores. The relationship is dynamic rather than stable, which helps explain why models predicting voter turnout are constantly being reformulated. For example, in the past, models anticipated finding a negative relationship between the size of the female voting population and voter turnout rates. Now, however, the reverse is true. Today, more women than men vote because of gains they have made in education, income, and employment opportunities, as well as the removal of stereotypes about "appropriate" female electoral behavior. The more the gap narrows between men and women on these dimensions, the less powerful gender will be as a predictor of voter turnout.

Socioeconomic attributes alone cannot predict turnout, although age is increasingly seen as the most powerful of these factors. For example, Rosenstone and Hansen, in *Mobilization, Participation, and Democracy in America,* found that 65-year-olds were 29 percent more likely to vote in presidential elections than 18-year-olds. In contrast, the wealthiest Americans were 16 percent more likely to vote in presidential elections than less affluent individuals. And college graduates were 17 percent more likely to vote in presidential elections than those with no more than an eighth-grade education. Those who had lived in their communities for forty or more years were 11 percent more likely to vote in presidential elections than those who had moved into their community within the year of the election. Homeowners were 7.5 percent more likely to vote in presidential years than renters, and people who attend church every week were 15 percent more likely to vote in presidential elections than those who never attend religious services.

In their multivariate model explaining the decline in voter turnout in presidential election years between the 1960s and 1980s,[45] Rosenstone and Hansen found that a younger electorate explained 17 percent of the decline, compared to weakened social involvement (9 percent), declining feelings of efficacy (9 percent), weakened attachment to and evaluations of the political parties and their candidates (11 percent), and education (0 percent!).[46] Their study and others showed that legal factors contribute little to explanatory models today since many obstacles to registration and voting have been removed.[47] In Rosenstone and Hansen's classic study, only a decline in mobilization—outreach efforts by political parties and candidates to get people interested enough in the election to go to the polls—explained more than age did (54 percent). Persons must be motivated to vote, and motivation can come either from the inner self (social-psychological attitudes) or external factors (the political environment).

Social-Psychological Attitudes

Individuals are motivated to cast their ballot for a variety of social and psychological reasons: out of a sense of civic duty, as a commitment to political parties or candidates, because they believe their votes count (political efficacy), because they think that government can be trusted to do what's right and be attentive and responsive to the citizenry, and because they are genuinely interested in politics and political outcomes.[48] Research has generally shown that "it is the concerned, the strong partisans, and the conscience-bound who have the highest probability of voting, all other things being equal."[49]

The Link Between Age, Social-Psychological Attributes, and Voter Turnout

Few studies have focused extensively on the linkage in turnout between each sociopsychological factor and age.[50] However, I have already shown a relationship between age and a belief that voting is a civic duty, an interest in politics, trust and confidence in government, and cynicism regarding the responsiveness of government. Younger voters are less likely to view voting as a civic duty or to feel guilty when they don't go to the polls.[51] They are also slightly less interested in politics, especially local politics. But younger voters are slightly more trustful of governments and their responsiveness—they are less cynical (although, as previously noted, few studies have found strong links between feelings of trust or beliefs about governmental responsiveness and voter turnout).

According to many voter turnout models, mostly of high-profile presidential elections, the more strongly a person identifies with a political party, the more likely that person will be to vote.[52] Rosenstone and Hansen, for instance, found that people who identified themselves as strong partisans were 11 percent more likely to vote than citizens who leaned toward neither party. Those who cared about the outcome of an election were 6 percent more likely to vote, and those who strongly preferred one candidate over another were also 6 percent more likely to vote.[53]

Historically, the young have had a weaker identification with parties. They are much more prone to describe themselves as independents than those who strongly identify with parties.[54] They are also less likely to care which political party—or even which candidate—wins an election. In sum, younger voters care less about election outcomes than older voters.[55] In part, this may be because many don't believe that voting is an effective way of trying to influence political outcomes (see Table 2.5).[56]

Age-based studies of political efficacy have found that the youngest and the oldest cohorts have the greatest sense of powerlessness—or the lowest levels of political efficacy because "both age-groups [are] effectively denied equal access to societal power and resources by the dominant middle-age groups."[57] But the same research also has concluded that "whereas the process of aging increases feelings of powerlessness for the old, it decreases such feelings for the young."

Economic Factors

The close relationship between economic and political cycles is well known.[58] What is more controversial is the degree to which an individual's current economic status or perception about his or her economic future prompts voting. Some have argued that if an individual is experiencing economic adversity (such as unemployment, a layoff, a change to part-time status, or a loss or reduction of health or pension benefits), that person is less likely to vote "because the stress and personal preoccupation of joblessness forces people into retreat from the public realm." Others have argued just the opposite—that "people who have suffered economic hardships of various sorts might well blame the government and go out to the polls to punish incumbents in the executive and legislative branches." Still others have observed that a better predictor is the individual's perception of his or her future economic status: A person who expects to be worse-off next year is more likely to vote than one who expects no change.[59]

As noted, public opinion surveys in recent years have shown that younger people tend to be pessimistic about their economic futures, often as a direct consequence of their perceived responsibility for financially supporting the elderly co-horts.[60] Older persons, particularly those near or already in retirement, are also pessimistic but for different reasons. First, they are more subject to layoffs and benefit reductions than younger workers because they earn more and because financially strapped businesses, nonprofit organizations, and governments will save more if these people are fired or laid off. Second, many fear they will lose everything if they get sick and their health benefits are exhausted.

Thus, for the age-extreme groups, especially the young, the economic motivation to vote has increased. This helps explain the narrowing of the gap in turnout rates between age-groups. (I will take a closer look at age-based turnout differentials later in the chapter.)

Political Mobilization Factors

Campaigns affect the profile of the electorate on election day.[61] They prompt some to vote and others to stay at home. Forecasters often plug a number of campaign variables into models for predicting voter turnout. Among the more common are campaign spending, media use (electronic and print), political party competitiveness, candidate competitiveness in high-profile races (which is often related to the presence or absence of an incumbent), personal contacts between candidate and voter, the degree to which a potential voter perceives that a candidate shares his or her interests, perceived closeness of the election, and voter perception that a clear and appealing choice is available among the candidates or issues.[62]

The more money spent in a political contest, the more likely it is that race will be highly competitive, featuring more than one serious or credible candidate, each of whom has a different stance on issues. Such contests also rely more heavily on the electronic media, especially television, to reach potential voters. Healthy funding also permits a candidate to have more direct contact with the electorate, either through the mass media or by direct mail. The premise is that candidates and their campaigns can stimulate voter interest (and turnout)—and the more money they have, the more easily they can drum up that interest. This does not always mean that the candidate who spends the most wins; rather, the races that feature higher spending by a variety of candidates may elicit greater voter interest and higher voter turnout.

Turnout also generally rises when two-party competition is strong.[63] But the perceived closeness of an election seems to stimulate turnout only when a voter thinks he or she will benefit by voting.[64]

Campaign attention theorists—who theorize about who watches political campaigns, why, and what difference it makes—argue that the decision about whether to vote is secondary. According to two scholars, "People decide for whom (if anyone) to vote before they decide whether to vote. Both answers depend on individuals' attention to the campaign. Increasing levels of campaign attention prompt individuals to gather information about candidates and issues, form judgments about them, establish preferences between the candidates, and *then* decide whether to vote" (italics added).[65] Those ultimately deciding not to vote fall into five categories: "politically ignorant voters (those who are uninformed about the campaign), indifferent voters (those who see no difference between the candidates), selectively aware nonvoters (those who are aware of only one candidate), dissatisfied nonvoters (those who dislike one or both candidates), and the conditionally inactive (those who do not participate because they are unemployed)."[66] Among the nonvoters, those in the indifferent and conditionally inactive categories tend to be younger.

The Link Between Age, Political Mobilization, and Voter Turnout

From an age perspective, several other observations stand out. First, because older voters are more likely to be interested in politics in general, it is often easier to arouse their interest in a particular contest or issue. Second, because older voters follow the news more attentively in a variety of media (electronic, print), they are more likely to both perceive differences among the candidates and see a contest as more personally relevant, thereby making it more likely that they will vote. Third, they are more likely to be strong partisans, thereby enhancing the likelihood that they will vote. In general, older persons "are comparatively more attentive to political campaigns than younger persons, . . . more likely to seek 'practical' knowledge about political events, . . . and use television more extensively than do persons at any other point in the life cycle," up to a certain age, when the trend reverses.[67]

Actually, younger persons may now be coming closer to their senior counterparts in terms of time spent watching television. The data clearly show that the young watch more programming on cable TV networks (e.g., MTV) than the old, and the schism between the young and old in types of television watched (cable versus network) has been used effectively by certain political candidates. They have found that these divergent viewing patterns make it easier to target political messages to different age-groups. As noted earlier, many credit the rise in youth turnout in the 1992 presidential election to MTV—a cable network aimed at the young. (I will say more about age, media, and attentiveness to political parties and election campaigns in Chapter 3.)

Voter Turnout by Age-Groups: The Nation

Turnout rates vary tremendously from election to election and race to race (because of roll-off). Moreover, the rates differ depending upon which of the two common methods of computing turnout are used (see Figure 2.1). The first method calculates the number of persons voting as a percent of the voting age population. The second calculates the number of persons voting as a percent of the total number of persons registered, yielding a higher percentage because the denominator is smaller. In reality, the two methods often serve different purposes.

In *The Election Data Book: A Statistical Portrait of Voting in America 1992*, Brace et al. were careful to point out that turnout calculated as a percent of VAP

FIGURE 2.1 Voter Turnout Rates Differ by Method of Calculation

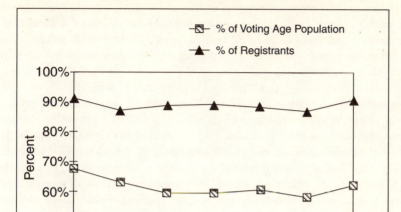

Source: Calculated from Jerry T. Jennings,*Voting and Registration in the Election of November, 1992*. Washington, D.C.: U.S. Bureau of the Census, Current Population Report P20-466, April 1993.

uses potential voters as the base (denominator). However, this number includes certain persons who are ineligible to register or vote, such as noncitizens, those with criminal records, those lacking mental capacity, or those who have not met state or local residency requirements. These VAP turnout rates can also vary depending on the source of the "voted" figure (the numerator). Some figures on the numbers who voted come from surveys in which respondents self-reported whether they did indeed vote (e.g., the Census Bureau's Current Population Survey and the University of Michigan's National Election Study). Other "voted" figures come from data reported by state election officials—the number of persons who actually voted or the number of valid votes cast for the office generating the most votes (e.g., *America Votes* series, *Election Data Book* series).[68] The turnout rate is generally higher when self-reported data form the numerator. For example, in the November 1992 election (during a presidential election year), the turnout rate calculated with self-reported data (in the CPS) was 61 percent. When calculated using valid vote figures supplied by state election officials, the turnout rate in the same election was 55 percent (*America Votes 20*).

Brace et al. acknowledged that academics and some practitioners still prefer turnout rates calculated as a percent of voting-age population because turnout rates calculated in this manner are somewhat more "comparable across jurisdictions, because (1) all voting age counts usually come from a single source (however flawed . . .) and (2) registration counts differ by jurisdiction due to registration practices and variable purging of 'deadwood.'"[69] As already noted, some states are more rigorous in keeping their voter registration rolls up to date than others.

The second method, in which turnout is calculated as a percentage of registered voters, gives election officials, candidates, political parties, interest groups, and even the press a sense of how well they have motivated registrants to get out and vote. Of course, as Brace et al. observed: "Turnout in any state may also be affected by the personalities of the candidates involved, the volatility of issues on the ballot, the level of demographic heterogeneity of the electorate, or even the weather," all of which make cross-jurisdiction comparisons difficult—and risky.[70]

States that have high turnout rates using one method of calculation may not rank as high using the other because the two figures measure different concepts. Neither measure is a perfect indicator of voter participation, but both can show, to some degree, how interested Americans are in electoral politics.

Turnout Rates: Presidential Election Years

A longitudinal look at self-reported voter turnout rates from 1960 to 1992 generated by the U.S. Bureau of the Census (calculated as a percent of voting-age population) shows a consistent gap between the turnout rates of younger and older voters. That gap widened each year from 1972 to 1988 but narrowed slightly from 1988 to 1992—from a 33 percent to a 27 percent difference between those 18 to 24 and those 65 and older. In 1992, turnout rates of 18- to 24-year-olds rose more sharply than those of the 65 and older group (up 6.6 and 1.3 percent, respectively), although those 65 and older still turned out at considerably higher rates than those 18 to 24 (70 percent versus 43 percent).

A more detailed age breakdown shows that between 1972 and 1992, the turnout rate declined for all age-groups except 65 to 74 and 75 and older; rates in those groups went up 6 and 9 percent, respectively (see Table 2.6). The consistently higher turnout of these groups, when the participation rates of other age-groups declined, is largely responsible for the notions that the old vote and the young don't and that the old are increasing their political clout at the expense of the young.

The consistency of older citizens' turnout rates during periods when trust and confidence in governments and elected officials are declining sharply among *all* age-groups brings us back to the civic duty issue. A 1992 study of factors affecting voter turnout among different age-groups concluded that "a diminished sense of voting as a civic duty may play a larger role in the turnout problem than such factors as voter anger, public disinterest in politics, and other often mentioned reasons for low turnout. . . . Among older people a sense of voting obligation keeps them going to the polls, even though they may not be knowledgeable about politics or even though they may be alienated from politics."[71] Among the younger cohorts, that sense of obligation, or civic duty, is missing, and younger people often know very little about public affairs.

Young and old alike are generally more poorly informed about issues and candidates in congressional or other midterm or off-year election contests (state or local). (A midterm election occurs in an even-numbered year in which there is no presidential election. An off-year election occurs in an odd-numbered year. Many state and local officials are elected in either midterm years, when Congress members are also elected, or off years.)[72]

Turnout Rates: Midterm (Congressional) Election Years

Although many voting analyses focus on turnout in the general election held in presidential election years, we can learn a great deal about age-group differentials by examining turnout in non–presidential election years as well. Younger voters, for example, are far less likely to vote in midterm elections than older voters. In 1990, 77 percent of those 65 and older said they voted, compared with only 18 percent of the 18- to 20-year-olds and 22 percent of the 21- to 24-year-olds. Going into the 1994 midterm elections, 80 percent of those 65 and over said they planned to vote in the election, compared to just 53 percent of those 18 to 29.[73] The actual turnout was lower for both groups.

The slight dip in the turnout rate of 18- to 20-years olds between 1992 and 1994 was attributed by some to the fact that MTV gave less coverage to the midterm elections (see Table 2.6). The inconsistency of the youth vote is troubling to leaders of groups like Lead . . . or Leave, who believe that changing this pattern is one of their biggest challenges. Said one leader, "It's crucial to convince the so-called Generation X that politics is not like a microwave breakfast burrito—you don't pop it in, and two minutes later it's done. We have to stay in the political arena for reasons besides MTV hype. That means voting in the off-term as well as the main elections."[74]

If this pattern continues, it will mean that the clout of older voters vis-à-vis the young will continue to escalate disproportionately in all types of elections (congressional, state, and local) held in non–presidential election years.

Voter Turnout in Florida

If Florida is any indication, the generational gap in turnout rates will narrow, not widen, as the nation's age profile changes. Between 1980 and 1992, the difference between the proportion of the Reagan and World War I generation members who claimed they voted in the presidential election was more than cut in half—from a 50 percent difference in 1980 to a 20 percent difference in 1992. The turnout rate gap in non–presidential election years (only two elections between 1987 and 1991) also shrank—from a 41 percent difference to a 36 percent difference. In each instance, the older generation turned out in greater numbers, as expected. Turnout rates for both groups were highest in the presidential election years.

Another interesting trend observed in Florida is that the increases in the self-reported turnout rates for the Reagan and World War II generations between 1988 and 1992 were virtually equal—quite different from the national pattern. This provides one more piece of evidence that Florida leads the nation in the pace at which younger and older voter participation rates are converging, albeit slowly.

At the same time that voter participation rates are converging, the gap between the youngest and oldest generations in terms of their interest in national politics is narrowing. The difference in the proportion of those saying they are "very interested" in national politics shrank from 22 percent in 1981 to 15 percent in 1993. Contrary to national patterns, the percentage of Florida's Reagan generation members saying they are "very interested" in national politics increased slightly (up 2 percent), while those of the World War I generation and the Depression/World War II generation declined slightly (down 5 and 3 percent, respectively), although these differences are not statistically significant.

As for Floridians' trust in the federal government, I see no closing of the generational gap. Paralleling national trends, the percent expressing trust in the federal government declined sharply between 1981 and 1993 across all generations. The biggest declines occurred among the youngest (Reagan) and oldest (World War II) generations, down 14 percent, assuring that the gap is not closing in this area. This phenomenon provides further evidence that eroding trust in government does not adequately explain voter turnout differentials across or between different generations. Campaign- and candidate-centered explanations are much more enlightening.

Why People Don't Always Vote: An Age-Group Analysis

Survey researchers have long thought that the best way to determine why people don't vote is, quite simply, to *ask* them. In a country that has many elections (a crowded election calendar) and media that tend to cover only the highest-profile races, it is not surprising that the primary reason why people don't always vote is because they don't have enough information about the candidates. Also, in an age when negative campaign ads are the norm, many say they don't vote because they don't like any of the candidates. A poll taken by the Times Mirror Center for The People & The Press in June 1992 found that Americans more often cited these two reasons for not always voting, rather than difficulties registering or getting to the polls, a general disinterest in politics, or a belief that who's elected makes little difference.[75]

However, some interesting age differences appear in the reasons given for not always voting. The 18- to 24-year-olds were more likely than those 65 and older to say they don't always vote because they sometimes don't like any of the candidates (71 percent versus 61 percent). Those 65 and older, by contrast, were more likely than the 18- to 24-year-olds to cite difficulties in registering (19 versus 14 percent), a desire to stay out of politics (34 versus 29 percent), or the belief that who's elected doesn't really matter that much (43 versus 31 percent).

Both the youngest and oldest cohorts were somewhat more likely than the middle-aged to say they don't vote because of registration complexities, difficulty getting to the polls, lack of interest, or insufficient information about the candidates (a curvilinear pattern). However, the underlying factors sometimes differ considerably. For example, younger persons have more difficulty getting to the polls because of time constraints at school or at work. For older persons, it's more a matter of physical inability. Among the young, low interest levels often reflect their failure to see politics as personally relevant; among the old, low interest levels stem more from disengagement because of infirmities or changes in living situation.

A 1988 Times Mirror survey focused specifically on why people do not vote in presidential elections, which are usually the highest-profile contests.[76] The responses fell into nine categories: (1) "not registered," (2) "away from home or out of town on election day," (3) "not interested in the campaign," (4) "don't like any of the candidates," (5) "illness," (6) "inconvenient," (7) "working/couldn't get off work," (8) "new resident," and (9) "no particular reason."

Those younger than 30 were considerably more likely to say they didn't vote in the presidential election because they weren't registered (16.5 percent versus less than 1 percent), were out of town on election day (20 percent versus less than 1 percent), or couldn't get off work (18 percent versus 3.6 percent). Older Americans were more likely than those younger than 30 to say they didn't vote because of illness (32 percent versus 3 percent) or because they didn't like any of the candidates (16 percent versus 2 percent). The two groups differed little in terms of residency and inconvenience reasons. A greater proportion of people 50 to 59 failed to give a specific reason for not voting, as compared to the younger or older cohorts. Overall, these differences track very closely with the individual's place in the life cycle.

SUMMARY

The young and old differ considerably in the extent to which they register and vote. Most of the differences can be explained by their relative stages in the life cycle—the maturation effect. The older one grows, the more likely one is to register and vote in a wide variety of elections (national, state, and local) and to participate in a number of other community activities and organizations (political, civic, church, and professional).

Furthermore, the older one grows, the more personally relevant politics and elections become, up until the point in life when a person begins to disengage from social and political activities. This disengagement takes place later today than it did even a decade ago. Past research claimed that older citizens' political participation rates started to fall once a person reached the mid-60s. Today, that point has been pushed to the mid-70s. In the coming years, disengagement will most likely take place even later in life as the average life span in the United States increases. If election laws catch up with technology and make it possible to register and vote electronically from a wide variety of locations (e.g., homes, hospitals, nursing homes, or other congregate care facilities), we may see even less disengagement.

The interest levels of the youngest and oldest cohorts are quite similar with regard to national affairs. But the gap between generations in this regard is widest in local affairs. As a consequence, older voters often flex their political muscle most effectively at the state and local levels.

Older persons generally stay more informed and knowledgeable about politics; they follow politics in detail in a wider range of news sources than do younger people. This, too, may change as the methods of delivering the news become more interesting and appealing to younger cohorts. Indeed, computer-based, interactive news-distribution mechanisms have the potential to capture the eyes and ears of the younger generations, who often feel more comfortable with high technology.

Although older Americans are more cynical and less trustful of government and elected officials than the young, this attitude does not seem to translate into nonparticipation. Overriding their cynicism is a strong belief that registering and voting are civic duties that ought to be taken seriously. Generational differences on this dimension are clear. Younger cohorts do not believe that voting is as essential or effective as their older counterparts do. Observers often blame this development on the disintegration of the family, coupled with less emphasis on patriotism and civics education in the schools.

The gaps in the registration and turnout rates between the young and the old may be narrowing. The gaps did close slightly between 1988 and 1992, lending support to voting theorists who espouse personal relevancy as a stronger impetus to voting than simple personal attributes (e.g., education, income, gender, or race). Evidence indicates that the young view their economic futures much more negatively than do older cohorts—and they are increasingly attributing their less-than-bright economic futures to retirees and baby boomers, with an us-against-them mentality. Thus, participation rates among the young likely will increase as intergenerational economic and social issues become more evident—and more personally relevant.

The reasons Americans give for not always voting vary according to their place in the life cycle. Younger voters show a greater tendency to belittle the quality of the candidates—that is, they don't like any of them. They are also more likely to say they are busy (at work or school), out of town, or not registered. Older persons who don't vote tend to attribute their nonvoting to illness, registration difficulties, a desire to stay out of politics, or their belief that who's elected doesn't really matter that much.

Persons of all age-groups cite insufficient information about candidates as the main reason they don't always vote. In Chapter 3, I will focus on the effectiveness of political parties and their candidates in getting information to potential voters. I will also look at differences in attentiveness and participation across various age-groups and generations.

TABLE 2.1 News Sources Regularly Relied upon by Different Age-Groups

	Age-Group			
	18-29	30-49	50-64	65+
Regular News Sources	(%)	(%)	(%)	(%)
ELECTRONIC MEDIA				
Television				
Local news about your viewing area	69.9	77.7	82.1	83.0
National network news on CBS, ABC, or NBC	45.6	55.5	72.8	75.1
Cable News Network (CNN)	31.6	33.3	38.5	40.8
MacNeil/Lehrer News Hour	2.9	8.3	16.6	16.1
C-Span	10.1	10.5	13.7	12.4
Sunday morning new shows (such as *Meet the Press*, *Face the Nation*, or *This Week with David Brinkley)*	7.4	17.0	25.1	29.4
News magazine shows (such as *60 Minutes* or *20/20)*	36.1	52.0	59.4	66.9
Talk shows (such as *Oprah, Donahue*, or *Geraldo)*	34.6	21.5	22.6	18.0
The Rush Limbaugh Show	8.1	6.7	4.2	8.8
The Larry King Show	3.1	3.6	6.3	9.8
Radio				
Programs on National Public Radio such as *Morning Edition* or *All Things Considered*	13.0	14.1	18.2	15.3
Call-in talk shows	12.4	17.1	22.8	15.0
PRINT MEDIA				
Newspapers				
Daily newspaper	56.5	65.6	69.9	75.4
Magazines				
News (such as *Time, US News & World Report*, or *Newsweek)*	18.8	25.2	24.1	26.4
Personality (such as *People* or *US)*	16.0	11.2	9.2	8.0

Note: Respondents were asked: "I'd like to know how often, if ever, you read certain types of publications, listen to the radio, or watch certain types of TV shows. For each that I read, tell me if you do it regularly, sometimes, hardly ever, or never. How often do you [X]?"

Source: Times Mirror Center for The People & The Press. Telephone survey of a nationally representative sample of 1,507 adults 18 years of age or older, conducted May 18–24, 1993. Reprinted with permission.

TABLE 2.2 Concerns About the Economic Future: Young Worried More Than Old (in percentages)

Concern	Age-Group			
	18-29	30-49	50-64	65+
Losing your job or taking a cut in pay	57.6	52.3	40.7	7.9
Losing your home because you can't afford to keep it/being able to own your own home	67.4	47.8	36.9	25.9
Not having enough money for retirement	77.4	80.1	70.6	40.7
Your children not having good job opportunities	78.8	80.9	70.3	46.2
Being unable to save enough money to put a child through college	73.4	67.9	28.8	19.9
Being unable to afford necessary health care when a family member gets sick	79.1	69.2	75.5	65.9

Note: Respondents were asked: "Now I'd like you to think about the future. As I read some different things that might affect your personal future, please tell me how concerned you are about each one happening to you. First, how concerned are you about [phrase]? Would you say very concerned, somewhat concerned, not too concerned, or not at all concerned?" Percentages reported are very and somewhat concerned.

Source: The Times Mirror Center for The People & The Press. Telephone survey of a nationally representative sample of 2,001 adults 18 years of age or older, conducted March 16-21, 1994. Reprinted with permission.

TABLE 2.3 National Registration Rates (as percent of voting-age population): 1972–1994, Presidential and Congressional (midterm) Election Years (in percentages)

	Percentage reporting they registered											
	Presidental election years						Congressional election years					
	1972	1976	1980	1984	1988	1992	1974	1978	1982	1986	1990	1994
Age												
18–20	58	47	45	47	45	48	36	35	35	35	35	37
21–24	59	55	53	54	51	55	45	45	48	47	43	45
25–34	68	62	62	63	58	61	54	56	57	56	52	51
35–44	74	70	71	71	69	69	66	67	68	68	66	63
45–64	79	76	76	77	76	75	73	74	76	75	71	71
65 and older	75	71	75	77	78	78	70	73	75	77	77	76
Race/ethnicity												
White	73	68	68	70	68	70	63	64	66	65	64	64
Black	65	59	60	66	65	64	54	57	59	64	59	58
Hispanic origin[a]	44	38	36	40	36	35	34	33	35	36	32	30
Hispanic citizen[a]	—	51	54	59	57	59	—	48	52	54	52	NA
Sex												
Male	73	67	67	67	65	67	62	63	64	63	61	61
Female	71	66	67	69	68	69	61	63	64	65	63	63
Region												
Northeast	—	66	65	67	65	67	62	62	63	62	61	61
Midwest	—	72	74	75	73	75	66	68	71	71	68	69
South	68	68	64	64	66	67	59	60	62	63	61	61
West	—	63	63	65	63	64	59	59	61	61	58	58
Employment												
Employed	74	69	69	69	67	70	63	63	66	64	63	63
Unemployed	58	52	50	54	50	54	44	44	50	49	45	46
Not in labor force	70	65	66	68	67	67	61	63	64	66	63	62
Education												
8 years or less	61	54	53	53	48	44	54	53	52	51	44	40
1–3 yrs high school	63	56	55	55	53	50	54	53	53	52	48	45
4 yrs high school	74	67	66	67	65	65	61	62	63	63	60	59
1–3 years college	81	75	74	76	74	75	66	69	70	70	69	68
4 or more yrs college	87	84	84	84	83	85	76	77	78	78	77	76
Total	72	67	67	68	67	68	62	62	64	64	62	62

Note:
[a]Persons of Hispanic origin may be of any race.
NA = not available.

Sources: U.S. Bureau of the Census, Current Population Reports, Voting and Registration in the Election of November 1976 (Washington, D.C.: U.S. Government Printing Office, 1993), Series P-20, no. 322, 11-12, 14-21, 57, 61; November 1978, no. 344, 8, 11-19, 60, 65; November 1980, no. 370, 10-20, 50, 56; November 1982, no. 383, 1-12, 46, 49; November 1984, no. 405, 13-24, 59; November 1986, no. 414, 11-22, 29, 31; November 1988, no. 440, 13-24, 48, 50; November 1990, no. 453, 1-2, 4, 13-14, 17; November 1992, no. 466, v-vii, 1, 5; November 1994, Table 14. Reported in Harold Stanley and Richard Niemi, Vital Statistics on American Politics, Washington, D.C.: CQ Press, 1988, 1993. Reprinted with permission

TABLE 2.4 Socioeconomic Characteristics: Different Age-Groups (in percentages)

	Age-Group			
Characteristic	18-29	30-44	45-64	65 & Over
Gender (1992)				
Male	50.6	49.6	48.1	40.2
Female	49.4	50.4	51.9	59.8
Race/Ethnicity (1992)				
American Indian/Aleut/Eskimo	0.9	0.8	0.6	0.4
Asian/Pacific Islander	3.3	3.3	2.6	1.5
Black	13.4	11.6	9.9	8.0
Hispanic Origin (any race)	11.6	8.6	6.3	3.7
White	71.5	76.3	81.0	86.6
Marital Status (1992)				
Single	61.5	16.6	5.6	4.6
Married	34.7	71.3	76.1	55.8
Spouse present	31.9	66.8	72.3	54.1
Spouse absent	2.8	4.5	3.8	1.7
Widowed	0.1	0.8	5.8	34.4
Divorced	3.7	11.4	12.5	5.3
Family Status				
In family	78.6	84.0	84.0	66.5
Not in family				
Nonfamily householder	11.5	11.2	13.7	32.0
Unrelated person in household	8.7	4.1	2.0	1.2
In group quarters	0.3	0.2	0.1	0.2
Home Ownership (1992)	26.8[a]	60.2	77.1	77.2
Education (1991)				
8 years or less	4.0	4.6	11.1	26.5
1–3 yrs. of high school	14.6	8.0	11.9	15.7
4 yrs. of high school	41.3	39.0	40.3	34.3
1–3 yrs. of college	25.5	22.1	16.4	11.4
4 yrs. college or more	14.6	26.3	20.4	12.1
Labor Force (1993)				
In labor force	79.7[a]	84.4	70.1	10.9
Employed	71.5[a]	78.6	66.3	10.5
Unemployed	8.2[a]	5.8	3.8	0.4
Not in labor force	20.3[a]	15.6	29.9	89.1
Keeping house	8.9	9.9	13.7	24.6
Going to school	6.9[a]	1.0	0.3	0.1
Unable to work	0.7[a]	1.4	3.5	4.0
Other reasons	3.8[a]	3.3	12.4	60.4
Poverty (1992)				
Receiving public assistance	26.5[b]	21.0[c]	15.2	18.1
Below the poverty line	18.0[b]	11.5[c]	8.9	12.9

(continues)

TABLE 2.4 (cont.)

Characteristic	Age-Group			
	18-29	30-44	45-64	65 & Over
Place of Residence (1990)				
Urban	79.6	75.3	72.8	75.4
Rural	20.4	24.7	27.2	24.6
Mobility				
Living in same residence as 1 yr. ago	66.1[a]	82.8	91.0	95.0
Moved	33.9[a]	17.2	9.0	5.0
To different state	5.6[a]	3.0	2.0	1.0

Notes:
[a]Age-group is 20–29.
[b]Age-group is 18–24.
[c]Age-group is 25–44.

Sources: Gender, race/ethnicity, marital status, and family status are from Arlene F. Saluter, *Marital Status and Living Arrangements: March 1992,* Washington, D.C.: Bureau of the Census, Current Population Reports, P20-468, December, 1992, Tables 1, 2. Urban-rural status figures are from *1990 Census of Population, General Population Characteristics United States,* Washington, D.C.: Bureau of the Census, 1990-CP1-1, November, 1992, Tables 14, 16. Education figures are from Robert Kominski and Andrea Adams, *Educational Attainment in the United States: March 1991 and 1990,* Washington, D.C.: Bureau of the Census, Current Population Reports, P-20, No. 462, May, 1992, Table 1. Poverty figures are from *Poverty in the United States: 1992,* Washington, D.C.: Bureau of the Census, Current Population Reports, Consumer Income, P60-185, September, 1993, Table 7. Mobility figures are from Diane DeAre, *Geographical Mobility: March 1990 to March 1991,* Washington, D.C.: Bureau of the Census, Current Population Reports, Population Characteristics, P-20-463, October 1992, Table F. Home ownership figures are from *Current Population Reports: Population Characteristics,* Washington, D.C.: Bureau of the Census, P-20-467, April 1993, Table 16. Labor force figures are from *Employment and Income,* Vol. 40, No. 2, Washington, D.C.: Bureau of Labor Statistics, February, 1993, Table A-4.

TABLE 2.5   Young Less Convinced Voting Is a Very Effective Way to Influence Government (in percentages)

	Total	Age-Group					
		18-24	25-29	30-34	35-49	50-64	65+
Effectiveness of making sure you vote in all elections							
Very effective	57	48	50	52	58	63	64
Fairly effective	27	34	34	31	28	20	19
Not too effective	10	10	10	10	10	11	9
Not at all effective	4	6	5	4	3	3	4
Don't know	2	2	1	3	1	3	4
Total	100	100	100	100	100	100	100

Note: Respondents were asked: "I'd like your opinion about the effectiveness of different ways of try-ing to influence the way government is run and influence which laws are passed. How effective is it to make sure you vote in all elections: very effective, fairly effective, not too effective, not at all effec-tive?"

Source: Times Mirror Center for The People & The Press, *The People, The Press, & Politics: Campaign '92: "The Generation Divide,"* July 8, 1992, p. 40. Telephone survey of a nationally repre-sentative sample of 3,517 adults 18 years of age or older, conducted May 28-June 10, 1992. Reprinted with permission.

TABLE 2.6 Self-Reported Voter Turnout (as a percent of voting-age population): Presidential and Midterm Election Years, 1972–1994

| | Percentage reporting they voted | | | | | | | | | | | |
| | Presidental election years | | | | | | Congressional election years | | | | | |
	1972	1976	1980	1984	1988	1992	1974	1978	1982	1986	1990	1994
Age												
18–20	48	38	36	37	33	38	20	20	20	19	18	16
21–24	50	46	43	44	38	46	26	26	28	24	22	22
25–34	59	55	55	55	48	53	37	38	40	35	34	32
35–44	66	63	64	64	61	64	49	50	52	49	48	46
45–64	70	69	69	70	68	70	56	59	62	59	75	56
65–74	68	66	69	72	73	74	56	60	65	65	64	64
75 and older	56	55	58	61	62	65	44	48	52	54	54	56
Race/ethnicity												
White	64	61	61	61	59	64	46	47	50	47	47	47
Black	52	49	51	56	52	54	33	37	43	43	39	37
Hispanic origin[a]	37	32	30	33	29	29	22	24	25	24	21	19
Hispanic citizen[a]	—	43	44	48	46	48	—	34	37	36	34	34
Sex												
Male	64	60	59	59	56	60	46	47	49	46	45	44
Female	62	59	59	61	58	62	43	45	48	46	45	45
Region												
Northeast	—	60	59	60	57	61	48	48	50	44	45	45
Midwest	—	65	66	66	63	67	49	51	55	50	49	49
South	55	55	56	57	55	59	36	40	42	43	42	40
West	—	58	57	59	56	59	48	48	51	48	45	46
Employment												
Employed	66	62	62	62	58	64	46	47	50	46	45	45
Unemployed	49	44	41	44	39	46	28	27	34	30	28	28
Not in labor force	59	57	57	59	57	59	43	46	49	48	47	45
Education												
8 years or less	47	44	43	43	37	35	34	35	36	33	28	23
1–3 yrs high school	52	47	46	44	41	41	35	35	38	34	31	27
4 yrs high school	65	59	59	59	55	58	44	45	47	44	42	40
1–3 years college	74	68	67	68	65	69	49	52	53	50	50	49
4 or more yrs college	83	80	80	79	78	81	61	64	67	63	63	63
Total	63	59	59	60	57	61	44	46	49	46	45	45

Notes:
[a]Persons of Hispanic origin may be of any race.

Sources: U.S. Bureau of the Census, Current Population Reports, *Voting and Registration in the Election of November 1976* Washington, D.C.: U.S. Government Printing Office, 1993, Series P-20, no. 322, 11-12, 14-21, 57, 61; *November 1978,* no. 344, 8, 11-19, 60, 65; *November 1980,* no. 370, 10-20, 50, 56; *November 1982,* no. 383, 1-12, 46, 49; *November 1984,* no. 405, 13-24, 59; *November 1986,* no. 414, 11-22, 29, 31; *November 1988,* no. 440, 13-24, 48, 50; *November 1990,* no. 453, 1-2, 4, 13-14, 17; *November 1992,* no. 466, v-vii, 1, 5. *November 1994.* As reported in Harold W. Stanley and Richard G. Niemi, *Vital Statistics on American Politics,* Washington, D.C.: CQ Press, 1988; pp. 66-67; 1994, pp. 86-87. Reprinted with permission.

3

Activism in Political Parties and Election Campaigns

Nearly all of us have heard someone say, "There's not a dime's worth of difference between the Democrats and the Republicans"[1] or "I vote for the person, not the party." Others, when pressed by friends or colleagues to identify whom they will vote for, acknowledge their preferred candidate is "NOTA" (none of the above)![2] Although many believe these antiparty attitudes have emerged relatively recently, some degree of cynicism has always existed toward political parties, especially the party holding power at a particular moment. Many years ago, Will Rogers said, "The more you read and observe about this Politics thing, you got to admit that each party is worse than the other. The one that's out always looks the best."[3]

Staunch believers in the U.S. political party system counter such negativism with statistics showing that an overwhelming majority of Americans still quite willingly identify themselves as Republicans, Democrats, Libertarians, or Ross Perot-United-We-Stand independents. In fact, they can do this almost as quickly as they can identify their religion, marital status, or favorite sports team! Party identification is learned at an early age, as young as 6 or 7,[4] and generally transmitted from parents to children in much the same manner as religious preference or cultural heritage.[5] Though some children ultimately reject their parents' party choice, most adopt that choice as their own. For these people, what is likely to change over the course of their lives is the strength of their identification with a particular party, their appraisal of its strengths and weaknesses, and their reliance on party label as a voting cue.

WHY POLITICAL PARTIES—AND ARE THEY STILL RELEVANT?

Why Care About Party Activism?

For some time, pundits have predicted that political parties in the United States are going the way of the dinosaur and that, in the process, democracy may be threatened. (As reported in Chapter 2, some observers link declining voter turnout rates to the failing strength and influence of political parties among the U.S. electorate.) As the parties grow weaker, so, too, their proponents fear, does the average citizen's personal interest and involvement in a wide variety of campaign activities that precede the act of voting—from watching party conventions and wearing campaign buttons to stumping for a candidate or giving money to a party or a cause.

In this chapter, I explore the validity of these claims, focusing squarely on the question of whether these phenomena have occurred at the same pace or even in the same direction across different generations. I also consider whether the media have dampened or sparked Americans' interest and participation in various party-related campaign activities and whether age makes any difference in terms of media influence.

Age and Partisanship

As is commonly perceived, older Americans are likely to be stronger partisans than younger Americans, for many reasons. First, as people grow older, they identify more strongly with organizations and institutions they have been associated with at some point in their lives.[6] An older person is often more loyal to his or her church or religion, community, school (alums always remember the good things!), or political party. This argument reflects the maturational effect.

The period effect comes into play in the concept of *partisan realignment.* Partisan realignment occurs when there "is a dramatic change in the composition of the electorate or its partisan preferences, or both,"[7] usually after a critical election.[8] People living through a major shift in the nation's partisan makeup are much more likely to retain a strong identification with their own party and to see clear differences between the two parties from that time forward.

Most political scientists agree that a major realignment occurred in the 1930s during the Depression. This shift, they say, helps explain why today's older generations more strongly identify with a political party, usually the Democratic Party, than the younger generations do. But scholars disagree considerably about whether that was the last realignment. Some believe we are in the midst of another partisan realignment at this moment; others think the most recent realignment occurred during the Reagan years. Scholars are carefully watching the party identification patterns of younger generations to affirm or disprove these new realignment theses.[9]

Partisan realignment also helps explain why the grandchildren of those living through a major shift in party allegiances are not as partisan as their grandparents.

> According to this theory, after a realignment occurs parents will be very conscious of the issues on which the new alignment has turned and will strongly transmit their partisan attachments to their offspring. These children of realignment, however, will be less successful in passing their party identification on to the next generation, because by this time the realigning issues will have faded as matters of serious political

concern. As a result, the entrance of this less partisan generation into the electorate will contribute to a process of dealignment.[10]

Dealignment occurs when large numbers of people reject parties and declare themselves independents "instead of changing from one party to another or joining one party in large numbers."[11] The dealignment theory has picked up steam lately, especially given the vote totals independent candidate Ross Perot received in the 1992 presidential election and the extensiveness of crossover voting in the 1994 midterm elections.

Another reason for variations in party affiliation and strength of identification across age-groups has to do with changing educational levels.[12] Many argue that younger generations identify less strongly with political parties because they are more educated and are taught to individually weigh each candidate's qualifications and positions on the issues rather than simply voting the party line. Voting a split ticket—that is, voting for a mix of Democrats, Republicans, and independents—is perceived as the thinking person's alternative to blind partisan allegiance. But others discount this argument because, regardless of educational level or age, split-ticket voting has increased. In their view, media coverage emphasizing individual candidate attributes rather than party affiliation has accelerated this split-ticket, or independent voter, phenomenon.[13] Another camp attributes the phenomenon to "the growth of issue-oriented politics that cuts across party lines for those voters who feel intensely about certain policy matters."[14]

Is the Party Over, or Is It Just the Intermission?

Public opinion surveys have consistently shown a decline in the strength of Americans' party identification over the past few decades. However, analysts strongly disagree about whether the decline has occurred because of anger or negativism toward political parties or simply because of growing indifference or neutrality, as Americans rely less on parties as relevant voting cues.

Proponents of the first view argue that this negativism toward political parties parallels a general decline in Americans' confidence in a whole array of institutions, governmental and nongovernmental. This decline tracks with the upward trend in cynicism, as observed in Chapter 2. Specifically, Americans gripe that the parties "are corrupt institutions, interested in the spoils of politics; they evade the issues; they fail to deliver on their promises; they have no new ideas; they follow public opinion rather than lead it; [and] are just one more special interest."[15]

Proponents of the latter thesis (indifference or irrelevancy) point an accusing finger at the media for focusing too intently on individual candidates, their personal attributes, and their issue stances while largely ignoring party positions, platforms, and policy successes and failures. In *The Media Game*, Stephen Ansolabehere, Roy Behr, and Shanto Iyengar reflected on this phenomenon in presidential elections: "Not only [have] campaigns become increasingly visible and audible to voters, but elections also [have become] much more than opportunities for voters to express their party loyalty. . . . The personal qualities and images of the candidates also come into play, with voters often deserting the candidate of their party because he projects (or fails to project) particular traits."[16] Others say that the strength of a person's identification with a party is irrelevant. What matters more is *consistency*—how often he or she votes the party line. They point to more optimistic evidence showing that regardless of how strongly a person feels about a party, a direct correlation exists between partisan leaning and support for at least some of that party's candidates at election time.

Political Parties and Activism in the American Political System

Close inspections of who is active in U.S. political parties typically concentrate on three groups: citizens, elected officials, and party officials. According to A. James Reichley in *The Life of the Parties: A History of American Political Parties:* "There are *parties in the electorate* (voters who align themselves with one or another of the parties); *parties in government* (elected public officials who have reached their posts by running on a party ticket or who join a party caucus in a legislative body); and *party organizations* (the formal structures that conduct election campaigns and perform other political functions in the party's name)."[17]

In this chapter, I focus primarily on parties in the electorate and party organizations, looking at the age breakdowns of those who participate in each aspect of party life to determine if there are generational differences. (I will discuss elected officials in Chapter 4.)

POLITICAL PARTIES IN THE ELECTORATE

Political parties are as American as mom, apple pie, and democracy.[18] More than fifty years ago, political scientist E. E. Schattschneider described the strong link between parties and democracy: "The political parties created democracy and modern democracy is unthinkable save in terms of the parties."[19] With all their flaws, political parties are still perceived as vital to the functioning of our representative democracy.

Party Functions

Parties perform a variety of services to the U.S. electorate. Among the most important are "organizing the competition, simplifying the choices, unifying the electorate, translating public preferences into policy, bridging the separation of powers by fostering cooperation among branches of government, providing loyal opposition, socializing and assisting immigrants, providing channels for upward mobility through patronage, and recruiting and nominating candidates for office."[20]

Two Parties Dominate

Two political parties have always dominated the U.S. political landscape. Third parties periodically appear on the horizon, especially in presidential elections, but their candidates typically have little success in getting elected. Third and minor parties typically have an ideological, single-issue, economic protest, or factional focus.[21] Often, their true impact in the long run is on the two major parties—forcing them to grapple with an issue or situation they have ignored in the past.[22] Third-party candidates have been slightly more successful at the state and local levels, but even there they take a back seat to the two major parties. The notion of two parties—Republican and Democrat—is firmly ingrained in most Americans' minds from childhood.

Throughout our lives, the notion of a two-party system is constantly reinforced. As children, we learn from our parents and schoolteachers that in matters of politics and voting, people are usually Democrats or Republicans. As we reach voting age, our election system strengthens this notion in a number of ways. In many states, we must choose a party affiliation at the time we register to vote. And most states restrict participation in party primary elections—that is, nominating party candidates to run in the general election against opposition party candidates—to those who formally declare their party affiliation; these are termed *closed primaries.*

Candidates for major offices typically run with a party label attached to their names.[23] Their political ads and campaign literature must report party affiliation. And the candidates' parties often supply both campaign workers and funds. In many states, the ballot format even makes it easiest to vote a straight party ticket. In others, party symbols are allowed on the ballot, along with party slogans. Thus, throughout the electoral process, we are encouraged or required to declare our party affiliation.

At the same time, we are subjected to counterpressures urging us to avoid using party label as our only voting cue. Schools, peers, individual candidates, and even the parties themselves, hoping to attract crossover voters, challenge us to focus more on a candidate's personal attributes and issue stances than on party label alone. On top of that, the negative nature of the media's coverage of candidates has, in the opinion of some, created the impression that little difference exists in the parties or in the quality of the candidates who run under their banners. Individuals running as independents or write-in candidates—a growing phenomenon—have also made a point of proclaiming that the two major political parties offer little real choice to the voter.

These two views of parties help explain why a large proportion of Americans can identify themselves with one party or the other when asked to do so, either by pollsters or by election officials. At the same time, these views help us understand why the strength of party identification has gradually declined since the early 1950s.

Strength of Party Identification

In the *American National Election Studies Data Sourcebook,* party identification was defined as "the psychological feeling of attachment to a political party." The

FIGURE 3.1 Strong Party Identifiers by Age Cohort: 1952–1992

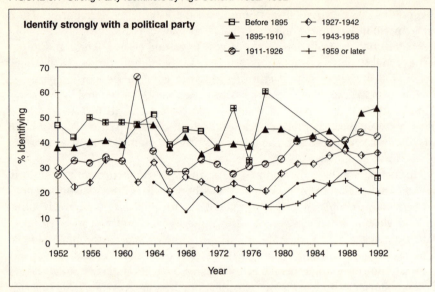

Source: Warren E. Miller and Santa A. Traugott, *American National Election Studies Data Sourcebook: 1952–1986,* Cambridge, MA: Havard University Press, 1989; 1988 & 1990 data from *U.S. Statistical Abstract 1990, 1992,* p. 270. 1992 figures provided by Lynn Vavreck. Reprinted by permission of the publishers from *American National Election Studies Data Sourcebook* by Warren Miller and Arthur Miller, Cambridge, Mass.: Harvard University Press, Copyright © 1980 by the President and Fellows of Harvard College.

authors of the *Sourcebook* made it clear that party identification "is to be distinguished from such behavior as party registration for primary elections or voting for candidates of a particular party." But they acknowledge that "although self-identification as a Republican or Democrat is separable from the act of voting, it nevertheless has a substantial impact on political attitudes, participation, and vote choice."[24]

Larry Sabato, in *The Party's Just Begun,* described how party identification works for the average American:

> Most American voters *identify* with a party but do not *belong* to it. There is no universal enrolled party membership; no prescribed dues; no formal rules concerning an individual's activities; no enforceable obligations to the party assumed by the voter. . . . Party identification or affiliation is an informal and impressionistic exercise whereby a citizen acquires a party label and accepts its standard as a shorthand summary of his or her political views and preferences. . . . The party label becomes a voter's central political reference symbol and perceptual screen, a prism or filter through which the world of politics and government flows and is interpreted. . . . On the whole, Americans [view their partisan affiliation] as a convenience rather than a necessity.[25]

Since 1952, the proportion of Americans who identify themselves as either strong Democrats or Republicans has declined (Figure 3.1), and the percent saying they are independents has increased. Exactly how much party identification has declined is often a function of how that identification is calculated.

For many years, public opinion surveys have asked respondents a series of questions aimed at determining the strength of their identification with a particular political party. The series goes as follows: "Generally speaking, in politics do you usually think of yourself as a Republican, a Democrat, an independent, or what?" Persons who say they are Republicans or Democrats are then asked: "Would you call yourself a strong or a not very strong Democrat/Republican?" Persons who initially identify themselves as independents are then asked: "Do you think of yourself as closer to the Republican or the Democratic Party?" If they say the Republican Party, they are classified as "independent Republican leaners"; if they say the Democratic Party, they are "independent Democratic leaners." Analysts using such a series of questions frequently construct a seven-category scale of party identifiers: (1) strong Republicans, (2) weak Republicans, (3) Republican leaners, (4) pure independents, (5) Democratic leaners, (6) weak Democrats, and (7) strong Democrats. Some add an eighth category—apoliticals, those who repeatedly refuse to indicate any affiliation whatsoever.

Often, the seven categories are condensed into three—Democrat, Republican, and independent—and used to test the proposition that Americans' attachment to parties is declining. (Apoliticals are excluded altogether.) When combining the categories, a key decision is how to treat the independent leaners. If they are treated as partisans (counted with the party they lean toward) rather than independents, party decline does not seem so marked. But if the independent leaners are counted in the independent total, party decline and the rise of independents appear to be much sharper trends.

Considering all the hype about the decline of political parties and what that means to their future, I find it noteworthy that so little has been written about the presence or absence of maturational, generational, or period effects on changes in the strength of party identification. One notable exception is the work of William Flanigan and Nancy Zingale regarding partisan change between 1952 and 1992. They found "a period effect that has resulted in an increasing independence in all age-groups, a generation effect that keeps Democratic partisan loyalty high in the generation that entered the election during the New Deal, and a life cycle effect that yields greater independence among the young than among their elders." (Their definitions of period, generation, and life-cycle effects, however, are somewhat different from those used by other scholars.[26])

Looking at trends in strength of party identification over time and across different generations (Table 3.1), we find that (1) the older one grows, the stronger one's party identification becomes—a maturational or life-cycle effect; (2) older generations are much more strongly identified with the Democratic Party than are the younger generations, especially the Reagan generation—a period effect; and (3) younger and older cohorts today are more likely to be independents than their counterparts in the past—a period effect but also a generational effect in that the incidence of independents is highest among the young.

To keep the facts in perspective, it is important to note that at least 85 percent of the members of each generation label themselves as identifying with one party more than the other. Only 15 percent or fewer are pure independents—refusing to lean in either party's direction, even when pollsters press them to do so.

Voting the Party Line or a Split Ticket?

Many political analysts, party activists, and candidates are more interested in the consistency issue: how often a party identifier, no matter how weak or strong, votes for the party's candidates on election day. Some regard this as a measure of how often voters use party labels as voting cues—and as a measure of how strongly the person believes in his or her party for whatever reason (i.e., voting the party line).

Many studies have found a rather close link between party identification and support for party candidates running for a variety of offices. But though still strong, this link is weakening. Today, there are higher incidences of divided party control between the executive and legislative bodies at the national level (involving the presidency and majority rule of the U.S. Senate and U.S. House of Representatives) and at the state level (involving the governorship and control of the state house and state senate). There are also more instances in which a district's voters support one party's candidate for chief executive but another party's candidate for a legislative seat.

Divided party control occurs when one party's candidate captures the executive post and the other party wins a majority of the seats in at least one of the two legislative chambers (senate and house).[27] Thus, it reflects split-ticket voting, and it happens quite commonly at the national level. Morris Fiorina pointed out that between 1832 and 1992, "national elections have created or continued a condition of divided government for 62 of 160 years, about 40 percent of our history."[28] Divided party control is also increasingly common at the state level.[29] According to one estimate, almost three-quarters of Americans live in divided-control states.[30]

Split-ticket voting has increased sharply since the late 1960s. As expected, however, it has increased most rapidly among the younger cohorts. Split-ticket voting is highest among young and middle-aged voters. Younger voters depend more upon television for their campaign information, and television is a forum that emphasizes personality more than party. (I will return to this point later in the chapter.) Although split-ticket voting concerns party officials, these facts should be kept in perspective. Most voters of all ages tend to vote for their party's candidates. The proportion is even higher in many state and local races, which get far less media attention than presidential elections. In fact, in the less-visible races, party may be the *only* voting cue, other than name recognition, available to the voter. In this media era, many voter perceptions of party differences (or lack thereof) are created by the form and content of the media messages, which may themselves be age-bound.

In situations in which a voter or potential voter does not see any difference between the two parties, that person will more often (1) choose the independent classification, (2) vote a split ticket, and (3) use media-delivered, candidate-centered information, as opposed to party label, as the primary voting cue.

THE ELECTORATE'S PERCEPTIONS OF PARTY DIFFERENCES

Each party's leaders are intent on showing that there are meaningful differences between parties and that *their* party and its candidates are better choices. Parties work hard to persuade people to see differences and to vote accordingly. Capturing public office is just the first step; the ultimate goal is to affect public policy outcomes. An equally important goal is to "deepen citizens' affections for the parties and their candidates"[31]—to strengthen the party system and ensure that it lives on. Two prominent political analysts put it this way: "Political parties live and die by the numbers—numbers of supporters, candidates, contributors, and especially voters."[32]

For all these reasons, political analysts and party activists are quite interested in whether the public sees more than "a dime's worth of difference" between the Democrats and Republicans. Having tracked this question for quite some time, they have found it necessary to ask more than "Do you see any differences between the two parties?" or "Do you think there are any important differences in what the Republicans and Democrats stand for?" Pollsters must probe more deeply, asking Americans whether they see any differences in the quality of the candidates run by the two parties, in party organizational abilities and management skills, or in each party's ability to lead the nation in a different direction. Pollsters also regularly ask a battery of issue-type questions: Which party is best able to address problem x, y, or z?

Not surprisingly, Americans generally identify more differences when asked detailed questions about various dimensions of party activities than when asked simply whether there's any difference. But even when asked the simple question, a majority of the electorate sees differences in what the two parties represent. A 1994 Times Mirror survey found that nearly one-fourth see "a great deal of difference" and that another 51 percent see "a fair amount"—little changed from a similar 1987 survey.[33]

Does a person's age affect the extent to which he or she perceives party distinctiveness? Presumably, yes—and for a variety of reasons: generational differences in terms of interest levels, knowledge, strength of party identification, and ideology (liberal or conservative). Older persons, being more interested in and informed about politics, more strongly attached to a party, and more conservative (or at least that's the common perception), are expected to see more differences in the aggregate.

However, it is assumed that a person's age is less likely to be a factor in perceiving differences in party organizational and governing capacities. Such contrasts are more likely to be period- and personality-bound, varying considerably more by who is in office than by the respondent's age. Again, few studies exist to enlighten us further in what we should expect to find.

The results of my analyses are quite surprising. In some instances, the assessments of older citizens differ markedly from their younger cohorts; in others, there is not much difference across age-groups.

Differences in What the Parties Stand For

In general, the proportion of voters who see important differences between what the two parties stand for increased sharply during the Reagan years and remains higher today than in the pre-1980 years. Older cohorts are somewhat more likely to see these differences than the young. However, the 1980 jump in the proportion who perceived differences was sharpest among the youngest and oldest cohorts. For the young, this probably reflected their first exposure to a more ideologically based presidential campaign, with candidates Ronald Reagan, Jimmy Carter, and John Anderson. For the oldest, the insertion of a high-profile, third-party candidate (Anderson) likely caused them to focus more clearly on party distinctions.

Surveys that place more emphasis on uncovering what the public thinks it means to be a Republican or a Democrat have shown that most Americans do have some idea of what these party labels mean, even if their responses are not always explicit or sophisticated. The Times Mirror Center for The People & The Press surveys occasionally ask those it polls two open-ended (fill-in-the-blank) questions: "What does it mean to you when someone says he or she is a Republican?" and "What does it mean to you when someone says he or she is a Democrat?" The most common descriptors are ideology (liberal/conservative), constituency base (poor/rich, labor/business), and government spending (for more spending/against more spending). These are standard, textbook delimiters of party differences that have shown up in other surveys using a similar question format.[34]

In these perceived distinctions, some age-group differences exist—but not many. As shown in Table 3.2, a much higher proportion of older persons are able to give a reply—that is, few give a "don't know" response. This supports the conclusion of a study completed more than twenty years ago that found that in stable party systems such as ours, older persons have a clearer idea of what party means as a "direct function of [their] continuing experience with the party system."[35] "The passage of time offers people repeated opportunities to support verbally, and vote for, a party and its candidates, resulting in learning by means of psychological reinforcement."[36] Older people also appear more likely to define party differences in terms of government spending levels, reflecting their years of experience with parties defined in such terms at election time. Finally, older persons are more likely to say there's little or no difference between the two parties, although this is still very much a minority viewpoint.[37] It is, however, further evidence of the more cynical attitudes of older persons as compared to the young.

Older persons are more likely to have clearer ideas of what they like and don't like about each political party. The National Election Study regularly asks its respondents, "Is there anything in particular you like/dislike about the Republican party?" "Is there anything in particular you like/dislike about the Democratic party?" Generally, the youngest cohort is the least able to articulate a specific like or dislike about either party. This fits with the notion that party distinctions (and support for a particular party) are less firm among the young.

On the matter of likes and dislikes, older persons are somewhat more negative toward parties, although this pattern spans all age-groups. Although it is, to a certain degree, human nature to articulate the bad in more detail than the good, this negativism distresses parties and their candidates. However, one of the difficulties they face is that the different age-groups vary in what they find appealing or unappealing about each party. Much of this difference can be traced to the political generation to which an individual belongs and the reputation or prestige and issue stances of each party at the time they came of voting age. But the differences can also be explained, to some extent, by each age-group's place in the life cycle. As will be shown in Chapters 5 and 6, an individual's policy priorities differ according to what stage of life he or she is in. Thus, they may affect specific likes or dislikes about a party depending upon how that party addresses a high-priority issue.

Specific Likes and Dislikes About the Democratic Party

Responses to the National Election Study questions on party likes and dislikes are often divided into four categories: group representation, ideology, economic, and government programs (tapping the extensiveness of the government's role in addressing societal problems). Among all age-cohorts, group representation (of the poor, the aged, the unemployed, farmers, the working class) is the most-cited "like" category regarding the Democratic Party; ideology is cited the least. The most common "dislike" category is economics, reflecting the perception among a sizable portion of the public that the Democratic Party favors more taxing and spending. In general, the youngest cohort (born in 1959 or later) likes the group representation and government programs positions of the Democratic Party more than its ideolgy or economic stances; generally, however, this group has fewer likes or dislikes regarding the party than the older cohorts do. The oldest cohort (born before 1895) most likes the party's group representation dimensions and most dislikes its economic positions. However, the generation born between 1895 and 1910 is the most favorable toward both.[38]

Specific Likes and Dislikes About the Republican Party

Generally, fewer likes or dislikes regarding the Republican Party are articulated in responses to public opinion surveys. In stark contrast to the data for the Democratic Party, the most common "like" category, especially among the youngest cohorts, is the Republican Party's ideology.[39] The most cited "dislikes" fall into the categories of group representation and economics. The middle-aged generations are the most critical of the party's constituency base and economics, although the percentage citing these dislikes is still relatively small.[40]

In general, when asked open-ended questions about what in particular they like or dislike about a political party, few respondents are able to articulate a specific attribute, but the older are slightly more capable than the youngest cohorts because they have had more experience with political parties and election campaigns where party themes are articulated.

What Party Means to Party Identifiers

To personalize the concept of political party, surveys often probe respondents' views about how the party label affects their political behavior—that is, the frequency of their support for party candidates, their degree of support for what the party stands for, their involvement in party activities, the importance attached to their party identification, and the degree to which that identification is simply an expression of strong anti–other-party feelings.

A 1987 Times Mirror survey along these lines shows that the biggest age-group differences emerged with regard to the importance of the party label and the consistency of support for party candidates. The young were less prone to view the party as "important to me" than the old. The old were more likely to describe themselves as "usually preferring [their party's] candidates, but sometimes supporting [the other party's]," although high proportions of each age-group described themselves in such a manner.[41] High proportions of all age-groups also considered themselves partisans but not always in complete agreement with what the party stands for, reflecting the rise in split-ticket voting. Only one-fifth of each age-group saw party identification as primarily an anti–other-party affiliation. In general, these findings underscore the greater partisan independence of younger cohorts.

Assessments of Party Organization, Management, and Effectiveness

Most Americans are quite capable of judging which party (if any) is superior to the other in its organization, capacity to manage the federal government, selection of candidates, and effectiveness as an agent of change. Surveys by the Times Mirror Center for The People & The Press have routinely shown that 90 percent of the public can make distinctions when asked, "Tell me whether you think [a specific attribute] better describes the Republican Party or the Democratic Party" (see Table 3.3).

Between 1987 and 1994, the Republican Party was consistently perceived as better organized than the Democratic Party. The Democratic Party was rated as a better agent of change, although the gap narrowed. The parties flip-flopped in the public's assessment of which could best manage the federal government (Democrats replaced Republicans in 1992 but, in turn, the Republicans recaptured this position by 1994). However, differences between the parties in terms of management ability have never been very wide. In fact, between one-fourth and one-fifth of the public regularly judges neither party as being particularly good at managing the government. Meanwhile, the parties have been judged virtually equal in their ability to select good candidates for office, although the Republican Party held a slight edge going into the 1994 elections.

Predictably, the Democratic Party has most often been perceived as "concerned with the needs and interests of the disadvantaged" and "the needs of people like me," and the Republican Party is seen as more concerned with "the needs and interests of business and other powerful groups," according to various Times Mirror surveys.[42]

In 1994, when probed about which party "governs in an honest and ethical way," 35 percent of the respondents identified the Democratic Party and 32 percent identified the Republican Party; significantly, 21 percent answered "neither" to this question. This reflects the growing distrust of both major U.S. political parties among the population at large (especially the national political parties).

Age breakdowns on questions about political party operations revealed differences hovering in the 10 percent range and reflected variations in the partisan base of each group. A higher proportion of those under age 30 were Republicans than were those over 30, accounting for the increasingly positive assessments of almost all attributes of the Republican Party among the 18- to 29-year-olds. In contrast, the older cohorts tended to give more positive assessments to the Democratic Party and its leaders, reflecting their own partisan leanings. (A November 1994 poll by the Times Mirror Center for The People & The Press showed that 44 percent of those 18 to 29 either labeled themselves as a Republican or leaning toward the Republican Party, compared to 38.8 percent of those 65 and over.)

A slightly higher proportion of older persons saw *neither* party as superior to the other. This is further evidence of the higher cynicism levels of the elderly. However, the proportion was relatively small—in most instances, below 20 percent. But it is surprising that more old than young said they don't know which party is better at issues such as organization, management, representation, and candidate selection. One explanation may be that textbooks and the media historically haven't used these factors as often as ideology, spending, or issue positions to distinguish between the two parties. Years of witnessing the same problems popping up over and over without much resolution may also prompt such a response. Moreover, more old than young generally give "don't know" responses to all public opinion surveys.

Perceptions About Party Capacity to Handle Major Public Policies

The success of political parties and their candidates often depends upon a majority of the voters perceiving that one party can best handle the pressing problems of the day. Often these problems are lumped into several categories: foreign policy/defense, social welfare, economic, and moral. Parties struggle, as one scholar put it, to "own" the public's confidence in their ability to handle certain issues.

Over the course of U.S. history, certain "issues become features of a party's policy agenda because the party's candidates and officials (who are disproportionately members of the groups demanding government action) respond to pressure from their constituents that the government do something about difficulties they (the constituents) are facing."[43]

The constituency (identifier) bases of each political party are different.[44] Democrats draw more support from African Americans, Hispanics (except Cubans), women, gays and lesbians, older voters, blue-collar workers, labor union members, those who have not graduated from college, Jews, Catholics, and those with no religious preference. Republicans have stronger bases among the young, whites, Cuban Americans, college graduates, the more affluent, Protestants (especially members of the more conservative religions), and Mormons.[45]

Although voters may not be able to identify the issue stances of many candidates, particularly in lower-profile races in a crowded election field, research shows "voters do harbor general impressions about the parties in terms of issues, and they are responsive to these perceptions."[46] When respondents are asked whether the Democrats or Republicans will do a better job of handling an issue, Democrats have historically scored better on the domestic front (social welfare and fairness issues). Republicans are generally regarded as more competent on foreign policy/defense issues and in promoting moral values. Economic issues have more of a "mixed ownership." Scholar John Petrocik described it this way: "Some [economic issues] are Democratic assets, some are owned by the GOP, and others are performance questions—where a recent record of success or failure provides a "lease" rather than a clear title. Spending, taxation, and inflation are traditional Republican issues. Unemployment was a Democratic strength until the economic turmoil of the Carter years and the prosperity of Reagan's terms . . . moved the GOP ahead or into a tied position on unemployment issues."[47] (The recession of the late 1980s and early 1990s made it a Democratic issue once again, although by the 1994 midterm elections, the gap had narrowed considerably.)

There is fairly strong support for Petrocik's thesis. Between 1987 and 1991, a souring economy, as evidenced by rising unemployment and slower rates of growth in the gross domestic product, changed the public's perception of which party could handle the economy best. We all know the rest of the story. The party holding the presidency during the downturn (Republican) lost to the out-party (Democratic) in the 1992 presidential election. Perceptions about which party could best handle social, foreign policy/defense, and moral issues were much more stable.

It is likely that economic issues will be preeminent in the 1996 election as well. The critical question is which party will be perceived by the public as best able to deal with the economy. By mid-1994, Republicans were being judged as more capable of "making America competitive in the world economy" (48 percent compared to Democrats' 35 percent) and doing "a better job of reducing the federal budget deficit" (42 percent compared to the Democrats' 36 percent), no doubt helping explain the Republicans' capture of both houses of Congress for the first time in forty years.[48] But there's no guarantee they will maintain the "upper hand." As noted, Americans' opinions about party handling of economic issues are the fastest to change—and they often have the greatest political consequences.

From my perspective, another interesting question about party issue-handling capacity is whether the young or the old are more likely to *change* their opinions. In *The Rational Public: Fifty Years of Trends in Americans' Policy Preferences*, Benjamin I. Page and Robert Shapiro found some—albeit marginal—support for the hypothesis that the young are more receptive to new circumstances and change their opinions at a more rapid rate than the old. They concluded: "All age-groups seem to be affected in roughly the same way by events and new information and changing societal conditions."[49] Based on their experiences, I was not surprised to come to a similar conclusion when comparing changes in age-group judgments regarding party capacity to handle various issues, even though my research certainly encompasses a shorter time frame.

Focusing exclusively on *changes* in age-group assessments of party capacity to handle specific issues, two observations stand out, even within a short time frame. First, younger respondents are quicker to abandon responses saying that neither party is best at handling an issue. Perhaps this reflects a sharper gain in knowledge about the issue among the young (who have a steeper learning curve than their elders), as well as the older cohorts' greater cynicism. Second, younger Americans are somewhat more likely to shift the intensity of their opinions toward the two parties' issue-handling capacity. Perhaps this reveals their less-firm understanding of how the parties differ or, again, their education or knowledge gains on the issues and the parties.

More Than a Dime's Worth of Difference

These observations don't lend much support to claims that there's no difference between Democrats and Republicans—at least in the minds of most Americans. The generations do vary in how much difference they see, a perception that is affected, no doubt, by the depth of their knowledge and experience with the party system. They differ less in their perceptions of which party is best at handling a specific issue. The economic issue, though belonging to neither party, can propel one party into power (the presidency) and yank the other out. In the years ahead, intergenerational economic issues will keep the economy at the forefront of the electorate's mind, lending further support to my thesis that participation rate gaps between the young and the old will continue to shrink.

THE ELECTORATE'S PARTICIPATION IN CAMPAIGN ACTIVITIES

People vary tremendously in the extent to which they participate in or follow the election season. To use a sports analogy, we can point to those who don't really get interested until the play-offs or even the Super Bowl, others who avidly follow the sport from preseason until the championship game, and still others whose interest waxes and wanes throughout the season, depending upon the publicity given a particular game or rivalry. Some are loyal to their favorite team until the bitter end no matter how far behind it is, believing that the game is truly not over until the clock runs out. Others shift loyalties rather easily, especially if their favorite team is losing, or they just turn off the game, saying, "Wait 'til next year." Some individuals never tune in at all, no matter what—they just aren't interested.

In many ways, political parties behave like marketing firms and cheerleaders. Their job is to mobilize support for the whole gamut of their team's operations: its players (the candidates), its game plan (the party platform), its coaches (the strategists and pollsters), its staff (party officers and workers), and its fans (the party identifiers, volunteers, and contributors). Their job isn't easy in light of the intense competition for the attention and loyalties of the public. But try they must. Their efforts are, in the words of scholars Rosenstone and Hansen, the key to getting people to the polls (and perpetuating the party system):

> People vote because they have the resources to bear the costs and because they have the interests and identities to appreciate the benefits. But people also turn out to vote substantially because somebody helps them or asks them to participate. The actions of parties, campaigns, and social movements mobilize public involvement in American elections. The "blame" for declining voter turnout, accordingly, rests as much on political [including party] leaders as on citizens themselves.[50]

Rosenstone and Hansen, along with a multitude of other researchers, found that using the personal touch is often the most effective strategy. Party volunteers go door to door, block by block, and talk face to face with residents about their party's candidates. Phone bank operators call potential voters on the phone, and other party workers or professional consultants mail campaign brochures or flyers directly to individual homes. On election day, party activists drive voters to the polls. The results of all these methods seem to be worthwhile: "When parties make the effort, the people they contact are far more likely to participate in electoral politics than the people they pass over."[51]

Party Strategies in Personal Contacting

Political parties are undoubtedly restrained in the amount of personal contacting they can do by the amount of their resources, primarily labor and money. In *Winning Local and State Elections: The Guide to Organizing Your Campaign,* campaign consultants Ann Beaudry and Bob Schaeffer strongly urged parties and potential candidates to target, unless money is no object (a rare circumstance):

By targeting you can identify those areas with the greatest concentrations of nonvoters and voters who consistently support candidates from the other political party. These areas should be a low priority, if they receive any resources at all. And likewise, targeting will pinpoint those areas where the greatest concentrations of potentially favorable and persuadable voters are located. *These are the voters who represent the margin of victory in a campaign.* It is in these high priority areas that you want to concentrate your campaign communications.[52]

Historically, political parties have targeted the following groups: (1) strong party identifiers, the surest votes; (2) key constituency groups with long histories of support for the party (e.g., labor for the Democrats, business for the Republicans); and (3) the social belongers, the longer-term residents who are active in community, church, and civic organizations. Since older persons are stronger party identifiers and more frequent social belongers, it is not surprising that parties and individual candidates target more of their limited resources toward contacting them rather than the very young.[53]

In spite of the effectiveness of personal contacting, parties are relying less on this method today. Larger districts, rising fear of crime and lawsuits, and greater difficulty in recruiting party volunteers have made door-to-door campaigning and election-day drives to the polls less attractive or viable, especially in major metropolitan areas.[54] An increase in the public's tendency to hang up on any type of phone solicitation, including that urging them to vote, has made phone banks a little less effective as well. Direct mail remains the most viable form of personal contacting, although the saturation of junk mail is also making it difficult to get people to pay attention to campaign literature. Consequently, it is not surprising that in recent years, political parties have been cutting back their personal contacting efforts and, by necessity, turning more to the media to engage the public in political campaign activities. The cutback has affected all age-groups in virtually the same way. The pattern is sharpest in the contacting activities of Democratic congressional candidates.

The Media, the Parties, and the Public

The public participates in political campaigns through its interaction with the media more than the average citizen realizes. Simple acts such as reading the newspaper, watching the evening news, tuning in to radio talk shows or late-night TV comedy programs, or watching political party conventions, candidate debates, and paid campaign advertisements all yield valuable information about politics, politicians, and public policies.

Although we know that older persons are generally more attentive to politics and gather their information from a wider array of sources, we don't know much about whether age makes any difference in which parts of the campaign season people view as the most interesting and influential. (For a good overview of the campaign season, see Table 3.4.) Surveys taken by the Times Mirror Center for

The Public & The Press at various stages of the 1988 and 1992 presidential campaigns offered some intriguing insights into Americans' attentiveness to and patience with what's considered by many to be long and drawn-out horse races. Actually, some consider a presidential campaign a never-ending horse race since the next campaign begins the day after election day—or sooner. Polls appear almost instantly, gauging who's in the lead for the next round of nominations, and they don't stop until election day four years later.[55]

Party Presidential Primaries and Caucuses. There are fifty paths to the presidency: Each state plays a formal role in the nomination and election of a president. The presidential campaign in each state typically begins either with a primary election (as occurred in thirty-two states in 1992) or a party caucus or convention. Depending upon the state and the political party, these primaries and caucuses give voters a chance to express their choice for the convention's nominee or select a party's delegates to attend the national party convention.[56] Ultimately, the whole process is intended to narrow each party's list of presidential wannabes to one. It often causes anxiety for party officials because "a genuine primary is a fight within the family of the party—a fight that can turn nasty as different factions within the family compete with each other to secure a place on the November ballot for their candidate."[57]

The nominating process is quite complicated. Larry Bartels, author of *Presidential Primaries and the Dynamics of Public Choice,* described the ordeal as follows: "Instead of two candidates there may be half a dozen or more. Some candidates may be well-known political figures; others may be virtually unknown to the electorate. The issues dividing them may have little to do with the issues on which the winner will eventually wage the general election campaign. And they compete in fifty separate state-level delegate selection processes governed by a bizarre assortment of complex rules."[58]

Such a process is tailor-made for the media and its captive audience, the public. As Bartels noted: "As the focus moves around the country from week to week, politicians, journalists, and the public use the results in each state to adjust their own expectations and behavior at subsequent stages in the process. One week's outcome becomes an important part of the political context shaping the following week's choices. Thus, each primary must be interpreted not as a final result but as a single episode in the series of interrelated political events that together determine the nominee."[59]

Earlier Is More Interesting—and Important. The nomination season starts with a bang and ends with a whimper. Voters in states holding their primaries or caucuses first, traditionally New Hampshire and Iowa, receive a disproportionate amount of attention from the media and the candidates.[60] For example, in 1992, the New Hampshire primary got 23 percent of all the TV news coverage of state primaries and caucuses. In contrast, the four largest states—New York, California, Texas, and Florida—received only 8, 5, 2, and 4 percent, respectively, for a total of only 19 percent![61]

In recent years, officials in many states whose primaries or caucuses used to fall at the end of the nomination season have now scheduled them earlier, often in concert, in order to get more clout and attention for their state or region. For example, in 1988, fourteen southern states agreed to hold their primaries on the same day, March 8, which has come to be called "Super Tuesday." (Moving primaries or caucuses to earlier dates is known as "front-loading.") According to one account, more than half of the delegates to both national party conventions are chosen before the end of April—and before the party's nominee is already obvious.[62]

Front-loading will intensify. In 1993, California moved its primary from June to March to give the state greater influence in the 1996 nomination process. New York, Florida, Ohio, and Georgia will also have their primaries in March 1996, which guarantees "that the parties [will] know the identity of their nominees by the end of March, 1996."[63] This will force parties and candidates to start working much earlier—and to rely on the media even more. According to political analyst Mark Shields:

> Changes in primary dates will make the 1996 nominating process a lot shorter, much more expensive and practically inaccessible for the underfinanced, overlooked long shot. . . . Within five weeks of the February 20 New Hampshire primary, 75 percent of the pledged delegates to the 1996 presidential nominating convention will have been chosen. . . . After they leave New Hampshire, the surviving 1996 presidential candidates will spend their time almost exclusively at airport tarmacs, before TV cameras, or on the phone, dialing desperately for campaign dollars.[64]

The edge in coverage will almost certainly go to the big states, although the states that begin the nominating process, no matter how large, will surely get more attention than those that pull up the rear.

Who Votes in Presidential Primaries? Some authorities contend that those who actually participate in their party's primaries and caucuses are the highly politically attentive and thus do not represent the overall constituency base of the party. According to this argument, such activists may choose party nominees who do not appeal to the majority of party identifiers. Yet, other authorities say choosing presidential favorites (and delegates bound to them) through the primary system makes the nominee *more* representative of the party rank and file than when party leaders or elites make the selection. The same debate applies to voter profiles of those who select party nominees for state and local positions using the primary system. At a minimum, all agree that older persons are typically more politically attentive than younger persons. Consequently, one would expect them to participate in presidential primaries at higher levels than their younger counterparts.

One Times Mirror survey, taken in January 1988 before the November presidential election, lent support to this thesis. Pollsters asked: "If there is a Presidential primary or a caucus in your state this year, how likely is it that you will participate? Is it very likely, somewhat likely, not too likely, or not at all likely?" Compared to younger citizens, nearly twice as many older citizens (except for the oldest) said they were "very likely" to participate, even though at this stage of a presidential election campaign, "most citizens . . . know little or nothing about most of the candidates or even who they are and, quite often, have thought little about public policies."[65]

Moreover, primary election results from two Florida counties in 1992 show that older voters turn out in droves. In Hillsborough County (Tampa) and in Pinellas County (St. Petersburg), half the voters 65 to 74 years of age cast ballots, compared to one-third of those 35 to 44 and less than one-fifth of those younger than 24.

Furthermore, the age profile of the delegates who attend the national party conventions shows that the median (half above, half below) age of the delegates to each party's convention is older than that of the party identifiers. Republican delegates, as a rule, are older than Democratic delegates; no doubt, the comparative youth of the Democrats stems from a change in the party's delegate selection rules in 1972, mandating greater inclusion of younger voters. The fact that both Republican and Democratic delegates are older than party identifiers does not come as a surprise. First, party activists tend to be older than party identifiers. Second, in a number of states, some delegate slots are reserved for elected party officials, who tend to be older than the average party identifier.

Voter turnout in presidential primaries is strongly related to the time at which those contests are held (earlier is better) and how much impact they are perceived to have on the eventual selection of a party's nominee (big states and states joining in regional coalitions have higher turnout). Economist Anthony Downs, author of *An Economic Theory of Democracy,* has argued that this is a good example of rational decisionmaking by the voters and nonvoters.[66]

Party Primary Effectiveness in Tapping Candidates. What do Americans think about the primary system's effectiveness in selecting the best-qualified nominee? According to Times Mirror surveys, the answer is a toss-up. Between the 1988 and 1992 presidential campaigns, the percentage of Americans who entered the presidential primary season thinking the primary system was an effective way to determine the best-qualified party nominee dropped from 61 to 51 percent.

Evidence also indicates that once a presidential primary season begins, criticism about the selection system intensifies. For example, between January and March 1992, the period of the first primaries and caucuses, the percentage of Americans who viewed primaries as an effective tool to measure candidate qualifications dropped from 51 to 31 percent. The 18- to 29-year-olds ended up more positive toward the primary method (41 percent) than the 65-and-older group (26 percent), although the two groups were much closer in their opinions at the outset.

Other data to be discussed later in the chapter suggest older voters get tired of the media-intense election hoopla much more quickly than younger voting-age people who are experiencing it for the first or second time. In deciding whom to vote for, older persons also tend to make up their minds more quickly, and they tend to get more disgusted when their favorite candidate is eliminated early in the primary season.

Party Primary Effectiveness at Holding Voter Interest. Data from the February 1992 New Hampshire primary indicate that the proportion of voters who followed the primary was relatively small but virtually the same for each party (around 15 to 30 percent, depending on age-group). Predictably, older voters across the United States were twice as attentive as younger voters to their party's first nomination fight.

As the primary and caucus season wore on, interest in the Democratic Party's nomination politics grew considerably across all age-groups, although older voters still were the most interested. The major Republican challenger to sitting President George Bush, Patrick Buchanan, dropped out of the race early, thereby deflating interest in the state Republican primaries. In the case of the Democrats, a larger number of contenders stayed in the contest for a longer period, creating a more suspenseful scenario.

In summary, older voters follow party primaries more closely than their younger counterparts, but changes in the level of competition evoke similar changes in interest levels across all age-groups.

Party Conventions: Who Watches and What Interests Them? Political party conventions are big media events, although network television coverage of them has declined in recent years. Only CNN and C-SPAN now offer gavel-to-gavel coverage. The highlight of each convention is the formal nomination of the party's candidate for the presidency and vice presidency, although nowadays, the outcome is often widely known before the convention.[67]

Conventions serve a number of other useful purposes for both the party and the electorate. The nominee typically gets a bump upward in the public opinion polls right after the convention, an average of seven points over the last thirty years.[68] Party activists get fired up to work on the campaign. Nominees have an easier time raising funds. And the voters learn a good deal more about the party platforms and the nominees. Some voters actually decide whom they will vote for during the conventions.

Political conventions are informative—and entertaining. Byron Shafer, author of *Bifurcated Politics: Evolution and Reform in the National Party Convention,* described them beautifully:

> For its audience, the charm of a national party convention remains a mix of what it has always been. There is the element of momentous decision, of course [the selection of the presidential nominee]. Even in an era when the convention merely ratifies rather than makes its central decision, that act still confirms one of two possible alternatives for the most important political office in the United States, and perhaps the world. There is the element of contention and conflict too. Few conventions occur without some evident struggle—over platform, over rules, perhaps over the

FIGURE 3.2 Young Heavily Dependent on Television for Campaign News

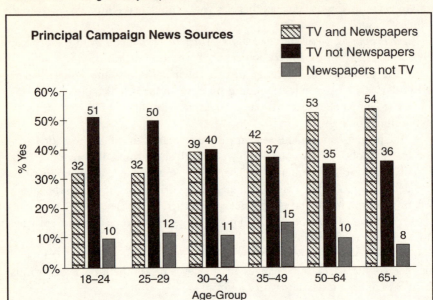

Note: Respondents were asked: "How have you been getting most of your news about the presidential election campaign? From television, from newspapers, from radio, or from magazines?

Source: Times Mirror Center for The People & The Press. Telephone survey of a nationally representative sample of 3,517 adults 18 years of age or older, conducted May 28-June 10, 1992. Reprinted with permission.

presidential nomination itself—and that struggle acquires the intrinsic attraction of disputes which are larger than those of daily life. Finally, there is the element of sheer spectacle as well. If this is the aspect most satirized in conventions, it still possesses an almost automatic, visceral fascination—the proverbial cast of thousands, the rhetoric and symbols of a rich national history, the high drama and low comedy of democratic politics in action.[69]

Some critics attack the conventions as nothing more than media events staged by each party, "replete with patriotism, traditional values, and reminders of their past accomplishments."[70] But many in the public view them with less cynicism and have some strong ideas about how much and what type of television coverage they would find most helpful. A series of questions asked in the days immediately preceding the 1992 Democratic National Convention give us some insights about whether age plays any role in these perceptions.

According to the preconvention survey, conducted by the Times Mirror Center for The People & The Press, younger persons were much more inclined to demand that television networks offer extensive coverage of the political convention proceedings (60 percent, versus 46 percent of the older cohorts). This is consistent with other Times Mirror surveys showing that more than half of those 18 to 24 and 25 to 29 acknowledged they get their news about the presidential election campaign almost exclusively from television (see Figure 3.2).

When watching the conventions, the public is most interested in learning about the party platforms (more than 70 percent of each age-group). Roughly half are interested in the roll call of states as their delegations cast ballots for the party nominees (typically lots of hoopla here), the nominees' acceptance speeches, and projected intraparty personality conflicts. The biggest age-group difference surfaces in terms of interest in the nominee's acceptance speech: Older voters are considerably more interested in watching this event than the young. Younger voters are slightly more interested in watching the state roll call and following intraparty personality conflicts.

Candidate Debates: How Many, What Format, How Helpful, Who Watches? Debates are high-visibility campaign events. Like party conventions, they capture the attention of some segments of the electorate more than others. During the presidential primary season, candidate debates take place between contenders for a party's nomination, although a sitting president who is seeking reelection rarely debates contenders within his own party. After the convention, debates pit the Democratic and Republican nominees (and major third-party or independent candidates, like Ross Perot in 1992) against each other. These debates typically attract a great deal of attention and are the most-watched events of an entire presidential campaign.

Those most likely to watch presidential debates, at any stage, are the more interested and knowledgeable members of the electorate. However, the media's tendency to turn debates into boxing matches, proclaiming winners and losers as soon as the sparring ends, creates more interest than usual *and* enhances the media's influence. Stephen Wayne, in *The Road to the White House 1992,* pointed out that the "[media's] evaluation conditions how the public judges the results. . . . Since most people do not follow the content [of the debate] very closely and do not put much faith in their own evaluation, media commentary can have a considerable impact on public opinion. It can modify the immediate impression people have, moving the public's assessment in the direction of an acknowledged winner."[71]

The public's enthusiasm for debates, especially those between party nominees, changes little over the course of the campaign. A Times Mirror survey conducted in October 1991, more than a year before the 1992 election, found strong support for the idea of having major presidential candidates appear on TV one evening a week in the nine weeks before the election to talk about the policies they plan to follow if elected, to answer questions about their policies, and to debate one another. A survey taken a year later asked whether respondents planned to watch the upcoming debate, and the percent who said yes was similar. (The proportion who actually watched was considerably lower, perhaps reflecting the tendency of survey respondents to give pollsters socially desirable answers about their political participation or to have had good intentions even if they didn't, in the end, watch.)

Younger voters are considerably more supportive of the idea of multiple weekly debates than those 50 and older (87 versus 66 percent), and they perceive such debates as helpful in determining for whom they will vote. This is not as surprising as it might initially seem. Because younger voters generally are less knowledgeable about politics and more likely to be independents or weak partisans, they are more likely to be influenced by the debates. For strong partisans, debates tend to solidify support; for "weaker partisans and independents, the debates are more likely to increase interest, and clarify, color, or even change perceptions."[72] Postelection surveys by Times Mirror in 1988 and 1992 confirmed that the youngest voters perceived debates as considerably more helpful in making the decision about which candidate to support on election day than older cohorts, although a majority of all age-groups found them useful.

Every election sends the media and the candidates in search of new debate formats. The 1992 election featured three different formats: The candidates were questioned by a panel of reporters, by selected voters, and by a single moderator with no other questioners. Across all age-groups, the least popular format was the questioning by reporters; the most popular was the questioning by voters. The youngest cohort was somewhat more favorably disposed to the voter-questioning format than those 65 and older (49 versus 38 percent). Older viewers may have thought that the selection of voter questioners was somewhat staged and that those individuals were a bit too disrespectful toward the candidates. (This opinion is solely based on comments I overheard after that debate.)

In summary, debates are popular ways of engaging and informing the electorate. They are more likely to solidify the opinions of older persons but to form or change those of younger voters. Both young and old alike prefer debate formats that feature questioning by either voters or a single moderator rather than reporters.

News Coverage of Campaigns: How Much and What? Candidates running for office are well aware of the two avenues to press coverage—one free, the other expensive—and they know that both are essential. Free media includes newspaper, radio, or television news, and coverage in organizational newsletters, bulletins, and other periodicals. Paid media "refers to electronic spots and print ads for which the campaign must buy time or space as well as literature and such campaign paraphernalia as buttons and bumper stickers."[73]

The vast majority of Americans of all ages generally follow campaigns via television news—network and local, and the proportion following campaigns on TV stays virtually the same throughout the whole process. The percentage using various print media—newspapers and magazines—increases as election day approaches, but it still lags behind the figure for those using TV. As Wayne stated, "News on television seems more believable. People can see what's happening. Being an action-oriented, visual medium, television reports the drama and excitement of the campaign: How are they doing? What is their strategy? Who is ahead? It is the campaign as contest that provides the principal focus for television, as well as for the print medium."[74]

The broadcast media have created a different world for politicians today. The authors of *The Media Game* painted the scenario well:

> Today, political leaders communicate with the public primarily through news media that *they do not control.* The news media now stand between politicians and their constituents. Politicians speak to the media; the media then speak to the voters. The media can filter, alter, distort, or ignore altogether what politicians have to say. The emergence of this two-step flow of communication has radically altered the behavior of politicians, and it has also dramatically affected the relation of individual citizens to the political process.[75]

Some of the media's toughest critics are staunch supporters of political parties who are convinced this new media politics has sapped their power and effectiveness. One of the harshest and most widely cited critiques came from Larry Sabato, in *Feeding Frenzy: How Attack Journalism Has Transformed American Politics.* He likened most news coverage of campaigns to tabloid journalism: "The sad conclusion is inescapable: The press has become obsessed with gossip rather than governance; it prefers to employ titillation rather than scrutiny; as a result, its political coverage produces trivialization rather than enlightenment."[76] He and a slew of others lay most of the blame on television news, with its focus on candidate personalities and character and on who's winning at the expense of issues, which typically receive only one-third of the coverage.

Other media analysts attribute the press's fixation on campaign strategy and candidate personality to training. Journalism schools teach reporters to focus on controversy because that's what tends to capture the attention of editors and the public at large. In *Out of Order,* longtime media analyst Thomas E. Patterson described the situation:

> For reporters, controversy is the real issue of campaign politics. The press deals with charges and countercharges, rarely digging into the details of the candidates' positions or the social conditions underlying policy problems. It is not simply that the press neglects issues in favor of the strategic game; issues, even when covered, are subordinated to the drama of the conflict generated between the opposing sides. In this sense, the press "depoliticizes" issues, treating them more as election ritual than as objects of serious debate.[77]

What does the public think about the debate over coverage of the issues versus coverage of the horse race? Do younger and older voters view the controversy differently? In advance of the 1992 election, the Times Mirror Center for The People & The Press set out to get some precise answers about what the public wants to see more and less of in presidential campaigns (see Figure 3.3).

FIGURE 3.3 Public Preference for Campaign News Coverage: How Much and What?

Preferred Level of Coverage

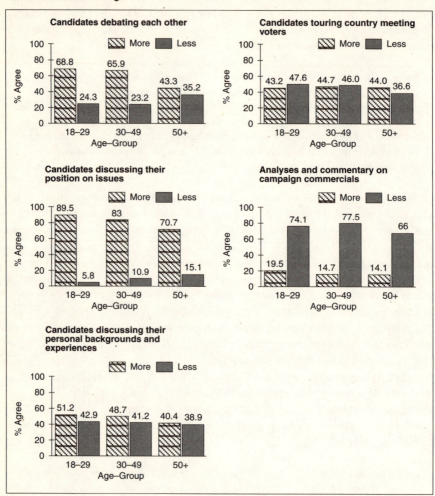

(*continues*)

Four points from that survey deserve mention. First, a huge portion of the electorate preferred more coverage of the candidates' issue positions and less analysis of or commentary on campaign commercials: They can interpret these for themselves, thank you! Second, younger persons generally wanted more coverage than older persons do on just about every facet of the campaign, reflecting their need to gather more information about the process, parties, and candidates. Third, a higher but still small proportion of older voters were satisfied with past

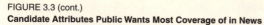

FIGURE 3.3 (cont.)
Candidate Attributes Public Wants Most Coverage of in News

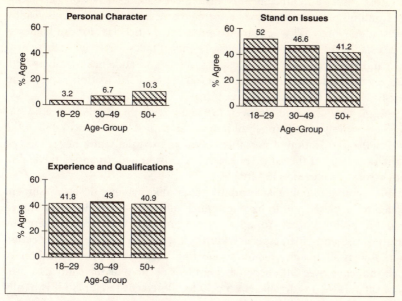

Notes: Respondents were asked: "I am going to read some things news organizations can do to cover a presidential election campaign. For each, tell me if it is something you would like to see more of, or like to see less of in coverage of the 1992 campaign than in previous presidential elections?" Respondents were asked: "In reporting on a presidential candidate, what one factor do you think news organizations should pay the most attention to: a candidate's personal character, a candidate's stand on issues, or a candidate's past experiences and qualifications?"

Source: The Times Mirror Center for The People & The Press. Telephone survey of a nationally representative sample of 1,211 adults 18 years of age or older, conducted October 3–6, 1991. Reprinted with permission.

levels of coverage. Fourth, across all age-groups, a candidate's personal character was *not* what they would most like the media to cover.

Polls taken later in the 1992 campaign affirmed what the public had said a year earlier and at the end of the 1988 campaign as well. When asked what they liked most about their favorite candidate, personality and character were far less frequently mentioned than issue stances, leadership, or experience. However, it is interesting to note that personality/character was a bigger factor in the vote decisions of older constituents rather than younger ones. Older voters also weighed experience more heavily, whereas younger voters counted leadership a bit more. Each individual's place in the life cycle explains this pattern. Younger persons are more subject to hero worship and are also more likely to see issues as cut and dried. By contrast, older persons more readily recognize the muddiness of issues and also put more faith in the ability of experienced people with strong character to tackle just about any issue placed before them. (Age matters!)

Quasi-News Coverage: Talk Shows and Late Night Comedy/Entertainment Hours. Candidates can get free news coverage by appearing on increasingly popular radio and television call-in talk shows and late-night comedy programs. In fact, the

1992 presidential campaign propelled the candidates who used these forums into stardom. Ross Perot's announcement of his bid for the presidency on *Larry King Live,* Bill Clinton's cameo saxophone performance on *Arsenio Hall* and his visit on *Donahue,* and Al Gore's MTV appearance represented a new way for candidates to bypass the establishment news media. Proponents of talk shows believe these programs expand the electorate: "By providing callers and audience members with direct access to candidates, the format enfranchises. Participation rather than spectatorship is invited by its interactive form."[78]

By 1992, the time was ripe. Between 1982 and 1991, the number of radio stations devoted entirely to talk, much of it political, tripled to 600, and 1,450 of the nation's 7,500 radio stations listed themselves as predominantly news, talk, or public affairs outlets. At the same time, cable television had expanded the dial in most cities from five channels to fifty.[79]

A sizable segment of politicians and the public alike perceive the establishment news media to be biased and to have too much influence over who is nominated and elected to political office. Younger persons are somewhat more bothered by this than those 65 and older, especially during the primary phase of the election campaign. Across all age-groups, the proportion believing the news media have too much influence over who becomes president declines as the campaign progresses, but it still is considerable (in the 40 to 50 percent range). So it is hardly surprising that the public, like the candidates, is quite receptive to new informational sources and formats.

Politically oriented talk shows on television and radio attract older persons more than younger ones, perhaps because the young have less time to listen or watch but probably because they are just somewhat less interested in politics. The young are more attracted to network television call-in shows like *Oprah* or *Geraldo* or infotainment shows with a less obvious political focus, such as *Entertainment Tonight* or *A Current Affair.* In general, younger persons are less drawn to traditional news sources, which has sent enterprising campaign media consultants in search of new venues.

Late-night comedy programs are to the young what news magazine shows such as *60 Minutes* or *20/20* are to the old—their best source of soft political news (see Table 3.5). One-fourth of those 18 to 29 are regular watchers of late-night shows, compared with less than 10 percent of those 65 and older. One-third of the 18- to 29-year-olds acknowledge they hear things on these programs about the candidates or the election campaign that they haven't heard before.

Late-night comedy programs are renowned for their political jokes, a phenomenon harking back to the early days of *Saturday Night Live.* Some analysts go so far as to analyze the jokes aired on these programs to make projections about winners and losers. Sabato, in *Feeding Frenzy,* noted that "for a politician in trouble, humor can be a deadly brew, a compound of sweet poison that finishes him or her off. . . . The most costly humor to a modern campaign is that sponsored by the princes of television comedy. . . . Their one-liners and skits reinforce and extend the disasters that befall candidates, transforming the pols from subjects of sympathy to objects of ridicule, changing the way voters perceive the real events on the campaign trail."[80] The biggest impact is on the youngest voters, who are most attentive to these "night-howl" fests.

Paid Advertising: What Appeals to the Public? Campaign ads can do a great deal to sell a candidate to the public, just as product ads sell soft drinks, cars, and headache remedies. Like quasi-news talk shows and infotainment programs, they give candidates a way to reach the potential voter without having their messages filtered or interpreted by news reporters.

Paid political advertisements appear in a wide variety of formats, including brochures, newsletters, questionnaires, letters, billboards, yard signs, bumper stickers, newspaper advertisements, magazine advertisements, matchbooks, buttons, pencils, and radio and television commercials.[81] Advertising, especially on television, is expensive but considered essential to reach large portions of the electorate.

In recent years, more candidates have used negative advertising strategies, taking a page from the private sector's advertising book. Attack ads, which emphasize the opposition's flaws and shortcomings, regularly outnumber promotional spots, which emphasize a candidate's strengths. Media consultants believe the negative approach works because "the public holds politicians in low esteem" and because "negative ads are more memorable than positive messages."[82] Many political scientists believe such ads, augmenting the negative tone of campaign news coverage, ultimately depress voter turnout.[83] Moreover, such ads give no guarantee of getting elected. In *Air Wars,* Darrell West warns that attack ads are undependable because "it is hard to get the benefits of attack without suffering the blame for an unpleasant campaign."[84]

But despite the fact that news people and even some laypersons may criticize the quality and tone of most political ads, voters still find them helpful. From their perspective, ads assist them in learning about the candidates and their platforms, priorities, and personae. But the main question is whether age makes any difference in what voters find useful about such ads.

During both the 1988 and the 1992 presidential campaigns, the Times Mirror Center for The People & The Press asked whether television ads made the public aware of candidates or helped them gain some sense of what a candidate was like. The pollsters also asked respondents to rank the utility of ads vis-à-vis regular news reports. Almost two-thirds of the electorate first became aware of a particular candidate through TV ads—the proportion rose in all age-groups between 1988 and 1992 (see Figure 3.4).

Younger persons are more prone to attribute their awareness of candidates to TV ads than are senior citizens, although the differences between the old and young in this respect are not great. For older citizens, the proportion who gained some knowledge about what the candidates were like through ads was about the same in 1988 and 1992 (63 percent). For younger persons, that proportion hovered around 50 percent in 1992, down slightly since the previous campaign.

The candidates' targeting strategies might account for the differences. Their campaign media consultants, for example, may have advised them to run televi-

FIGURE 3.4 Electorate "Connects" with the Campaign via Candidate Advertisements

<u>Candidate Awareness</u>

I often don't become aware of political candidates until I see their advertising on TV

<u>Knowledge of Candidate</u>

I get some sense of what a candidate is like through his or her TV commercials

<u>A Helpful Voting Cue</u>

Candidate commercials were helpful to me in deciding which candidate to vote for

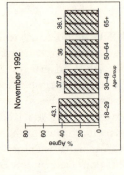

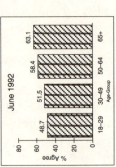

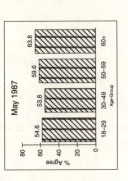

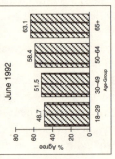

Notes: In May 1987 and June 1992, respondents were asked: "For each statement, please tell me whether you completely agree with it, mostly agree with it, mostly disagree with it, or completely disagree with it: [I don't often become aware of political candidates until I see the advertising on television; I get some sense of what a candidate is like through his or her TV commercials]. Percentages reported are completely and mostly agree. In November 1992, respondents were asked: "How helpful were the candidates' commercials to you in deciding which candidate to vote for? Would you say they were very helpful, somewhat helpful, not too helpful, or not at all helpful?" Percentages reported are very helpful and somewhat helpful.

Source: The Times Mirror Center for The People & The Press. Face-to-face survey of a nationally representative sample of 4,244 adults 18 years of age or older, conducted April 25–May 10, 1987; telephone survey of a nationally representative sample of 3,517 adults 18 years of age or older, conducted May 28–June 10, 1992; telephone survey of a nationally representative sample of 1,012 adults 18 years of age or older, conducted November 5–8, 1992. Reprinted with permission.

sion ads to target the older voters during prime-time periods and to rely on pop culture approaches such as MTV and late-night programs to reach the younger voters.

Regardless of viewers' age, the new and unusual ad format usually catches the most attention—and turns out to be the most memorable. In 1992, the new format was the infomercial—a regular program-length commercial paid for by the candidate. Ross Perot popularized this format (which itself became a topic in the news), and postelection surveys rated his ads as the best of the campaign. Actually, many budget analysts felt that most Americans learned more about the economy from Perot's thirty-minute infomercials than they had in school or from regular news sources. However, Times Mirror surveys probing respondents' reactions to the Perot commercials found that although a high percentage saw and learned something from them, they were not persuaded to change their minds about whether to vote for Perot because of those ads.

In 1996, media strategists will be searching for a new or vastly improved type of ad or paid program to educate the voters about their candidates. One veteran campaign consultant and observer explained it this way: "Campaign handlers are taking a wild ride down the information super highway, and it is changing the way elections are won, and lost. Successful campaigns in the new media age are meaner, faster, livelier—and they are all driven by data. ... What counts are tracking polls, focus groups, dial groups, 'wave fronts,' and digital-TV editing machines, and a candidate [or political party] capable of raising the huge amounts of cash needed to pay for the technology."[85]

Paid media messages will continue to be an important part of a campaign because voters find them useful and are influenced by them. A 1992 postelection survey showed that well over one-third of the electorate credited ads as being helpful in deciding for whom to vote, with the younger voters being slightly more swayed by them.

Other survey results suggest that the figure may not be quite that high but that it is still high enough to matter. Times Mirror surveys taken in the middle of the 1988 and 1992 campaigns showed that approximately three-fourths of each age-group said news reports gave them a better idea of the candidates' issue stances and personae than commercials. However, between 15 and 20 percent cited commercials as the best source. For many candidates (national, state, or local), 15 to 20 percent is often the margin of victory, which guarantees that ads will continue to be campaign staples. The key question is whether the ads will get more negative. Some say yes; others disagree. But all agree that technology is rapidly changing the art of political advertising.

GETTING PERSONALLY INVOLVED IN THE CAMPAIGN

Most Americans do not become actively engaged in political campaigns. Only a small percentage volunteer to work in a party's headquarters, go door to door for a candidate, attend a political rally, wear a campaign button, put a campaign bumper sticker on their car, or give money to a political party or a candidate. In fact, National Election Studies have consistently found that 10 percent or less of all Americans tend to do such things, although a third or so admit they talk to friends, neighbors, and coworkers and try to influence their vote.

Age makes a difference in whether people become politically active. Rosenstone and Hansen found that middle-aged persons were nearly twice as likely as the young to work for a party or candidate; 80-year-olds were more than twice as likely as 18-year-olds to contribute money to a party or candidate. They concluded: "Consistent with life-experience explanation, participation in electoral politics increases throughout life. . . . Except where participation taxes physical stamina, except where infirmity defeats experience, participation rises consistently with age."[86]

But even though many Americans choose not to get involved personally, they still think that working in political campaigns and joining a local political party can be effective ways of trying to influence the way government is run. A Times Mirror survey in the middle of the 1992 presidential campaign season found that two-thirds of its respondents believed in the effectiveness of getting involved in political campaigns and that 56 percent believed in joining local political parties. Though not rated quite as highly as the actual act of voting (judged as effective by more than 80 percent), these forms of political participation are still seen as worth the effort by more than half the citizenry. Younger constituents were somewhat more positive in their assessments in this area than those 65 and older, reflecting higher rates of cynicism among the latter group—a theme observed throughout this chapter.

Joining Political Party Organizations

Each state determines the conditions that must be met for a group to be formally recognized as a political party. States also determine how party nominees for state and local offices will be selected, whether by direct primaries, caucuses, or conventions.[87] In addition, state laws outline party governance structures—all the way from local party committees at the grassroots level to state executive committees.

Actions of the national party governing bodies, the Democratic and Republican National Committees, often get most of the media attention, especially during presidential and congressional campaigns. The national committees contribute some of the party monies to candidates, and they set the rules governing the selection and seating of delegates, who still come from each of the states, to the national party conventions.

However, the *real* backbone of our political party system consists of thousands of local (precinct, ward, city, or county), congressional district, and state party committees. These committees engage in a wide range of campaign activities: They sponsor voter registration and get-out-the-vote drives, hold political rallies, recruit candidates and party volunteers, work with their candidates' campaign coordinators, and establish party issue positions. Party committee members are typically elected, most commonly at local and state party conventions attended by party activists.

One study has found that young party activists lean more toward campaign involvement than older activists (see Table 3.6). On the other hand, older party activists in both parties "are more likely to be involved in registration drives, the contacting of voters generally and new voters specifically, local candidate recruitment efforts, and county party organizational work and party business meetings."[88]

People who actually join party organizations, not just verbally identify with a party, tend to be strong party identifiers. They see sharper differences between the two major political parties than the average person. Many also have political ambitions—to win an elective office or be appointed to a high-level post—and begin by becoming active in their local party organizations. Party activists normally work their way up the party committee chain. Service on a higher-level committee (e.g., at the county level) or in a committee leadership role (e.g., committee chair) often comes as a reward for hard work on another level (e.g., in the precinct), although in some instances a top leadership position in the party goes with one's election to office.

Various differences between activists in old and young age-groups presumably stem from their differing attitudes about their parties. In this regard, older activists believe strongly in what their party stands for, and younger activists (although not the youngest cohort) focus more on using their party service as a ticket to elected office. Because the more politically ambitious are more eager to take on party leadership positions (such as the committee chair), it is thought that the median age of those holding such positions would be lower than the median age of those serving on party committees. There seems to be some support for these notions.

A study of party activists at the county level (county committee chairs and precinct committee members) in eleven southern states found that a considerably higher percentage of those serving as county chairs (Democrats and Republicans alike) were 30 to 49 years of age, as compared to those 65 and older.[89] Those serving on county executive committees were more likely to be middle-aged rather than either very young or of retirement age.

The energy and commitment of many people are needed to propel political parties through the long, arduous, and often acrimonious election campaigns that seem to pile one on top of the other. Regardless of their party or age, party activists are more heavily involved in the nitty-gritty of campaigns than the average voter. And every stage of the campaign is important to the parties and their candidates because people decide how they're going to vote—or if they'll vote at all—at different times.

When Individuals Decide Whom They Will Vote For. Everyone—be it pollsters, media consultants, TV networks, party leaders, or the candidates themselves—is curious about *when* people make up their minds about whom they will support. Each is searching for successful formulas to use the next time around. A comparison of the decision times in the 1988 and 1992 presidential campaigns reveals certain patterns, a few of which are age-specific (see Table 3.7).

Times Mirror postelection surveys of those who actually voted have shown that older persons make up their minds earlier, perhaps reflecting their stronger partisanship. Around 10 to 15 percent of those 60 and older knew whom—or at least which party's candidate—they would support before the election year even began. Another one-fifth made up their minds by the time the party primaries ended but before the party conventions began. Just 5 percent or so waited until election day or the day before to make up their minds. In contrast, among those 18 to 29, only 5 to 10 percent knew whom they would support before the election year began; 15 to 18 percent knew by the end of the primaries, and 17 percent did not know until election day.

Among all age-groups, the biggest boosts accrue to candidates during and right after the party conventions, as mentioned earlier, and after the presidential debates. (Vice presidential debates seem to influence only the candidates' long-lost school chums and neighbors.) By the end of the election, a high proportion of the electorate—especially older voters—say they are tired of the campaign. Just prior to election day in 1992, for example, 82 percent of those 65 and older said they were tired of the campaign, compared to 65 percent of the 18- to 29-year-olds. Older constituents are the most bored because they have made up their minds far sooner than the younger cohorts. But when all is said and done, the voters give themselves a big pat on the back for their behavior during the campaign season.

The Voters Grade the Campaign Participants

After the 1988 and 1992 presidential races and the 1994 midterm elections, the Times Mirror Center for The People & The Press asked the voters to give letter grades to the press, pollsters, campaign consultants, each political party, and each presidential nominee. They were also asked to grade their own conduct over the course of the campaign. Results show that voters generally gave themselves higher marks than the other campaign actors, with the exception of the winning nominee, who enjoyed an initial honeymoon. (One wonders if this is the voters' way of saying that democracy works and that they are quite capable of sorting through the spin of all the other players.) More than one-half to two-thirds of the voters failed to give the press, pollsters, or campaign consultants As or Bs. And as expected, older Americans gave poorer grades to the campaign participants than the young did, but they surely didn't let their cynicism keep them from the polls, as mentioned in Chapter 2. The good news is that the grades for all but the losing party and its candidate improved between 1988 and 1992.

Florida's Party Identifiers and Party Activists: Any Lessons for the Future?

Florida's political party system is highly competitive. By 1990, the affiliations of Florida's registered voters were as follows: Democrats, 52 percent; Republicans, 41

FIGURE 3.5 Floridians See Sharper Differences Between Political Parties

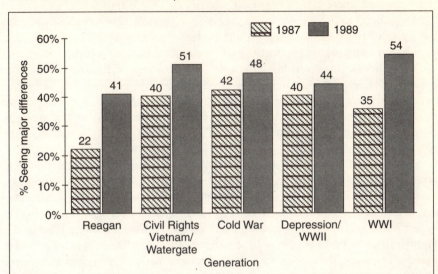

Note: Respondents were asked: "Do you think there are major differences between what the two parties stand for, minor differences, or no difference at all between the two parties?"

Source: Suzanne L. Parker, Florida Annual Policy Survey, Tallahassee, FL: Survey Research Laboratory, Policy Sciences Program, Florida State University. Reprinted with permission.

percent; and independents and third-party members, 7 percent. By 1994, the Democrats had only a plurality (49+ percent). Much of the change in the state's party system—Florida used to be the classic one-party, southern Democratic state—can be traced to the influx of retirees from the Midwest and Northeast who have brought their Republican registrations with them.[90] A heavy influx of immigrants from Cuba who lean heavily toward the Republican Party has also bolstered the party's strength. However, it should be noted that a large percentage of new immigrants from various South and Latin American countries are not citizens and thus cannot register to vote. They, like many other immigrant groups across the nation, are somewhat slow in making the decision to become naturalized citizens. Finally, the state's younger cohorts, the Reagan generation, have also tended to identify with the Republican Party, like their counterparts throughout the nation.[91]

When political parties are highly competitive, their differences become clearer to the public, and party-line voting increases. Such has been the case in Florida. The proportion of the public who see major differences between the Republicans and Democrats has increased significantly in Florida—much more so than in the country at large.[92] The greatest jump has taken place among the youngest and oldest generations: Between 1987 and 1989, the proportion of each group seeing sharp contrasts increased by nearly 20 percent (see Figure 3.5).

It is difficult to use Florida's data for broader generalizations because the state has a unique party membership profile: Higher proportions of older persons are Republicans, and higher proportions of Hispanics, primarily Cuban Americans, are Republicans. But given this limitation, the data suggest that those who fear political parties will wither and die are overly pessimistic. However, the larger gap between the young and the old that is observable in Florida (with the young being less likely to see major differences between parties) suggests there will be less support in the future for the old notion that party identification strengthens with age.

The profile of party leadership in Florida gives us some hints about what may take place nationally. The age gap between party activists holding leadership positions (committee chairs) and those serving on local party committees is narrowing, although the median age of persons holding chair positions is still slightly higher.[93] As I will show in Chapter 5, part of the explanation is an increase in the number of older persons who want to run for office. Another part is the growing number of young persons who see themselves as independents rather than party regulars.

SUMMARY

How active a person chooses to be in a political party depends on a variety of factors, including age. The older one grows, the more likely one will strongly identify with a party, seeing sharper differences between the two major political parties. Older persons also have more explicit likes and dislikes toward each political party. Younger persons are more likely to classify themselves as political independents and to vote a split ticket.

Age-groups differ slightly in their judgments of which party is superior to the other in organization, capacity to manage the government, candidate selection, and effectiveness as an agent of change. Age-groups also vary little in terms of which party they regard as best able to deal with major public policy problems, although younger Americans are a little more likely to emphasize the two parties' issue-handling capacity. Democrats historically score better on the domestic front, Republicans on the foreign policy/defense front. Judgments on which party is best able to handle economic issues change with the state of the economy and depend on which party is in office at the time.

Participation in various political campaign activities, from simply watching and reading about the race to actually working in a campaign or giving money to a party or candidate, varies considerably by age. Older constituents are more politically attentive to all phases of a campaign, relying on a broader range of media (electronic and print) for their information about candidates. However, they are generally more critical of the media's coverage, get tired of the campaign more quickly, and decide whom they will vote for much earlier than the youngest cohorts.

Younger cohorts depend much more heavily on television to keep them informed about the campaign. They generally want more coverage than older persons do on just about every facet of the campaign, reflecting their need to gather more information about the process, parties, and candidates. However, they are more heavily influenced by less traditional, quasi-news sources, such as television talk and infotainment shows, late-night comedians, and political commercials.

In general, voters of all ages want to know more about candidates' issue stances and experience than about their personalities or character. However, older persons do weigh personality and character a bit more heavily than the young.

Clear age-group differences exist in the degree to which people volunteer to work in a political campaign, attend political rallies, wear campaign buttons, or make financial contributions to candidates. As with other forms of individual campaign participation (voting in primaries or tuning in to party conventions and candidate debates), older persons are more likely to engage themselves in the nuts and bolts of campaigns. But it is the middle-aged persons who are most active in political party organizations at all levels—local, state, and national committees.

Florida's experience suggests there will be less support in the future for any strong relationship between aging and the strengthening of party identification. While today's younger cohorts are more likely to see major differences between the two parties, they are much more likely to see themselves as independents and split-ticket voters.

TABLE 3.1 Party Identification by Age-Cohort Groups: 1952–1994 (in percentages)

Cohort	1952	1954	1956	1958	1960	1962	1964	1966	1968	1970	1972	1974
1959 or later	*	*	*	*	*	*	*	*	*	*	*	*
	*	*	*	*	*	*	*	*	*	*	*	*
	*	*	*	*	*	*	*	*	*	*	*	*
	*	*	*	*	*	*	*	*	*	*	*	*
	*	*	*	*	*	*	*	*	*	*	*	*
	*	*	*	*	*	*	*	*	*	*	*	*
	*	*	*	*	*	*	*	*	*	*	*	*
	*	*	*	*	*	*	*	*	*	*	*	*
1943–1958	*	*	*	*	*	*	20	11	8	13	8	14
	*	*	*	*	*	*	32	30	24	24	25	22
	*	*	*	*	*	*	12	11	22	15	18	18
	*	*	*	*	*	*	8	16	17	19	18	20
	*	*	*	*	*	*	8	13	15	11	14	8
	*	*	*	*	*	*	12	11	7	12	9	10
	*	*	*	*	*	*	4	8	4	6	6	4
	*	*	*	*	*	*	4	0	3	1	1	4
1927–1942	22	14	17	26	18	18	24	14	20	17	13	16
	30	27	24	24	27	27	26	31	26	24	26	21
	9	12	11	9	8	11	13	12	11	14	11	12
	6	10	10	9	12	9	9	13	10	13	15	14
	9	11	13	6	6	10	7	9	11	11	12	12
	11	11	13	14	10	16	13	14	15	15	14	17
	8	8	7	7	15	6	8	6	6	7	8	7
	4	7	5	5	4	3	1	1	2	0	1	2
1911–1926	20	23	20	26	19	23	27	18	19	24	19	17
	31	28	26	26	27	27	26	28	26	25	27	22

1976	1978	1980	1982	1984	1986	1988	1990	1992	1994	Party Identification
*	7	11	8	9	13	13	11	9	11	Strong Dem
*	16	21	26	21	20	15	17	19	20	Weak Dem
*	16	18	13	16	9	16	15	17	16	Independent Dem
*	27	18	15	13	16	14	15	16	11	Independent
*	7	9	8	15	12	15	14	15	11	Independent Rep
*	8	15	17	15	15	16	16	15	16	Weak Rep
*	7	3	7	9	10	11	9	9	14	Strong Rep
*	11	5	5	4	5	2	2	2	1	Apolitical
10	9	12	16	12	14	14	20	18	15	Strong Dem
25	25	25	25	21	22	19	22	19	17	Weak Dem
16	19	13	14	12	14	12	14	15	14	Independent Dem
19	17	17	14	13	13	13	10	11	10	Independent
12	10	11	10	13	12	15	10	13	11	Independent Rep
13	12	13	13	16	15	12	15	13	14	Weak Rep
5	5	6	7	12	8	14	8	11	18	Strong Rep
1	3	3	2	2	2	1	2	1	1	Apolitical
13	13	16	21	20	20	22	24	22	18	Strong Dem
24	28	22	24	23	22	18	17	17	19	Weak Dem
12	14	11	12	11	10	12	11	12	10	Independent Dem
16	11	10	10	7	10	7	9	11	7	Independent
10	11	13	8	13	10	13	14	11	16	Independent Rep
16	15	16	15	14	13	14	13	13	12	Weak Rep
8	7	11	10	11	14	14	10	13	17	Strong Rep
1	2	1	2	2	1	1	1	1	(Z)	Apolitical
19	21	26	29	26	28	23	30	29	26	Strong Dem
27	24	23	21	18	25	18	22	15	19	Weak Dem

(continues)

100

TABLE 3.1   (cont.)

Cohort	1952	1954	1956	1958	1960	1962	1964	1966	1968	1970	1972	1974
	10	9	7	7	9	6	9	9	10	8	9	13
	5	7	9	7	10	10	9	11	11	12	9	12
	9	6	8	6	7	5	6	5	8	5	8	7
	15	13	14	16	14	14	14	17	17	16	16	16
	7	10	12	8	13	10	9	10	9	9	12	10
	3	4	3	4	2	4	0	2	1	1	1	3
1895–1910	22	22	21	28	23	29	32	23	27	21	22	25
	23	25	21	19	22	19	23	23	24	23	25	18
	11	7	4	7	4	5	6	6	5	8	6	9
	6	8	9	7	9	4	7	13	10	11	10	9
	5	7	7	4	9	5	3	7	6	6	7	8
	14	14	15	18	15	16	13	16	14	16	13	16
	16	16	19	13	16	18	15	13	15	14	16	14
	2	2	4	3	3	5	1	0	1	1	2	2
Before 1895	25	23	26	24	23	25	27	25	23	27	13	32
	17	19	16	17	21	15	19	27	26	19	23	21
	7	7	3	5	3	5	3	3	4	3	5	0
	7	7	6	5	9	4	4	10	3	9	3	9
	6	1	6	4	2	3	6	4	2	3	5	5
	13	19	14	19	17	21	17	15	15	23	23	12
	22	19	24	24	25	22	24	14	22	17	24	21
	4	6	4	3	2	4	1	3	4	0	4	0

Notes: *indicates cohort not of voting age.

Z = less than 0.5 percent.

Sources: 1952–1986 data are from Warren E. Miller and Santa A. Traugott, *American National Election Studies Data Sourcebook, 1952-1986*, Cambridge, MA: Harvard University Press, 1989, p. 82. 1988 and 1990 data are from the *Statistical Abstract of the United States, 1990 and 1992*, Washington, D.C.: U.S. Government Printing Office. 1992 and 1994 NES data generated by Lynn Vavreck. Reprinted by permission of the publishers from *American National Election Studies Data Sourcebook* by Warren Miller and Arthur Miller, Cambridge, Mass.: Harvard University Press, Copyright © 1980 by the President and Fellows of Harvard College.

1976	1978	1980	1982	1984	1986	1988	1990	1992	1994	Party Identification
8	11	9	9	8	8	9	7	12	5	Independent Dem
10	11	8	7	10	7	7	6	8	10	Independent
9	9	10	8	11	7	9	10	10	10	Independent Rep
14	13	14	14	13	14	13	13	14	14	Weak Rep
11	10	7	11	15	11	17	13	12	14	Strong Rep
1	2	1	1	1	1	2	1	(Z)	1	Apolitical
23	29	27	25	27	27	26	43	32	9	Strong Dem
23	18	22	26	12	18	18	14	12	24	Weak Dem
9	8	8	3	6	3	4	9	8	12	Independent Dem
9	9	9	7	10	7	9	5	8	9	Independent
6	5	5	2	7	10	10	2	7	6	Independent Rep
14	13	11	18	16	16	20	19	11	24	Weak Rep
15	16	18	16	21	17	12	9	21	12	Strong Rep
2	3	1	3	1	2	3	(Z)	0	3	Apolitical
19	36	-	-	-	-	-	-	-	-	Strong Dem
16	24	-	-	-	-	-	-	-	-	Weak Dem
3	0	-	-	-	-	-	-	-	-	Independent Dem
3	8	-	-	-	-	-	-	-	-	Independent
6	0	-	-	-	-	-	-	-	-	Independent Rep
37	8	-	-	-	-	-	-	-	-	Weak Rep
13	24	-	-	-	-	-	-	-	-	Strong Rep
3	0	-	-	-	-	-	-	-	-	Apolitical

TABLE 3.2 Age Breakdowns by 1987 and 1990 Times Mirror Data of What It Means to Be a Republican or Democrat (in percentages)

	May 1987[a]						May 1990[a]					
	18-24	25-29	30-39	40-49	50-59	60+	18-24	25-29	30-39	40-49	50-59	60+
What is a Republican?												
Conservative	15.3	22.0	26.8	20.6	22.1	17.0	14.6	19.4	26.6	27.3	22.9	18.3
Rich, powerful, monied interest	19.5	14.5	18.2	17.9	19.4	17.6	21.7	17.7	24.8	19.6	17.3	18.5
Business-oriented	13.3	11.4	16.5	17.0	9.9	7.5	5.3	10.2	11.4	13.1	12.0	7.1
Conservative levels of gov't spending	1.5	5.1	4.7	3.8	7.0	6.0	2.1	5.4	8.6	7.2	5.8	4.0
Agrees with Party platform	6.8	6.0	8.4	10.4	7.2	8.6						
Identifies with/believes in Party	1.8	1.6	4.4	5.6	7.4	5.6						
Unconcerned with needs of people	4.0	5.0	5.0	5.5	4.4	5.5	4.3	3.9	3.9	5.1	2.1	3.2
Lower taxes	0.9	1.3	1.1			0.3	1.4	1.0	1.3	1.0	1.1	1.0
Nothing/no difference between Parties	9.0	13.1	10.7	11.9	16.1	19.1						
Don't know	21.3	15.4	13.4	14.6	13.6	13.3	47.7	49.0	40.3	42.1	42.7	50.9
What is a Democrat?												
Liberal	15.2	21.0	21.6	18.8	18.4	15.0	13.2	16.1	20.5	24.0	19.2	13.7
Cares for poor, disadvantaged	6.6	5.3	7.1	8.2	9.1	7.4	5.3	9.7	7.1	5.2	6.9	9.8
For working people	17.9	18.6	20.8	23.1	23.0	20.2	16.0	18.8	19.5	19.6	19.9	16.1
Heavy levels of gov't spending	5.3	7.5	5.9	8.8	7.8	9.1	1.2	1.3	3.1	4.2	3.6	5.0
Identifies with/believes in Party	8.7	5.9	10.3	12.2	6.8	9.9	5.0	8.7	10.4	12.7	12.3	6.1
Interested in social programs	6.6	7.0	12.6	6.9	2.3	4.9	1.4	2.2	1.0	1.5	0.7	1.0
Higher taxes	1.9	0.6	2.3	1.9	1.2	2.1						
Nothing/no difference between Parties	8.2	12.2	10.3	12.1	15.8	17.6						
Don't know/no answer[b]	22.5	14.4	13.2	13.2	12.0	11.5	52.5	50.3	42.2	41.3	44.3	51.0

Notes: [a]The interviewers' probes were much more rigorous in 1987 than in 1990.
[b]Respondents were asked: "What does it mean to you when someone says he or she is a Republican? a Democrat?"

Source: The Times Mirror Center for The People & The Press. Face-to-face survey of a representative sample of 2,169 adults 18 years of age or older, conducted April 25–May 10, 1987; face-to-face survey of a representative sample of 3,004 adults 18 years of age or older, conducted May 1–31, 1990. Reprinted

TABLE 3.3 Age-Group Assessments of Political Party Organizational and Governing Capacity (in percentages)

Assessment	Republican			Democrat			Both			Neither			Don't know		
	18-29	30-49	50+	18-29	30-49	50+	18-29	30-49	50+	18-29	30-49	50+	18-29	30-49	50+
Well organized															
May 1987	33.6	33.7	36.0	18.2	17.7	20.3	24.1	27.3	22.1	12.7	14.2	13.3	11.4	7.0	8.3
July 1992	55.7	46.7	41.0	26.8	24.2	21.5	4.0	7.1	5.6	9.3	14.7	18.0	4.3	7.2	13.9
May 1993	49.2	43.9	34.3	32.6	32.8	36.9	1.8	7.4	8.0	8.1	10.6	9.8	8.3	5.2	11.0
July 1994	54.6	49.9	41.7	27.6	26.2	29.1	4.9	7.2	7.5	10.0	13.2	13.8	2.9	3.5	7.9
Selects good candidates for office															
May 1987	30.9	26.7	25.6	26.0	24.9	27.2	23.0	25.9	24.5	10.1	15.4	13.4	10.1	7.0	9.4
July 1992	43.9	37.0	25.3	33.2	32.6	34.8	0.8	4.4	4.9	12.4	18.4	13.8	9.7	7.7	21.2
May 1993	45.3	39.3	26.0	38.4	36.6	37.8	2.7	4.9	7.3	5.0	11.3	10.2	8.7	7.9	18.8
July 1994	49.3	39.4	34.7	33.6	36.4	36.6	4.0	5.9	8.2	9.3	14.7	12.0	3.7	3.7	8.5
Able to manage the federal government well															
May 1987	29.2	24.2	21.7	22.7	22.3	28.9	15.5	13.6	11.6	20.4	31.5	28.5	12.1	8.4	9.3
July 1992	39.6	28.8	24.5	38.6	34.8	35.2	0.5	2.1	1.1	15.5	26.3	23.8	5.9	7.9	15.5
May 1993	42.9	37.6	31.1	37.6	28.4	31.6	1.3	2.2	3.0	7.2	23.5	15.6	11.0	8.3	18.7
July 1994	48.7	43.7	39.8	31.8	29.3	32.4	4.0	3.1	3.6	10.8	20.4	17.6	4.6	3.4	6.6
Can bring about the kind of changes the country needs															
May 1987	32.3	25.6	22.1	30.9	35.6	41.5	14.9	14.1	12.6	10.9	16.0	13.2	10.9	8.6	10.6
July 1992	25.3	27.4	17.4	54.9	44.2	44.9	1.2	2.9	2.4	11.8	17.7	16.8	6.7	7.9	18.4
May 1993	36.7	30.0	25.7	49.8	50.2	48.0	1.4	2.7	3.3	5.5	12.1	9.1	6.7	5.0	13.9
July 1994	44.5	38.9	35.2	40.4	42.3	42.8	5.3	4.0	4.2	7.0	11.7	9.2	2.8	3.2	8.6

(continues)

TABLE 3.3 (cont.)

Assessment	Republican			Democrat			Both			Neither			Don't know		
	18-29	30-49	50+	18-29	30-49	50+	18-29	30-49	50+	18-29	30-49	50+	18-29	30-49	50+
Is concerned with the needs of people like me															
January 1988	18.4	24.0	22.8	49.1	46.9	46.4	12.4	10.4	10.7	11.6	12.5	13.1	8.4	6.3	7.0
May 1988	25.6	19.6	24.6	48.4	54.5	48.5	9.3	8.7	7.0	9.9	12.3	10.8	6.8	4.9	9.2
July 1994	37.9	33.8	33.4	48.4	49.7	48.2	3.2	3.6	4.9	7.4	9.3	7.4	3.1	3.6	6.2
Is concerned with the needs and interests of the disadvantaged															
May 1987	16.3	8.9	10.5	54.8	64.5	61.1	12.4	13.9	15.8	7.7	6.0	6.5	8.8	6.7	6.1
July 1994	23.5	18.5	22.2	66.6	69.8	59.0	2.2	2.7	5.3	4.4	4.5	5.4	3.2	4.5	8.2
Is concerned with the needs and interests of business and other powerful groups															
May 1987	57.4	59.5	56.4	14.2	13.7	16.4	13.9	16.5	15.5	3.5	3.1	3.6	11.1	7.2	8.2
July 1994	67.8	69.4	60.6	25.4	20.9	23.1	2.7	5.2	5.7	1.1	1.2	1.8	2.9	3.4	8.8
Governs in an honest & ethical way															
July 1994	39.1	28.8	29.9	33.8	37.2	33.6	4.7	4.4	7.5	18.3	24.8	19.8	4.2	4.8	9.1

Notes: Respondents were asked: "Now I am going to read a few phrases. For each tell me whether you think the phrase better describes the Republican party or the Democratic party. [Phrase] Does that more accurately describe the Republican party and its leaders or does it more accurately describe the Democratic party and its leaders?" The surveys conducted prior to 1992 were personal interviews where respondents were more likely to volunteer the "both" response, and less likely to name either party. Trends on these measures should be judged with that in mind.

Source: Times Mirror Center for The People & The Press. Face-to-face survey of a nationally representative sample of 4,244 adults 18 years of age or older, conducted April 25-May 10, 1987; face-to-face survey of a nationally representative sample of 3,021 adults, conducted May 13-22, 1988; telephone survey of a nationally representative sample of 1,009 adults 18 years of age or older, conducted April-29 May 2, 1993; telephone survey of a nationally representative sample of 3,800 adults 18 years of age and older, living in the continental United States, conducted July 12-27, 1994. Reprinted with permission.

TABLE 3.4 Typical Presidential Campaign Timetable for Parties, Their Candidates, and the Media

Stage	Nomination Politics	
	What the candidate does	**What the media does**
The Preliminary Period Begins 18–24 months before November general election	All potential Democratic and Republican candidates form exploratory committees and begin fundraising and issue development. Candidates attempt to secure the support of important political leaders and groups, especially in key primary and caucus states.	The press plays the part of the "Great Mentioner," speculating as to which candidates will enter the race and which are the true "heavyweights."
The Early Rounds January–February of election year	Iowa's party caucuses and New Hampshire's primary are the first tests of voter response to the candidates; candidates begin advertising blitzes in states with upcoming primaries.	Media focus heavy attention on the candidates who do well or better than expected.
The Long Haul March–May of election year	Serious contenders emerge in both parties as more states hold primaries or caucuses to select delegates to the upcoming national conventions.	Media scrutinize all aspects of front-running candidates; attention turns away from weaker candidates, further depleting their ability to raise money and support.
The Final Races May–June of election year	If the race within a party is close, the final states' primaries can be very decisive. Most often, races are decided before the final primaries.	Media begin comparisons of leading Democratic and Republican candidates and speculations on potential vice presidential nominees.
The National Party Conventions July of election year	In separate national conventions, the Democratic and Republican delegates chosen in preceding state races meet to cast ballots for the party's presidential nominee. The chosen nominee's first duty at the convention is selecting a vice presidential running mate to complete the party's ticket.	The conventions are media events carefully orchestrated to appeal to a national viewing audience. The media analysts scrutinize the acceptance speech, which usually contains some hints about the candidate' issues and positions as reflected in the party platform adopted at the convention.

(continues)

TABLE 3.4 (cont.)

Election Politics		
The General Election Campaigns August through national election day, first Tuesday after the first Monday in November	The two presidential tickets now tour the country in media-oriented stops. The official campaigns are paid by public funds. Both campaigns use "tracking polls" to adjust their message daily. Especially during the final days of the race, campaign resources are devoted to winning pivotal states in the Electoral College. Independent groups also sponsor ads, both negative and positive, on behalf of the candidates.	The media give scrutiny to each member of the ticket. More often than not, media coverage focuses on candidates' gaffes and errors, on polling results, and on other "horse race" aspects of the race rather than on the details of the candidates' policy promises. The media bore in on the candidates' performances in televised debates.

Source: Myron A. Levine, *Presidential Campaigns and Elections: Issues, Images, and Partisanship*, Itasca, IL: F.E. Peacock Publishers, Inc., 1992, p. 15. Reprinted by permission of the publisher.

TABLE 3.5 The "Quasi-News" Media: News Magazines, Infotainment, and Late-Night Comedy Shows in 1992 (in percentages)

Late-Night Comedians or Comedy Shows

Regular watchers of comedy shows				
Show	18–29	30–49	50–64	65+
Johnny Carson	8.0	4.7	6.7	6.7
Jay Leno	6.3	3.6	4.1	4.1
David Letterman	7.7	1.7	0.4	0.8
Arsenio Hall	19.5	6.5	2.9	3.7
Saturday Night Live	22.4	4.3	5.4	1.0
Dennis Miller	5.0	1.4	0.0	1.0

Late-night comedy show with best political humor			
18–29	30–49	50–64	65+
14.6	17.8	24.3	16.6
5.4	9.0	5.0	7.1
8.2	3.2	2.3	2.2
20.2	13.5	5.9	1.9
20.3	10.0	4.1	1.1
5.8	3.2	0.2	0.0

Hear things about candidate or election campaign on shows that haven't heard before				
	18–29	30–49	50–64	65+
Yes	32.5	20.2	13.9	12.3
No	56.1	56.1	49.0	44.0
Never watch	8.2	19.5	28.7	37.7
Don't know	3.1	4.2	8.4	5.9

(continues)

TABLE 3.5 (cont.)

News Magazine Shows and Infotainment Shows

Show	Regularly watch					
	18–24	25–29	30–34	35–49	50–64	65+
News Magazine						
News magazine shows such as *60 Minutes* or *20/20*	30	33	40	44	56	63
Sunday morning news shows such as *Meet the Press, Face the Nation,* or *This Week with David Brinkley*	6	9	12	10	19	28
Infotainment						
Entertainment Tonight	13	12	13	10	12	8
A Current Affair	25	20	16	16	24	18

Note: Respondents were asked: "I'd like to know how often, if ever, you watch any of these late-night comedians or comedy programs. For each one, tell me if you watch regularly, sometimes, hardly ever, or never?" [show] "Do you ever hear things about the candidates or the Presidential election campaign on these shows that you haven't heard before?" "Which one of the late-night comedians or comedy shows has the best political humor this year—the best jokes about the Presidential candidates and the campaign?" [show] Respondents were asked: "I'd like to know how often you watch or regularly listen to certain programs. For each that I read, tell me if you watch or listen to it regularly, sometimes, hardly ever, or never?" [show]

Source: The Times Mirror Center for The People & The Press. Telephone survey of a nationally representative sample of 1,301 adults 18 years of age or older, conducted April 30–May 3, 1992; telephone survey of a nationally representative sample of 1,759 adults, conducted May 28–June 10, 1992. Reprinted with permission.

TABLE 3.6 Activities Performed in Current Party Position by Grassroots Party Activists (in percentages)

Activity	Democrats					Republicans				
	Under 40	40-49	50-59	60-69	70+	Under 40	40-49	50-59	60-69	70+
Contacting voters	82	80	84	87	87*	82	82	87	88	88*
Raising money	55	55	51	53	51	50	56	59	58	60*
Getting people to register to vote	79	79	84	89	91*	74	77	84	84	87*
Campaigning	79	74	73	73	72*	80	79	79	73	69*
Public relations	74	73	77	77	76	69	70	76	74	70*
Contacting new voters	72	68	76	80	81*	67	70	77	79	78*
Participate in Party meetings/business	81	79	83	85	87	80	80	85	86	87*
Recruiting and organizing workers	69	66	70	69	67	66	67	72	69	65*
County Party organizational work	67	66	72	72	71*	62	66	69	71	73*
Increasing political info for voters	75	74	76	76	78	76	80	79	79	80
Policy formulation	56	55	58	59	59	54	59	60	60	62*
Getting candidates for local office	60	60	63	68	65*	61	66	69	69	68*
Other nominating activities	46	41	46	47	40*	40	46	46	46	41*

Notes:

*Indicates statistically significant relationship using chi square at 0.05 level.

Data are from the eleven-state Southern Grassroots Party Activists Project, a collaborative effort funded by the National Science Foundation and administered through the University of New Orleans.

Source: Stephen D. Shaffer and David Breaux. "Generational Differences Among Southern Grassroots Party Workers," paper presented at the 1992 Annual Meeting of the American Political Science Association, Chicago, IL, September 3-6, 1992, p. 25. Reprinted with permission of the American Political Science Association and the authors.

TABLE 3.7 Decision Day: When Individuals Make Their Vote Choice (in percentages)

Decision Time	Age-Group			
1988	**18-29**	**30-49**	**50-59**	**60+**
On election day	7.0	6.9	3.5	5.7
On day before election	3.4	2.1	2.5	3.1
Weekend before election	1.9	2.5	2.6	2.5
During week before election	4.9	4.4	3.4	4.3
During two weeks before election	5.4	5.6	5.9	5.6
After second presidential debate	13.0	7.8	8.6	7.2
After the vice presidential debate	2.0	1.8	1.3	0.5
After first presidential debate	6.8	5.7	6.4	3.4
In September after the party conventions	16.8	16.6	14.3	17.9
During the summer/around the conventions	13.4	16.6	17.8	13.7
During the party primaries (before the summer conventions)	18.4	18.1	19.0	22.7
Before 1988	5.1	9.4	11.6	11.3
Don't know	1.9	2.4	3.0	2.0
1992	**18-29**	**30-49**	**50-64**	**65+**
On election day (11/3)	12.9	10.3	5.5	4.2
On day before election (11/2)	5.1	3.1	5.5	1.7
Weekend before election	3.3	4.2	5.1	3.8
During week before election	8.0	7.9	8.1	7.5
During or just after the presidential debates (10/11; 10/19)	17.5	11.9	6.5	11.6
After the vice presidential debate	1.9	1.0	2.4	0.0
When Ross Perot reentered the race (9/30)	0.7	3.6	3.4	1.2
In September after the party conventions	0.4	5.0	4.7	2.1
During or after the Republican Convention (8/15–23)	4.2	2.7	3.0	1.2
During or after the Democratic Convention (7/11–19)	6.2	6.4	5.4	4.6
When Perot first dropped out of race	2.4	3.0	5.0	5.0
During the party primaries (before the summer conventions (2/17–6/2)	15.7	15.7	19.6	21.8
Before 1992	9.8	11.9	13.7	14.8
Other	8.6	7.6	7.1	8.8

Note: Respondents were asked: "When did you make up your mind definitely to vote for [candidate you said you voted for]?" (open-ended question).

Sources: The Times Mirror Center for The People & The Press. Telephone survey of a nationally representative sample of 2,022 registered voters, conducted November, 1988 (postelection); telephone survey of a nationally representative sample of 1,012 registered voters, conducted November 5-8, 1992. Reprinted with permission.

4

Individual and Group Activism: From Writing Letters to Running for Office

"When something gets my dander up, I'm not going to sit idly by. Somebody's going to hear about it." Whether it's a pothole that needs filling, a bill to increase college tuition, a budget proposal calling for higher taxes, or an elected official's push to legalize casinos—almost any action, or inaction, by government can provoke Americans to mobilize and organize. Just as an old law of physics states that for every action there's an equal and opposite reaction, so in politics one can say that for every issue there are likely to be equally vociferous proponents *and* opponents. The old saying "There's strength in numbers" also applies.

CITIZENS CONNECTING WITH THEIR GOVERNMENTS

Citizens give guidance to their governments—national, state, and local—on everything from issues to personnel. By expressing their opinions and policy preferences, individuals and the groups that represent them help ensure that ours remains a government of, by, and for the people. Naturally, not everyone is equally concerned with every issue or situation. The vast diversity of our nation's populace virtually guarantees that those who get involved will differ from issue to issue.

Why They Get Involved

The reasons *why* people get involved are likely to be quite different as well. Some get involved to affect political outcomes—the ultimate victory or defeat of a candidate or party, the passage or defeat of a referendum or initiative, the enactment or defeat of a particular law or ordinance, the enforcement of a law or policy through the drafting or implementation of particular regulations, or the appointment or removal of a particular citizen advisory board member, government contractor, or public employee. Others get involved for more personal reasons. They simply enjoy participation in politics for its own sake, they like and benefit from the social contacts they make, or they derive satisfaction from contributing to a cause in which they believe.[1]

How They Get Involved

Americans' choices of *how* to get involved also vary. For some, it is calling an elected official's office or a local radio or TV talk show to express an opinion. For others, it is writing letters, sending faxes, signing petitions, or responding to surveys conducted by officeholders, interest groups, or the press. A sizable (although smaller) number actually go to the trouble to attend city council meetings, participate in public hearings, or take part in marches or protest demonstrations.

In a nation of joiners, many Americans belong to groups that may mobilize politically, depending on the situation and issue at hand. Some are only passive members, belonging by virtue of a personal attribute such as age, gender, race, or religion. Or they may join a group but rarely attend meetings or assume leadership roles.

Ardent group members, who often have strong beliefs about a given issue, may go so far as to contribute money to political action committees (PACs) or to personally lobby government officials. Group leaders often decide to run for office themselves to ensure representation of their group's—and their personal—perspectives.

The Backbone of Participatory Democracy

Although these forms of individual and group activism may not always evoke the high levels of publicity that voting and election campaigns command, they are viewed by many to be the real backbone of participatory democracy—the key to keeping government accountable to the citizenry. And as with voting and campaign activity, conventional wisdom says that one's place in the life cycle makes a difference in the quantity and form of one's nonvoting activism. However, participation in these nonvoting types of political activity seems to peak at a younger age than does voting activity. Several decades ago, political scientists Sidney Verba and Norman I. Nie concluded that these forms of activism peak in the 50s, whereas voting peaks in the 60s.[2] But with longer life expectancies and new forms of interactive communications, is this still true?

FORMS OF PARTICIPATION: WHO ACTS AND WHY?

Some types of participation take more personal effort and physical mobility than others. It is easier to call a Congress member's office to express an opinion about an issue than to draft and send a personal letter (not a form letter) to a government official or newspaper editor. Likewise, it takes more personal initiative to speak at a public hearing or city council meeting or to organize a march than it does to simply attend. For some, physical mobility difficulties make activities requiring attendance almost impossible. Other forms of participation, such as contributing to a PAC or filing a lawsuit against a governmental entity or official, may be restricted by a person's financial status or expertise.

Not surprisingly, fewer people participate in activities that require real effort or are considered to be outside the mainstream. For most Americans, contacting is easier than attending; attending is more within their means in terms of both money and expertise than contributing; and contributing requires less effort than litigating, protesting, leading, organizing, or running for political office.

Age-Based Expectations About Individual Activism

The young presumably are more likely than the old to engage in activities that re-quire attendance and physical effort, especially door-to-door petition drives, walks, marches, and protests. After all, the young have higher levels of physical mobility, stamina, and idealism.

Older persons, by contrast, are more active contacters and contributors. They have more experience in dealing with government, greater knowledge of issues and processes, and more personal interest in things politic. They are also gener-ally in a better financial position than the young and can contribute to interest groups, PACs, or candidates running for office (although they are less able to do so than persons of working age at the height of their careers). Limited mobility makes older persons more likely to engage in activities they can do in their own homes.

The middle-aged are presumed to be the most active attenders, organizers, so-cial activists, litigators, and office-seekers.[3] Higher levels of education and experi-ence, wider work and social networks, and the fact that issues are more relevant to them prompt this age-group to take part in more communal or group-related ac-tivism, often orchestrating efforts designed to prompt the young and the old to act as well.

In other words, age-based expectations regarding participation stem from the no-tion that the young are in a start-up mode and that the old are in a slow-down mode. Verba and Nie painted this picture of the situation: "[The young] are still unsettled; they are likely to be residentially and occupationally mobile. They have yet to develop the stake in the politics of a particular locality that comes with extended residence, with home ownership, with children in school, and the like.... Old age brings with it sociological withdrawal as individuals retire from active employment. And it brings as well physical infirmities and fatigue that lower the rate of political activity."[4]

Contacting Public Officials

Traditionally, studies tracking the level of citizen contacting have focused on the in-cidence of people contacting a government official.[5] A 1976 survey of the U.S. pub-lic found that 20 percent had, at some time or another, contacted a local govern-ment official about an issue or problem; 18 percent had contacted a state or national government official.[6] Since that time, the percentage has increased. By 1993, 29 per-cent of Americans surveyed acknowledged they had written a letter to an elected of-ficial; 39 percent had called or sent a letter to their Congress member; and 15 per-cent said they had called or sent a letter to the White House (see Table 4.1).[7]

Technological advancements have caused pollsters to revise the wording of their questions on contacting. By 1994, they were asking whether a person had ever written, called, or faxed a letter to a given person or entity. E-mail will be next. Technological improvements and the facilitative efforts of groups and government officials have made it easier for people to contact their governments: "Interest groups facilitate the whole procedure by urging communications and supplying guidelines. Politicians also reduce the effort involved by inviting communications and by sending out questionnaires."[8]

The young (under 34) contact public officials less than any other age-group. Contacting levels of those 45 and older vary little and certainly do not lend strong support to the notion that older persons disengage rapidly from contacting. Some attribute the sustained interest of seniors in contacting to their greater awareness of age-related issues and consequences. This awareness is heightened through their membership in organizations like the American Association for Retired Persons (AARP) and through media attention to the effectiveness of such efforts.[9] It is now commonplace for the evening news to report how many thousands of phone calls, letters, and faxes the White House and Congress members have received on impending legislation as a crucial vote nears.

Contacting the Media: A Back Door to Get Officials' Attention

Increasingly, the populace believes that public officials are heavily influenced by the press. Some even say we are now a nation governed by polls, which are highly visible in the media. A 1994 survey asked Americans, "Which one of the following groups plays the most influential role in determining which issues and events are considered important these days: business leaders, political leaders in Washington, the press, religious leaders, or Hollywood?" Forty-four percent identified the press, followed by political leaders in Washington (22 percent), business leaders (12 percent), Hollywood (10 percent), and religious leaders (7 percent).[10] All age-groups ranked the press as the most influential, although a higher proportion of those 18 to 29 years of age rated it highest, as compared to those 65 and older (47 and 34 percent, respectively).

Perceiving that elected officials pay attention to what ends up in print or on the airwaves, a sizable and growing number of citizens use the press as an indirect way of contacting politicos. The press has worked hard to solidify its image as "a new intermediary in the American political system," linking the public and government.[11] Newspapers have promoted and encouraged this indirect citizen communication with elected officials by expanding their letters to the editor and op-ed (opposite the editorial page) sections. They frequently solicit opinions and print surveys that readers can answer easily and mail back quickly. The paper then reports the results in a news story.[12] Similarly, radio stations have increased the number of public affairs talk shows that conduct call-in polls,[13] and television has made it fashionable to phone in questions and opinions to leaders appearing on light news, "town meeting" programs. Television also has used 1-800 and 1-900 numbers to conduct instant polls on fast-breaking news events, public officials' speeches and actions, and legislation.[14] The high profile given to public opinion polls has prompted many interest groups to jump on the bandwagon and send out their own surveys. Once a survey of this type is completed, the group distributes a press release on the results, hoping it will become a news story in and of itself.

Some of these new or improved methods of indirect contacting have been more popular than others. A 1994 survey showed that efforts by groups, television stations, and newspapers to encourage people to express their opinions on public issues and politicians generate higher levels of contacting than talk shows or letters to the editor.[15] However, more people are using these forums today than in the past, despite the fact that it's hard to get through on talk-show phone lines and that letters to the editor are difficult to write and get published. A 1976 study found that just over 3 percent of all Americans had ever written a letter to the editor;[16] by 1993, the percentage had jumped to 13 percent. And call-in talk shows, which were virtually nonexistent in the past, flood the airwaves today.

These new indirect forms of contacting seem to be used as much as or more by the young than the old. As shown in Table 4.1, persons younger than 30 are more likely than those 65 or older to have dialed a 1-800 or 1-900 number to express an opinion on some issue of public concern, participated in a poll sent to them by an interest group to which they belong, called in or sent a response to a question or issue put up for discussion by a newspaper or TV station, tried to call in to a talk show to discuss views on a public or political issue, or called a television or cable company with a complaint about a program. Older persons are only marginally more inclined to write letters to the editor than younger people (13 versus 11 percent).

Actually, the most active group in these types of indirect contacting, as expected, are the middle-aged, those between 35 and 54 years old. The one exception is that 55- to 64-year-olds are more likely to call a television station or cable company to complain about the nature or content of a program, reflecting the strong, conservative opinions held by this age-group on moral and crime issues. (I will return to this point in Chapter 6.)

The biggest difference between the young and old occurs in the contacting efforts they make after media prompts. The young are much more likely to respond than the old, which is consistent with earlier findings that the young are more tuned in and responsive to interactive types of programming. As noted in Chapter 3, the attractiveness of these alternative forms of individual contacting has the potential to reduce historical participation gaps between the young and the old.

Moreover, the increasing types of interactive media are likely to ignite more political involvement in all phases of politics. Developments such as direct broadcast satellite conferencing and computer conferencing are decentralizing control over mass communications, making it possible for voters and candidates to exchange information without regard to real time and space and indeed bursting through all previous boundaries on the amount of information that can be exchanged.

Attending Public Hearings, Council or Commission Hearings, and Public Affairs Forums

It is far easier to engage in attendance-related activities that take place in one's own community or neighborhood: Not everyone has the time or resources to go to the state capital or Washington, D.C., to express their opinions about an issue. Even so, few people regularly attend local public hearings, city council, county commission or school board meetings, or public affairs forums. Not until an issue or problem affects them personally do they get upset or concerned enough to attend such events.

Issues that commonly stimulate attendance at public forums, whether governmental or group-sponsored, include:

- land use issues—such as zoning changes or the taking of private land for public improvements like roads, prisons, and landfills
- moral, privacy, and individual rights issues—for example, abortion, prayer in schools, gay and lesbian rights, pornography, or gun control
- the government's unresponsiveness to a problem—potholes, pollution, deteriorating neighborhoods, and so forth
- proposed tax increases
- crime and safety issues arising after a terrible incident or natural disaster

The more directly a problem or issue affects an individual and the greater the perceived magnitude of it, the more likely a person is to show up and vent his or her feelings, especially if this can be done without much difficulty.[17]

Governments, like the press, are making it easier for individuals to take part in deliberations. Many hold meetings in the evenings or on weekends to accommodate those who work during the day. Increasingly, agencies hold hearings and meetings in different parts of the community to make them more convenient to attend. Some large cities and counties even televise their council or commission meetings and public hearings and permit viewers to phone in reactions, which amounts to mini "televotes."[18] Groups, too, are better at informing their members about how and when to attend, even sometimes providing transportation (especially for the old and poor). These efforts appear to be paying off.

The percentage of persons who said they had attended a city council or town meeting rose from 21 percent in 1976 to 30 percent in 1993. The percent who had attended a public hearing reached 34 percent by 1993.[19] And a comparison of changes between 1987 and 1992 in the proportion of Americans who "attended a public hearing or a meeting of a special interest organization" shows that participation went up substantially across all age-groups.[20]

Middle-aged persons, in the 45 to 54 and 55 to 64 age-groups, are the heaviest attenders (in the 30 to 40 percent range), as expected, followed by those 65 and older and then the younger cohorts (see Table 4.1). But it is the oldest cohort that is most likely to have *spoken* at a public forum.[21]

Interestingly, though, among the youngest age-group (18 to 29), more (28 percent) have attended a public hearing than have engaged in contacting or any other type of attendance activity. Other evidence shows the young have attended demonstrations, protests, and sit-ins at higher rates than the old, reflecting youthful idealism and the influence of the college environment.[22]

Demonstrations, Protests, and Civil Disobedience

The notion that demonstrations, protests, and civil disobedience are the province of college youth stems from analyses showing that the majority of those who took part in such activities associated with the civil rights and anti–Vietnam War movements were young.[23] But in the 1980s and 1990s, "rather staid and conservative groups" with older profiles,[24] such as those affiliated with the right-to-life movement, have taken to the streets alongside more liberal younger-to-middle-aged gay rights protesters and pro-choice advocates of all ages. None of the current national movements is based primarily on college campuses, as were the protest movements of the 1960s.

Today's demonstrators, like those of earlier decades, occasionally willfully break what they perceive to be unfair or unjust laws to make their point and to call attention to their plight by gaining extensive media coverage of their protests. Indeed, the way the media cover protests makes or breaks them. Although journalists are trained to search out bizarre, unusual, and extreme behaviors, they do not necessarily react favorably to every protest group. Because journalists are also trained to seek out the views of official governmental spokespersons, their coverage may focus more on questions of the legality of the protesters' actions as opposed to the morality of the issues involved; therefore, they may "legitimize official authority and marginalize radical protest groups."[25]

When lawbreaking occurs peacefully, it is known as civil disobedience.[26] Those who engage in such activities invite police arrest. "By willingly accepting punishment for the violation of an unjust law, people who practice civil disobedience demonstrate their sincerity. They hope to shame public officials and make them ask themselves how far they are willing to go to protect the status quo."[27]

Breaking the law through violent means such as murder, bombings, terrorism, rioting, burning, looting, and kidnapping is regarded as criminal activity—an unacceptable form of protest. All age-groups view civil disobedience more positively than violence, although the young are more likely than the old to see both types of actions as acceptable expressions of individual rights of assembly and free speech.

Mass demonstrations and marches are not the only form of protest. Economic boycotts threatening the loss of tax revenue and jobs are the newest protest tools used by individuals and groups, both liberal and conservative, in pushing communities, states, and public and private entities to implement or reverse certain public policies.

National Election Studies conducted in the mid-1970s asked their survey respondents whether they had participated in sit-ins, demonstrations, or protests. Just 1.5 percent acknowledged they had done so at the national level, and less than 3 percent said they had done so at the local level.[28] The young were more active protesters than the old. These studies did not ask specifically about willfully breaking the law or engaging in boycotts.

Recent and more comprehensive surveys show that younger adults, including those in the Civil Rights/Vietnam War generation,[29] are considerably more likely to be protesters, boycotters, and civil disobedients than older persons (see Figure 4.1). Of these forms of action, boycotts are the most common. By 1992, more than one-fifth of the respondents reported they had boycotted a company, up from 14 percent in 1987. The proportion who reported they had taken part in a public demonstration also rose above the level observed in the mid-1970s (rising to 9 percent). The percent who believed staging protests is an effective way to influence government stood at 45 percent overall and 57 percent among those 18 to 29. Civil disobedience levels remained low; only 1 percent of all those surveyed in 1987 reported they had broken the law for a political or social cause. The figure was 2 percent among those younger than 30 years of age.

Petitions: Signing and Circulating

Many activists have turned to more political ways of changing public policy. In *Citizen Lawmakers,* David D. Schmidt reported: "Grassroots citizen groups are finding ballot Initiatives [put on the ballot through citizen petition signatures] to be far more effective in bringing issues to public consciousness than such traditional political activities as protest marches, letter-writing campaigns, and lending support to sympathetic candidates."[30] Petitions have replaced protests, which are hard to sustain and which, if too radical, may ultimately provoke a negative backlash affecting the opinion of both the public and government officials.

Groups use petitions to get the government's attention, and they often succeed in this regard because petitions frequently get the media's attention first. In fact, in describing how to successfully conduct a petition campaign, Schmidt advised petition-drive leaders to "hold news conferences, mail out regular press releases, stage attention-grabbing 'media events,' and court the editorial boards of newspapers and television and radio stations." He also recommended that petition-drive leaders "begin educating reporters and editors about the issue even before the petition drive begins, and keep sending them information."[31]

Petitions provide a way of showing how widespread public sentiment is on a particular topic. In certain situations, they are used like public opinion polls to register citizen discontent (or content) on a wide range of issues and situations— from a parks department's proposed increase in softball-team registration fees to state adoption policies to national medical experiments involving human subjects.

FIGURE 4.1 Low but Rising Levels of Participation in Demonstrations, Boycotts, and Civil Disobedience

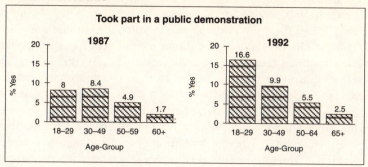

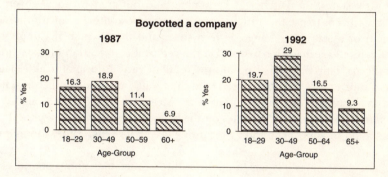

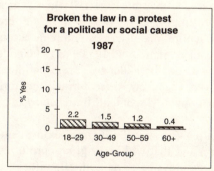

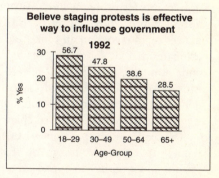

Note: In 1987, respondents were asked: "The following are actions people have taken to express their views on issues that concern them. For each, please tell me if you have done it over the last four years or so to express your view on any issue?" In 1992, respondents were asked: "Which of these things have you done in the past year to express your opinions on issues that concern you?" (took part in public demonstration; boycotted a company . . .). In 1992, respondents were also asked: "I'd like your opinion about the effectiveness of different ways of trying to influence the way the government is run and influence which laws are passed." Percentages reported are for those who answered "very or fairly effective."

Source: The Times Mirror Center for The People & The Press. Telephone survey of a nationally representative sample of 4,244 adults 18 years of age or older, conducted April 25–May 10, 1987; telephone survey of a nationally representative sample of 3,517 adults 18 years of age or older, conducted May 28–June 10, 1992. Reprinted with permission.

Petitions are also used in more formal ways to enable citizens to intervene directly in the legislative process. Each of the three tools of direct democracy—initiative, referendum, and recall—has a petition element. In *Direct Democracy,* Thomas Cronin noted that "the *initiative* allows voters to propose a legislative measure (statutory initiative) or a constitutional amendment (constitutional initiative) by filing a *petition* bearing a required number of valid citizen signatures." A petition referendum allows voters to demand a chance to vote on legislation already passed by the legislature but not yet in effect if enough eligible citizens sign a petition within a specified time.[32] "The *recall* allows voters to remove or discharge a public official from office by filing a *petition* bearing a specific number of valid signatures demanding a vote on the official's continued tenure in office."[33] Some states permit all three types of direct citizen initiatives; others permit none.

Twenty-six states, the District of Columbia, and hundreds of local governments allow citizens to use the initiative process to propose either a constitutional amendment or a statutory change. Fifteen states and the District of Columbia provide for recall mechanisms to vote on the removal or retention of statewide elected officials. Thirty-six states permit the recall of various local officials.[34] The initiative is much more frequently used than the recall,[35] and the number of state initiatives has escalated sharply in recent years. Meanwhile, citizen petitions have directly placed a wide variety of issues on the ballot in recent years or prompted legislators to do so—most commonly regarding tax, civil rights, crime, and moral issues.[36]

Each state determines its own rules, procedures, timetables, and signature requirements for using the initiative and recall at the state level. Local governments also have procedures citizens can use to propose changes to local or city ordinances or to revote on an officeholder's tenure in a given position. One account estimates that local governments in the United States hold 10,000 to 15,000 referenda annually, although not all are placed on the ballot by citizen petitions.[37] Most involve tax and bond issues. Used effectively, these formal and direct democracy mechanisms "not only *vent* popular discontent, but *channel it constructively*" to make the desired changes.[38]

The explosion in petition drives has revived several criticisms about them—namely, that there are too many of them and that whichever group, pro or con, has the most money to spend on an issue prevails.[39] The political editor of the *Miami Herald* articulated these concerns well:

> Despite its populist clothing, direct democracy is, in actuality, special democracy. To put an initiative on Florida's ballot today costs hundreds of thousands of dollars—a price tag far beyond Joe Citizen's means. As a result, those that make it [get enough signatures from registered voters] are usually backed by a special interest with the ability to raise big sums, produce compelling television and run a full-bore campaign. And not surprisingly, the measure is often tailored to yield that interest direct results. Shouldn't one wonder why, for example, the impending casino amendment

only benefits pari-mutuel licensees and doesn't allow hotels and riverboats to operate them? Answer: The money behind the casino amendment comes from the former, not the latter.[40]

Tom Fiedler wrote this after twenty-three separate petition drives had formally begun to put proposals on the ballot dealing with everything from legalizing casino gambling, fixing prison sentences, taxing sugar to pay for the Everglades cleanup, outlawing gay rights ordinances, and guaranteeing gay rights (nothing like competing petitions!), to prohibiting gill nets that might trap sea turtles. To get on the ballot, each proposal needed 430,000 valid signatures from registered voters—a monumental task for individuals or groups without the funds to hire professional signature collectors. (Florida is one of only a few states that permit the hiring of signature collectors.)[41]

But proponents of direct democracy counter these arguments by citing evidence showing little relationship between money spent and referenda outcomes. They also discount the influence of self-serving special interest groups. As Schmidt said in *Citizen Lawmakers:* "The 'special interest' label is ambiguous; one person's 'special interest group' is another's 'public interest group.' . . . Ultimately, Initiatives are controlled neither by the Right, Left, nor special interests, but by the people. The people exercise their control not only by voting, but also by signing (or refusing to sign) petitions to put Initiative questions on the ballot, and by circulating these petitions."[42]

The use of direct democracy tools has exploded over the past several decades. The 1976 National Election Study found that 11 percent of all respondents had signed a petition aimed at national policies, and 22 percent had signed one aimed at local entities and policies. By 1987, a Times Mirror survey showed that 55 percent of the U.S. populace had signed a petition within the past four years; another 10 percent had actually circulated one. And by 1992, 53 percent acknowledged they had signed a petition within the past year alone.

In line with patterns mentioned earlier, middle-aged and young voters are more active in signing and circulating petitions.[43] Some analysts attribute young people's greater enthusiasm for signing petitions to their higher educational levels, which make them more susceptible to the kind of appeals commonly used by those collecting petition signatures: "'Well,' says the person at the table, 'won't you help us to get it on the ballot so it can get a full public debate and so it can be put on the ballot in November?'"[44]

GROUP-BASED ACTIVISM

Americans are joiners, to say the least! The *1994 Encyclopedia of Associations* listed nearly 23,000 national organizations and more than 53,000 regional, state, and local organizations.[45] Though these numbers appear staggering, they are actually quite conservative: Thousands of other small, remote, or informal groups and associations are not listed. The *Encyclopedia* classifies its listed groups by their *primary* interests (although some have multiple interests), using the following categories:

- trade, business, and commercial
- environmental and agricultural
- legal, governmental, public administration, and military
- engineering, technological, and natural and social science
- educational
- cultural
- social welfare
- health and medical
- public affairs
- fraternal, foreign interest, nationality, and ethnic
- religious
- veterans, hereditary, and patriotic
- hobby and avocational
- athletic and sports
- labor unions, associations, and federations
- chambers of commerce, trade, and tourism
- Greek letter and related organizations
- fan clubs (Elvis lives!)

Some organizations have huge memberships, others small. Some are quite broad in their focus, others quite narrow. Some have lots of money, fancy newsletters, paid staffs, and Washington offices. Others operate on a shoestring, are staffed primarily by volunteers, and are headquartered in someone's basement. But each means something special to those who belong to it.

Why Belong?

Political interest groups offer their members a number of benefits.[46] First of all, they promote communication between constituents and their representatives: "They are a primary link between citizens and their government, forming a channel of access through which members voice their opinions to those who govern them."[47] In addition, groups are an invaluable source of information for their members, and they help educate both members and the public at large about important issues. In fact, groups are often the first to call attention to a problem. Groups also often serve as watchdogs—closely monitoring the operations and effectiveness of various officials, policies, and programs.

Because Americans have so many groups to chose from, they often sustain their memberships in the ones that offer them the most personal benefits and pleasure.[48] For some, the greatest benefit is that through group activism, they can play a larger, more focused, and more constant role in the policy-influencing process than by just voting every couple of years. Furthermore, those who are active in groups are also more likely to vote than those who are not.

Popular Groups Not Commonly Thought of as "Political"

Many Americans participate in groups or organizations they do not think of as remotely political in nature. For example, they rarely think about their church, their sports league, or their fraternal, social, or civic club as being involved in politics. However, depending on the situation, these basically nonpolitical groups can become quite political if their interests are threatened by impending government legislation or inaction.[49] (Later in the chapter, I will show how involved these types of groups can be in representing the views of the young and old to legislators.)

Interest Groups That Hope to Influence Public Policy

Organizations more commonly seen as highly political are labeled *interest groups.* In *The Interest Group Society,* Jeffrey M. Berry defined an interest group as "an *organized* body of individuals who share some goals and who try to influence public policy."[50] However, even for these groups, rarely is politics the primary glue that holds the members together. Rather, it is the common area or areas of interest that attracted these people to join the group in the first place (i.e., the many categories listed in the *Encyclopedia of Associations* or common personal attributes such as age, race, gender, or ideology—liberal or conservative). By every account, the number of special interest groups has escalated sharply since the early 1980s.[51] Between 1987 and 1993, the proportion of Americans who acknowledged they had recently "joined an organization in support of a particular cause" increased from 17 to 27 percent.[52]

Developing Links Between Constituents and Their Governments

Groups, like the individuals who compose them, try to get government's attention in both direct and indirect ways. Using direct, face-to-face interactions with group members or their representatives (lobbyists) to more indirect, grassroots lobbying, campaign contributions through PACs, or litigation efforts, groups try to affect public policy outcomes. In fact, what groups do is to orchestrate joint action by their members—creating a larger pool of concerned voters (strength in numbers) than would be possible if individuals were left to initiate such action on their own.

Sponsoring public rallies, attending public meetings with government officials en masse, and orchestrating mail-ins, call-ins, fax-ins, or "electronic-mail-ins" to politicians are common examples of grassroots lobbying. To rally the troops, group leaders or staff first contact their own members via direct mail, faxes, or phone banks to urge them to respond to a looming piece of legislation or a public policy or a situation they find critical to their members' interests. Larger, more established and resource-rich groups even have elaborate computerized membership mobilization files that enable them to target voters in specific congressional or legislative districts, or those with some common attribute (e.g., retirees with a military background or families with children in private schools). Mobilization techniques are as varied as the skills and resources of the interest groups themselves and the communication technologies available to them.

Age and Group Activism

Group activism seems to peak during middle age (although, as already seen, certain types of group activism, such as protests, are associated more strongly with the youngest cohorts). The youngest and oldest cohorts presumably will not be as active in groups as those in between because income affects group activism much more than other forms of political participation. As Kay L. Schlotzman and John T. Tierney, in *Organized Interests in American Society,* argued: "Membership in organizations makes special demands of a material nature that many other forms of political participation do not. . . . For those with greater resources, the costs of organizational membership and activity—from paying dues to paying a baby-sitter—represent much less of a drain."[53] But such characterizations may not be as accurate today as they once were.

Group participation, like the other forms of participation that I have examined, is now more interactive and less demanding in terms of physical attendance. People can participate from their kitchen tables via telephone, fax, letters, and monetary contributions. Organizations clearly recognize this fact and court participation through these means.[54]

Groups Focused on Aging and Retirement

"The aging of the population and the growth of age-based and retirement-based programs and benefits have contributed to [greater] political consciousness and activism among the elderly," noted one scholar.[55] Participation in groups that focus on aging and retirement make older Americans among the best organized of all U.S. citizens.[56] As of 1994, sixty-one national social welfare organizations represented the interests of older citizens. (There are thousands of others that are purely local, state, or regional in focus.) Of these national groups, nearly half (41 percent) have headquarters in Washington; the others are based in twenty different states. Moreover, nearly three-fourths (72 percent) were founded between 1970 and 1990, reflecting the onslaught of interest groups in recent years and the aging of the U.S. population.[57]

The AARP, the National Council of Senior Citizens, the Gray Panthers, and the National Alliance of Senior Citizens are among the most prominent national mass membership organizations for seniors.[58] The largest and most powerful is the AARP, with 33 million members and a staff of 1,200. In fact, the only organization bigger than the AARP is the Catholic Church. Besides being a powerful lobbying group, AARP sustains its membership levels by offering a great many services to those who belong. For example, the organization either directly or indirectly (through outside firms) makes available an extensive and efficient pharmacy service, group health insurance, car and homeowners insurance, mobile-home insurance, an investment program, a Visa credit card program, a travel program, rental car and hotel discounts, and even emergency road service.[59]

As the population ages, the membership lists of organizations serving seniors will swell. AARP projects its membership will double over the next two decades, and it expects "to increase its formidable political power on core issues ranging from health care to safeguarding Social Security benefits."[60]

However, because of their higher educational levels, the new seniors are expected to be "more independent and willing to buck the group in pursuit of their individual interests."[61] Indeed, some argue that divergent opinions are inevitable in a group of such mammoth size, and they predict that members of this group will begin fighting among themselves—e.g., upper-income elderly will fight against lower-income elderly, or working elderly will be at odds with nonworking elderly.[62] With so many members, the elderly have become a large political target, and people at the grassroots level may be more likely to sit back and wait for someone else to lobby on issues affecting senior citizens.[63]

Groups Focusing on Infants, Children, and Youth

Groups representing infants, children, and youth have always been fairly independent of one another. Compared with groups representing the elderly, youth-serving groups are older and are more likely to be oriented toward a single purpose and headquartered outside the nation's capital. Of the 116 youth-oriented national social welfare organizations listed in the *1994 Encyclopedia of Associations,* 40 percent were founded prior to the 1970s; 86 percent are headquartered outside Washington, D.C.

One of the most widely known organizations serving the young is the Children's Defense Fund, a nonmembership advocacy group. It provides "systematic, long-range advocacy on behalf of the nation's children and teenagers [and] engages in research, public education, monitoring of federal agencies, litigation, legislative drafting and testimony assistance to state and local groups, and community organizations in areas of child welfare, child health, adolescent pregnancy prevention, child care and development, family services and child mental health."[64] Founded in 1973, it has a budget of nearly $9 million and a staff of 100.

Other powerful groups are the traditional youth club organizations such as 4-H, YMCA, YWCA, Big Brothers/Big Sisters, Camp Fire Boys and Camp Fire Girls, Boy Scouts and Girl Scouts, and Girls Clubs and Boys Clubs; sports organizations such as police athletic clubs and Little League; and church youth groups. None of these long-established youth-oriented groups, individually or collectively, is as powerful as the AARP. However, many are now emphasizing collective action and community service designed to highlight their importance and effectiveness as well as to help bridge the generation gap.[65]

Youth-oriented groups are likely to coalesce more in the future once resources start flowing disproportionately to seniors in the coming decades. At the same time, coalitions, though effective, are often difficult to sustain over time, as even the groups representing the elderly have discovered.[66]

The newest types of groups representing the younger adult population focus heavily on economics. One of the first and most powerful is Americans for Generational Equity (AGE). Many credit this organization with "*creating* the notion that the problem of inadequate societal resources for children [is] a product of excessive benefits for the aged."[67] Founded in 1984, it attracted 600 members in its first year of operation and raised considerable amounts of money, which helped it publicize its concerns about the future of the Social Security system. Some credit—or blame—the organization for popularizing the concept of generational equity.

The Third Millennium and Lead . . . or Leave, both formed in 1992, are the newest youth advocacy groups with a clearly economic focus. The two groups have formed chapters around the country to speak for the more than 40 million Americans of Generation X born after 1960. The New York–based Third Millennium, which has enrolled 1,100 dues-paying members, says its purpose is to represent the concerns of "young adults worried about the economic and social burdens they see as the looming legacy of their elders."[68] The group particularly objects to the government's borrowing from the Social Security fund to finance operations. "We don't believe in Social Security, the way it is now constituted, any more than we believe in the tooth fairy or Santa Claus," says Deroy Murdock, 30, a founder.[69]

Lead . . . or Leave was founded in August 1992 as a Washington-based organization by two young men in their twenties, Rob Nelson and Jon Cowan, to target the federal deficit. Says cofounder Rob Nelson, 30, "The deficit is our Vietnam."[70] Embittered at the prospect of paying off huge debts inherited from previous generations and having nothing left for their own vision, the group hopes to mobilize 18- to 30-year-olds at the ballot box to oust elected officials who are afraid to rid the nation's budget of its red ink. But Lead . . . or Leave is also interested in getting young people to register and vote, providing forums for younger voices and bringing their concerns to the attention of national leaders, distributing the group's *Revolution X* (a "survival guide" on how the group thinks the United States can be fixed), and building a constituency that can advance an agenda for the next generation.[71]

At one time, the organization was touted to have had over a million members, chapters in all fifty states, and affiliations with sixty-three college campuses and three student organizations. But by 1995, it had become a smaller, more locally based group (primarily composed of chapters at various universities). That year, its popular, highly visible founders closed their Washington office and moved on to other things, although they still retained their positions on the group's board of directors.

Lead . . . or Leave's experiences (and also those of AGE, now defunct) demonstrate some of the unique hurdles young adult–focused groups have to overcome. First and foremost is the tendency of these new groups to be identified with the specific personalities who found them, most often on a shoestring budget, and to be geared toward their "pet" projects and issues. Once these founders move into middle–age, they resign and leave the organization with a huge leadership vacuum at the top, along with a miniscule budget. Fund-raising is very difficult for young adult–focused groups. They have more difficulty attracting dues-paying members because the young have far less disposable income than the older cohorts for such activities. These groups also find it very difficult to get large contributions from major foundations or individual donors. Nonetheless, I predict that the number of young adult–oriented interest groups will continue to grow and their memberships will swell as intergenerational economic tension escalates.

Groups Influential in Representing the Young and Old at the State Level

National mass membership groups and nonmembership organizations with national funding bases quite naturally target national-level decisionmakers. But who speaks for the young and the old at the grassroots level?[72] To get an answer, a 1994 survey asked Florida's legislators to name the groups in their respective districts that were most active in promoting issues important to their younger and older constituents. Ironically, the legislators identified many groups whose members would probably not label them as highly political—for example, civic, church, and social groups. But many were politically focused interest groups, encompassing environmental activists, homeowners and taxpayers, good-government proponents, service providers and users, and people of various political persuasions.

Paralleling patterns at the national level, Florida's legislators identified a wider array of groups representing the young than the old. The groups they most commonly named as representing the interests of younger constituents were those with education, civic affairs, the environment, or business as their primary focus. Also important were political groups like the Young Democrats and Young Republicans. Although this political linkage is a natural one (future political activists linking up with current officeholders), it is often ignored by those who write about interest groups.

Among the Florida legislators, much more consensus existed about which groups were most active in representing the interests of their older constituents. More than two-thirds identified AARP. Homeowner/taxpayer, health, and veterans groups were also perceived as quite active in representing the interests of senior citizens. These groups are powerful in districts with large older populations, and they are typically better organized and funded than the groups representing the young.

These findings bolster other Florida-based studies that have found that the clout of public interest, citizens, health care, and education groups has increased as the state's age profile has changed.[73]

Groups as Contributors: Political Action Committees

Today's interest group activities often demonstrate there is strength in dollars. By pooling individual members' monetary contributions, groups can exercise more influence over elected officials, either directly through group donations to a candidate's campaign fund or indirectly through independent advertisements calling for the election or defeat of a candidate, often because of the candidate's position on issues of interest to the group. In addition, groups can and do raise and spend money to mobilize their own memberships to action. Some describe this as a "'triple-threat' offensive: skillful mobilization of public opinion through large, well-financed public relations campaigns; direct assistance to friendly candidates (usually incumbents) in the form of campaign contributions as well as 'education' of the voters by independent expenditures on mailings, advertisements, and the like; and direct influence on officeholders through lobbying."[74]

Federal election laws, established under the Federal Election Campaign Act of 1971 and its amendments, govern who can contribute (individuals, interest groups, and political parties) and how much they can give to presidential and congressional election campaigns. States establish their own contribution laws for state and local elections, many of which are patterned after national laws.

What Is a PAC?

Federal laws permit business, labor, trade association, and other interest groups to raise money on a voluntary basis from members, stockholders, or employees to contribute to candidates' political campaigns and to political parties as well.[75] These individually contributed but collectively expended funds are disbursed by PACs. Paralleling the sharp increase in the number of interest groups, there has been a tremendous upsurge in the number of PACs—from 608 in 1974 to 4,195 by the end of 1992.[76] PACs spend millions of dollars to lobby elected officials directly and indirectly.

PACs have become "the dominant organizations through which interest groups raise and spend money."[77] In *Inside Campaign Finance*, Frank J. Sorauf characterized them as "conspicuous icons [that] dominate the media-born images of campaign funding and embody most of the public fears about a campaign finance that relies on voluntary private largesse." At the same time, Sorauf acknowledged that "both contributors and candidates [have] rediscovered one of the immutable laws of political action: organized, aggregated activity achieves more political goals more effectively."[78]

In deciding how to spend their contributors' money, PACs typically examine a candidate's campaign platform, voting record (if he or she is an incumbent), and likelihood of winning; they also consider whether the candidate will be receptive to PAC lobbying. Critics and reformers see PACs as a "system of legal bribery" that is unfairly tilted toward groups with large, affluent memberships.[79] Defenders see PACs as clear-cut examples of the exercise of individual rights of assembly and freedom of speech. Proponents also point out that most elected officials get PAC money from a variety of interest groups, making it hard to demonstrate that a single group dictates their vote on bills.[80]

Who Gives to PACs? Young or Old?

Contributing is generally thought to be the domain of middle-aged and older persons. The young often do not yet have the financial resources to make PAC contributions. Nor are the young as involved in organized interest groups as their older counterparts, making it less likely they will be asked by a business, trade association, or other organization to donate to a PAC. In contrast, older persons are better able to give and are more aware of the utility of PACs from a business, partisan, personal, or ideological perspective. Older people also find contributing easier and more appealing than group activities that require physical attendance.

Two recent surveys show not only that more older persons contribute to PACs but also that the generation gap is widening. In 1987, roughly 10 to 15 percent of all age-cohorts said they had contributed to a political action group that supported or opposed a particular candidate in an election (see Figure 4.2). By 1993, the percentages of contributors among those 55 and older had risen to 17 to 18 percent, while the percentage in the youngest cohort had dropped to 9 percent. Thus, there is little evidence that those of retirement age stop making PAC contributions once they leave the workforce (see Table 4.1). Moreover, the most active PAC contributors are those between 55 and 64—at the peak of their professional careers in terms of position, leadership, and income.

Litigation Strategies: Using the Courts to Achieve Group Goals

A decade ago, a major study of interest groups concluded that "if an interest group is to maximize its influence in the policy-making process, it must stand ready to use litigation as one of its lobbying tactics."[81] Ours is an increasingly litigious society. Groups, like individuals, have recognized that the courts often appear to be the only way left to get a public policy changed or to stop one from being implemented.[82] The litigation strategies used successfully by civil rights groups in the 1960s and 1970s have prompted conservative and nonideological groups alike to adopt similar strategies in the 1980s and 1990s.[83]

Why Sue?

Today, groups of all types file lawsuits for a variety of reasons: "to safeguard the interests of their members, promote test cases or class action suits to secure judicial favor for a particular principle, defend against formal charges rather than settle out of court, and file amicus [friend of the court] briefs to provide new information to courts hearing disputes between others."[84] Groups often file lawsuits when they perceive they have been shut out of the regular political process. In the courtroom, "one does not have to demonstrate the size of one's constituency or what one can do for the policymaker if one has the law on one's side." It's "the strength of one's case in law, rather than one's backers in politics," that dictates the outcome.[85]

FIGURE 4.2 PAC Contributions: Generational Gap Widening

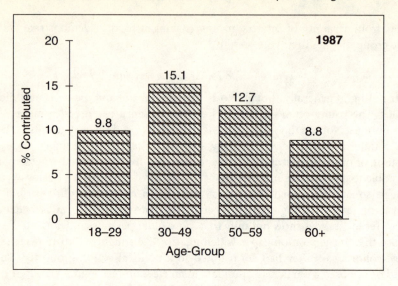

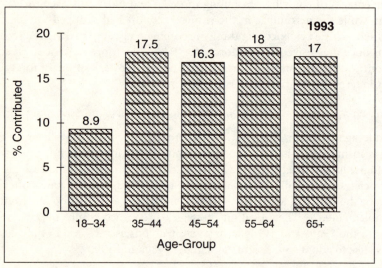

Note: In 1987 respondents were asked: "Which of the following things, if any, have you done in the last 4 years or so to help a party or candidate win an election? (Contributed to political action groups that supported or opposed particular candidates in an election?)." In 1993 respondents were asked: "People express their opinions about politics and current events in a number of ways besides voting. I'm going to read you a list of these ways. Please tell me whether you have ever [contributed to a PAC]?"

Source: The Times Mirror Center for The People & The Press. Face-to-face survey of a nationally representative sample of 4,244 adults 18 years of age or older, conducted April 25–May 10, 1987; telephone survey of a nationally representative sample of 1,003 adults, conducted June 2–6, 1993. Reprinted with permission.

Types of Groups Most Likely to Sue

Some groups are in a better position organizationally, legally,[86] or financially to use litigation as a policymaking tool. One intriguing study found that the groups most likely to sue are the well-established organizations with more resources that have been involved in "structured, recurring, and intense conflict with the same opponents" and whose "political fortunes change drastically with changes in [political] administration."[87] In addition, groups that employ both inside and outside strategies of policy influence use the courts more often than those that are less active. Trade associations and unions, which clearly have more resources and are more likely to have in-house counsel, sue more than citizen groups.

Contrary to conventional wisdom, "the groups that are in the courts most often are those profit sector groups and unions who are protecting their members' professional or business interests and not the cause-oriented groups pressing for the expansion of civil liberties or for the expansion of governmental benefits to outsiders."[88] In other words, the desire to protect a group's economic interests is more likely to spark litigation than its concern with individual or civil rights, although the latter certainly has occurred frequently throughout U.S. history.

Age Groups and Litigation

The economic impetus for group use of litigation strategies will probably intensify as intergenerational economic tensions increase. Recent analyses of group use of litigation already hint that groups representing younger Americans will likely file equity suits questioning the fairness of government spending patterns.[89] Groups representing older Americans will no doubt litigate should the sources of income for the elderly, including entitlements, retirement benefits, or jobs, be threatened.[90] The number of age-based discrimination complaints filed with the Equal Employment Opportunity Commission is already substantial and is escalating sharply.[91]

To be a party to a lawsuit, either as an individual or as part of a class action group, often requires a lot of time, energy, and money. Thus, it is not unreasonable to expect that individuals who show their political activism by engaging in lawsuits are older but are not retirees. Many retirees, after all, are on fixed incomes and prefer not to spend their time in the courtroom. However, since we now know that younger persons are more likely to break the law in a protest for a political or social cause, we might expect higher numbers of them to be parties to lawsuits with this purpose in mind.

In a 1987 survey by the Times Mirror Center for The People & The Press, 7 percent of the respondents indicated they had "initiated or participated in a lawsuit." (The survey did not ask whether their lawsuit involvement was part of a group effort.) The highest incidences of litigation activism occurred among 30- to 49-year-olds (9 percent) and 50- to 59-year-olds (8 percent), lending support to the thesis that the middle-aged are in the best position to sue. But 6 percent of

FIGURE 4.3 Few Want a Family Member to Go into Politics as a Career: Young More Positively Inclined Than Old

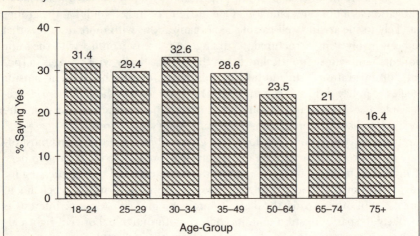

Note: Respondents were asked: "Would you like your son or daughter or other member of your family to go into politics as a career?"

Source: The Times Mirror Center for The People & The Press. Telephone survey of a nationally representative sample of 3,517 adults 18 years of age and older, conducted May 28-June 10, 1992. Reprinted with permission.

the 18- to 29-year-olds also said they had played an active role in a litigation effort. The least litigious were those 60 and older, less than 3 percent of whom reported they had played such a role within the past four years or so.[92] (Based on the survey, it is not unreasonable to speculate that more might have done so earlier in their lives, although the litigation explosion really began in the 1960s.)

RUNNING FOR AND HOLDING ELECTIVE OFFICE

By most accounts, only one out of a hundred Americans ever runs for elective office. This form of political participation is the most demanding, regardless of whether one's decision to run is purely individual or prompted by a person's political party or interest group. Most Americans simply don't want to run for political office, even at the local level. Some are reluctant to run because they think people like themselves, whether defined by gender, race, income, education, political party, ideology, or some other trait, cannot win.[93] Others believe they haven't participated enough in community groups or political party organizations to have gained leadership experience, stature, or name recognition among the electorate.

Many recognize the headaches and personal sacrifices it takes even to serve on a local school board or city council. Their reluctance extends to other members of their families. When a Times Mirror survey in June 1992 asked, "Would you like your son or daughter or other members of your family to go into politics as a career?" just over one-fourth (27 percent) said yes. Younger cohorts view a political career much more positively than the older ones (see Figure 4.3). For example, among those 18 to 24 years of age, 31 percent answered yes, compared to just 21 percent of those 65 to 74 and only 16 percent of those 75 and older.

Running for and holding office often takes a heavy toll on a person's time, family, finances, and privacy. Depending upon the office sought, it may require lots of traveling, even the maintenance of a second home and a relocation. Alan Ehrenhalt, in *The United States of Ambition,* argued that seeking and holding office in the United States today is far more demanding than it was a generation ago. He claimed that the biggest barriers to seeking a political career are "the burdens of time, physical effort, and financial sacrifice."[94] Others would add loss of privacy and a hostile press to the list. Indeed, surveys have shown that many Americans, especially the young, see press coverage of the personal and ethical behavior of elected officials as excessive and ineffective. Young and old alike perceive such coverage to be a formidable deterrent to getting good people to run for public office. Ehrenhalt warned that our democratic system suffers when individuals willing to "submerge their personal preferences for the common good" are not willing to run for office.

Why Seek Office?

People choose to run for office with one or more expectations in mind. Some run for a position not expecting to hold it for long, perhaps just long enough to resolve one or more issues they deem important. Others run for a position expecting to make a career out of that office but not anticipating a run for any other office. Still others run for one office, hoping that their experience there will catapult them into a higher office. In the landmark study *Ambition and Politics,* Joseph Schlesinger labeled these three types of ambition as "discrete," "static," and "progressive," respectively.[95]

The reasons people seek office range from grudge to glory. They may have been recruited by their political party. They may believe that holding office is a good way to serve a neighborhood, community, or state. They may hope to increase business contacts or build up name recognition and gain experience to run for office again (this is often the attitude when making one's first run for office). They may be motivated by the personal thrill of receiving media attention. Or they may simply enjoy politics.[96] In spite of the self-serving nature of many of these motivations, far more officeseekers enter politics for service reasons than is commonly perceived. Ehrenhalt's study of officeholders concluded: "What stands out . . . is that for most of them the commitment to a political life has been accompanied by a positive attitude toward government itself as an instrument for doing valuable work in American society."[97]

Deciding Which Office to Seek

The United States has 86,743 governments—one national, fifty state, and 86,692 local, which includes county, municipal, township and town, school district, and special district groups.[98] At the national level, we elect a president and vice president, 435 U.S. House members, and 100 U.S. senators. Many states also have a substantial number of elective positions—executive, legislative, and judicial.[99] So, too, do local governments. For example, it is not uncommon for residents of a city to separately elect a mayor, several city council members, municipal judges, and an assortment of other municipal officers (e.g., treasurer, controller, and clerk). Because of the sheer number of elective posts available at the local level, many politicians begin—and end—their careers there, especially those with discrete or static ambitions.

Holding a local office is often less disruptive to one's family and career, although some in such posts do exhibit progressive ambitions. That is, they may move from an elective legislative post in a smaller jurisdiction (e.g., a city council) to one governing a larger entity (e.g., a county commission) or to an executive (e.g., mayoral) or judicial post but still within the same community. The part-time nature of many local positions permits officeholders both to have more discretion over their time and to hold private jobs.

The higher an office on the political career ladder (from local to statewide to national), the more difficult it becomes to run, especially if one must leave a safe position behind and relocate. Also, the higher one climbs, the more likely the office is to be a full-time rather than a part-time post. For those with lucrative careers in the private sector, running for such a position may be unattractive in terms of both time and money. Ehrenhalt said it well: "Politics in the 1990s is for people who are willing to give it vast amounts of their time. It is also for people who are not particularly concerned about making money."[100] Age often is a key factor in deciding whether to run for office or to move up the political ladder.

Age and Running for Office

Age affects a person's decision to run in a number of ways. First, some positions have minimum age requirements. For example, the U.S. Constitution requires that an individual be at least 35 to hold the office of president, 30 to be a U.S. senator, and 25 to serve in the U.S. House of Representatives. A number of state constitutions and state statutes also establish minimum age requirements for governors, state legislators, and certain other state officials, although for most state and local positions, the minimum age is the same as the voting age—18. When test cases have challenged minimum age requirements at the state and local levels, the courts have generally ruled them valid on the rationale that "it takes someone with more maturity to administer a public office than to vote for someone to administer that office."[101] The latest cases dispute maximum age requirements or mandatory retirement ages. In particular, judges in a number of states have challenged laws denying them the right to run for office after a certain age.

Naturally, the age requirements of an office affect the age of entry into it. So, too, does its place in the hierarchy of political offices. The more prestigious the office and the larger the constituency, the less likely it is that that office will be the point of entry into politics. In *Ambition and Politics,* Schlesinger identifies four base offices that were frequently held by governors and U.S. senators before they ran for their prestigious statewide positions. These are (1) local elective offices, such as city council member, alder, county supervisor or commissioner, and mayor, (2) state legislative offices, (3) administrative or appointive posts in the government, and (4) law enforcement or judicial positions, such as sheriff, judge, or district attorney.

More recent studies have found similar results: It is common for persons to start their political careers at any of these base points. But it is uncommon for someone to run for a statewide office (governor, lieutenant governor, secretary of state, treasurer, auditor, attorney general, supreme court justice) or a congressional seat (House or Senate) without having first held a base position. When this does occur, the candidate is more likely to be an older person who has achieved recognition as a result of accomplishments in his or her profession rather than in politics.

Age of Entry

Minimum age requirements and the stepping-stone nature of higher-level positions explain why the age at which a person decides to run for a particular political office differs by the post. Schlesinger's study found that the most common age of entry into the U.S. House of Representatives is 35 to 40. For governors, it is 45 to 50. (A governorship is regarded as a higher political office than a U.S. House seat because a governor has a statewide rather than a district constituency.) For presidents, most are older than 50 when first inaugurated (see Table 4.2). Almost one-fifth of the nation's vice presidents began one or more terms after reaching age 65.[102]

The age at which one runs for his or her *first* office, often a base office, is much lower. For example, Schlesinger found that half the state and national officeholders he studied had run for their first elective office when they were between 25 and 34 years of age. But these are the politicians whose careers suggest they entered politics with progressive political ambitions. For the many whose first office may be their only office, the age of entry is typically older. For example, most persons are middle-aged (39 to 45) when they first run for and win a seat on a city council.[103] In Florida, with its numerous smaller cities with large concentrations of retirees, many are even choosing to enter politics at the city council level as they reach retirement age.[104]

There is little evidence to suggest that advanced age is a liability once someone decides to run for local office. In fact, it may actually be an advantage as the overall population ages.

At the same time, there is little evidence showing that older persons are more likely to favor older candidates over younger ones. A survey taken by the Times Mirror

Center for The People & The Press in the middle of the 1992 presidential campaign found that those 65 and older were as amenable to the notion of younger candidates as were those 18 to 29; in fact, they were even slightly more amenable to the idea than those in the middle-aged cohorts. But across all age-groups, the youth of the Democratic candidates—Bill Clinton and Al Gore—was *not* seen as a liability.[105]

In summary, age is more likely to affect a person's decision to run than it is to hinder a person's chance of winning once the decision to run is made. Age may also affect a person's decision to leave one office and run for another, but even this may be changing.

Age and Progressive Political Ambitions

Age affects a person's progressive political ambitions. Numerous studies of politicians at all levels have found that the older one grows, the less likely one is to seek a higher office (a maturational effect).[106] Older people are often reluctant to run for higher positions, especially those that require relocation. One study of who runs for Congress found that for many, the personal costs of having to leave home are just too great. Among these costs were "cutting off valued relationships with family and friends, abandoning established careers, and endangering their sense of self as they left behind local roots and familiar habits and entered the new world of politics in Washington."[107]

Many state and local elected officials in their late 40s and early 50s also hesitate to run for Congress because they perceive it will take them a decade or so to gain influence there—that is, to attain seniority-based committee assignments and party leadership positions. They are unwilling to trade the influence they have in their current state and local positions for less influence in Congress. However, the prospect of term limits may prompt more state and local officials to leap into the fray or get out of politics altogether, an option that many find even more distasteful.

The decision to retire from politics looms larger as one grows older. Politicians typically say they are dropping out "to spend more time with the family," which often means with the grandchildren. Upon announcing his decision not to seek another term, Representative Alfred A. McCandless, a Republican from California, pointed to the birth of his first two grandchildren as the major factor: "Parenting, and grandparenting, are life-changing events. They profoundly mark the passage of time. As I looked at these two baby girls, it struck me that at my present pace, I would have little time to see them grow up."[108]

For those who contemplate entering elective politics with a political career in mind, most experts advise starting young. More specifically, one expert has urged city council hopefuls aiming ultimately for the governorship or a position in Congress "to arrive on the (city) council at a young age—before thirty-five—and move on to an intermediate office after one, or at most two four-year terms on the council."[109] Persons most likely to stay on the city council for their entire political careers are those who first get elected when they are between 35 and 50 years of age, followed by those older than 50.

Changing Age Profiles of Officeholders

The aging of the population, in combination with a rising number of elected offi-cials with discrete or static ambitions (which some refer to as the "incumbent lock") suggests that the age profiles of those holding base and higher-level offices are rising. An inspection of city council and school board members confirms that this is true. Turning first to city councils between 1981 and 1991, the proportion of persons 60 or older increased from 19 to 23 percent (see Table 4.3). On school boards, the percentage of members older than 60 rose from 11 to 14 percent in al-most the same period.[110] Moreover, in 1993 alone, more than half of the county supervisors or commissioners in large U.S. counties were 50 or older, and nearly one-fifth were 60 or older.[111]

Similar trends are occurring among Congress members. The percent of House members and senators younger than 40 declined between 1977 and 1991 (down 10 and 6 percent, respectively). Meanwhile, the percentage of House members 60 and older increased from 20 to 25 percent. In the Senate, it actually declined from 33 to 31 percent, reflecting a growing tendency among those at the head of the of-fice pecking order, short of the presidency, to retire earlier.[112]

These age trends alarm many youth advocacy groups and their representatives. They fear that older officeholders will have far different perspectives on the needs and concerns of the young. (However, my study of Florida legislators does not bear out this fear.) At any rate, groups representing the young often push younger persons to seek political office, and in Florida, they seem to be succeeding.

The Career Paths of Florida's Legislators

Twenty-nine percent of Florida's legislators in office in 1994 were younger than 40; 15 percent were 60 or older. For many, their political ambitions began quite early.[113] According to a 1994 survey, more than half (52 percent) of the legislators had been elected to their high school's student council (a third had been presi-dent), and 39 percent had held an elective post in another student organization (most often the presidency) (see Table 4.4). A third had been elected to a student government position in college. Most of these college officeholders had served in the student senate, but some also had held judicial posts or were student body presidents.

In their adult years, three-fourths had held an elective post, generally the pres-idency, in a nonpolitical organization—civic, professional, cultural, church, busi-ness, or service. Ten percent had held elective posts in more than one of these types of organizations, and 38 percent had held some elective post in their politi-cal party. Thus, many of Florida's legislators exhibited high levels of interest in politics, group involvement, and progressive ambition before formally seeking public office.

When these electoral histories are broken down by the age of the legislator, it is clear that higher proportions of the younger legislators (under age 40) have fol-lowed a more politically oriented elective path (high school organization, college student government, political party), as compared to the older legislators, who have followed the community organizational leadership mode.

A major change is the increasing similarity of career paths taken by younger men and women. In the past, women entering state legislatures were older than men, had less previous involvement in political parties or student government, and had worked more in civic and service organizations. Some speculate that this change has occurred because of the efforts to promote gender equity in our schools, universities, and political parties. In addition, with increasing numbers of females in political offices, young women have more role models, a factor that helps to even out the playing field of elective politics.[114]

It is also clear that a higher proportion of the younger Florida legislators started their political careers at the state legislative level rather than in local elective offices. Since these younger legislators' backgrounds suggest they are likely to have progressive ambitions, one can speculate that age profiles of Florida's statewide and congressional delegations may actually decline in future years.

But a considerable number of candidates still delay running for public office, even at the local level, until they reach their 50s or 60s. If this trend continues, given the aging of our population, we may revise the old notion that an older candidate lacks progressive political ambitions. At the same time, we may also revise the notion that an older officeholder's career path is always up or out. The recent chronologies of Florida's governor and U.S. senator suggest that older U.S. Congress members may return home from Washington and seek office at the state or local level rather than retire from politics altogether. For example, Lawton Chiles left the U.S. Senate to run for governor at age 60. Chiles's success has led some political pundits to speculate that U.S. Senator Bob Graham, who left the governor's office at age 50 to run for the Senate, may take the same route as he tires of the arduous trips back and forth to Washington. Both Chiles and Graham started their political careers in the Florida House of Representatives when they were quite young (Chiles at 28; Graham at 30).

But Florida's other U.S. senator, Connie Mack, started his career by successfully running for the U.S. House of Representatives at age 43 and for the U.S. Senate at age 49. I agree with Schlesinger: Ambition will always override conventional notions of the proper age to run for a position. And those who run will always make up a small proportion of the population because seeking office is the most difficult form of political participation.

WHO DOES IT ALL? THE TOTAL ACTIVISTS

If we take into account the multiple forms of individual and group participation outlined in this chapter and the age profiles of those engaged in each type, we can assume that middle-aged persons come the closest to being the total activists. A 1993 Times Mirror Center for The People & The Press survey confirmed this assumption. Persons 30 to 49 years of age were much more likely to have participated in multiple forms of activism than those younger than 30 or those 50 or older. Among the 30- to 49-year-olds, one-fifth engaged in seven or more of the fifteen forms of activism included in the 1993 Times Mirror survey questions.[115] Among those 50 or older, only 14 percent were that active, compared to only 5 percent of those younger than 30.

To test whether the total participation levels of different generations have changed much in recent years, I used the Florida Annual Policy Survey participatory index. This additive index incorporates six types of participatory acts: (1) attending a meeting for a candidate; (2) contributing to a candidate or political party; (3) displaying a sign, wearing a political button, or showing a bumper sticker; (4) working for a political party, candidate, or issue; (5) writing to a public official; and (6) running for office. For the past twelve years, the baby boomer generation (the 35- to 50-year-olds) have been the most active, which complements the Times Mirror data.

The Florida data show slightly greater increases in the number of participatory acts performed by the younger age-groups as compared to the older cohorts. However, the participation rates have changed little for any of the generations over the twelve-year period examined, although these six activities represent a rather short list of the various types of participation now possible. By 1993, the differences between the participation rates of Florida's younger and older generations were insignificant—again, I believe, a harbinger of what will occur at the national level as the country ages.

SUMMARY

People can be active in the political process in many ways beyond voting, belonging to a political party, or following a political campaign. Individuals, either alone or in tandem with others, can express their pleasure or displeasure about an issue by contacting a public official, be it in person or via phone, pen, or fax. Contact can also take place through the press—newspapers, radio, and television—as citizens let their representatives know what they think about various public policies. Participating in these forms of activism is easier than contributing to candidates, groups, or political action committees or litigating, protesting, or running for public office.

A person's age often affects the forms of individual and group activism that he or she chooses. But in general, participation is becoming easier with the emergence of new technologies (e.g., call-in interactive TV and radio shows) and greater sensitivity on the part of government, interest group leaders, and the press to the mobility and resource limitations of various age-groups. Across the generations, there are fewer differences in nonvoting activism than in voter turnout rates today. Still, differences do exist.

Compared to younger Americans, larger proportions of older citizens engage in the more traditional forms of political participation: contacting a public official, attending a public meeting or forum, speaking at a forum, or contributing to a PAC. For many older persons, it is difficult to engage in the more physically demanding and time-consuming forms of activism, such as demonstrating or litigating.

Younger people participate to a greater degree than their older counterparts in more physically demanding and more radical activities, such as circulating petitions, taking part in demonstrations or boycotts, or performing acts of civil disobedience. They are also more likely than older persons to express their opinions indirectly through the press via the new forms of communication: 1-800 or 1-900 numbers soliciting opinions, interest group polls, newspaper polls, and call-in talk shows.

But it is the middle-aged who are the most involved in many of these nonvoting forms of political activism. They, more than the youngest and oldest cohorts, attend public meetings and forums and sign and circulate petitions. They are the most likely to join a group in support of a particular cause, the heaviest financial contributors to PACs (they enjoy the best financial positions), and the most active litigators and boycotters. And they are also the most likely to hold political office. In sum, the middle-aged come the closest to being total activists than do members of any other age-group.

Age makes a difference in whether a person decides to run for political office, in which office will be sought, and in whether he or she will leave that position to run for another post higher up the political career ladder. But at the same time, age is less of a factor in whether the person will win once the decision to run is made. There is little evidence that the old vote against younger candidates because of their age. Moreover, the older one grows, the less likely he or she is to leave one post and run for another, although that is changing somewhat as term limits kick in.

Traditional views of age and office are changing. Florida data show that many younger and older persons are bypassing traditional base positions (usually local-level elective posts) and running for state or congressional positions. But the data also reveal that more older persons are deciding to run for office as they reach retirement age and that as Congress members age, they may increasingly decide to return to state- and local-level politics, which require less travel and permit more time with their families, especially the grandchildren.

A comparison of generational nonvoting activism over the past twelve years in Florida shows a slight increase in activity among the younger cohorts, but there is also a remarkable stability and a fairly narrow gap between old and young. Increasingly, people of all ages get involved via individual and group forms of activism when something arouses their interest. And it is easier to get involved today than it has ever been before.

TABLE 4.1   Participation in Nonvoting Forms of Political Activity by Age-Group
(in percentages)

Political Activity	Age-Group				
	18-34	35-44	45-54	55-64	65+
Direct Contacting					
Written a letter to any elected official	21.1	32.6	41.2	28.3	33.8
Called or sent a letter to your Congress member	23.5	42.9	48.0	50.1	53.9
Called or sent a letter to the White House	6.9	14.4	21.9	22.3	21.3
Indirect Contacting					
Written a letter to the editor of a newspaper	11.0	16.0	16.6	12.9	12.7
Called into a television station or cable company to complain about a program	11.3	9.9	9.5	14.4	7.6
Called in or sent a response to a question or issue put up for discussion by a newspaper or TV station	13.4	17.1	20.3	12.9	7.3
Tried to call into a talk show to discuss views on a public or political issue	7.9	14.7	5.9	7.8	7.6
Dialed an 800 or 900 number to register an opinion on some issue of public concern	14.2	20.6	13.8	15.3	10.1
Participated in a poll sent by a group one belongs to	22.3	33.5	38.9	31.2	19.8
Joining/Attending					
Joined an organization in support of a particular cause	19.9	24.9	27.1	20.1	15.2
Attended a city or town meeting in one's community	21.7	27.5	33.4	39.8	38.6
Attended a public hearing	27.7	34.4	43.9	40.6	35.6
Participated in a "town meeting" or public affairs discussion group	17.7	28.1	30.6	32.8	24.5
Contributing					
Contributed money to a PAC	8.9	17.5	16.3	18.0	17.0
Contributed money to a candidate running for public office	10.7	21.4	26.9	23.1	26.9

Note: Respondents were asked: "People express their opinions about politics and current events in a number of ways besides voting. I'm going to read a list of some of these ways. Please just tell me if you have or have not ever done each. Have you ever [X]?"

Source: The Times Mirror Center for The People & The Press. Telephone survey of a nationally representative sample of 1,507 adults 18 years of age or older, conducted May 18-24, 1993. Reprinted with permission.

TABLE 4.2   Age of Presidents at Inauguration

Age at inauguration	1700–1799		1800–1899		1900–Present	
	N	Percent	N	Percent	N	Percent
35–45	0	0.0	0	0.0	2	6.9
46–55	0	0.0	15	51.7	11	37.9
56–65	3	100.0	12	41.4	13	44.8
Over 65	0	0.0	2	6.9	3	10.3
Total	3	100.0	29	100.0	29	100.0

Note: Data is categorized based on age at beginning of term. For terms that begin in one century and end in another, data are recorded for the century in which the term began.

Source: Calculated from data reported in Harold W. Stanley and Richard G. Niemi, *Vital Statistics on American Politics,* 4th ed., Washington, D.C.: CQ Press, 1994, pp. 257–259.

TABLE 4.3 Changing Age Profiles of Elected Legislative Posts: Local, State, Congress (in percentages)

Age-Group	City Council 1981	1991	Change 81–91
18–22	0.0	0.1	+0.1
22–29	2.6	1.9	-0.7
30–39	20.5	16.7	-3.8
40–49	30.8	32.5	+1.7
50–59	27.2	26.2	-1.0
60 and over	18.9	22.6	+3.7
Total	100.0	100.0	

Age-Group	School Boards 1982	1992	Change 82–92
25 or less	0.6	0.2	-0.4
26–35	9.2	3.8	-5.4
36–40	17.8	14.2	-3.6
41–50	38.7	47.2	+8.5
51–60	23.0	20.9	-2.1
Over 60	10.7	13.7	+3.0
Total	100.0	100.0	

Age-Group	County Commissions/Boards of Supervisors 1982[a]	1993	Change 82–93
18–29	NA	2.0	—
30–39	NA	15.4	—
40–49	NA	31.9	—
50–59	NA	31.8	—
60 and over	NA	18.9	—
Total		100.0	—

(continues)

TABLE 4.3 (cont.)

Age-Group	Florida State Legislature 1982	1994	Change 82–94
House			
18–25	2.6	0	-2.6
26–29	1.7	2.5	+0.8
30–39	41.9	29.2	-12.7
40–49	31.6	39.2	+7.6
50–59	17.1	14.2	-2.9
60 and over	5.1	15.0	+9.9
Senate			
18–25	0	0	—
26–29	0	0	—
30–39	25.0	22.5	-2.5
40–49	35.0	22.5	-12.5
50–59	27.5	40.0	+12.5
60 and over	12.5	15.0	+2.5

Age-Group	U.S. Congress 1977	1987	1991	Change 77–91
House of Representatives				
Under 40	18.6	14.5	9.0	-9.6
40–49	27.8	35.2	34.9	+7.1
50–59	33.8	31.5	30.8	-3.0
60–69	16.3	12.9	19.8	+3.5
70–79	3.5	5.5	4.6	+1.1
80 and over	0.0	0.4	0.9	+0.9
Senate				
Under 40	6.0	5.0	0.0	-6.0
40–49	26.0	30.0	23.0	-3.0
50–59	35.0	36.0	46.0	+11.0
60–69	21.0	22.0	24.0	+3.0
70–79	10.0	5.0	5.0	-5.0
80 and over	2.0	2.0	2.0	—

Note: [a]Data not available for 1982.

Sources: Council member data from International City/County Management Association, Washington, D.C. School board data from National School Boards Association, Alexandria, VA, 1993. County data from mail survey of county governing board clerks in 93 large U.S. counties (over 423,380 population), conducted December, 1992-January, 1993 by Susan A. MacManus. Florida State Legislature data calculated from *Clerk's Manual 1982-1984,* Tallahassee, FL: House of Representatives, 1983 (3 legislators missing—did not report date of birth); and John D. McKinnon, *Guidebook to Florida Legislators 1993-1994,* Baltimore, MD: Legislative Guidebooks, Inc, 1993. U.S. Congress data from Bureau of the Census, *Statistical Abstract of the United States 1992,* Washington, DC: U.S. Government Printing Office, 1992, calculated from Table 426, p. 264.

TABLE 4.4 Electoral Chronologies: Florida Legislators (in percentages)

Electoral Chronology	Entire Legislature	Senate	House	Current Age 18–39	40–49	50 & over
Number of cases						
(respondents)	(n=82)	(n=19)	(n=63)	(n=28)	(n=22)	(n=32)
PRE-PUBLIC OFFICE						
High School						
Student council	53.2	50.0	54.1	57.7	59.1	45.2
President[a]	30.6	16.7	33.3	46.2	25.0	18.2
Other student organization	37.8	46.7	35.6	39.1	50.0	29.0
College						
Student Government	32.9	31.3	33.3	46.2	38.1	17.2
Senate[b]	50.0	100.0	41.2	60.0	50.0	0.0
Student body president[b]	15.0	0.0	17.6	20.0	12.5	0.0
Judiciary[b]	30.0	0.0	35.3	30.0	37.5	0.0
Other	6.1	2.5	6.3	2.1	1.8	5.4
Adulthood						
Nonpolitical organization	72.5	66.7	74.2	52.0	90.9	75.8
Political party organization	38.3	36.8	38.7	44.0	27.3	41.2
PUBLIC OFFICE						
First Public Office Sought						
City council	16.5	17.6	17.7	7.1	27.3	19.4
Mayor	2.5	0.0	3.2	3.6	0.0	3.2
County commission	10.1	17.6	3.3	3.6	9.1	12.9
School board	3.8	5.9	3.2	3.6	0.0	6.5
Fla. House of Reps.	60.8	29.4	69.4	71.4	50.0	54.8
Fla. Senate	3.8	17.6	0.0	3.6	4.5	3.2
Other	2.5	11.8	0.0	0.0	9.1	0.0
Age at time						
18–24	6.3	16.7	3.2	15.4	4.5	3.1
26–29	13.7	11.1	14.5	26.9	13.7	0.0
30–39	42.5	44.4	42.0	57.7	54.5	21.9
40–49	27.5	22.2	29.0	—	27.3	50.0
50–59	5.0	5.6	4.8	—	—	12.5
60 or older	5.0	0.0	6.5	—	—	12.5
First Public Office Won						
City council	18.5	11.1	22.2	3.8	36.4	21.2
Mayor	2.5	0.0	3.2	3.8	0.0	3.0
County commission	6.2	11.1	3.2	3.8	4.5	6.1
School board	3.7	11.1	1.6	0.0	0.0	9.1
Fla. House of Reps.	61.7	33.3	69.8	80.8	45.5	57.6
Fla. Senate	7.4	33.3	0.0	4.3	13.6	3.0

(continues)

TABLE 4.4 (cont.)

Electoral Chronology	Entire Legislature	Senate	House	Current Age 18–39	40–49	50 & over
Age at time						
18–24	2.5	5.3	1.6	2.1	4.5	0.0
25–29	13.5	15.8	12.9	30.8	9.1	3.0
30–39	38.3	36.8	38.7	65.4	31.9	21.2
40–49	33.4	31.6	33.9	—	54.5	45.5
50–59	7.4	10.5	6.4	—	—	18.2
60 or older	4.9	0.0	6.5	—	—	12.1
Age first elected to current position						
18–24	1.2	0.0	1.6	3.8	0.0	0.0
25–29	6.2	0.0	8.1	19.3	0.0	0.0
30–39	35.8	42.1	33.8	76.9	27.3	9.1
40–49	37.0	31.6	38.8	—	72.7	42.4
50–59	13.6	21.1	11.2	—	—	33.3
60 or older	6.2	5.3	6.5	—	—	15.2
No. of terms in position						
1	50.0	63.2	46.0	61.5	50.0	41.2
2–3	25.6	31.6	23.8	27.0	36.4	17.6
4–5	12.2	0.0	15.9	7.7	9.1	17.7
6–7	7.3	5.3	8.0	0.0	4.5	14.7
8–9	3.7	0.0	4.7	0.0	0.0	8.8
10+	1.2	0.0	1.6	3.8	0.0	0.0
No. of times run before winning current position						
won first time	82.9	94.7	79.4	96.2	77.3	76.5
2 times	14.6	5.3	17.5	3.8	18.2	20.6
3 times	2.4	0.0	3.2	0.0	1.8	2.9

Notes:
[a] Percent of those elected to student council.
[b] Percent of those elected to student government.
NS-not significant at the .05 level.

Sources: Current profile information was abstracted from John D. McKinnon, *Guidebook to Florida Legislators 1993-94,* Baltimore, MD: Legislative Guidebooks, Inc., 1993 and from Tom Fiedler and Margaret Kempf, *Almanac of Florida Politics 1994,* Miami, FL: *The Miami Herald,* A Division of Knight-Ridder, 1993. Data on electoral histories are from a survey of Florida legislators conducted January-February, 1994, by Susan A. MacManus.

PART III

Differences in Public Policy Preferences and Priorities

5

Taxing and Spending Preferences: Different Generational Priorities?

The biggest fights in households across the United States take place over money: how to raise, spend, and save it. These skirmishes sometimes are filled with such rancor that they lead to divorce or estrangement of the parties involved. More often, they lead to bruised feelings that are slow to heal.

In government, too, some of the biggest battles are waged over money. Combatants often cast government taxing and spending policies as zero-sum situations—us-against-them scenarios in which someone wins and, at the same time, someone else loses. Debates involving money often become explosive, and the protagonists naturally assume a protectionist stance, whether the topic is cigarette taxes, student loans, or Social Security. When people perceive a threat to their livelihood, current or future, they tend to become entrenched in their opinions and intensify their political activism.

As the U.S. population ages, tensions will probably escalate over the proper allocation of public funds and the tax policies designed to generate the dollars to cover expenditure demands. Fears of the future abound among all generations. Older persons fear impoverishment in old age. "Increasing life expectancy, the fact that few private or public pension and retirement programs are adjusted for inflation, and the incidence of reductions and bankruptcy among pension and retiree health-care plans, further the concern among many individuals that they could become destitute," concluded Fernando M. Torres-Gil in *The New Aging*.[1] The young face rather grim statistics predicting they will experience downward mobility, be unable to afford a home, confront stiff competition in the workforce for high-paying jobs, witness reductions in their health and pension plans, and find it difficult to save.[2]

SELF-CENTERED OR ALTRUISTIC?

The media has often painted a picture of both age-extreme groups, the youngest and the oldest, as self-centered, with labels such as the "spoiled, selfish Generation X" and the "greedy geezers." However, many politicos and groups representing these generations disagree with these labels and are somewhat more optimistic that generational warfare can be avoided. They believe a bridge between the age-extreme groups can be built by successfully appealing to the older generation's concern for the fiscal future of their children and grandchildren and the younger generation's feelings of indebtedness to their parents and grandparents for support during their childhood and young adult years. These optimists also point to research showing that many Americans are more "public-regarding" and less "private-regarding" than normally assumed when it comes to spending public funds.[3]

Of course, much of one's generosity depends upon one's economic condition at the time. Both the young and the old, compared to their middle-aged counterparts, are perceived to be more economically vulnerable, which explains why the two age-extreme groups are often portrayed as self-centered. However, in recent years, the elderly "appear to have improved their position considerably relative to the rest of society, so that old persons today face a smaller probability of being poor than at any time in our nation's history."[4] Meanwhile, the youngest generation is projected to "become the only generation born this century to suffer a one-generation backstep in living standards."[5] Many already believe their prospects for achievement are worse than their parents'. This pessimistic outlook is certainly evident in Florida, where 44 percent of the two youngest generations (Reagan and Civil Rights) see their lives as harder than their parents', compared to just 19 percent of the oldest generation (World War I).

Major changes in government taxing and spending policies frequently mobilize the young and old alike. But do they always pit one age-group against the other? If so, are some of the schisms driven by age-group differences in ideology (liberal versus conservative) and perspectives on governmental efficiency? I look first at the issue of taxes.

GENERATIONAL DIFFERENCES: TAXES

In 1789, Benjamin Franklin wrote, "In this world nothing can be said to be certain, except death and taxes."[6] (Today, some of us are not sure which is the worst of the two!) But as the sage U.S. Supreme Court Justice Oliver Wendell Holmes, Jr., penned nearly a century ago, "Taxes are what we pay for civilized society."[7]

Purposes of Taxes

In *Federal Tax Policy*, an excellent historical overview of taxation in the United States, Joseph Pechman spelled out the three major goals of taxation. The first is to "transfer resources from the private to the public sector" to pay for governmental services and activities. The second is to "distribute the cost of government fairly by income classes and among people in the same economic circumstances"—to raise money in an equitable fashion. The third is to "promote economic growth, stability, and efficiency."[8] Sometimes, taxation also serves as a regulatory instrument—to deter businesses or individuals from undesirable behavior (e.g., pollution taxes). In other instances, taxes are used as incentives to encourage businesses or individuals to engage in certain types of activity. For example, governments sometimes give tax breaks for agricultural property or to businesses relocating in inner-city neighborhoods. One thing is sure, taxation as a major instrument of social and economic policy is not value-free.

Tax Definition and Types

Webster's dictionary defines a tax as "a charge usually of money imposed by authority on persons or property for public purposes."[9] Taxes are levied on three broad bases—income, consumption, and property—on either individuals or corporations. Since the early 1930s, the income tax has been the primary tax of the federal government; the consumption (sales) tax, that of state governments; and the property tax, that of local governments. These patterns still prevail to a certain degree. However, as resource pressures have mounted over the years, the proprietary nature of each of these taxes has eroded so that today all but seven states tax personal income,[10] and in some states, even local governments can levy their own income and sales taxes on top of those imposed by the federal and state governments. Nonetheless, local governments remain the most restricted in the types of taxes they are legally permitted to collect; indeed, they are often limited to collecting the property tax.[11]

Other Sources of Revenue: User Taxes, Borrowing, and Grants-in-Aid

Governments raise revenue from a variety of other nontax sources:[12] lotteries,[13] user charges, impact fees (e.g., requiring a real estate developer to create a public park in exchange for a construction permit),[14] fines and forfeitures, interest earned from the investment of idle revenues, money raised from the sale or lease of government property (land, buildings, used equipment, or unclaimed stolen property), and borrowing funds (bond sales or short-term loans from banks).[15]

In some places, property tax revolts have led to restrictions on raising such taxes at rates faster than the rate of growth in the consumer price index or inflation. When that has happened, state and local governments have had few options other than to assess fees and charges to meet rising expenditure demands. Although fees and charges are technically not taxes, Americans are increasingly viewing them as such; in fact, a number of taxpayer groups have started referring to them as "user taxes" or "fee taxes." Still, these fees, along with sales taxes of all types, are less despised as revenue-raising alternatives than the traditional income and property taxes.

State and local governments often receive grants-in-aid from other levels of government or payments from other governments for services rendered or commodities sold (e.g., a large city may provide police and fire services or sell water to a smaller one). These moneys are known as intergovernmental revenues. In many instances, the grants-in-aid are pass-through tax revenues rather than nontax revenues. (For example, federal grants-in-aid to state and local governments come from monies collected via the federal income tax.) The amount and timing of these revenues are often quite uncertain, creating pressures on recipient governments to find other, more stable sources of funds.

Declining Federal Aid, Fiscal Stress, Public Cynicism, and Tax Revolts

Federal aid, especially to localities, has been more unpredictable in recent years—declining in the late 1970s and 1980s and rising slightly in the early 1990s—as the federal budget deficit has swelled.[16] Because of the unpredictability of federal aid, a recession, Americans' growing skepticism about the ability of public officials and governments to spend money wisely, fairly, or efficiently, and the perception that the tax system is either unfair (with too many loopholes and exemptions) or overly burdensome—or some combination thereof—it has become necessary for states and localities to search for other ways to raise revenue or reduce spending—or both.[17]

In some places, tax hikes have sparked revolts. These tax revolts are more successful at the state and local levels because of citizen initiative or referendum laws permitting taxpayers to put such issues directly on the ballot for a vote (see Chapter 4). To impose a comparable measure, like a balanced-budget amendment, on the federal government requires a two-thirds vote in both houses of Congress and the ratification by three-fourths of the state legislatures—a much more difficult task.[18] Naturally, the heavy media exposure after California's Proposition 13 tax revolt in 1978 gave credence to taxpayer-initiated revolts and prompted citizens in other states and localities to launch similar protests.

Governments that have been successful at fending off such efforts have often done so by threatening to cut popular services or by earmarking any proposed tax increase to a popular functional area, often related to public safety (e.g., police). They base such a strategy on public opinion surveys showing that when respondents are confronted "with a *direct trade-off* between reducing taxes or cutting public services, pluralities favor keeping taxes 'about the same,' rather than 'increasing' or 'reducing' them."[19] But there's evidence the public is wising up about this strategy and coming to see it as a shell game.[20] Others have expressed concern that certain age-groups, most notably the elderly, are playing their own shell game—pushing governments for lower taxes while pressing for higher spending on services of which they are the primary beneficiaries.[21] But past research has often found that older persons are no more likely than the young to favor higher spending on elderly oriented programs like Social Security or Medicare.[22]

The Link Between Age and Tax Preferences

Extensive longitudinal reviews of public attitudes toward taxes all come to the same conclusion: Most Americans abhor paying taxes and think the taxes they personally pay are too high.[23] When Gallup and the National Opinion Research Center asked respondents whether the federal income taxes that they themselves pay were "too high," "too low," or "about right," a majority said "too high." Only 2 percent said they were "too low."

That's not to say, however, that most Americans necessarily believe the taxes *others* pay are too high! Questions about tax fairness often reveal that many see certain taxes as unfair and propose closing tax loopholes as a way to make others pay their fair share—in other words, more.[24] With few exceptions, the middle-aged see taxes as less fair than either the young or old, primarily because they bear the heaviest burdens.

Tax Burdens: Who Sees Theirs as Heaviest? In *The Changing American Mind*, William G. Mayer concluded that age-groups differ in their perspectives of whether taxes are too high for them personally primarily because of a life-cycle effect. It is the middle-aged who see their taxes as too high, not the young or the old. Mayer contended that employment status, related to the life cycle, offers the best explanation:

> When a cohort first enters the adult population, it contains a sizable number of students and part-time workers, who pay little or no federal income tax and hence complain about it somewhat less. However, once the average age of a cohort reaches about twenty-eight and its members have largely entered the workforce, the difference vanishes. At the other end of the age distribution, after a cohort reaches the age of sixty-five, its members begin to retire, social security payments are nontaxable [up to a point], and, hence, its tax worries are reduced.[25]

Tax Fairness. Fairness often means something different to the individual taxpayer than it does to a public finance expert. To the expert, fairness, or equity, means a tax is progressive in nature—that is, that it takes a proportionately heavier chunk from those who are more affluent. The progressive nature of a tax reflects the principle that one's taxes should rise based on one's ability to pay. To the average taxpayer, who has a limited understanding of economic theory, fairness often means that everybody should pay the same percentage. This perspective helps explain why taxpayers are less upset about (and actually prefer) regressive but flat-rate sales taxes to the more progressive federal income or property taxes.[26]

Studies of Americans' opinions of tax fairness have been commissioned by the U.S. Advisory Commission on Intergovernmental Relations (ACIR) annually since 1972. The question posed to respondents is, "Which do you think is the worst tax—that is, the least fair? the federal income tax? state income tax? state sales tax? or local property tax?" Consistently, the federal income tax and local property tax have been ranked as the least fair, followed by the state sales tax, then the state income taxes. Although state income tax brackets are narrower and the gradation is steeper than in the federal income tax, they also terminate at a much lower income level. Thus, they are far less progressive than the federal income tax and more like flat-rate taxes. They can also be deducted from an individual's federal income tax, thereby making them more attractive because they keep tax money at home rather than sending it to Washington.[27]

When attitudes toward tax fairness are broken out by age, several clear patterns emerge. First, over the years, older persons have generally rated the property tax as the least fair; younger persons, by contrast, have named the federal income tax. Second, older persons are more consistent in their rankings. Between 1982 and 1993,[28] a plurality of those older than 65 rated the property tax as the worst, or least fair, tax nearly every year. In contrast, during this same period, a plurality of persons 18 to 24 rated the federal income tax as the worst half of the time and the property tax as the worst the other half of the time. Moreover, in two of those years, the younger group rated the federal income tax and another tax (the property tax once and the state sales tax once) as equally bad. Third, with regard to state taxes, the gap between the two age-extreme groups is quite narrow. The percent differences were 5 percent or less for the state sales tax nearly every year, as were the percentages for the state income tax about half of the time. Fourth, since 1982, the young have become more antagonistic toward the federal income tax; while the old have become more positive. However, the middle-aged are the most antagonistic toward the federal income tax and consistently rate it as the least fair tax, a predictable response in light of the fact that they bear the heaviest tax burden.

The Social Security Tax. Since 1988, the ACIR survey has occasionally included the Social Security tax in the "least fair" tax inquiry. Respondents are asked, "Which do you think is the worst tax—that is, the least fair—including Social Security?" The results, shown in Table 5.1, are quite surprising in light of the forecasts predicting deep schisms on this issue in the coming decades. None of the age-groups have rated Social Security as the worst tax and, in fact, the gap between the youngest and oldest cohorts in terms of the fairness of this tax closed between 1988 and 1992. This outcome was no doubt affected to some extent by the heavily publicized proposals to impose steeper income taxes on the affluent elderly, which did come to pass in 1993 and made the tax seem fairer.[29] The ACIR survey results also support what public opinion surveys from earlier decades have shown—namely, a feeling that Social Security taxes are "about right."[30]

Age-group differences with regard to the Social Security tax reappear when it is compared to the federal income tax. Data from the 1993 Florida Annual Policy Survey showed that almost half the young saw the Social Security tax as more unfair than the federal income tax, compared to only a third of those from the Cold War and Depression generations. A major explanation for these differences lies in the responses to another question, one asking Floridians whether they believed they would receive more in Social Security benefits than they paid in. Only 17 percent of the youngest generation believed they would, compared to more than half of the Depression generation. This is hardly surprising in light of the fact that the Social Security Administration is constantly changing its forecast of when the system will go bankrupt. A report released in 1994 predicted 2029 as the bankruptcy date—not that far off.

These grim forecasts have shaken the young's faith in government-based retirement systems. A December 1993 survey by the Gallup Organization for the Employee Benefit Research Institute asked its respondents: "When thinking about

FIGURE 5.1 Tax Social Security at Same Rate as Other Income

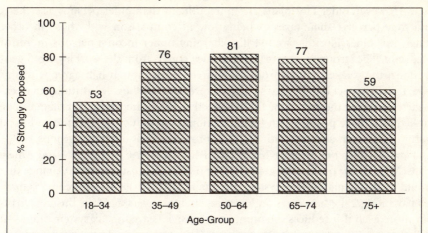

Note: Respondents were asked: "Do you favor or oppose taxing Social Security payments to the elderly just like any other source of income?" [Some respondents volunteered "neither" as an answer.] "Do you strongly or not so strongly favor (oppose) taxing Social Security payments?"

Source: Warren E. Miller, Donald R. Kinder, Steven J. Rosenstone and the National Election Studies, American National Election Study: 1990-1991. *Panel Study of the Political Consequences of War/1991 Pilot Study,* Ann Arbor, MI: University of Michigan Center for Political Studies, 1991. As reported in Christine L. Day, "Public Opinion Toward Costs and Benefits of Social Security and Medicare," paper presented at the Annual Meeting of the American Political Science Association, Chicago, IL, September 3–6, 1992. Reprinted by permission of the American Political Science Association and Christine L. Day.

health and retirement, do you have more confidence in an employer or the government when it comes to paying the employee pension or government Social Security benefits that have been promised?" Among those 18 to 34 years of age, 61 percent expressed more confidence in their employer, compared to only 37 percent of those 55 and older. When asked whether "you would like to contribute half of your Social Security taxes to an IRA (Individual Retirement Account) now and take a smaller Social Security benefit when you retire," 54 percent of the 18 to 34 year olds said yes, compared to just 37 percent of those 55 and older, reflecting the young's concern about government-provided retirement income. [31]

Age-groups also differ when asked whether Social Security income should be taxed (see Figure 5.1). A survey taken in 1991 found those older than 35 were considerably more opposed to "taxing Social Security payments to the elderly just like any other source of income" than were the young or the very old.[32] The greatest opposition came from those closest to becoming recipients (50- to 64-year-olds), 81 percent of whom strongly opposed such a tax, compared to 53 percent of the 18- to 35-year-olds. Fissures in intergenerational harmony showed up again when questions were asked about which programs should be sustained and which should be cut in the face of a budget deficit reduction.

Floridians' attitudes toward taxing Social Security income seem counter to this view. However, older Floridians are more affluent than older persons elsewhere, and they perceive their taxes as being low in comparison with those in other states. But older Floridians don't like charging upper-income persons more for Medicare. The strongest support for this idea comes from the working-aged generations; the weakest comes from the retirees, even though half agree with this idea, too. (The fact that Florida's elderly expressed "less hostile" attitudes than expected regarding means testing for benefits that most directly impact them can be viewed as a more positive sign for the nation, especially if the income and fiscal status of older Americans continues to improve vis-à-vis other age-groups.)

Ways to Make the Nation's Tax System Fairer. One ACIR survey asked Americans, "Which *one* of the changes would be the single most important change that would make the nation's tax system more fair? 1. Make the upper income taxpayers pay more; 2. Reduce taxes on lower income taxpayers; 3. Make business firms pay more even if it reduces the number of jobs; 4. Leave the tax system alone—it is about as fair as you are ever going to get?"[33] Not surprisingly, the most common response across all age-groups was to "make the upper income taxpayers pay more" (see Table 5.2). Nearly half (49 percent) of the population chose that response, followed by 16 percent who favored leaving the tax system alone and 13 percent who thought businesses should pay more. It is the middle-aged who favored more progressive solutions, preferring that the rich pay more. (One never thinks of oneself as rich!)

How to Improve Federal Income Tax Collections. According to the ACIR survey, of all the ways to increase federal income tax collections, the most popular solution (39 percent) was to cut back on all itemized deductions, such as those for state and local taxes, interest paid on mortgages and consumer loans, and charitable contributions. The next most popular solution (21 percent) was to raise individual income taxes, followed by cutting back on current tax exemptions, such as Social Security, pensions, and interest on municipal bonds (14 percent).[34] But, according to this survey, more than one-fourth of Americans did not know *how* to improve collections.

When the responses were broken down by age-group, it was clear that a higher proportion of the elderly than the young said they didn't know of any solutions. (Other studies have found that "don't know" responses are somewhat more common among the elderly, regardless of the topic.[35]) Among each of the other age-groups, the strongest support went to cutting back on itemized deductions. This solution enjoyed the highest favor among the youngest cohort—no wonder, since they are the least likely to itemize! The strongest support for raising individual income taxes came from the middle-aged—the group most likely to itemize.

How Best to Raise Federal Taxes When Things Get Tight. Occasionally (usually when the economy slips into a recession), pollsters ask Americans how they think taxes could best be raised. One ACIR survey asked, "Suppose the Federal government must raise taxes substantially, which of these do you think would be the best way to do it: 1. Have a form of national sales tax on things other than food and similar necessities; 2. Raise individual income tax rates; or 3. Raise money by reducing special tax treatment for capital gains and cutting tax deduction allowances for charitable contributions, state and local taxes, medical expenses, etc.?"[36]

Again, across all age-groups, a plurality favored closing loopholes rather than creating new taxes or raising individual income tax rates. The elderly were the most evenly split in their opinions, divided between closing loopholes and imposing a national sales tax. But among all age-groups, imposing a national sales tax was far preferable to raising individual income tax rates, which most respondents interpreted to mean as their own rates. This finding affirms a point I made earlier, namely, that sales taxes are more popular as budget-balancing approaches, even if they are new taxes, than raising the federal income tax. The term *federal income tax* itself has come to have a pejorative meaning.

Reducing the Federal Budget Deficit: Revenue Alternatives. In one survey, ACIR pointedly asked its respondents which revenue-raising approach they would favor to reduce the federal deficit. Among the choices presented were: (1) an increase in gasoline and diesel fuel taxes (sales or excise taxes); (2) an increase in individual income tax rates; (3) a national lottery; (4) a national sales tax on all purchases other than food; and (5) an increase in user fees or charges for things such as use of national parks and forests, passports, customs inspections, and Coast Guard services for boaters.[37]

Reflecting the rapid spread of state lotteries, nearly half (47 percent) of all Americans expressed a preference for a national lottery. The next most common preference was for increases in federal user fees (15 percent). However, there were some clear age-group differences in this regard (see Table 5.3).

Older persons were less enthusiastic about a lottery than the youngest cohorts, an attitude related to their greater conservatism on moral issues, a point I will return to in Chapter 6. Older persons were also more likely to volunteer that they favored *no* new or increased taxes. (I will address this point shortly when I look at opinions about policy choices offered in a trade-off context.)

Raising State Revenues in Tough Times. Recognizing that state governments are also facing fiscal stress, ACIR asked which revenue alternatives taxpayers preferred at the state level, with the focus on sales and income taxes and on user fees and charges: "If your state government decided to raise a small amount of additional revenue to help meet costs and improve services, which one of these would you prefer: 1. An increase in cigarette and liquor taxes ['sin' taxes]; 2. An increase in the general state sales tax; 3. An increase in gasoline and diesel fuel taxes; 4. An increase in state income tax rates, or an income tax if your state does not now have one; or 5. An increase in user fees or charges for things like the use of state parks, automobile registration, boating licenses, or toll roads?"[38]

There were few age-group differences about the best ways to raise money for states in need (which is different from responses regarding federal and local taxes); the differences between age-groups on various approaches to generating funds for state coffers were in the range of 3 to 5 percent. By far the most popular choice (54 percent) across all age-groups was to raise cigarette and liquor taxes; respondents seemed to say, "Let the sinners pay!" This choice was followed by increasing user fees or charges (13 percent). The popularity of user fees and charges stems from the existence of a direct, discernible link between the money paid and the benefit received. With user fees and charges, taxpayers see what they are getting for their money. However, the biggest age-group difference, although still narrow, occurred with regard to increasing user fees or charges for the use of state parks, for automobile registration, for boating licenses, or for toll roads. Only 10 percent of those 65 and over favored this approach, compared to around 15 percent of the other age-groups. I suspect these fees were more strongly opposed by the elderly because they tend to see such fees as "required spending" (especially fees for automobile registration), the effect of which is to take a bigger bite out of their fixed incomes. Similar fears were observable when local property tax was involved.

Raising Local Revenue in Tough Times. The public seems to be fairly evenly split over which revenue enhancement strategies their local governments should use during economic downturns. ACIR posed this question in a 1987 survey: "If your local government decided to raise a small amount of additional revenue to help meet costs and improve services, which one of these would you prefer: 1. A local income or wage tax, or an increase in existing local income or wage tax rates; 2. A local sales tax, or an increase in the existing local sales tax; 3. An increase in property tax rates; or 4. An increase in user fees or charges for things like the use of local parks and swimming pools, parking, library use, garbage pick-up, or ambulance service?"[39]

There was a clear preference across all age-groups for either increases in user fees or local sales taxes, and the most opposition was expressed toward local income or property tax increases, although far less than a majority favored any single revenue source. Overall, the youngest cohort was the most supportive of each alternative.[40] The greatest age-group differential appeared in regard to the property tax. Older citizens were far less enthusiastic about this approach.[41]

What's Unpopular About the Property Tax? ACIR has surveyed taxpayers on several occasions—both before and after California's famous Proposition 13 tax revolt in 1978—asking them what they found most offensive about the property tax.[42] Respondents were asked to choose from a list of property tax "negatives": "1. It is hardest on low-income families [regressivity]; 2. It is based on estimates of home value that are not always fair; 3. Reassessments may sometimes result in a shocking tax bill increase; 4. It discourages homeowning; 5. It taxes any increase in the value of a home over the original purchase price, even though that increase is only on paper and not in the homeowner's hands unless he or she sells the house; or 6. Property taxes have been going up faster than other taxes." The responses were remarkably similar year to year, demonstrating that the public's opinions about the tax are fairly consistent.

Responses were quite mixed across age-groups, although the tax's regressivity was most often-cited "negative" (27 percent). Those 60 years and older were more prone to cite regressivity and the relative rate of increase in the property tax than those 18 to 29 years of age.[43] The youngest were slightly more likely to mention the tax's deterrent effect on home ownership.[44] Each of these responses reflected the individual's place in the life cycle: The young were concerned about owning a home and its appreciation in value; the old were more concerned about any revenue source that appeared to take a consistently bigger chunk out of their relatively fixed incomes.

Property Taxes, Schools, and Age

School districts across the United States are primarily funded by property taxes. In recent years, the fairness of this method of paying for schools has become a hot issue. Poorer school districts have successfully filed lawsuits calling for states to equalize per-student spending across school districts either through state aid to the districts or revised property tax laws.[45] It is often thought that support for equalization comes both from poorer school districts *and* from districts with heavy concentrations of older persons, who are presumed to oppose raising local property taxes to pay for schools. But is this latter assumption true?

In 1993, ACIR posed this question to its respondents: "Some states are thinking about taking some property tax money from upper income school districts and giving it to lower income school districts in order to ensure equal, or nearly equal, spending on education for each public school student in the state. If this were proposed in your state, would you strongly favor, somewhat favor, somewhat oppose, or strongly oppose the idea?"[46] A majority of all age-groups favored such a proposal. Predictably, the strongest support came from the 18- to 24-year-olds, 62 percent of whom favored it, compared to just 52 percent of those older than 65 (although this still represented a majority). The relatively strong support from those 65 and over no doubt tracked with that group's anticipated property tax relief following the adoption of new equalization-driven financing schemes.

The property tax has been criticized in a number of states for promoting inequalities across school districts, which has sent state and local lawmakers in search of funding alternatives. The most interesting and most closely watched case occurred in Michigan. There, voters were recently presented with an either-or choice on how to pay for schools, and raising the local property tax was not one of the choices. Intense controversies in the state legislature over school finance inequities, which rekindled contempt for the property tax, led to the passage of a bill eliminating property taxes as a primary source of school funding. Voters had to choose between increasing either the state sales or income tax. Predictably, an overwhelming majority of all age-groups chose the sales tax.[47] Older voters, although not necessarily thrilled about higher taxes, were often quoted as saying that anything was better than raising the local property tax. "Supporting it [education] with the sales tax is about the fairest way. Property owners have been bearing the load for too long," said one Michigan retiree. "I haven't had kids in school for 30 years. I think my dues are paid by now. And now they raised my evaluation another $700."[48]

Overall, there were no marked generational differences regarding the equalization of school district financing, although there was some variation with regard to what tax should be used (or not used) to accomplish the goal. The older generation's stronger opposition to the property tax is attributable to its fixed-income status. Might we expect similar life-cycle explanations on the spending side of the budgetary ledger?

GENERATIONAL DIFFERENCES: GOVERNMENT SPENDING

Generational differences on government spending preferences vary according to the manner in which opinions are tapped. Some surveys present respondents with a list of items or programs on which government regularly spends money and ask whether it should be spending more, less, or about the same amount. In others, respondents are offered a slightly different scenario. They are given a list of current problems and asked whether the government is spending too much, too little, or about the right amount in addressing each.[49] The problem list constantly changes in response to new circumstances and the mass media's coverage of them, often limiting the availability of longitudinal data on specific spending priorities (and making it extremely difficult to sort out generational, period, and cohort effects). The latest trend is to ask respondents trade-off questions linking taxing and spending or questions regarding spending cuts they personally find most unacceptable. As I will show, it is the latter type of question that often reveals the most distinct intergenerational differences. But all these approaches yield important insights into the U.S. public's spending preferences.

The National Opinion Research Center and the Roper Organization have been asking the traditionally worded spending priority questions for the longest period, since 1973. Responses show that the most consistent support has been for increased spending for education and for programs aimed at controlling crime, improving health, combating drug addiction, and protecting the environment.[50] Increased spending for public welfare and transportation has been less popular. Growing numbers of Americans believe public welfare is already funded at too high a level, and most feel transportation is funded at about the right level.

Experts in examining long-term trends in U.S. public opinion see a great deal of order in these opinions. For example, Benjamin I. Page and Robert Y. Shapiro, in *The Rational Public,* concluded:

> This configuration of preferences reflects a fundamental individualism that esteems individual responsibility and individual initiative, and relies primarily upon free enterprise capitalism for economic production and distribution. Yet it also reflects a sense of societal obligation, a strong commitment to government action in order to smooth capitalism's rough edges, to regulate its excesses, to protect the helpless, and to provide a substantial degree of equal opportunity for all.[51]

Spending Preferences and Age: Rational Self-Interest?

At the center of the long-running and intense debate about the relationship between age and spending preferences is the thesis that people's preferences in this area reflect their own needs—this is the rational self-interest, or a "private-regarding," view. Underlying this debate are several other premises. The first is that the needs of the young and the old differ sharply. The second is that there is a fairly high level of consensus within each age-group about spending priorities. Third and most disturbing to advocates for the elderly is the "gray peril" hypothesis: "It expresses a fear that increasing numbers combined with widespread political activism among older persons will result in resistance to . . . government taxing and spending for programs lacking immediate benefits for aging people and increasing demands for services benefiting principally the elderly population at the expense of younger persons."[52]

To test these theories, some researchers have compared age-groups' preferred spending levels for programs that benefit people markedly different in age—for example, education and public assistance (welfare) for the young and Social Security and Medicare for the old. Others have focused on a wider array of programs with less clear-cut age-based backing, such as crime, the environment, transportation, parks and recreation, libraries, and economic development.[53]

Most of these studies have come to the same conclusion. They have found that the young more often support higher federal spending for elderly programs (Social Security and health programs) than the old themselves, although the differences are not great.[54] At first glance, this pattern appears to refute the gray peril hypothesis. However, these studies have also found that older persons do not support increasing educational spending as much as the young do,[55] although findings are more mixed with regard to the elderly's support for school bonds (borrowing).[56]

On other issues, National Opinion Research Center surveys have shown that the young prefer higher spending levels than the old do for the environment. Older people tend to be less supportive of federal spending on space exploration, cities, minority programs, and parks.[57] In the past, the elderly were considerably more supportive of higher spending for national defense, but by the mid-1980s, a majority of both the young and the old favored spending less on defense. On welfare spending, it's the middle-aged who are the most opposed; they bear the major portion of the costs of welfare programs. The young and the old differ on welfare spending, although the young lean more toward increased spending levels, as they do for most social programs.[58]

The bottom line is that when survey respondents are questioned about their preferences on federal spending levels for various policy and program areas, different age-groups generally give responses closely resembling the priorities that would be expected of persons at their point in the life cycle. The same pattern prevails in terms of preferences on state and local government spending levels.

State Spending Priorities in Florida. Few studies have looked at spending priorities below the federal level. But since 1981, the Florida Annual Policy Survey has asked whether "the amount now being spent [in the state of Florida] on [a given program area] should be increased, kept at the present level, or decreased." The programs cluster into four broad policy areas: (1) social services, which include programs for the elderly, assistance for low-income families with children, and health care; (2) education, typically public schools (kindergarten through twelfth grade) and colleges and universities; (3) law enforcement, including prisons and programs for combating crime; and (4) economic development, which consists of programs for developing industry, promoting tourism, and building roads and highways.[59] (The survey also has inquired about environmental protection, an area that does not fall neatly into any of these four categories.) An analysis of Floridians' support for increased state spending levels in each of these four broad areas confirms some bits of conventional wisdom and rejects others (see Figure 5.2).[60]

For example, conventional wisdom would suggest that the youngest cohorts would favor higher spending for education. However, the oldest generation (World War I) is considerably more supportive of educational funding than the Depression generation, reflecting an increasingly common argument—that the oldest-old differ considerably from the young-old in their policy preferences.[61] Also flying in the face of conventional wisdom is the fact that the greatest jump in support for more educational spending has occurred among members of the oldest generations (World War I and Depression). These findings, viewed in tandem, suggest that period and maturational effects may be interacting. The normal tendency for people to grow less supportive of educational spending as they grow older (with their children out of school) has been offset somewhat by a deluge of news stories about how the United States is falling behind other countries in its educational achievements and how Florida is falling behind other states in this area.

On social service spending, Florida's generational differences are considerably wider and more volatile. Predictably, the younger generations (Reagan and Civil Rights/Vietnam/Watergate) are more supportive of higher spending on social services than the older ones. However, between 1981 and 1993, preferences for higher spending on social services escalated across all generations except the oldest (World War I), although this support began to weaken in the early 1990s. Perhaps signaling what is to come, the Cold War/Sputnik generation, which is nearing retirement, is the only one to increase its support for higher state social service spending in the 1990s. This suggests that as the intergenerational competition for scarce resources intensifies, the older generations may actually push for greater government spending while the younger generations push for reductions—a reversal of the spending preference patterns observed to this point.

Preferences on law enforcement spending reflect a dichotomy in the attitudes of the young and the old. On the one hand, the elderly feel much more vulnerable

FIGURE 5.2 Generational Differences in Support for Spending on State Programs

Preferences for Educational Spending
(Mean number of programs to increase)

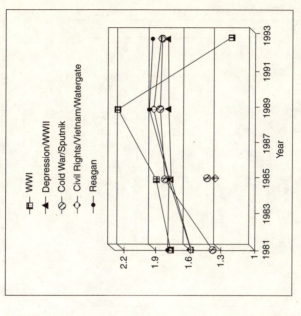

Note: Respondents were asked: "Do you think spending for educational programs should be increased, kept at the present level, or decreased?"

Source: Suzanne L. Parker, Florida Annual Policy Survey, Tallahassee, FL: Policy Sciences Program, Florida State University.

Preferences for Social Spending
(Mean number of programs to increase)

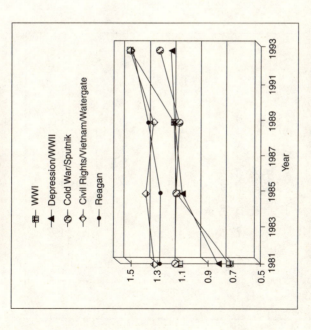

Note: Respondents were asked: "Do you think spending for social programs should be increased, kept at the present level, or decreased?"

Source: Suzanne L. Parker Florida Annual Policy Survey, Tallahassee, FL: Policy Sciences Program, Florida State University.

(continues)

FIGURE 5.2 (cont.)

Preferences for Law Enforcement Spending
(Mean number of programs to increase)

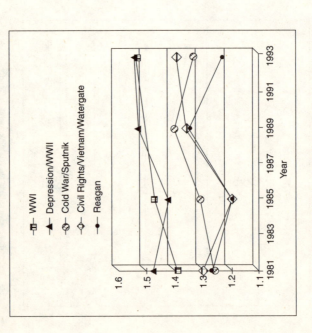

Note: Respondents were asked: "Do you think spending for law enforcement programs should be increased, kept at the present level, or decreased?"

Source: Suzanne L. Parker Florida Annual Policy Survey, Tallahassee, FL: Policy Sciences Program, Florida State University.

Note: Respondents were asked: "Now I'm going to ask you some questions about spending by the state government in Tallahassee. Please bear in mind that eventually all government spending comes out of the taxes you and other Floridians pay. As I mention each program area, tell me whether you think the amount now being spent should be increased, kept at the present level, or decreased." (Lead-in question format)

Preferences for Spending on Economic Development
(Mean number of programs to increase)

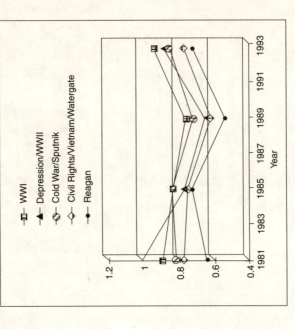

Note: Respondents were asked: "Do you think spending for economic development programs should be increased, kept at the present level, or decreased?"

Source: Suzanne L. Parker Florida Annual Policy Survey, Tallahassee, FL: Policy Sciences Program, Florida State University.

to attack than the young. On the other hand, younger persons often have a more antagonistic attitude toward the police and law enforcement. Consequently, the oldest generations (World War I, Depression) are consistently the most supportive of increased spending for law enforcement. In the 1990s, their support for more spending in this policy area rose sharply. This parallels the escalation of crime to the top of the list of their most important problems, a point I will examine in more detail in Chapter 6.

Of the four broad policy areas examined, economic development spending appears to be the least affected by age-group differences, although the older generations are slightly more supportive of such spending than the young. But as shown in Figure 5.2, support for heavier spending in this area fluctuates across all generations, tracking closely with the rise and fall of the economy. At the depths of a recession, spending on economic development appears to be a lower priority than other types of spending.[62] Support for heavier spending on economic development tends to increase after the economy is well on its way to recovery, as in 1983 and 1993.

State Spending Priorities: Lessons from Floridians. Unfortunately, few national polls ask their respondents to rank order or prioritize their spending preferences. Consequently, studies that merely focus on who favors growth in spending for certain types of programs may get a more optimistic view of that support than actually exists in the real world of limited revenues. Results from the Florida Annual Policy Survey show how spending support patterns change when respondents are asked to identify not only which program areas should receive increased or decreased funding but also which of those programs should be the *top* priority for an increase or decrease.

Since 1983, little consensus has existed among Florida's oldest and youngest cohorts on the top priorities for funding increases (see Table 5.4). Predictably, the youngest cohorts have chosen education as their top funding priority; the oldest cohorts select programs to combat crime. Is it any surprise, then, that the major debate in recent sessions of the Florida legislature has concerned the proportional amounts of money to put into education and crime control? These results suggest there is more of a generation-based rational self-interest aspect to spending priorities than is commonly found by looking only at age-group spending preferences for individual policy areas.

TAXING AND SPENDING PREFERENCES IN EITHER-OR SITUATIONS

Budgetary ledgers have two sides: revenues and expenditures. Most people believe the two sides should balance because they look at a governmental or private sector budget much as they look at their own checkbooks.

In the public sector, a budget can be balanced in a number of ways. Spending levels can be cut while keeping revenues (taxes) the same. Revenues can be raised to meet expenditure demands. Or both approaches can be combined, raising some revenues and reducing some spending. Mass publicity—and hysteria—about the rising national debt and federal budget deficit have prompted pollsters to begin posing their taxing and spending questions in the context of choices or trade-offs.[63] As noted, such questions generally permit more careful testing of the "self-interested" fiscal preferences of various age-groups.

Raising Taxes Versus Cutting Spending

A 1989 ABC News/Washington Post survey asked Americans how they would prefer to reduce the federal budget deficit (which is not exactly the same as asking how to balance the budget but is close in the public's mind). Their choices were a tax increase or a spending cut, although the second choice was split into two parts—social or military. When the question was posed in such a manner, all age-groups overwhelmingly preferred spending cuts to tax increases. However, the older cohorts were slightly more supportive of raising taxes and less supportive of cutting spending than the youngest cohorts.[64] This finding clearly suggests that there may be an economically based generational standoff down the road as the size disparity between the age-cohorts widens. It reflects the trend observed earlier in the Florida spending priorities—namely, that as the nation ages, the older are more likely to support government growth than the young, reversing the trend of the 1980s and 1990s.

Spending Cuts Versus a Tax Increase/Spending Cut Combination

A Times Mirror Center for The People & The Press survey, perhaps recognizing that tax increases generate little support, posed the "choice" question somewhat differently. Respondents were asked to choose between spending cuts and a tax increase/spending cut combination.[65] This may be a more realistic question given today's limited resources and the public's animosity toward taxes. When the question was posed in this manner, the age-group differences were a little narrower, with the older cohorts (but not the oldest) slightly more in favor of spending cuts.[66] Still, this question, like the one pitting a tax increase against a spending cut, tells us little about *which* programs different age-groups would or would not approve of cutting to reduce the federal budget deficit.

In Favor of Higher Spending Even if New Taxes Are Required

The same Times Mirror survey presented its respondents with a list of economic and social issues facing the nation and asked whether each "is not much of a problem, is a problem but no government action is required, is a problem that requires government action but only if no new taxes are required, or is a problem that requires government action even if new taxes are required." Support for heavier spending even in the face of higher taxes was strongest for programs designed to combat the war on drugs (crime), make sure the elderly enjoy a decent standard of living, provide medical care for the indigent and health insurance for major illnesses, and promote literacy. But with the exception of the war on drugs, support for greater spending on these critical issues rarely exceeded the 40 to 50 percent range in any age-group (see Table 5.5). With few exceptions, younger Americans saw more need for government intervention, even if this required higher taxes and included greater spending on programs primarily benefiting the aged. However, there were some signs that the young's attitudes become more "self-regarding" once they enter the workforce and take on the responsibilities of raising a family.

Tax Increases Versus Spending Cuts Versus Privatization

A 1988 Times Mirror survey also presented respondents with "a list of ways in which government revenues could be increased or government expenses could be cut" and asked them to identify "each action, if any, that you would support in order to reduce the federal deficit." Although limited to a single point in time, the results clearly showed that more inclusive choices (specific tax increases versus specific program cuts) produced the strongest support across all age-groups for increases in selective sales taxes (alcohol, tobacco) and income taxes on the wealthy, as opposed to specific spending cuts. But results also showed that when *freezing* spending was offered as a separate choice from *cutting* specific programs, there was more support for freezing, except in the area of defense. Support for freezing was somewhat stronger among the older and middle-aged cohorts.[67]

Support was only lukewarm for privatizing the U.S. Postal Service or the federal prison system. Privatization can be viewed as an approach that combines revenue-raising and spending-reduction. Privatizing the post office could effectively raise revenue (those buying the right to take over delivery would pay a fee to the federal government), and it could also produce a cost savings, or a spending cut, once the government divested itself of financial responsibility for providing the mail service. Survey responses revealed no clear generational schisms in this regard.

Unacceptable Spending Cuts: Generational Self-Interest or Not?

When a more inclusive choice scenario was given, responses by the old and young alike to questions on spending cut preferences did not initially appear to be overly self-centered. Heavy proportions of the elderly did not prefer cuts in public education nor did large proportions of the younger cohorts favor cutting back Medicare benefits or eliminating the automatic cost-of-living (COLA) increase in Social Security payments as ways to reduce the federal deficit. But a somewhat different pattern emerged when the respondents were asked, "Which of these ways of reducing the federal budget deficit would you *strongly oppose*?"

Age-group beneficiaries were most intransigent regarding age-targeted programs. As shown in Table 5.6, the older cohorts (50 and older) were most opposed to cutting spending for Medicare and Social Security COLAs. The younger cohorts were most opposed to cutting spending for public education and Medicare. The young were also less supportive of cuts in social and entitlement programs such as food stamps and minority aid, which have predominantly

younger beneficiaries. This sets the stage for what many forecasters have predicted—namely, that the greatest intergenerational battles will take place over
Social Security and other entitlement programs.[68]

As Senators Warren B. Rudman and Paul E. Tsongas have warned:

> To cut the deficit, we must debate and enact concrete reforms in our trillion-dollar
> system of federal entitlements from Social Security, Medicare, and civil service and
> military pensions to farm supports and to the employer-paid health-care exclusion.
> We must direct our reform efforts to where these programs provide windfalls to
> those who don't really need them. . . . As we grow older, the overriding importance
> of our children becomes even clearer. It is not simply economically destructive to
> bequeath them an inheritance of diminished investment, productivity, and compet-
> itiveness—along with the debts for our past consumption. It is immoral.[69]

The Either-Or Question at the State and Local Level: Florida. Most state and local governments are required to balance their budgets, which means that deficit
spending like that engaged in by the federal government is not an option!
Consequently, state and local governments are often forced to address the revenue
side of the budget. In such instances, elected officials have given their constituents
the choice of either tax cuts (and service reductions) or tax stability (and the
maintenance of current service levels). The Florida Annual Policy Survey asked
the question in this manner: "Some people think state and local taxes should be
reduced even if public services have to be cut. Others say we need these public services even if it means paying the same taxes. Which do you prefer?"

Floridians of all age-groups clearly prefer maintaining current service levels
over tax cuts. The percent favoring tax cuts actually dropped between 1981 and
1993. Not atypically, support for tax cuts in Florida was strongest when the state's
economy had fallen into deep recession (1981 and 1991).

Florida's older generations are more in favor of maintaining current service
levels even when taxes cannot be cut. This finding has two possible explanations.
First, older Floridians, a large number of whom have come from other states where
taxes are higher, see Florida's taxes as being low in the first place.[70] Another is that
they may see Florida's service offerings as less extensive, more restrictive, and less
generous than those of other states, such as New York. (This is true for most social
services.) Nonetheless, in the survey data, there is a reoccurring pattern—namely,
older persons are more strongly supportive of protecting government spending
levels than younger persons, even when such a strategy may prohibit lowering tax
rates, although a majority of all age-groups still prefer spending cuts.

IDEOLOGY, GOVERNMENTAL RESPONSIVENESS, AND ECONOMICS

In *The Changing American Mind,* Mayer made a powerful argument linking
Americans' opinions on taxes and spending with their ideologies (liberal or con-
servative) and outlooks on governmental size, effectiveness, and efficiency.[71]
"American liberals," he said, "have rarely flirted with government ownership or

centralized planning, but they have believed in a strong role for government, particularly the federal government, in providing welfare, regulating business, and coordinating fiscal and monetary policy."

In contrast, conservative Americans have been more intent on "stressing the need for low taxes, a limited welfare state, and freedom for businesses and entrepreneurs to expand and develop according to the dictates of the free market." When government intervention is called for, conservatives prefer that it be done by state and local governments.[72]

Ideology: A Confusing Term

Ideology in its more technical sense "refers to the structure of a person's ideas or beliefs about political values and the role of government."[73] Those who study U.S. political ideology often portray it as having two dimensions: "One dimension is [a person's] attitude toward government intervention in the economy, and the other is [an] attitude toward the maintenance or expansion of personal freedoms."[74]

Do Americans see ideology in those terms? A 1987 survey by the Times Mirror Center for The People & The Press asked, "What does it mean to you when someone says he or she is a liberal? a conservative?" Nearly one-fifth of all adults gave an economic explanation.[75] Virtually the same proportion (17 to 21 percent) defined ideology more in terms of whether a person is amenable or resistant to change (old-fashioned). Only 6 to 8 percent gave individual rights–related responses, and few gave a partisan-oriented definition. When these responses were broken down by age, it is not surprising that the older appeared more likely to define ideology in economic terms; the young, in terms of change (see Table 5.7).

Actually, a prominent study has identified four ideologies common among Americans today: liberal, conservative, libertarian, and populist. In *Beyond Liberal and Conservative*, William S. Mattox and Stuart A. Lilie defined each ideology: "Liberals support government economic intervention and expansion of personal freedoms; conservatives oppose both. Libertarians support expanded individual freedom but oppose government economic intervention; populists oppose expansion of individual freedom but support government intervention in the economy."[76]

To be sure, however, these four are not the *only* ideologies espoused by Americans. For example, socialism, the belief that we should have "an economic and governmental system based on public ownership of the means of production and exchange,"[77] has long been promoted by a small portion of the U.S. populace. And "ideologies within ideologies," such as "neoliberalism" and "neoconservativism," often emerge in reaction to changing societal conditions.[78]

Are Americans Highly Ideological?

Experts argue over whether most Americans have neatly packaged belief systems. Many believe that Americans are rarely ideologically consistent in their preferences for political candidates, parties, and public policies. Others give the citizenry more credit for being able to identify, although in quite general terms, the ideological tilt of candidates, parties, and issue positions.[79] When prompted by pollsters, Americans *can* place themselves on an ideological continuum ranging from the far Left (liberal) to the far Right (conservative) or identify themselves as liberals, conservatives, or middle-of-the-roaders.

Regardless of the question format, the majority of Americans tend to place themselves in the middle, much as they tend to classify themselves as middle-income rather than rich or poor. Since 1972, when surveys begin to ask ideological predisposition questions, middle-of-the-roaders, also known as moderates or "nonideologues,"[80] have outnumbered conservatives and liberals. Moreover, conservatives have outnumbered liberals (see Figure 5.3). But just as more Americans are seeing themselves as political independents rather than Democrats or Republicans, more are classifying themselves as nonideologicals rather than as liberals or conservatives.[81]

Links Between Age and Ideology

Some believe that as we age, we become more conservative. If so, we could be in for a conservative boom in light of the nation's changing age profile. To date, however, there is little research to support "the notion that increasing conservatism is an inevitable part of the political life cycle" (an aging effect).[82] However, research does show that a higher proportion of older persons label themselves conservative. (If this sounds confusing, it is!) Ideology, even more than party identification, often means different things to different people, depending upon social and political conditions dominating society at the time the individuals came of age politically.[83] The failure to recognize this fact, experts say, could lead to erroneous conclusions about the changing relationship between age and ideology:

> Orientations deemed "liberal" by society in an earlier era (which constituted the formative years of political socialization for a contemporary-aged generation) may become socially defined as "conservative" as the person ages. . . . Thus at least part of the observed "shift to the right" with age may be a product of society's definition of a person's political stance, not merely a shift of perspective within the individual per se. Whether or not the political orientations of older persons are conservative is a combined product of both personal and social-historical factors.[84]

The Ideological Dispositions of Different Age-Groups

Unquestionably, what's considered liberal by some today may be viewed as conservative by others in the future, making it difficult to conclude that a person grows more conservative over time. Nonetheless, the ideological self-labeling of different age-groups across time can be compared. One recent study tracked the ideological identifications of 20- to 29-year-olds between 1974 and 1991. Over this period, the proportion of the young who identified themselves as liberals declined by 8 percent, while the percent who called themselves conservatives increased by 12 percent[85]—overall, not a drastic swing. The ideological leanings of older cohorts

FIGURE 5.3 Americans' Ideology: A Cross-Time Look

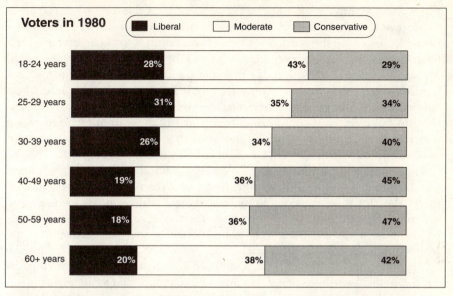

Note: Respondents were asked: "Regardless of the party you may favor, do you lean more toward the liberal side or the conservative side politically?" Sample=9,431 voters as they left voting booths.
Source: Survey by ABC News, November 4, 1980. Reported in *The American Enterprise* 4 (March/April 1993), p. 86.

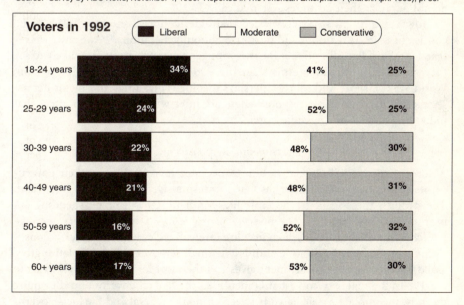

Note: Respondents were asked: "On most political matters, do you consider yourself liberal, moderate, or conservative?" Sample=7,000+ voters as they left voting booths.

Source: Survey conducted November 3, 1992, by Voter Research & Surveys, a consortium of ABC News, CNN, and NBC News. Reported in *The American Enterprise* 4 (March/April 1993), p. 86. Reprinted with permission.

have been even more stable and somewhat more conservative, and they remain that way in the early 1990s.

More older Floridians label themselves conservative than do older persons nationwide. Reflecting the transient nature of what constitutes a conservative (or a liberal for that matter), the percentage who said they were conservative fluctuated considerably across all age-groups over the period examined. The ideological leanings of the young fluctuated most sharply, in line with what other researchers have observed. And younger Floridians, like young persons elsewhere, were less likely to call themselves conservative. Nearly half of those from each generation preferred to think of themselves as middle-of-the-roaders; the young have been more prone to see themselves in that light but only marginally so.

How an individual uses ideology in making political decisions depends upon who is running for office and what the issues are. When economic issues surface, those who clearly see ideology in more economic terms will use ideology as a screening mechanism. When the issues are social or moral, those who see ideology in those terms are more likely to be affected by that perspective. In truth, many Americans feel quite comfortable supporting a liberal candidate in one race and a more conservative one in another. Furthermore, a 1990 Times Mirror survey found that two-thirds of voters across all age-groups said a candidate's ideology (liberal or conservative) was not too important.[86] Political scientists tend to agree that "most Americans are unconstrained by a patterned ideology.... [They] do not organize their attitudes systematically."[87]

However, a recent study concluded that older cohorts were more likely to be consistent than baby boom and post–baby boom generations.[88] And my own research on Floridians found that the two younger generations were less likely to say they think in ideological terms than the two oldest generations (Depression, World War I). More and more, a person's ideological leanings and his or her assessments of government responsiveness are intertwined—and both affect that individual's taxing and spending preferences.

Governmental Responsiveness

According to one widespread notion, Americans increasingly see their governments (federal, state, and local) as being unresponsive, wasteful, and inefficient. The stronger these feelings, the more likely individuals will prefer spending-cut over tax-increase solutions to budgetary problems—a more conservative approach. (As noted earlier, such choices are rarely that clear-cut, however.)

Since 1972, the Advisory Commission on Intergovernmental Relations has asked, "Which level of government gives you the most for your money?" Prior to the 1980s, the majority consistently identified the federal government. But more recently, the public has vacillated between citing the federal and the local government (although local government has been rated the most cost-effective since 1989) (see Table 5.8). State government has nearly always been ranked at the bottom, largely because it delivers services in a less direct fashion than either the federal or local government. In light of these general patterns, should we expect to find age-group differences?

Age, Governmental Responsiveness, and Rational Self-Interest

Based purely on the theory of rational self-interest, it would seem that older persons would see a more direct linkage between benefits and the services of the federal government because of Social Security and Medicare. Similarly, the young would be expected to cite state and local governments since they play the biggest role in providing education. However, certain other facts challenge this rather simple hypothesis. Because conservatives are more likely to be hostile toward bigger (i.e., federal) government,[89] viewing it as inefficient and unresponsive, and because a higher proportion of the older cohorts are conservative, would it not be reasonable to expect more of the elderly to regard the state and local governments as more efficient? (The problem with the latter argument, of course, is that the linkage between age and ideology is somewhat weak in the first place.)

The ACIR survey results supported the rational self-interest thesis, albeit weakly. Between 1972 and 1993, a plurality of the oldest cohort consistently cited the federal government as giving them the most for their money. But so, too, did a plurality of the youngest cohort. However, a *majority* of the younger cohorts selected either the local or state government, whereas only a plurality of the older cohorts chose those governments. About one-fourth of the oldest cohort said they did not know which government gave them the most for their money. As previously noted, some have speculated that giving "don't-know" answers is simply a common pattern in older persons' responses to surveys.

The real explanation may be that a number of older people think none of the three governments gives them the most for their money. That explanation makes sense in light of a 1989 ACIR survey question about which of the three levels of government needed more power. More than one-third of those older than 65 volunteered that none of them did, compared to just 14 percent of those 18 to 24.[90] This negativity was consistent with the elderly's greater cynicism toward government.

Few people in any age-group identified the federal government as most in need of more power. Older cohorts were more evenly divided about whether state or local government needed more power the most, leaning slightly toward the local. In contrast, the youngest cohorts leaned much more strongly in the direction of giving the local government more power.[91]

SUMMARY

Regardless of age, Americans tend to be rational in their support for various fiscal policies. An individual tends to judge as most cost-effective and responsive the government that delivers more of the services from which he or she benefits most directly. The willingness to pay is also stronger when benefits received are greater, especially when such benefits are threatened by shrinking revenues. As has been shown, no generation or age-cohort is exempt from the criticism that it is self-centered on taxing and spending issues. How this self-centeredness projects itself with regard to taxing and spending preferences is best explained by an individual's stage in the life cycle.

The middle-aged are the most likely to believe their taxes are too high because with their higher income they bear the heaviest tax burden. Older persons consistently see the property tax as the least-fair tax, whereas the middle-aged and younger cohorts find the federal income tax more onerous. For older persons, the concern with the property tax stems from the fact that their incomes are fixed: Any time property values go up, a bigger chunk of their income must be used to pay those taxes. For the middle-aged and younger cohorts in the workforce, the major concern is the federal income tax because the more money these groups make, the more the federal government takes.

The young and old vary little in their views on Social Security taxes; most feel the tax levels are about right. However, on the issue of taxing the Social Security earnings of the elderly, the younger cohorts are much more inclined to tax those payments just like any other revenue source. The greatest opposition to this comes from those closest to recipient age.

When asked how to make tax systems fairer, most Americans, regardless of age, favor more progressive solutions (making upper-income persons pay more and closing loopholes perceived to primarily benefit the affluent). The strongest support for closing loopholes comes from the youngest cohorts—those least likely to itemize. The strongest support for raising individual income taxes in general comes from the middle-aged—those most likely to itemize.

Regardless of the level of government involved, when budget shortfalls necessitate raising revenues, Americans favor selective sales taxes (on cigarettes, alcohol, or gambling) over general sales taxes, sales taxes over user fees, and any of these over income tax hikes. Older persons are more likely to favor no new or increased taxes—unless this is linked with the alternative of service reductions. Then, they are more likely to opt for higher taxes or, at a minimum, sustained tax rates. They are also more opposed to the use of lotteries as revenue enhancers, reflecting their more conservative ideological leanings.

On the spending side of the budget, the great debate has focused on the gray peril hypothesis, which asserts that older persons exhibit more self-centeredness when it comes to spending priorities. The truth is that all age-groups exhibit some degree of rational self-interest behavior, depending upon how spending questions are asked. If asked whether they favor spending increases or decreases, the young tend to want to spend more on almost everything, including programs targeted toward the elderly (Social Security or Medicare). The elderly, in contrast, are somewhat less enthusiastic about spending more on education, social services, and other entitlement programs, thus suggesting that older Americans are more self-centered.

When asked which specific programs should get top ranking, virtually every age-group exhibits some self-centeredness. For example, when asked to identify their top priority for spending, the young and middle-aged, who typically have children, choose education, and the old choose law enforcement or health. These choices are natural products of their stages in the life cycle.

When questions are phrased in either-or terms (higher taxes or lower spending), most age-groups appear self-centered. For example, when given the either-or choice at the federal level, the older cohorts are slightly more likely to choose tax increases, which is not surprising since they are the most likely to receive direct benefits in the form of federal Social Security and Medicare payments. The reverse is true for the younger cohorts. The self-centered view shows up even more clearly when persons are asked about which budget-balancing approaches they oppose most adamantly. Predictably, the younger cohorts are most opposed to cutting education, social services, and entitlement programs that have predominantly younger beneficiaries (although they also strongly oppose cutting Medicare). Older persons are most strongly opposed to cutting Social Security cost-of-living adjustments and Medicare.

Further insight on Americans' taxing and spending preferences comes from their judgments about which level of government gives them the most for their money (cost-effectiveness). A plurality of each age-group regards the federal government as the most cost effective, but the elderly do so most consistently, no doubt reflecting the priority they give to Social Security and Medicare. A majority of the younger cohorts, by contrast, choose either local or state government—the primary deliverers of education and the other services they use more heavily than the elderly.

Some choices are simply a matter of one's ideological predisposition. For example, the young tend to favor more government intervention to deal with social and economic problems, even when doing so requires paying higher taxes. This reflects their more liberal ideological leanings but it also has to do with the lighter tax burden they bear compared to their middle-aged and young-old counterparts. In turn, greater support among the older cohorts for spending freezes reflects the more status quo–oriented behavior associated with a more conservative ideology. So, too, does the elderly's belief than none of the three government levels needs more power.

The generational differences vis-à-vis taxing and spending observed in this chapter suggest there may be a role reversal as the population ages. Signs indicate that as intergenerational competition for scarce resources intensifies, the older generations may actually push for *greater* government spending while the younger generations push for *reductions*—a real reversal of the spending preference patterns observed up to this point.

The increasing diversity of the older population, as exhibited by the growing lack of consensus in this group, is likely to provoke more us-against-them and either-higher-taxes-or-lower-spending battles within the older cohort itself. However, this *intra*generational divisiveness will only blur—not erase—*inter*generational fights over governmental taxing and spending priorities.

The key question that remains is whether these growing economic differences and fears will be the sparks that finally ignite the political participation fuse under the heretofore low-turnout younger generations. Rising turnout rates among younger voters in the 1992 presidential election lead some to believe it will.

But in terms of sheer numbers, older generations will increasingly have an advantage in influencing the taxing and spending choices at all levels, especially as the baby boomer generation edges toward retirement age. The biggest tax-related disputes are likely to center on the federal income tax—base, rates, and deductions. The spending areas where generational differences will matter most are education and social insurance entitlements.

Finally, to better understand the dynamics of generational differences in taxing and spending preferences, public opinion survey questions need to be framed in trade-off or choice formats. In the real world of government finance, the key choices are more often "either-or" rather than "more-or-less" decisions.

TABLE 5.1 Age-Group Opinions About Which Is the Worst Tax—Including Social Security (in percentages)

Year / Age-Group	Federal Income Tax	Social Security Tax	State Income Tax	State Sales Tax	Local Property Tax	Don't Know
1988						
18–24	26	24	10	11	16	13
25–34	30	19	9	16	19	7
35–44	26	15	10	15	26	8
45–65	26	12	9	18	27	8
Over 65	20	16	4	14	33	13
1989						
18–24	15	19	11	8	33	14
25–34	21	21	9	15	26	8
35–44	29	17	11	12	24	7
45–65	18	17	7	18	31	9
Over 65	23	16	5	12	29	15
1990						
18–24	18	17	11	16	31	9
25–34	29	21	8	10	25	7
35–44	30	11	12	14	25	8
45–65	27	14	12	11	30	7
Over 65	21	12	7	14	33	14
1992						
18–24	22	7	13	22	21	15
25–34	30	13	9	14	23	11
35–44	28	15	7	17	23	11
45–65	24	8	9	17	27	15
Over 65	20	7	9	8	28	29

Note: Respondents were asked: "Which do you think is the worst tax—that is, the least fair—including Social Security?"

Source: U.S. Advisory Commission on Intergovernmental Relations, *Changing Public Attitudes on Government and Taxes,* Washington, D.C.: ACIR, 1989–1992.

TABLE 5.2 Age-Group Perspectives on How to Make the Nation's Tax System Fairer (in percentages)

	Age-Group				
Changes	18–24	25–34	35–44	45–64	65 and over
Make the upper income taxpayers pay more	38	53	54	52	41
Reduce taxes on lower income taxpayers	17	13	12	12	14
Make business firms pay more even if it reduces the number of jobs	11	5	6	6	4
Leave the tax system alone - it is about as fair as you are ever going to get	18	14	13	15	22
None of the above	5	7	6	8	5
Don't know	11	8	9	6	14

Note: Respondents were asked: "Which one of the changes would be the single most important change that would make the nation's tax system more fair?"

Source: U.S. Advisory Commission on Intergovernmental Relations, Changing Public Attitudes on Government and Taxes, Washington, D.C.: ACIR, 1983, p.13.

TABLE 5.3 Age-Group Perspectives on Revenue Alternatives to Reduce the Federal Deficit (in percentages)

	Age–Group				
Revenue alternative to reduce Federal deficit	18–24	25–34	35–44	45–64	65 and over
An increase in gasoline and diesel fuel taxes	3	10	7	9	10
An increase in individual income tax rates	6	6	7	8	6
A national lottery	57	52	46	42	33
A national sales tax on all purchases other than food	11	5	15	9	16
An increase in user fees or charges for things like the use of national parks and forests, passports, customs inspections, and Coast Guard services for boaters	12	16	14	19	13
(Volunteered) No tax increase/no new taxes	5	5	7	5	11
Don't know/no answer	6	6	4	8	11

Note: Respondents were asked: "If the Federal government decided to raise a small amount of additional revenue to help meet costs and reduce the deficit, which one of these would you prefer?"

Source: U.S. Advisory Commission on Intergovernmental Relations, Changing Public Attitudes on Government and Taxes, Washington, D.C.: ACIR, 1987, p. 23.

TABLE 5.4 Top Spending Priorities by Generation: Florida, 1981–1993

Cohort	1981	Percent	Top Spending Priority By Generation 1985	Percent	1989	Percent	1993	Percent
1959–1973	Crime	35	Public schools	20	Public Schools	24	Public schools	35
	Low income families	12	Environment	18	Crime	18	Health	12
	Elderly	10	Combat crime	17	Low income families	11	Environment	11
	Public schools	7	Elderly	11	Environment	10	Crime	11
1943–1958	Crime	21	Public schools	30	Public schools	28	Public schools	38
	Public schools	20	Combat crime	18	Crime	18	Crime	15
	Elderly	18	Elderly	12	Low income families	10	Health care	14
	Drug law	9	Low income families	9	Elderly, Environment, Health care	8.5	Economic development	8
1927–1942	Crime	26	Elderly	24	Crime	26	Public schools	24
	Elderly	23	Public schools	18	Public schools	18	Health care	22
	Drug Law	14	Combat crime	17	Elderly	15	Crime	14
	Public schools	10	Environment	9	Highways	10	Elderly	14
1911–1926	Crime	32	Combat Crime	30	Crime	26	Crime	22
	Elderly	19	Elderly	17	Public schools	17	Health care	20
	Drug law	17	Public schools	12	Elderly	16	Elderly	14
	Low income families	6	Environment	10	Environment	12	Public schools	12
1899–1910	Crime	29	Combat Crime	32	Elderly	25	Crime	37
	Elderly	25	Elderly	23	Crime	20	Public schools	21
	Drug law	18	Low income families	11	Public schools	16	Highways	16
	Prison, Health care	5	Highways	10	Highways	9.1	Health care	16
					Environment, Health care			

Source: Suzanne L. Parker, Florida Annual Policy Survey. Tallahassee, FL: Survey Research Laboratory, Policy Sciences Program, Florida State University.

TABLE 5.5 Problem So Critical Government Action Is Needed Even if New Taxes Are Required (in percentages)

Problem	Age-Group						
	18–24	25–29	30–39	40–49	50–59	60–69	70+
Ensuring that every American has a place to sleep and food to eat	44.1	42.8	43.3	36.9	33.0	36.9	31.9
Ensuring that the quality of TV programs improves	4.6	3.9	6.8	7.0	4.4	6.2	7.3
Providing a job for everyone who wants one˙	27.5	21.8	23.5	23.3	21.1	20.4	19.7
Providing adequate medical care for all who need it but can't afford it	57.3	51.6	51.8	47.7	48.5	51.7	45.6
Providing health insurance for major illnesses	46.9	41.1	44.3	44.8	44.4	48.9	43.8
Ensuring that every American can read and write	41.1	51.6	46.1	45.5	31.2	33.4	25.5
Providing for a decent standard of living for the elderly	59.3	65.1	61.6	57.1	51.6	47.4	42.7
Ensuring that every American can afford to send their child to college	21.8	17.8	22.9	23.8	12.4	13.9	9.6
Improving the quality of education in the public school system	53.6	59.0	55.1	50.4	38.0	36.2	31.7
Ensuring that every American has equal opportunities for a job	28.8	22.4	27.4	24.0	18.2	17.9	15.7
Protecting American workers from sudden layoffs	25.2	20.5	19.1	19.6	14.5	10.8	14.8
Halting the smuggling of drugs into the U.S. from other countries	65.2	65.2	64.5	70.5	66.7	70.0	60.3

Note: Respondents were asked: "I am going to read you a list of problems facing the United States, and for each one, please tell me whether you think it is not much of a problem, is a problem but no government activism is required, is a problem that requires government action but only if no new taxes are required, or is a problem that requires government action *even* if new taxes are required?"

Source: The Times Mirror Center for The People & The Press. Face-to-face survey of a nationally representative sample of 3,021 adults 18 years of age or older, conducted May 13-22, 1988. Reprinted with permission.

TABLE 5.6   Federal Budget Deficit Reduction Strategies Most Strongly Opposed (in percentages)

Strategy opposed	Age-Group						
	18–24	25–29	30–39	40–49	50–59	60–69	70+
Taxing							
Increase taxes on alcoholic beverages	5.6	5.2	3.9	2.3	3.0	4.6	4.1
Increase income taxes for those earning more than $80,000 per year	3.9	3.6	3.6	4.7	5.5	3.2	1.8
Increase taxes on tobacco products	6.7	6.2	3.9	4.1	2.9	5.8	4.0
Establish a national sales tax	12.2	15.9	16.1	18.7	24.4	20.0	13.9
Increase taxes on gasoline	15.5	13.0	14.0	17.3	16.6	17.7	10.5
Spending							
Cut spending for defense	14.6	16.6	13.2	17.9	21.6	15.9	13.6
Freeze all federal spending at current levels, except education and AIDS research, until the budget is balanced	12.3	12.6	9.7	9.3	9.0	7.0	6.2
Freeze all federal spending at current levels until the budget is balanced	10.2	5.9	7.9	7.0	10.0	7.8	5.2
Eliminate the Strategic Defense Initiative or "Star Wars" Program	10.8	9.5	10.2	12.2	13.8	10.2	8.3
Remove American troops from Korea and Europe	8.6	11.5	11.8	9.8	10.9	7.7	4.8
Eliminate the space shuttle program	14.1	12.5	11.8	13.9	14.1	12.2	6.5
Cut spending on programs that assist blacks other minorities	15.8	13.2	19.0	15.7	12.8	10.3	9.1
End price supports for farmers	23.3	24.9	15.7	15.6	12.1	12.4	13.7
Eliminate the food stamp program	32.2	23.9	31.2	26.6	27.2	23.1	21.3
Cut spending for scientific research	23.1	21.1	20.6	22.3	21.1	17.8	13.3
Eliminate automatic cost-of-living increases in payments to Social Security beneficiaries	27.1	29.3	33.1	35.7	41.3	45.6	41.6
Cut spending for public education	48.6	44.5	49.4	44.4	43.0	34.5	26.2
Cut back Medicare benefits	46.0	43.6	44.8	46.2	54.1	55.3	57.6
Privatization							
Turn over management of federal prisons to private companies to operate for a fee	9.0	8.0	8.2	7.9	10.1	12.3	12.5
Turn over management of the U.S. Postal Service to private companies to operate for a fee	13.5	11.8	9.3	7.4	9.3	10.4	9.3

Note: Respondents were asked: "Here is a list of ways in which government revenues could be increased or government expenses could be cut. Please circle the number for each action, if any, that you would support in order to reduce the federal deficit. Then just read me the numbers you circled." Respondents were then asked: "Are there any of these ways of reducing the federal budget deficit that you would strongly oppose?" (Multiple responses possible.)

Source: The Times Mirror Center for The People & The Press. Face-to-face survey of a nationally representative sample of 3,021 adults 18 years or age or older, conducted May 13–22, 1988. Reprinted with permission.

TABLE 5.7 Older See Ideology in Economic Terms; Young in Terms of Reaction to Change (in percentages)

Attribute	Age-Group					
	18–24	25–29	30–39	40–49	50–59	60+
Liberal						
Economic						
Support programs that increase spending	10.4	8.0	16.4	15.6	20.5	23.4
Role of government/Individual rights & responsibilities/Values						
Like government involvement	1.3	2.0	1.1	2.9	1.7	3.0
Favor social programs	9.3	8.7	11.9	10.5	6.1	5.8
Support for environment	—	0.2	1.5	0.3	—	0.2
No morals/loose life style	1.2	1.3	1.2	1.4	0.6	0.7
Believe in rights of all people	10.1	5.8	8.1	8.5	7.6	8.1
A socialist/communist	1.4	1.0	3.6	2.9	1.5	1.5
Reaction to Change						
Acceptable to change/flexible	19.0	19.6	17.3	17.4	18.6	13.0
Open-minded	13.7	19.3	12.8	18.0	10.0	8.4
Progressive, forward thinking	1.3	2.5	3.0	2.6	3.1	2.3
Partisan						
Democratic	0.3	2.8	4.1	0.5	1.5	1.1
Other						
Trustworthy	0.3	—	—	—	0.4	—
Unthoughtful/indecisive/not practical	4.5	6.7	7.4	9.3	14.5	7.2
Independent thinker	3.2	9.6	6.5	4.2	3.1	3.5
Uncaring/selfish	1.9	2.5	2.1	2.9	1.9	2.7
Miscellaneous	15.9	8.3	9.3	11.2	8.9	8.2
No opinion/don't know	28.2	19.5	16.3	14.2	20.1	25.9
Conservative						
Economic						
Thrifty	16.4	12.4	12.5	15.5	16.5	24.5
Budget-minded	1.1	1.7	4.6	4.2	4.8	5.3
Business-oriented	2.5	5.5	9.5	3.1	2.1	2.4
Wealthy, very rich	1.1	1.2	2.1	1.2	1.2	0.9
Support military spending	1.2	1.8	2.5	0.8	0.3	0.5
Role of government/Individual rights & responsibilities/Values						
Less government involvement	1.3	0.9	1.3	2.1	2.0	1.2
Belief in Constitutional freedom	1.9	1.3	2.1	1.4	0.5	1.0
Moral/strong values	2.0	4.4	5.1	3.1	3.5	3.1
Narrow-minded, prejudiced	3.4	7.5	6.8	7.9	6.8	3.2
Reaction to Change						
Resistant to change	22.8	23.6	21.3	24.5	22.2	15.0
Traditional/old fashioned	7.4	9.0	9.1	12.1	9.2	5.6

(continues)

TABLE 5.7 (cont.)

Attribute	Age-Group					
	18–24	25–29	30–39	40–49	50–59	60+
Partisan						
Republican	1.5	1.1	4.3	0.4	—	1.3
Other						
Reasonable, practical	7.3	13.8	7.5	7.8	9.6	7.4
Independent, secure	2.6	3.0	2.1	2.6	5.6	4.5
Opposite of liberal	—	1.3	0.6	0.3	0.7	0.5
Miscellaneous	8.0	6.3	9.7	10.4	8.1	5.2
Middle of the road	2.3	6.6	3.5	6.1	5.4	4.8
No opinion/don't know	25.6	16.6	13.9	11.3	18.4	21.3

Note: Respondents were asked: "What does it mean to you when someone says they are a *liberal/conservative?"*

Source: The Times Mirror Center for The People & The Press. Face-to-face interviews of a nationally representative sample of 4,244 adults 18 years of age or older, conducted April 25–May 10, 1987. Reprinted with permission.

TABLE 5.8 Age-Group Differences on Which Level of Government Gives One the Most For One's Money (in percentages)

Year/ Age-Group	Federal	State	Local	Don't Know
1983				
18–24	36	24	23	17
25–34	27	23	35	15
35–44	27	22	37	15
45–65	30	18	32	20
Over 65	37	11	26	25
1984				
18–24	21	36	28	15
25–34	22	33	37	8
35–44	21	26	38	15
45–65	26	23	37	14
Over 65	32	18	33	17
1985				
18–24	35	26	27	12
25–34	29	28	28	15
35–44	28	21	38	13
45–65	36	19	30	15
Over 65	33	17	29	21
1986				
18–24	33	29	26	12
25–34	31	26	36	7
35–44	28	24	37	11
45–65	30	19	37	14
Over 65	43	16	21	20
1987				
18–24	34	27	16	23
25–34	27	32	28	13
35–44	21	23	40	16
45–65	26	16	31	27
Over 65	38	14	24	24
1988				
18–24	30	29	25	16
25–34	29	33	26	12
35–44	22	25	38	15
45–65	26	26	34	14
Over 65	34	23	20	23
1989				
18–24	31	27	22	20
25–34	32	29	26	13
35–44	28	22	35	15
45–65	36	21	29	14
Over 65	38	13	32	17

(continues)

TABLE 5.8 (cont.)

Year/ Age-Group	Federal	State	Local	Don't Know
1991				
18–24	21	33	23	24
25–34	25	26	29	20
35–44	24	20	37	20
45–65	27	18	34	22
Over 65	32	13	28	27
1993				
18–24	23	16	37	24
25–34	24	25	32	19
35–44	24	18	41	17
45–65	22	21	39	18
Over 65	20	17	40	23

Notes: Respondents were asked: "From which level of government do you feel you get the most for your money—federal, state, or local?"

Source: U.S. Advisory Commission on Intergovernmental Relations, *Changing Public Attitudes on Government and Taxes,* Washington, D.C.: ACIR, annual.

6

Domestic and Foreign Policy: Generational Outlooks and Preferences

Headline news stories, whether in the electronic or the print media, signal "what's hot and what's not" to millions of Americans. From one day to the next, the lead stories may shift from what's happening at home to what's happening abroad. Some topics capture the headlines for days, even months, others for only a day or two.

For some Americans, the sheer volume of press coverage strongly affects how they react to the latest policy proposals—whether on the domestic or the foreign policy front. Others are more strongly influenced by the period in which they came of age. But sometimes, an individual's reaction to various proposals is driven more by his or her personal situation (economic, ideological, social, or political), which in turn often depends on where that person is in the life cycle. In many instances, Americans' outlooks and opinions are shaped by each of these factors to one extent or another.

Actually, public opinion changes incrementally rather than radically. History tells us that relatively few issues provoke drastic shifts in the direction of public opinion—or even in the intensity of public opinion. In *The Rational Public: Fifty Years of Trends in Americans' Policy Preferences,* Page and Shapiro concluded: "The American public, as a collectivity, holds a number of real, stable, and sensible opinions about public policy and these opinions develop and change in a reasonable fashion, responding to changing circumstances and to new information."[1]

Frequently, public policymakers are less interested in how much opinion has changed over time than in what the public thinks about the details of a new policy proposal or what should be done to deal with a current situation. Generally, more consensus exists about how important a problem is rather than how to address it. Once specific proposals are placed before the public and proponents and opponents have had a chance to make their case, the public tends to favor more incremental solutions, rather than drastic ones.

AGE AND PROBLEM-SOLVING APPROACHES

The common perception is that older persons are more likely than younger persons to prefer conservative or status quo approaches to dealing with current problems, rather than radical or sharp-change tactics. But is this true? And if so, does the pattern apply in regard to both domestic and foreign issues? Is it equally true across all domestic issues or all foreign issues? In this chapter, I will attempt to answer these questions. I am particularly interested in whether there are generational differences in the types of problems judged as most urgent and in the ideas on how to deal with them. I will also look at whether different age-groups have dissimilar assessments of the ability of governmental institutions and leaders to deal with pressing problems confronting the nation.

GENERATIONAL PERSPECTIVES
ON THE NATION'S URGENT PROBLEMS

Beginning in September 1935 and continuing to the present, the Gallup survey has asked the public: "What do you think is the most important problem facing this country today?" Most other major survey organizations also regularly ask this type of question. (Indeed, only a question on the president's popularity is asked more frequently.) Pollsters pose the question in an open-ended fashion, allowing respondents to say whatever is on their minds.

Most Important Problem: Domestic Outweighs Foreign

Frequently, the responses to "most important problem" questions fall into two broad categories—domestic and foreign. For the past several decades, domestic issues, particularly economic ones, have predominated. Occasionally, other domestic issues—such as civil rights in the early 1960s and welfare concerns (poverty, slums, education, and health care) and environmental issues in the early 1970s—have surfaced at or near the top.[2] By contrast, foreign policy concerns prevailed in the earlier periods, except during the Great Depression.

The specific problem identified as the most important fluctuates considerably. As Page and Shapiro aptly noted: "Responses to it [the question asking what is the most important problem facing the nation] naturally jump around as dramatic events occur and as the media devote coverage to one issue and then another."[3] Across age-groups, differences are greater in respect to specific problems than for rank orderings across broad categories. For example, in 1987 and 1993, all age-groups agreed that their topmost concern was the broad category of economic issues. But they differed on specific problems. In 1987, the young considered unemployment/recession/depression a more important economic concern than the federal deficit, but the reverse was true for those 60 and older. In 1993, all three of the youngest cohorts' most important problems were economic in nature (the general state of the economy, the federal deficit and national debt, and unemployment). For those 60 and older, unemployment and the federal deficit ranked at the top, followed by two noneconomic domestic problems—health care and crime. These generational differences should not come as any surprise, nor should shifts in rankings that have subsequently taken place in response to changing political and economic conditions.

Past research and my analysis of taxing and spending priorities in Chapter 5 have shown that certain issues are simply more important and relevant at different stages in one's life. I have also found that the more a person thinks a noneconomic issue will have an economic dimension that directly affects him or her, the more likely that person will be to consider the issue important. For the older generations, health and, lately, crime are clearly such issues and are themselves linked. For the young, the issues are more likely to be education and employment.

When economic issues dominate the concerns of most Americans, it generally means that domestic issues prevail over foreign ones. It also means that foreign policy problems and solutions will be judged on the basis of how they affect the domestic economy.[4]

Critical Issues for the Future: Young Middle-Aged Identify More

Periodically, pollsters ask the public which issues are most important to the nation in a more structured, or closed-ended, and futuristic manner. The structured issue list is constantly changing as new situations emerge and more specific policy proposals come before the U.S. public. Though making it difficult to measure change, such questions can still yield valuable insights into the types of issues seen as critical by different age-groups.

Typical of this approach, the Times Mirror Center for The People & The Press surveys regularly present their respondents with a list of issues the country will face over the next few years and ask whether "you personally feel it is a critical issue facing the country, a very important issue, or one that is somewhat important." One interesting finding from these inquiries is that the young middle-aged (30- to 49-year-olds) tend to judge considerably *more* problems as "critical" than the other age-groups. This is the age-group that has the most contact with and responsibility for the young (their children) and the old (their parents and grandparents), which probably means that its members see more issues in personal terms (the economy, jobs, schools, health, crime, the environment, and family values).

Age-groups vary little in their judgments about the critical nature of some issues—namely, abortion, gay rights, or dealing with changes and conflicts in other parts of the world. This does not mean that age-groups don't differ on these issues; rather, it means that from a broad perspective, these issues are not perceived to be as important as other issues. Age-groups do differ considerably on the critical nature of certain other issues, and they differ in the expected direction. For example, the young are more likely than the older cohorts to judge economic conditions, protection of U.S. jobs, improving public school education, protecting the environment, and dealing with the homeless as critical issues.

However, on several issues—for example, developing a health care plan for all Americans, reducing the federal deficit, and reducing crime—age-group differences go in a direction opposite to what we might expect. For example, more young than old see health care and crime reduction as critical issues facing the nation. How can this be explained? On closer inspection, this pattern is not as unusual as it may seem. Recall that in Chapter 5, I noted that the young were willing to spend more on Social Security, Medicare, and other social problems than the elderly themselves were. Though skeptical about how much in benefits they will receive in retirement, the young are nonetheless enthusiastic in supporting those programs. Moreover, older persons as a rule are less inclined to label a problem as "critical" or to believe that government intervention is necessarily the best way— or even an effective way—to solve societal problems either at home or abroad. (I will discuss the last point later in this chapter.)

DOMESTIC POLICY ISSUES

In 1996, the largest generation ever in U.S. history will start turning 50. The baby boomers, those 76 million people born between 1946 and 1963, will greet middle age with their own expectations of how they will live and work. "They will make middle age and old age the dominant focus of society, just as they did youth in the '60s and '70s and yuppies in the '80s," remarked Ken Dychtwald, who made baby boomers the focus of his book *Age Wave.*[5] Experts agree that the "graying of America" will affect a multitude of domestic issues, particularly health care and Social Security. "But people may not realize that it's going to affect what we see on TV, how we drive, what kind of housing is built, and what's for sale in the grocery store."[6]

In looking at how age-groups view domestic issues, it is difficult to determine precisely whether the differences in the attitudes they express are the result of a maturational, period, or cohort effect (for a review of these terms, see Chapter 1). As previously noted, surveys that attempt to gauge public reaction to new or revised policy proposals rarely repeat exactly the same questions at different points in time or track the same respondents from one poll to the next. But even with less-than-ideal data, certain patterns can be observed in the responses.

General Policy Stances of Older Americans

In *What Older Americans Think,* Christine Day reviewed a large number of studies that contrasted the opinions of older and younger Americans prior to the 1990s. Focusing on older Americans, she identified certain opinion patterns:

Older Americans, while showing little ideological consistency across issues, tend to be more favorable toward policies of particular importance to the elderly, both compared to other age groups and relative to other types of issues. . . . Older people [are] generally more conservative on social issues such as abortion, pollution, legalization of marijuana, and women's roles, as well as on questions of civil rights and law and order. Their foreign policy opinions tend to be more isolationist. Their positions on domestic economic policy are more mixed, but tend to fall along group-interest lines.[7]

It is true, as revealed in Chapter 5, that attitudes on domestic economic issues reflect the rational self-interests of an age group. Deeper insight into the attitudes of older Americans can be gained by remembering the historical periods through which they lived. As James Michener, at age 86, wrote:

> We survived a depression, fought and won a world conflict and helped establish a new world order. In peace, our enthusiasm and energy enabled our country to become the richest and most powerful of nations. And we pioneered social innovations like accepting African-Americans to full membership in the armed services, opening opportunities for women, and laws which gave the less fortunate segments of our population better breaks. . . . And because we had been separated from our families for protracted periods, we rushed to produce an enormous crop of babies who would form a new generation to replace us.[8]

General Policy Stances of Younger Americans

Other studies have focused on uncovering patterns in the opinions of the young. Historically, these overviews have concluded that younger Americans are "more liberal in terms of racial equality, sexual equality, political tolerance, and . . . two social issues (pornography and marijuana)."[9]

Most attribute the young's more liberal inclinations to changes in society at large over the past several decades: "Older people grew up at a time when the country was more conservative on these issues; but the country as a whole has become more and more liberal on noneconomic issues (except for certain social issues) over the last thirty years, and younger people have adopted the more liberal norms at a faster rate than the older people."[10] Studies prior to the 1990s found few differences between the young and the old on capital punishment, abortion, and gun control.

A more recent study examined changes in the issue stances of 20- to 29-year-olds between 1972 and 1991. It concluded that although they have become more liberal on racial equality and sexual equality issues, the young have become more conservative on certain social and crime-related issues, such as abortion, pornography, marijuana, treatment of criminals, and capital punishment.[11] But so have older persons, suggesting that more of a period effect rather than a maturational effect comes into play here.

The growing conservatism among the young no doubt reflects their experiences with current social problems. One widely quoted assessment by 29-year-old Robert Lukefahr summed up this attitude: "Free love got the Boomers laid; it gave us AIDS. Marijuana, cocaine and LSD brought Boomers the 'enlightenment' to believe Jim Morrison was a poet; it brought us gang warfare. When Boomers pursued alternative family structures, they got a chance to pursue their ambitions; we got absentee parents and latchkeys."[12]

Another young writer, 27-year-old Ian Williams, contrasted his generation's view of the future with that of the baby boomers in this way:

Have you ever lived in a time when you felt America was on the right path, heading in the right direction, with a wonderful future? With few exceptions, anyone born after 1960 cannot. Even the brief moment of national hubris that erupted when Reagan took office seems like a good dinner date that went awry. We have lived our entire lives in this country without a blueprint for national sanity, whereas boomers grew up with some sense of convention, potential, and stability. In simpler terms, we wouldn't know a truly wonderful world if it slapped us in the face.[13]

I will now consider the domestic issues followed most closely by the young and the old and those projected to spark the greatest intergenerational conflicts in the 1990s. When possible, I will focus on reactions to specific policy proposals, rather than simple attitudes toward the problem in general.

What Do Elected Officials See as Major Policy Concerns of Each Generation?

A 1994 survey of Florida's state legislators showed that on the economic front, the young were most concerned about the economy and jobs; the old, about taxes and government spending (see Table 6.1). On noneconomic domestic issues, the young were most attentive to crime, educational, environmental, and moral issues. The old closely followed crime, health, social service, and moral issues.

Florida's legislators have identified moral, tax, social service, and health issues as those evoking the most intergenerational conflicts. These perceived conflict-generating issues form the primary focus of my discussion of domestic policy. Many new legislative proposals aimed at addressing each have been introduced or reintroduced at the national, state, and local levels since the beginning of the 1990s. The most sweeping proposals have been in regard to health care.

Health Care Policy

One-seventh of the U.S. economy is devoted to health care. This sector exceeds the military industrial complex in terms of spending, employment, exports, or installations. Nearly half (47 percent) of all the dollars spent on health go to hospitals and nursing homes; 28 percent to physicians, dentists, and other professionals; 9 percent to drugs and medical devices; 3 percent to public health programs; 1.5 percent to research; 1 percent to construction; 4 percent to home care of the elderly and disabled and to school and industrial infirmaries; and 6 percent to administrative costs. The rising cost of health care evokes nearly as much concern as the number of uninsured or underinsured Americans.

Many studies have focused on Americans' attitudes toward government spending on health care, as noted in Chapter 5. "General support for government spending on medical care has tended to rise and fall somewhat with the strength of the economy and the perceived urgency of medical costs and problems, but it has always been quite high," according to Page and Shapiro in *The Rational Public*.

They concluded: "Most Americans favor certain kinds of government help with medical care, especially health insurance, medical care for the needy, and promotion of medical research." In fact, "assistance with medical care has come to be viewed as an entitlement, with popularity comparable to that of Social Security."[14]

Over the years, pollsters have asked Americans whether they favor a universal health care system and how health insurance should be provided—via government or the private sector. As Page and Shapiro noted, "Many survey questions have indicated that large majorities [in the 70 percentiles] favor a 'national health insurance system' that would cover everyone [universal coverage]." But when respondents are asked whether they favor a government health insurance plan or a system financed via individual contributions and private insurance, support for a government health insurance plan drops closer to or below 50 percent.

Since the 1970s, support for government-financed health insurance has dwindled somewhat across all age-groups. The drop-off has been sharpest among the oldest cohort. By 1994, a considerably higher percentage of young, as compared to old, believed that the government should bear the greatest responsibility for making sure Americans are covered by health insurance. The oldest cohort laid more of the responsibility on individuals and their families.[15]

Increased spending on health care in the United States has had some positive and negative consequences. Allen Schick, a noted budget analyst, put it this way: "Increased spending has vastly improved access to medical care, modestly extended life expectancy, and somewhat relieved the financial strains of illness. It has also led to a great deal of complaining about the health care system. Physicians gripe about the paperwork and the controls, hospitals about cost pressures and frequent rules changes, and patients about inadequate coverage. Just about everyone complains . . . yet costs continue to soar."[16]

Cost Control Versus Universal Access. Prompted by the development and release of President Clinton's health care reform bill, public opinion surveys began asking trade-off questions to better discern the public's stance on the issue of cost control versus expanded access. An April 1993 question by the Times Mirror Center for The People & The Press asked: "What do you think is a more important goal for the nation: to find a way to limit the overall annual increase in health care costs, or to change the system so that all Americans are guaranteed access to all medically necessary care?"[17] Across all age-groups, the overwhelming majority chose universal access. In line with other findings, the youngest cohort was the most supportive of the universal access choice (81 percent); the oldest cohort was the least supportive (67.5 percent). The elderly's more lukewarm reaction to universal health care was related to their concerns about the government's role in such a system.

Most Significant Health Care Problems Facing the United States. Recent surveys of the U.S. public have asked respondents to identify the most important health care issues facing the country today. A Times Mirror survey taken near the beginning of the Clinton national health care reform debate asked this open-ended question: "What do you think is the most significant health care problem facing the country today?"[18] Among the youngest cohort (18 to 29), the two most commonly cited problems were the cost of health care (28 percent) and AIDS/HIV (17 percent). Among the other age-groups, these same two issues were also cited most frequently, although the relative proportion of respondents citing costs was higher, especially in the 30- to 49-year-old group. These rankings reflect the heavy media focus on these issues around the time the survey was taken. They also reflect a greater awareness of health care costs among the older cohorts.

Major Health Problems for Individuals and Their Families. Conventional wisdom suggests that "Americans evaluate health care reform mainly in terms of how it affects them personally."[19] Clear differences among age-groups exist in the rankings and intensity of their attitudes. For the youngest cohort, the major problems were security—the possibility of losing insurance if one changes or loses a job—and the cost of paying for a major illness, which were cited by 64 and 60 percent, respectively. Among the oldest cohorts, the most-often cited problem was the prospect of paying the cost of long-term care in a nursing home (70 to 78 percent).[20]

The most-stressed group seemed to be the 30-to 49-year-olds. High and nearly equal proportions (60 to 70 percent) of them cited four major problems: paying for long-term health care for themselves or a family member (mostly the latter), possibly losing their insurance as a consequence of changing or losing a job, paying the cost of a major illness, and possibly having an employer cut back their health care benefits or having to pay a larger share of their own health care costs.[21] Their higher levels of concern reflect their status as the "sandwich generation," charged with caring for the youngest and oldest cohorts of our society.

It is not surprising that a large percentage of each age-group mentioned long-term care and nursing home expenses as a major problem. Individuals and their families pay nearly half (44 percent) of the costs of nursing homes. In fact, for the nonpoor elderly, a substantial portion of their health care (37 percent) is not paid for by any government program, including Medicare. The need for long-term care will only escalate as the nation grows older.[22] And costs will rise as more of the elderly who need nursing home care stay there longer.

In the future, more older people with infirmities are likely to choose home or hospice care over moving into a nursing home or a child's home, thanks to technological advancements. As noted in *American Demographics* magazine, "Portable respirators and infusion pumps allow people with cancer, internal infections, and other serious medical problems to get effective treatment at home."[23] This change will require that some tough decisions be made on rationing health care. Currently, at least two-thirds of all home care assistance is provided free by family or friends—and that situation is not likely to continue.

Health Care Reform Priorities. Naturally, the health care problems experienced by different age-groups affect their priorities vis-à-vis health care reform. When asked whether various reform proposals "should be a top priority of health care reform, important but not a top priority, or not too important," the age-groups differed most with regard to reducing the amount of paperwork involved in health care, making long-term nursing home care more affordable, and making health insurance coverage universal. Predictably, the oldest cohort ranked affordable long-term nursing home care and reduction of paperwork much higher than the youngest cohort, most of whom face neither of these problems at their stage of life. Conversely, providing health insurance coverage for those who cannot now afford it ranked as a much higher priority for the youngest cohort,[24] who were more likely to be in lower-paying or part-time jobs, with few or no health benefits.

The strongest support for reforms encouraging preventive care came from the 30-to 49-year-olds—those who were most aware of the benefits and cost-savings of such approaches due to their own experiences with children and with elderly relatives who have not taken care of themselves.[25]

Reform Versus Service Reductions: Little Consensus. When strong support exists for both cost reduction and major restructuring of a service delivery system, something has to give. And usually, the major restructuring is scaled back. Early phases of the national health care reform debate have shown how this happens.

The pressure for major health care reform escalated sharply in the early 1990s. Surveys by Louis Harris and Associates revealed that the percent of Americans believing "our health care system has so much wrong with it that we need to completely rebuild it" jumped from 28 percent in 1982 to 42 percent in 1991.[26] By April 1993, it had leaped to 55 percent.[27] But by January 1994, it had dipped back down to 42 percent.[28] As the debate over reform further educated the public about the choices that would have to be made to rebuild the system, support for radical reform began to diminish. Warning signs that this would happen appeared even in the early polls.

Health care reform without cost—and tax—increases is not easy to achieve, economically or politically. Surveys show that a majority of Americans favor government limits on health care spending if there's no other way to control costs, but there is no strong consensus on this approach, although a majority favor it. Those between 30 and 49 years of age were the most supportive of this approach (62 percent); the least supportive were those 65 and older (55 percent).[29]

There is even less consensus on what changes people are willing to accept in a new health care system. A Times Mirror survey inquired about Americans' willingness to accept (1) a slower introduction of new medical procedures and technologies into hospitals, (2) longer waiting periods for nonemergency medical and hospital care, and (3) more restrictions on one's choice of doctors and hospitals (see Table 6.2). A majority of those younger than 65 preferred to wait longer for nonemergency medical and hospital care. Among those 65 and older, less than a majority were willing to accept *any* of these sacrifices. Of the three sacrifices, they tended to favor slowing the introduction of new medical procedures and technologies, although not by much.

All three groups gave the least support for restricting one's choice of doctors, although this option was more popular among the 30- to 49-year-olds than any other age-group. Higher proportions of the younger cohorts are in health maintenance organization (HMO) insurance plans that already restrict doctor choice.

Any plan, governmental or private, that is perceived as restricting the right to choose one's own doctor generates concern. Surveys such as the one conducted in June 1993 by the Gallup Organization for *Phi Delta Kappan* have shown that a majority of Americans (58 percent) would choose an "expensive health care program that allows you to choose your own doctor" over an "inexpensive health care program that does not allow you to choose your own doctor."[30]

Concern for the Role of Government in Health Care. Another part of the explanation for the drop in support for the original Clinton health care reform package was concern over the role of government. As previously noted, polls have long shown that the stronger the role of government in health care is, the less enthusiastic the public becomes. By September 1993, the public had already figured out that the government's role would expand tremendously under the health care reform package introduced in early 1993. A majority of all age-groups said that under the Clinton health care reform plan, the government would have the most influence—more than doctors, hospitals, and insurance companies.[31]

Americans more readily accept government intervention in health concerns that are viewed as harmful to individuals and society at large, as long as they do not involve moral issues. Government policies (especially educational ones) aimed at reducing smoking and alcohol abuse have been popular across all age-groups[32]—and effective as well.[33] Even so, when respondents are asked whether the government should interfere with the right of individuals to make their own choices and then penalize them for making those choices, including the choice to use tobacco, support drops.[34]

Government policies and social programs aimed at reducing teen-aged pregnancies, sexually transmitted diseases, and drug abuse are more controversial. For example, a June 1993 *Wall Street Journal*/NBC News poll found that only 55 percent of Americans agree with the idea of distributing condoms in schools to prevent diseases and unwanted pregnancies. The public is also skeptical about whether government-run programs work, especially in drug abuse prevention and treatment.[35] Predictably, government intervention programs aimed at the young are more strongly supported by the younger cohorts than the older ones.

Euthanasia—the taking of life to relieve suffering—has evoked strong support across all age-groups, especially among the elderly, for quite some time. Some authorities distinguish between passive and active euthanasia. In passive euthanasia, a person who chooses to die is allowed to die, usually by having life-sustaining medical treatment withheld in a terminal illness. In active euthanasia, a doctor or someone else helps a patient bring life to an end, as publicized in court cases involving Dr. Jack Kevorkian and a number of assisted suicides.[36] A September 1993 survey by Voter/Consumer Research for the Family Research Council found that almost two-thirds (62 percent) of the public agreed "that it should be legal to help people who do not want to live any longer to end their life."[37] A similar question has been asked regularly by the National Opinion Research Center. Between 1977 and 1985, support for laws allowing a doctor "to end the patient's life by some painless means if the patient and his family requested it" ranged from 60 to 80 percent.

Age differences clearly exist on the right-to-die issue (see Figure 6.1). The old are much more in favor of stopping treatment if there is no hope of recovery or if illness makes a person too dependent upon others. However, the old are far less supportive of taking the life of a spouse suffering from a terminal disease.

Intergenerational conflicts in health care policy will intensify in situations in which health care rationing becomes necessary. This overview of age-group attitudes toward choices has shown that the preferences of the young and old often differ considerably. When disease-specific funding and care choices are posed to the public, the differences will be even more dramatic—and controversial—in a world of limited resources. Studies are finding that an imbalance in health care spending between the young and the elderly already exists, especially for children in families with low incomes.[38] The long-standing argument about prevention versus reaction lies at the heart of this debate. Children's advocates clearly stress the prevention dimension in health care and other social issues (see Figure 6.2).

Crime and Criminal Justice Policy

As an issue, crime evokes fear and dread across all age-groups. A May 1988 survey that asked respondents whether they were concerned about becoming a crime victim found that more than 70 percent of each age-group, except those older than 70 (65 percent), admitted to having this fear.[39] By the mid-1990s, survey after survey showed that two-thirds of Americans worried more about crime than they had five years earlier; only one in twenty-five worried less.[40] And they feared that crime was coming closer to home. More than half of those 65 and older could point to an area within a mile of their homes where they were afraid to walk alone at night.

Punishment Versus Rehabilitation: Young and Old Alike Are Hard-Liners. Since the early 1970s, Americans have increasingly supported stringent punishment for criminals. One study examining survey results between 1960 and 1988 reported, "From the mid-1960s to the mid-1980s, support for the death penalty increased by about 30 percentage points, and the number of Americans saying that courts were treating criminals too leniently jumped by almost 40 percentage points."[41] Rising crime rates prompted these responses and narrowed the gaps between the young and the old.

Harris surveys found that between 1970 and 1982, the percent who said the main emphasis in most prisons should be on punishing the individual and protecting society from future crimes, rather than on rehabilitation, rose from 21 to 54 percent.[42] And Gallup surveys showed that the percent who thought it more im-

FIGURE 6.1 Views on a Person's Right to Die: Older More in Favor—Up to a Point

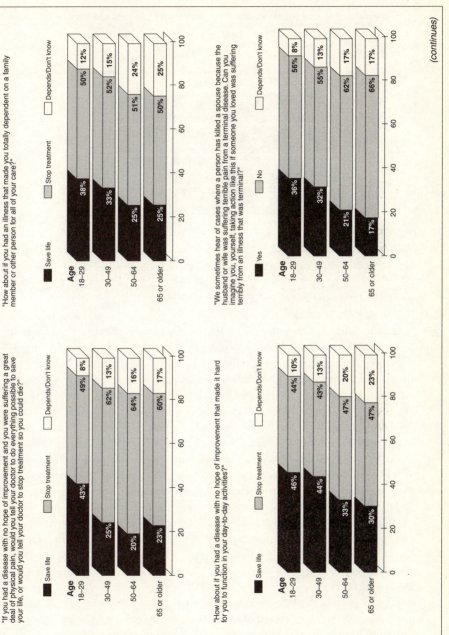

"If you had a disease with no hope of improvement and you were suffering a great deal of physical pain, would you tell your doctor to do everything possible to save your life, or would you tell your doctor to stop treatment so you could die?"

■ Save life ▨ Stop treatment □ Depends/Don't know

Age
18–29   43%   49%   8%
30–49   25%   62%   13%
50–64   20%   64%   16%
65 or older   23%   60%   17%

"How about if you had a disease with no hope of improvement that made it hard for you to function in your day-to-day activities?"

■ Save life ▨ Stop treatment □ Depends/Don't know

Age
18–29   46%   44%   10%
30–49   44%   43%   13%
50–64   33%   47%   20%
65 or older   30%   47%   23%

"How about if you had an illness that made you totally dependent on a family member or other person for all of your care?"

■ Save life ▨ Stop treatment □ Depends/Don't know

Age
18–29   38%   50%   12%
30–49   33%   52%   15%
50–64   25%   51%   24%
65 or older   25%   50%   25%

"We sometimes hear of cases where a person has killed a spouse because the husband or wife was suffering terrible pain from a terminal disease. Can you imagine you, yourself, taking action like this if someone you loved was suffering terribly from an illness that was terminal?"

■ Yes ▨ No □ Depends/Don't know

Age
18–29   36%   56%   8%
30–49   32%   55%   13%
50–64   21%   62%   17%
65 or older   17%   66%   17%

(continues)

FIGURE 6.1 *(cont.)*

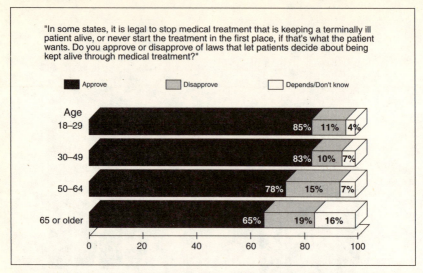

"In some states, it is legal to stop medical treatment that is keeping a terminally ill patient alive, or never start the treatment in the first place, if that's what the patient wants. Do you approve or disapprove of laws that let patients decide about being kept alive through medical treatment?"

Approve ▮   Disapprove ▨   Depends/Don't know □

Age	Approve	Disapprove	Depends/Don't know
18–29	85%	11%	4%
30–49	83%	10%	7%
50–64	78%	15%	7%
65 or older	65%	19%	16%

Source: The Times Mirror Center for The People & The Press, *Reflections of the Times: The Right to Die,* Washington, D.C.: Times Mirror Center for The People & The Press, 1990, pp. 10–13. Based on a telephone survey of a nationally representative sample of 1,213 adults age 18 years of age or older, conducted May 1-5, 1990. Reprinted with permission.

portant to "punish [those in prison] for their crimes," rather than "get them started 'on the right road,'" rose from 17 percent in July 1955 to 44 percent by June 1989.[43]

Americans also have increasingly supported victim rights and the right of society to be protected from criminals. In situations where the choice is protection of the rights of the accused (individual rights) versus protection of society at large, they have opted for the latter. For example, the percentage of Americans who agreed that "the police should be allowed to search the houses of known drug dealers without a court order" jumped from 48 percent in 1987 to 58 percent in 1990—in just three years' time.[44] Traditionally, younger cohorts have been less supportive than the old of diluting the rights of the accused, but the gap has narrowed; in May 1990, it was only 6 percent (59 percent among the young and 65 percent among the old).

Another area in which a sizable portion of the public favors the protection and safety of society over individual rights is drug testing of government employees. The two oldest cohorts are much more in favor of mandatory drug tests for government employees than the two youngest cohorts. The least supportive is the 30- to 49-year-old group—those socialized in the 1960s and the heaviest users of illegal substances today. However, even a majority of these people approve drug testing: 59 percent, as compared to 74 percent of those 60 and older, 71 percent of those 50 to 59, and 64 percent of those younger than 30.[45]

Crime in the 1990s: The Role of the Media. The media and entertainment industries often bear the brunt of the blame for creating the public's growing frenzy

FIGURE 6.2 Children Are a Good Investment

▶ **$1** spent on childhood immunizations or **$10** in later medical costs.

▶ **$1** spent on quality pre-school education or **$4.75** for later special education, crime, welfare, and other costs.

▶ **$765** spent per month for homelessness prevention and support services or **$3,000** to shelter a homeless family.

▶ **$3,925** spent for complete prenatal care and obstetric health package or **$70,000** for the first year of a baby born with low birth-weight and with developmental delays.

▶ **$5,000** spent on drug treatment services for an addicted mother for nine months or **$30,000** for medical care of a drug-exposed baby for 20 days.

▶ **$6,700** spent per youth per year for intensive community-based services or **$40,000** to maintain a youth at a correctional facility.

Source: Children's Board of Hillsborough County, "A Community That Cares," *The Tampa Tribune*, August 26, 1993, p. 2. Reprinted with permission.

of fear about crime and violence. A February 1993 survey by the Times Mirror Center for The People & The Press asked a series of questions on the media's role in promoting fear—and crime itself. The results showed clear age-group differences in the responses to most of these inquiries. Younger cohorts were less bothered by TV violence and saw a weaker link between the media's crime coverage and violent behavior.[46]

Nonetheless, overwhelming majorities of all age-groups (80 to 89 percent) agreed that "television news stories about violence have made Americans more fearful than they were in the days before there was television." They also agreed that "violence on TV shows is harmful to society" (77 to 84 percent) and that "television shows so much violence that people grow up not being shocked by violence" (75 to 81 percent).[47]

The most troubling part of the last statistic is that the young are by far the heaviest viewers of violence[48]—and the group that has contributed most to the sharp rise in its occurrence. In 1991 alone, 57 percent of all those arrested and charged with committing serious crimes were younger than 25 years of age;[49] this age-group also made up 55 percent of those arrested for murder and non-negligent manslaughter. According to FBI statistics, arrests of juveniles younger than 18 for violent offenses increased by more than 57 percent between 1983 and 1992. In that same period, weapons violations among juveniles increased 117 percent, and murder and non-negligent manslaughter rose 128 percent. In addition, the young are more often victims of violent crime than the old.

Ways to Reduce Violent Crime. The extensive press coverage and growing popularity of three-strikes-and-you're-out laws limiting a criminal's chances for parole have created the perception that little support exists for more preventive approaches. This is not totally the case, although there is certainly more support for getting tough with criminals.

A December 1993 survey that asked which techniques "would reduce violent crime in this country a lot, a little, or not at all" showed variance between different age-groups (see Table 6.3). The youngest cohort gave equal support (58 percent) to longer jail terms for those convicted of violent crimes (a punishment approach) and to jobs programs for inner-city areas (a preventive approach). The oldest cohort saw longer jail terms (65 percent) and more restrictions on the amount of violence shown on TV (65 percent) as the most promising ways to reduce violent crime, although more than half (54 percent) of this group also mentioned jobs programs for inner-city areas. Less than half of any age-group saw stricter gun control laws as effective, even after the debate surrounding passage of the Brady Bill, which provided for handgun control through registration and background checks.

Citizen Involvement to Reduce Crime. A 1994 survey by the Times Mirror Center for The People & The Press asked respondents what kinds of personal sacrifices they would be willing to make to reduce crime. More than 60 percent of each age-group indicated they were willing to pay higher taxes for more police and law enforcement. There was also strong support for joining neighborhood Crime Watch groups, although the elderly were less likely to see themselves doing so, most likely because of their physical limitations. The greatest age differences appeared in regard to volunteering personal time to work with young people from poor families in the inner cities (87 percent of those 18 to 29, 46 percent of those 65 and older) and in support of gun control. The elderly were far less supportive of limiting their right to own a gun for sport or personal protection, which is not surprising in light of their higher fear levels.[50]

Gun Control

Analysts warn that although gun control "is obviously connected with issues of crime and punishment, the relationship is not as straightforward as one might think."[51] The way in which questions on gun control are asked makes a world of difference. Surveys that ask whether gun ownership should be prohibited outright yield vastly different results than those asking whether certain types of guns should be prohibited, restricted in their use, registered, or subjected to a waiting period before purchase.

Although the proportion of those favoring some sort of gun control has jumped, paralleling rising crime rates and public angst and anger, there is still no strong consensus on this issue. The public is divided on whether it's more important to control guns (protect society) or to protect an individual's right to own a gun. Among the youngest cohort, there's considerably more support for controlling guns (64 percent). Older people are more evenly divided, although they still give more importance to gun control than to the right to own a gun.[52]

But when it comes to whether one "would favor or oppose a law that banned the sale of handguns," a majority of all age-groups, except those 65 and older, oppose such an outright ban.[53] The percent favoring the restriction of handgun sales dropped between 1990 and 1993 across all age-groups. These patterns reflect an underlying fear that "if guns are outlawed, only outlaws will have guns." They also demonstrate the public's concern that there are not enough police on the streets to deal with the crime problems affecting the average person, which means that individuals are often left to protect themselves. Media reports of successful acts of self-defense by average citizens against intruders or attackers has sparked the sale of handguns and other personal defense mechanisms to the public, especially women.

On crime, the key generational differences lie in the degree to which punishment, or reactive, strategies should prevail over more preventive strategies and in how closely violent criminal behavior is linked to violent program content in the media (news and entertainment). Generational outlooks and preferences on crime, though different, are still more similar than those on moral issues.

Moral and Social Issue Policy

Moral issues evoke vastly different opinions across the generations. Government policies promoting new forms of individual expression or alternative lifestyles often generate intense debate. At issue is whether these new social policies designed to protect individual rights weaken U.S. society as a whole. Another critical element of this debate is the extent of governmental involvement in regulating actions that are perceived by many Americans to be highly personal—and private.

It used to be that a moral issue was one that challenged traditional values and whose supporters and opponents were divided along religious and ideological lines. Some examples are abortion, prayer in the schools, and gay rights. In contrast, a social issue was one affecting society at large but some groups more than others. Examples are poverty, crime, education, and race relations. However, by the mid-1990s, many Americans perceived that moral (or values) issues were connected to social issues: "Even those who deeply disagree about how to handle social problems are coming to agree on the importance of values issues."[54]

The public's growing concern for the values issues has paralleled the sharp increases in juvenile crime, teenaged pregnancy, and school dropout rates. By mid-1993, three-fourths of the Americans surveyed strongly agreed that "traditional values have grown weaker and need to be strengthened." Strong support came from all age-groups but was strongest among the older cohorts, who tended to stress the importance of the traditional family unit (see Figure 6.3). At the same time, 77 percent agreed that the government should not pass laws regulating

FIGURE 6.3 Age & Perceptions of What Constitutes "Family Values"

Family values as a campaign theme is a big smoke screen. Let's talk about the real problems we all face. Family values are whatever any family sees as important in their family's life (love, trust, etc.). Since it cannot be defined, it makes a great issue, if we can't see through it. Get real! *73-year-old Presbyterian female.*

Self-discipline, self-reliance, integrity and honesty, love (of) neighbor, service to humankind, accepting those whose beliefs are different. *69-year-old United Methodist male.*

The way I think of family values is, so long as my child does not steal, murder or hurt anyone else or the environment, then he's fine. The rest are religious moral issues which keep the USA backward compared to Europe or the rest of modern society. *28-year-old female.*

Teaching the Golden Rule to children and the meaning of truth, caring and sharing. Most families are so busy just living day to day and making ends meet, it seems they have no time to teach ... life's lessons. *42-year-old Catholic female.*

... Bonding together in love of family members, friends and neighbors and reaching out in time of need to help one another, emotionally, spiritually and, if necessary, financially. It's being there for one another. *57-year-old Catholic female.*

Family values cannot be generalized. One family does not need to agree with another, and no candidate should run on a platform of trying to instill his family's values on the rest of the country. *20-year-old female.*

Teach children to respect and understand people, regardless of race, color, religion, and sexual orientation. Education in the home and school is the key. *34-year-old male non-practicing Catholic.*

A home where the parent or parents not only teach but themselves practice decent morals, thus giving the children incentive and motivation to grow up and continue to be morally responsible adults, parents ... and citizens. *64-year-old female.*

All people are loving members of the human family, with no exclusion of any individual. *52-year-old male.*

Do the best you can with what you have. Put your kids first and be open and honest with them. The lines of communication must stay open at all times. *32-year-old female.*

It's about as clear to me as the term "the cultural elite." *43-year-old Methodist female.*

Live to the best and highest standard your family can achieve, then try to understand and relate to standards of others. *75-year-old male.*

Family values is whatever it means to the individual and his or her private family. We're too diversified to set any strong guidelines. I do believe most families are a sick mess in the U.S. TV and the movies (have) a lot to do about it. *37-year-old female.*

Nurturing and caring for one another. Being honest and truthful, instilling a sense of ethics, morality, fair play and tolerance to our fellow humans of all races and faiths. To allow one another to make their own choices and support their right to do so. To promote an open communication, to give to and help those less fortunate. To be kind and to always live by the Golden Rule and the Ten Commandments. *46-year-old Lutheran female.*

Two or more people with a common interest who are supportive of each other. *60-year-old male.*

Teaching respect, compassion for others regardless of race, gender, illness, religion, income or sexual preference or orientation. *36-year-old male.*

Family values is not something anyone else can define for me, especially a politician. Family values cannot be dictated by anyone other than the individual. *39-year-old female.*

An environment in which older and younger persons can effectively communicate to one another, which stimulates the thoughts and beliefs that ultimately provide the foundation for decision-making among the younger persons. *27-year-old male.*

"Family values" is political nonsense, a phrase used by those who have nothing to offer to gain votes from people unwilling or unable to think through the real issues. *51-year-old female.*

Family values to me means love and compassion for others, a love for home and family and country, and Christian values. I believe too much stress is placed on the typical (so-called) family unit (father, mother and children) when many remain single through choice or otherwise, and are just as deserving of respect and recognition. (I am married with children and grandchildren.) *73-year-old Southern Baptist female.*

Does anyone know exactly what family values are? A perfect family would be wonderful, but who is to say what's "perfect" and what's not? *81-year-old Catholic female.*

Source: Associated Press, "Minority Population to Keep Growing," *St. Petersburg Times,* September 29, 1993, p. 1A. Reprinted with permission.

morality and how people live their private lives.[55] The young voiced more support for this view than the old but not by much.

The Cause of Moral Decline. The public is far more divided on what has prompted the breakdown of traditional values. A 1993 survey by *The Wall Street Journal*/NBC News showed "a deep split among Americans on whether today's social problems are caused by economic stresses and strains that tear at the fabric of the traditional family structure, or by more basic changes in the soul of the country."[56] Not surprisingly, the young were more likely to cite economics, the old, the decline of the traditional family structure.

In the 1990s, the most publicized public policy issues regarded as having strong moral and social overtones are abortion, gay rights, school prayer, pornography, women's and minorities' rights, adoption rights, and medical ethics, especially with regard to procreation. Based on previous age-group patterns, one would expect that on all these issues, older persons would favor the more traditional, or status quo, approaches.

Abortion. Abortion is a multifaceted issue that can evoke widely fluctuating opinions depending upon how questions are posed. The issue itself "raises a tangle of questions involving a woman's right to control her body (e.g., after rape or incest), the proper treatment of fetuses with genetic defects, and the sanctity of human life—along with the question of when human life begins."[57]

If simply asked whether "women should have the right to choose an abortion," two-thirds of Americans agreed.[58] Higher percentages (in the 80 percentiles) supported the right to have an abortion under certain circumstances: when pregnancy poses a health danger to the woman, if the baby might have a defect, or if the pregnancy resulted from a rape or incest. Smaller percentages (40 to 46 percent) favored allowing abortion if the family could not afford any more children, if a married woman simply did not want any more children, if an unmarried woman did not want to marry the father, or because the woman wanted the abortion for whatever reason.[59] In each instance, the young were more supportive of abortion rights than the old.

The *Webster* ruling by the U.S. Supreme Court in 1989 allowed states to restrict abortion. Few states have done so, primarily because support for laws making it tougher for a woman to get an abortion has been slipping. Support for more restrictive laws governing abortion has dropped off the most among 30- to 49-year-old women and elderly women. By 1993, there was little difference between the oldest and youngest cohorts on the right to obtain an abortion in most situations. Some opinion analysts, like Mayer, say this pattern refutes the thesis that "the elderly become more rigid and set in their opinions and thus more resistant to any kind of change."[60]

Clearer age-group distinctions still existed when the abortion-related restriction question was whether the government should require parental consent before girls younger than 18 can have an abortion. Predictably, the young were much less in favor of such an approach. Overall, two-thirds of Americans, more older than younger, believed that requiring parental consent is one governmental approach that might strengthen families and family values.[61]

Gay Rights. Americans' personal opinions about homosexuality differ sharply from their notions about how government should respond to this issue. Throughout the 1970s and 1980s, surveys consistently showed that between 70 and 80 percent of the U.S. public personally believed that homosexual relations are wrong. Less than half of any age group felt "homosexuality is a lifestyle that should be accepted by society."[62] The gulf between the young and the old on gay rights issues has always been wide and remains so in the 1990s.

Surveys between the 1970s and early 1990s tended to focus on whether Americans thought homosexuality should be legalized and whether gays and lesbians should be restricted by law from certain occupations. On the question of legalization, support fluctuated between 38 and 57 percent. Support dropped when AIDS first hit the press and was defined as a gay disease, but it has gone up again as the public has become more educated about the disease. Nonetheless, a survey showed that a sizable portion of Americans still thought "AIDS might be God's punishment for immoral sexual behavior" (35 percent of those 18 to 29, 42 percent of those 65 and older).[63]

Although support for equal job opportunities for gays has grown stronger, nearly half the public still expressed uneasiness with gays serving in the military or as high school teachers, members of the clergy, or elementary school teachers.[64] The young favored restrictions far less than the old.[65]

Even on this highly charged issue, Americans still showed some reluctance about government intrusion into an individual's private life. For example, a June 1993 *Wall Street Journal*/NBC News survey found that only 21 percent opposed gays and lesbians serving in the military under any conditions. Another 38 percent said they "should be allowed to serve as long as they keep their homosexuality private, and the military should not ask them about sexual orientation." The remaining 40 percent said they "should be allowed to serve openly, as long as they follow the same rules of conduct as other military personnel while they are on base." The young were much more likely to express support for gays in military service.[66]

Americans of all age-groups apparently are still quite unwilling to endorse laws making it legal for homosexual couples to marry or adopt children, that is, to act as a traditional family unit.

School Prayer. The United States is a religious nation.[67] Surveys over time show few fluctuations in the large proportions of Americans who say that prayer is an important part of their daily lives, that we will all be called before God on Judgment Day to answer for our sins, that even today miracles are performed by the power of God, that they are quite conscious of the presence of God, and that they don't doubt the existence of God. Age makes little difference in these views, with the exception of daily prayer (the elderly pray more).[68] Even when U.S. Supreme Court rulings have restricted prayer in the schools, the support for school prayer among the public has never wavered much.

In June 1993, the U.S. Supreme Court let stand without comment a 1992 ruling by the Fifth U.S. Circuit Court of Appeals in Houston (*Jones* v. *Clearcreek Independent School District*), which concluded that student-initiated prayers were nonproselytizing and nonsectarian and could be read at graduation ceremonies.[69] Since that time, a number of state legislatures across the United States have introduced legislation encouraging voluntary school prayer, permitting daily moments of quiet reflection, or allowing students to lead prayers at various school events. What has brought this issue to the forefront so quickly, when civil libertarians have for so long regarded such legislation as clearly a violation of the separation of church and state? The answer lies in the growing tendency to link moral and social issues.

A *Washington Post* story portrayed the development in this fashion: "The lawmakers, claiming that American public education has lost its moral bearings, insist that in a country where metal detectors are ubiquitous in schools, students deserve to hear the word 'God' again. . . . There's a frustration that for 30 years the ability to pray in school has been taken away, while society has grown more violent, more sexually demonstrative and somehow less morally guided."[70]

Florida State Representative Beryl Burke, a black female legislator representing Miami's mostly black Liberty City neighborhood, expressed this concern well: "We're bringing back to our children the recognition that there is a place for spiritual and moral enlightenment. The whole country is realizing that there were decades when God was left out of our society. We're seeing the error of our ways, and returning to what was good. There's a feeling, 'Let's stop all the talking. Let's just look at where we were before and how things were then.' I really think the people support us on this one."[71]

The old's concern for prayer opportunities for the young has changed little in recent years; one study showed three-fourths of the oldest cohort favored a constitutional amendment to permit prayer in the public schools. However, support among the youngest cohorts has slipped, although not by much. The survey also found that more than 60 percent of them approve of school prayer as well.[72]

Pornography. Americans have never been favorably disposed toward unrestricted access to pornographic materials—or toward pornography in general. Rising crime rates, especially sexual attacks against women and children, have increased concern about this issue. In *American Public Opinion,* Michael Corbett reviewed a number of surveys by Gallup and the National Opinion Research Center and concluded, "The majority position [of Americans] seems to be that pornography should be allowed for adults only, provided it does not involve children or sexual violence. [However,] a substantial minority completely opposes pornography."[73] The young find pornography less harmful than the old, although all age-groups are less willing to regard it as harmless adult entertainment than in the past.

More explicit sexual scenes and topics on television, on the Internet, and in the movies have also prompted various citizens' groups to endorse proposals for heavier government regulation of television and entertainment programming. Nearly a third of all Americans say that the amount of sex on television bothers them even more than the amount of violence—and many see the two as linked. Little difference exists across age-groups on this response.[74] A 1993 *Wall Street Journal*/NBC News poll found that more than half of its respondents, the old more than the young, believed that passing stricter laws regulating violence and sex on television and in the movies would strengthen families and family values.[75] Still, a sizable portion of Americans oppose regulating the press or engaging in anything that looks like government censorship.

Women's Rights. Public support for equality for women has increased significantly since the early 1970s. Support has grown stronger for equal employment opportunities for women and for their election to public office, including the presidency. The notion that women should stay at home with the children rather than work tapered off during the 1970s and 1980s, although the older cohorts always were and still are more in favor of a traditional role for women than the younger cohorts. In a May 1990 survey, more than 45 percent of those 65 and older agreed that "women should return to their traditional role in society," compared to just 23 percent of those younger than 30.[76]

Though favoring equal employment opportunities for women, persons of all age-groups are greatly concerned about the impact of women working on the rearing of America's children. Surveys show a growing concern among a large segment of the population and in all age-groups that "too many children are being raised in day care centers these days."[77] A June 1993 survey found that nearly two-thirds of Americans felt that "passing tax incentives to help mothers of young children stay in the home and not work" would strengthen families and family values.[78] But for many women with young children, that option is simply not economically feasible or even desirable from a professional advancement perspective.

Americans of all ages overwhelmingly support doing "what is necessary to make sure that everyone has an equal opportunity to succeed." Despite agreement among age-groups on this general principle, considerable differences exist in terms of society's pace at achieving this goal. Some 58 percent of those 65 and older think "we have gone too far in pushing equal rights in this country," compared to just 36 percent of those younger than 30. The percentages with this view have inched up in recent years, causing many to project a backlash against affirmative action programs in both the public and private sectors (see Table 6.4).

A majority of the population continues to acknowledge that women have not yet achieved equal employment opportunities (see Figure 6.4), but there is still strong opposition to government-imposed hiring quotas or preferential treatment to achieve balance in the workforce. For example, a 1985 survey by the National Opinion Research Center found that only 12 percent favored giving women preferential treatment when applying for jobs or promotions.[79] Similar patterns show up on racial equality questions.

Racial Equality. Since the mid-1960s, when many civil rights acts were passed, there have been major changes in Americans' attitudes toward racial equality, with the public becoming much more liberal and egalitarian. Over the years, voluminous numbers of survey questions, too many to report here, have tracked the

FIGURE 6.4 Discrimination Against Women: The Glass Ceiling

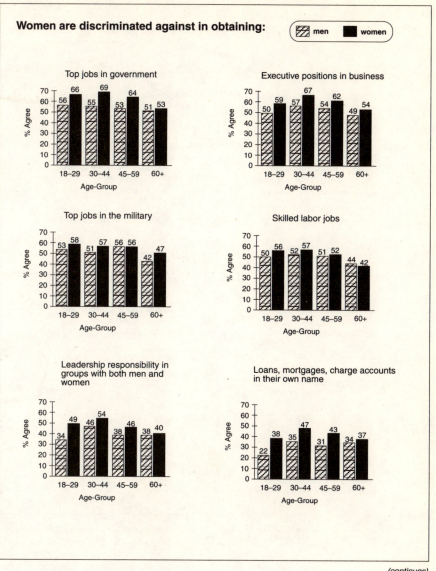

(continues)

FIGURE 6.4 (cont.)

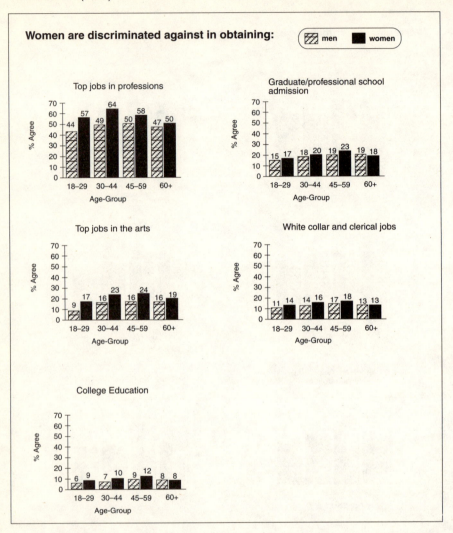

Women are discriminated against in obtaining:

men women

Top jobs in professions

Graduate/professional school admission

Top jobs in the arts

White collar and clerical jobs

College Education

Source: Virginia Slims Poll, conducted by Roper Organization July 22–August 12, 1989 (n = 3,001 adult women; 1,001 adult men). Data were provided by The Roper Center at the University of Connecticut

racial dimension of public opinion in a wide range of public policy areas: education, transportation, employment (public and private), housing, interpersonal relations such as interracial marriages, and blacks in elective public office (the presidency).[80] The adoption of more pro–civil rights attitudes occurred fairly rapidly in the 1960s and early 1970s and tapered off somewhat in the 1980s, although support for open housing and busing jumped significantly during this period. By the beginning of the 1990s, "the principle of desegregation was almost universally accepted, and substantial majorities favored government policies to enforce legal equality and to bring about certain kinds and degrees of desegregation."[81]

Naturally, the opinions of whites have changed considerably more than those of blacks. And as expected, the views of the young have liberalized more rapidly than the opinions of the elderly, although they, too, have become more liberal in their outlooks. Nonetheless, older cohorts are still more conservative on racial issues than the young.

To many civil rights proponents, it appears that support for racial equality, most notably for blacks, has stalled in the 1990s. Most Americans agree. Across all age-groups, there is a growing feeling that "in the past few years there hasn't been much real improvement in the position of black people in this country." Furthermore, the proportions of Americans who said that "discriminations against blacks are rare today" dropped between 1987 and 1993, meaning that more Americans think that discrimination still occurs. The older cohorts are the most likely to say that discrimination is rare, although only 25 percent of those 65 and older say this is true, compared to 17 percent of those younger than 30.[82]

The two most controversial types of government-imposed racial equality policies have been busing and affirmative action. Mayer, in *The Changing American Mind,* attributed this controversy to the use of government authority to dictate a certain result.[83]

During the 1980s, public opposition toward busing and affirmative action policies weakened, and the nation as a whole become became more pro–civil rights (liberal). However, as data from the Florida Annual Policy Survey indicated, opposition toward affirmative action began building again in the early 1990s. Opposition increased among all but the Reagan generation, whose opinions were more stable and slightly less pessimistic. However, when it comes to affirmative action on school admissions, the young are even more strongly opposed than the old, although certainly less of an age-group difference exists on this issue within racial minority groups. But in general, Florida data mirror a pattern noted earlier—a growing feeling that government intervention is exacerbating, rather than eradicating, inequalities.[84]

Some have painted the growing interest in and support for school choice as a racial issue. School choice laws allow students and their parents to choose which public schools the students will attend. Although a number of minority parent groups have endorsed this concept, it enjoys support across the entire populace. A 1993 Gallup survey found that nearly two-thirds (65 percent) of all Americans favor school choice, even though it has not yet been officially adopted in a large number of jurisdictions. The strongest support came from middle-aged cohorts, those with children in school.[85]

Social Welfare and Employment Policy

Public opinion surveys have consistently shown Americans to be concerned about the plight of the less fortunate in our society and to favor government assistance to the poor, up to a point. Between 60 and 70 percent of each age-group believe that "it is the responsibility of the government to take care of people who can't take care of themselves" and that "the government should guarantee every citizen enough to eat and a place to sleep."[86] In each instance, the younger cohorts are more supportive of government involvement than the older ones, which is consistent with findings reported throughout this chapter.

But Americans also strongly support—and demand—individual initiative and responsibility. Finding the right balance between the role of government and the role of the individual has been difficult. In fact, some public opinion experts have concluded that "public assistance for the poor has been the most controversial social welfare issue ever since the 1930s."[87] However, it should be noted that social welfare programs benefit more than just the poor.[88]

One excellent overview of Americans' beliefs about social welfare prior to the 1990s summarized them as follows:

- The public believes that the government should help poor people at least at a subsistence level.
- The public believes that many of those who receive public assistance are cheats who do not really qualify.
- The public believes that welfare programs can have bad effects on people as well as good effects.
- The public believes that public assistance and antipoverty programs are not run properly by government.
- The public believes in "workfare"; that people who receive public assistance should do some sort of work in return, even if the work serves no useful purpose.
- The public also believes that income inequality in the United States is too great.[89]

Social Welfare in the 1990s. Growing numbers of people on public assistance and at least one president (Clinton, who ran on a platform of welfare reform) have moved support for social welfare policy more in the direction of approaches that emphasize individual responsibility and away from purely government-provider initiatives. Between 1987 and 1993, support for the proposition that government should take care of people who can't take care of themselves dropped across all age-groups, although the decline was marginal among the youngest cohort (18- to 29-year-olds).[90]

A faltering economy had something to do with this decline, as indicated by similar drops (10 to 15 percent) in affirmative responses to the notion that "the government should help more needy people even if it means going deeper in debt."[91] But mounting disappointment with government public assistance programs also dampened enthusiasm for governmental approaches to solving poverty and unemployment problems. By 1994, more than three-fourths of all Americans felt that the system had made "able-bodied people too dependent on government aid." Negligible differences existed across the age-groups on this score, although a slightly higher percentage of the older cohort viewed welfare in this manner.[92]

Even more Americans think the welfare system should be changed than favor a drastic overhaul of the health care system. A Time/CNN survey taken in May 1992 showed that when asked, "Do you think the welfare system is working well in its current form or should the welfare system be changed?" 90 percent favored change. They laid more of the blame on flaws of the system than on the individual actions of welfare recipients. Eighty-two percent said the "current welfare system discourages people from finding work." In contrast, just over half (52 percent)—still a considerable percentage—agreed that "most people who receive welfare payments are taking advantage of the system." Those under 40 and those 65 and older were more inclined than younger cohorts to believe that recipients are exploiting the system (in the mid-to-high 50 percentiles).[93]

How to Change the System: Self-Sufficiency More Important Than Cost Savings. When presented with a list of possible changes to the welfare system, the public most strongly endorses those that they perceive will help recipients become more self-sufficient. Ninety-three percent think "giving poor people the skills they need to become self-sufficient" is a more important goal of a reformed system than "cutting the cost of welfare programs by removing people from the welfare rolls."[94]

The public is strongly committed to giving welfare recipients the chance to become self-sufficient—and it expects them to do so if possible. According to survey data, an overwhelming majority (87 percent) favored government forcing people on welfare to either work or learn a job skill while giving them every opportunity to do so.[95] More than 90 percent favored "spending extra money to provide free day care to allow poor mothers to work or take classes during the day."[96] Ninety-three percent also endorsed "taking money out of the paychecks and tax refunds of fathers who refuse to make child support payments that a court has ordered."[97]

There is weaker support for punitive approaches to welfare reform. A majority of the public opposed "ending increases in welfare payments to women who give birth to children while on welfare" (59 percent), "cutting the amount of money given to all people on welfare" (75 percent), or "eliminating all welfare programs entirely" (opposed by 93 percent). The 18 to 29, 30 to 49, and 65 and older cohorts were the most likely to oppose punitive approaches because they are more prone to see children and grandchildren as bearing the brunt of such policies. (Children make up a much higher proportion of those below the poverty line than do the elderly.) Overall, the 50 to 64 age-group was the most supportive of policies aimed at getting people off welfare using whatever method that takes (see Table 6.5).

Employment: Government Versus Individual Responsibility? The shift toward individual responsibility in the 1990s is revealed in answers to survey questions such as: "Should the government in Washington see to it that every person has a job and a good standard of living? Or should the government just let each person get ahead on his (or her) own? Or do you feel you are in the middle between these two positions?" In 1981, when the Florida Annual Policy Survey began posing such questions, more than half of each generation favored the individual responsibility approach.

Between 1981 and 1991, the proportion of those in favor of letting people go their own way rather sharply declined across each generation (see Figure 6.5). However, in 1993, the trend line headed in the opposite direction for all but the Reagan generation. In my opinion, this is yet another indication of this genera-

FIGURE 6.5   Government Job Guarantees or Individual Responsibility?

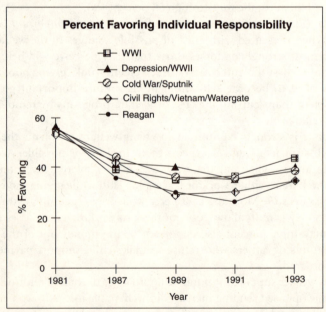

Note: Respondents were asked: "Should the government in Washington see to it that every person has a job and a good standard of living? Or should the government just let each person get ahead on his/her own? Or do you feel you are in the middle between these two positions?"

Source: Suzanne L. Parker, Florida Annual Policy Survey, Tallahassee, FL: Survey Research Laboratory, Policy Sciences Program, Florida State University.

tion's growing pessimism about their economic future. This pessimism even shows up in attitudes toward foreign and defense policy issues.

When asked a series of questions about how to improve the job situation in the United States, nearly three-fourths of each age-group favored restricting the number of immigrants coming in to the country each year (see Table 6.6.). The age-groups disagreed most over approaches involving more government taxing, spending, and trade restrictions. For example, the young, more than the old, tended to support spending more money on education, increasing the minimum wage, and increasing taxes on imported products—anything that would give them an edge in the job market.

FOREIGN AND DEFENSE POLICY ISSUES

Throughout U.S. history, domestic and foreign policy issues have been highly interrelated. Two leading scholars have put it succinctly: "Even if one sought to understand only U.S. domestic politics, data on international relations would be essential."[98]

The world's economy is much more global today than even a few years ago, and the U.S. economy has become much more interwoven with the economies of other nations. What happens abroad affects us domestically and vice versa, whether the issue is related to international trade pacts like the North American Free Trade Agreement (NAFTA), foreign investment regulations, U.S. military assistance and intervention, foreign aid, immigration, or involvement in international peacekeeping organizations like the United Nations and the North Atlantic Treaty Organization (NATO).

When things at home are tough economically, Americans lessen their support for foreign and defense policies that they perceive will either drain money from the domestic economy or result in the loss of jobs at home. In other words, they become somewhat more isolationist and protectionist, although such attitudes may not always be in their long-term self-interest. Ideology also affects a person's outlook on foreign policy issues, as does the generation in which he or she matured politically.

Liberal Versus Conservative Preferences in U.S. Foreign Policy

Historically, liberals (known as "doves") have favored defense cuts, détente, and arms control. Conservatives (often referred to as "hawks") have preferred increases in defense spending and getting tough with international rogues who oppose democratic principles. However, both liberals and conservatives have leaned more heavily toward international involvement than isolation.

In *The Changing American Mind,* Mayer cited a number of studies showing that both liberals and conservatives have called for "substantial American intervention in world affairs, although they differed, of course, about the means and goals of that intervention." Mayer went on to note that "conservatives see international involvement primarily as a way of containing communism and place greater emphasis on military forms of intervention" and that liberals are "more inclined toward economic aid, want the United States to advance the causes of economic justice and human rights in the Third World, and are more favorably disposed toward multilateral action through such international organizations as the United Nations."[99]

Sharp Shifts in Public Opinion Common

Public opinion changes much more sharply on foreign policy issues than on domestic policy issues, which, as we have seen, are largely incremental. In their analyses of fifty years of surveys, Page and Shapiro found that "foreign policy opinion changes were nearly three times as rapid as domestic, on the average, presumably because circumstances tend to change more quickly in international affairs." They observed that "most abrupt foreign policy opinion changes have followed wars, confrontations, or crises, in which major actions of the United States or other nations have understandably affected calculations about the costs and benefits of alternative policies."[100]

A person's outlook toward the U.S. role in foreign affairs is often permanently affected by the outcome of U.S. involvement in such a crisis, especially if he or she came of age politically at that time. If the U.S. involvement was generally judged successful, people tend to be more positive toward future U.S. involvement. If it was a failure, as perceived in Vietnam, the reverse is true. This tendency is evident in opinion patterns in the 1990s.

Americans More Isolationist in the 1990s: Young More Than the Old

A September 1993 survey by the Times Mirror Center for The People & The Press, comparing Americans' current opinions about international policies to those in the past, concluded:

> The general public is distinctly more pessimistic and inclined toward a new but unique kind of isolationism compared to [their] leaders. They want a foreign policy that serves the domestic agenda of the United States, and they would treat each global issue according to its impact on that agenda. . . . The American people now take a clearly protective, America-First stance on international issues, particularly those affecting their pocket books. A major exception is the public's concern for protecting the global environment.[101]

Over several prior years, surveys by other major polling firms as well as Times Mirror had detected a shift in the public attitude toward protectionism and isolationism, tracking closely with a declining economy. These earlier surveys showed increasing support for protecting U.S. jobs. A 1991 survey showed that 80 percent of each age-group agreed that "U.S. jobs should be protected from foreign competition." By April 1993, similar percentages agreed that the "U.S. should concentrate more on our own national problems" than on foreign policy—reflecting an isolationist attitude that had thrust President Clinton into the White House in 1992. However, that attitude could change sharply, especially if some international situation erupts and threatens our domestic economy. Increasingly, as noted, casting issues as either domestic or foreign is a questionable approach: The two areas are *not* mutually exclusive!

Foreign Policy Priorities in the Early 1990s: Age-Group Differences

When presented with a list of foreign policy problems facing the United States, Americans of all age-groups tend to rate economic and trade issues as more pressing than peace and power issues. Even issues such as stopping the international drug traffic and the flow of immigrants into the United States have strong economic overtones. Drugs are perceived as a major contributor to rising public assistance rolls and crime. And a considerable portion of the U.S. public believes immigrants take jobs away from Americans and add to the public assistance rolls as well.[102]

Reflecting clear generational differences in experiences, a much higher proportion of those 65 and older consider "countering the threat of North Korean militarism," "guarding against a resurgent Germany," "monitoring the emergence of China as a world power," and "bringing about a permanent settlement between Israel and the Arabs" as high priorities for the U.S. government. The percentage of elderly seeing these problems as high priorities is often double or triple that of those younger than 30.[103] But even among the elderly, more give higher priority to economic foreign policy issues.

Generational differences also appear in terms of how high a priority the U.S. government should place on addressing certain types of foreign policy issues. The youngest cohorts see protection of the global environment as much more important than the older cohorts do, by a spread of 20 percent.[104] In fact, a majority of the young have consistently favored increasing environmental controls, even if that reduces employment opportunities.[105] Among the older cohorts, however, support for environmental controls in the face of job losses has declined sharply in the 1990s.[106]

Long-Term U.S. Foreign Policy Goals. When Americans are asked about their long-term priorities for U.S. foreign policy, economic and defense issues (including economic self-defense—protection of energy supplies, reduction of our foreign trade deficit) are still rated as more important than the promotion of democracy, human rights, or multilateral organizations (see Table 6.7). In fact, there is more consensus across the age-groups on which long-term goals should be classified as top priority than on which current problem is most important. The exception is the protection of the global environment: Considerably more of the youngest cohort (64 percent) rate this as a top long-range priority, as compared to those 65 or older (47 percent).

U.S. Foreign Policy Trade-Offs. As in all policy areas, selecting one foreign policy approach over another involves serious trade-offs. To test Americans' support for certain principles and actions once they were informed of the possible negative consequences, the Times Mirror Center for The People & The Press asked a series of trade-off questions.[107] The responses showed that Americans clearly recognize that a strict imposition of our democratic values on other countries with different value systems and cultures may not always be a desirable foreign policy goal or have a positive outcome at home.

A third or less of any age-group agreed that the United States "should be willing to promote democracy around the world even if it risks the election of totalitarian, anti-American governments." Less than one-fifth believed the United States "should promote free markets and economic capitalism around the world, even if it seriously risks exploitation of underdeveloped peoples by western businesses." And no more than one-fifth of any group agreed that the United States "should promote self-determination of local ethnic groups within long-standing nations of the world, even if it would seriously risk the break-up of these nations into warring ethnic regions." Less than a third believed the United States "should insist on applying its human and civil rights standards throughout the world, even if it seriously risks antagonizing friendly nations whose traditions do not conform to our ideals."

The younger cohorts are consistently more dogmatic about spreading democratic principles across the globe, regardless of the consequences, although, as stated, there is no strong consensus for this approach among any generation. Again, the younger cohorts have had more positive experiences with aggressive intervention than the nation's older cohorts.

Foreign Aid: Too Much, Not Appreciated

The lack of enthusiasm for getting involved in the affairs of other nations can be traced in part to economics; and in part to foreign reactions to our do-goodism. Since 1973, the National Opinion Research Center surveys have asked Americans whether we spend too much, too little, or about the right amount on foreign aid. Consistently, between 68 and 79 percent of respondents have said too much.[108] Older persons have been more critical of foreign aid spending than the younger cohorts, although an overwhelming proportion of all age-groups have considered aid levels too high.

Older persons are also much more cynical about foreign aid's impact. More than 80 percent of those 65 and older think "most of the countries that have gotten help from America end up resenting us." Among the youngest cohort, only 60 percent feel this way, again reflecting their relative positivism and, perhaps, their lower levels of familiarity with the nation's fiscal history.[109]

Their strong feelings that foreign aid efforts are expensive and unappreciated make Americans less likely to espouse much support for U.S. military intervention in foreign countries, unless national security is at stake.

Sending U.S. Military Forces Abroad: Young More in Favor Than Old

Historically, Americans' responses to hypothetical questions about situations in which they would support U.S. military intervention in foreign countries have always been lukewarm. Responses to such questions are no different in the 1990s. Rarely do even a simple majority favor sending U.S. troops into other countries in an interventionist role. But Americans are more supportive of intervention for humanitarian aims and economic reasons, such as protecting oil supplies in the Middle East or improving trade, than for political goals such as restoring law and order in strife-torn countries.

Regardless of the reason, the young are more willing than the old to send U.S. troops abroad, with differences between the groups often ranging in the 20 percentiles (see Table 6.8). Their experiences with U.S. military intervention abroad, particularly in the Persian Gulf War and in response to the widespread starvation and violence in Somalia, have been more positive than those of other age-groups.

Defense Spending: Young More in Favor of Cutbacks Than the Old

Americans' support for defense spending has always fluctuated significantly, depending upon the condition of the domestic economy, world situations and perceptions of the threat they pose to the United States, and estimates about how much our foreign competitors are spending. In recent years, the young have been more likely to favor cutbacks in defense spending. Older Americans, who grew up in a period when the nation was at war or when the fear of war was great—for example, the red scare days of the Cold War—are less prone to say we spend too much than the young, even in tough economic times.

However, in the mid-1990s, enthusiasm for cutbacks in federal defense spending waned across all groups as serious conflicts (or threats thereof) appeared on just about every continent. Also, highly publicized defense budget cuts were beginning to have negative economic impacts in many communities throughout the United States. This swing in opinion largely reflects the highly volatile nature of opinion on defense spending levels, rather than any permanent shift.

Fear of the Spread of Nuclear Weapons

Americans have long feared that nuclear weapons would someday get in the hands of less responsible Third World nations. That fear persists today. The 1993 Times Mirror survey on Americans' attitudes toward international relations found that the "proliferation of weapons of mass destruction" was seen as dangerous to world stability by more respondents than nationalism or ethnic hatreds (although this category was a close second), religious fanaticism, population growth, international trade conflicts, or environmental pollution.[110]

Younger cohorts were the most fearful about the spread of nuclear weapons.[111] Slightly more young than old (though still less than a majority) also saw nationalism and ethnic hatreds[112] and environmental pollution[113] as threats to world stability. However, more old than young saw population growth[114] and religious fanaticism[115] as threats. But these pale in comparison with concerns about nuclear weapon proliferation.

The United States as World Leader: Past, Present, Future

Most Americans believe the U.S. role in world affairs is at least as important and powerful today—if not more so—than it was a decade ago. This perception holds true across all age-groups, although the young are somewhat more likely than the old to have seen an escalation in the U.S. role.[116] (Their comparative time line is much shorter.)

Americans of all ages remain committed to the idea of the United States playing an active role in world affairs. However, only 10 percent think the United States should be the single world leader. (My other findings strongly suggest that economic realities lie at the heart of this response.) Even fewer believe the United States should play no leadership role at all. By far the most common preference (in the 80 percentiles) is for the United States to be "no more or less active than other leading nations."[117]

Americans also support cooperation with other nations in peacekeeping activities around the globe, especially when funding and personnel responsibilities are shared. But in such situations, an overwhelming majority strongly believe that "American forces should always remain under an American officer rather than under United Nations Command when part of a permanent United Nations Command." The youngest and oldest cohorts feel most strongly about this: 74 percent of each of these groups agree, compared to 67 percent of those 30 to 49 and 62 percent of those 50 to 64 years of age.[118] Even in the face of declining confidence in their own governmental institutions and leaders, Americans still have more confidence in our nation's leaders than in those from other nations.

THE DECLINE IN THE PUBLIC'S TRUST AND CONFIDENCE IN GOVERNMENT

It's no secret that Americans' trust and confidence in government, especially the federal government, has been declining for quite some time.[119] More Americans today than in the past see government as too big, wasteful, and inefficient. The majority believes government has difficulty solving problems, creates more problems than it solves, and rarely does what's right. Since 1985, the proportion who "favor smaller government with fewer services over large government with many services" has jumped from 49 to 67 percent,[120] mostly in reaction to a rapidly expanding federal bureaucracy. Moreover, three-fourths of each age-group favors term limits for members of Congress.[121] Analysts disagree about what these figures mean to the future of democracy, but at a minimum, these trust and confidence statistics help explain the often less than enthusiastic responses we have seen for public policy approaches calling for heavy intervention by the government.

Trust, Confidence, and U.S. Democracy

The beginning of the dip in trust and confidence is often traced back to the events of the late 1960s and early 1970s, that is, from the Vietnam War to urban riots to Watergate.[122] Some see Americans' declining trust and confidence in government as a real threat to our democratic system. For a democratic system to survive, they argue, the citizenry must have some positive attachments to the system and give "the political system some degree of leeway to act."[123] Others see declining trust and confidence figures as evidence of the public's increasing irritation at individuals in government, especially incumbents, rather than at our democratic form of government.[124]

There is a widespread belief that these figures are greatly affected by the media's coverage of domestic and foreign policy issues and U.S. governmental leaders' responses to them. In *Feeding Frenzy: How Attack Journalism Has Transformed American Politics,* Larry Sabato stated this position well: "How the voters view politics at any given time—whether the electorate is optimistic or pessimistic, idealistic or cynical—is partly a by-product of what they learn about the subject from the news media. And above all, the dozens of feeding frenzies in recent times have had substantial and cumulative effects on the American political system."[125]

Age and the Trust and Confidence Issue

Do we lose faith in government's ability to solve problems in an expeditious, effective manner the older we grow? Or do some age-groups have less faith than others simply because of the period in history during which they came of age politically (e.g., the Civil Rights/Vietnam/Watergate generation)? Or has the decline in trust and confidence occurred at the same pace across all age-groups? Survey results show that there's a little evidence to support each position.

National surveys have consistently shown the young to be less critical of the wastefulness and inefficiencies of the federal government and less prone to see it as too intrusive in their personal lives than the old—by a spread of about 20 percent. Surveys also show that the Civil Rights/Vietnam/Watergate generation is the least likely to believe that "when the government decides to solve a problem that it will actually be solved" or that government can be trusted "to do what is right just about always/most of the time," although that age-group's responses vary only slightly from those of other age groups. By 1993, the gap between the young and the old on these problem-solving questions had narrowed considerably. The good news is that a majority, although a slim one, has confidence in Washington's ability to solve a problem. The bad news is that only a fourth or less believes the federal government can be trusted to do what's right.

A Closer Look at Declining Trust and Confidence: Florida

Data on changes in Floridians' trust and confidence in the federal government between 1981 and 1993 show, even more sharply than national data, a net decline.

By 1993, the generational gap had narrowed considerably, although the Civil Rights/Vietnam/Watergate and Cold War generations were still the least trusting. The sharpest decline occurred among the youngest (Reagan) generation. In my opinion, this reflects the disillusionment that members of that generation feel about the government's handling of economic problems, as well as their growing concern about their economic future.

Declining Trust and Confidence in Institutions and Elected Officials

To determine the extent to which Americans are annoyed with politicians more than with the system as a whole, surveys by the National Opinion Research Center and various other polling firms have asked: "As far as the people running these institutions (executive branch, U.S. Supreme Court, or Congress), would you say that you have a great deal of confidence, only some confidence, or hardly any confidence at all in them?"

The results show a steady decline in confidence since 1973, especially with regard to those running Congress and the executive branch. The same annual NORC survey asks Americans to assess the leaders of the press, military, organized labor, major companies, banks, medicine, television, education, and organized religion. Most believe that "nearly all these institutions have suffered a decline in [public] esteem since the early 1970s."[126] In fact, the public's confidence in those running the press, television, and organized labor is as low as it is for those running government. The highest ratings go to those leading the military and medical sectors.

A similar survey in 1994 by the Times Mirror Center for The People & The Press, with a somewhat different list of institutions and groups, showed some marked age differences in such assessments (see Table 6.9). The age-groups differ least in their assessments of newspapers, Congress, the U.S. Supreme Court, the military, business corporations, and Evangelical Christians. They differ most in their opinions regarding the two political parties, the United Nations, Wall Street investors, tobacco and insurance companies, most interest groups, and the media. The young tend to be more supportive of Republicans, the United Nations, Wall Street, tobacco companies, virtually every conceivable type of interest group, and MTV. The old are more supportive of Democrats, insurance companies, and network TV. These age-group differences reflect the younger generation's typically less cynical evaluations of most institutions, their more open views on alternative lifestyles, and their political party socialization patterns (see Chapter 3). But what about the views of various age-groups toward elected officials' performance in office?

More Negative Evaluations of Elected Officials' Performance: Florida

Many polls, including the Florida Annual Policy Survey, regularly ask the public to evaluate the overall job being done by various elected officials, most often chief executives (the president, the governor) and legislators (Congress members, state legislators). Typically, they ask whether certain officials are doing an excellent, good, fair, or poor job. To track general trends in the public's feeling about the performance of executive leaders and legislatures at the national *and* state levels (cumulatively), an index of executive performance and another of legislative performance were constructed based on Floridians' responses to the FAPS between 1981 and 1993.[127] The results amplified the national trends. Over time, the number of Floridians who failed to give any positive evaluations to the president or governor rose significantly, from close to 20 percent in 1981 to more than one-third in 1993 (see Figure 6.6). Each successive age-group grew significantly less positive toward their executive leaders. By 1993, younger cohorts in Florida were less positive toward chief executives than were older cohorts.

Similar patterns are evident in Floridians' assessment of legislative institutional performance. Although evaluations of legislative institutions have traditionally been more negative than those of individual Congress members or legislators,[128] the trends are nonetheless startling (see Figure 6.6). The percentage of Floridians failing to give a positive evaluation to either legislative institution (Congress or the state legislature) rose from close to half the public in 1981 to two-thirds in 1993. Again, the sharpest increase in negative evaluations occurred among the youngest (Reagan) generation. By 1993, the gap between the generations had closed considerably, with the Reagan generation slightly more positive than the older generations, reflecting the young's slightly less cynical view toward government.

What Does This Mean?

These trends make it difficult for elected officials to build a consensus among the public on policy alternatives. They also inhibit the coalition-building efforts of leaders and groups. In his work on political leadership, William Gamson stated the significance of the problem in this manner: "The effectiveness of political leadership . . . depends on the ability of authorities to claim the loyal cooperation of members of the system without having to specify in advance what such cooperation will entail. Within certain limits, effectiveness depends on a blank check. The importance of trust becomes apparent: the loss of system power, the loss of generalized capacity for authorities to commit resources to attain collective goals."[129]

In times of acrimony between different segments of society, such as young people versus older groups, this type of trust and confidence may be particularly necessary to arbitrate societal disputes. Cynicism about government's ability to solve problems will certainly hamper the reallocation of scarce resources. However, as this overview of Americans' attitudes toward various domestic and foreign policy issues and alternatives has shown, the public has never really strongly believed that exclusively government-driven solutions are necessarily the best.

FIGURE 6.6 Negative Performance Ratings: Executive and Legislative Officials (Percent Giving No Positive Evaluations)

Executive Officials

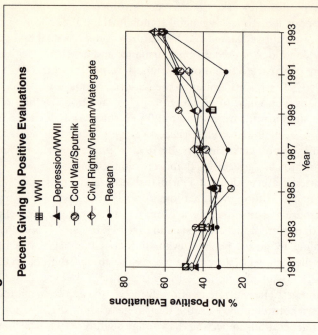

Legislative Institutions

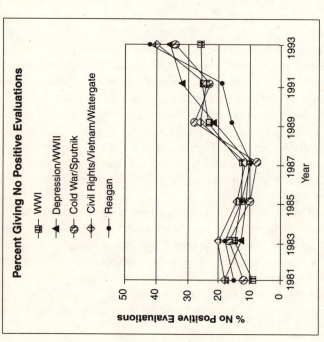

Note: Respondents were asked: "How would you rate the job the U.S. Congress (the Florida Legislature in Tallahassee) is doing? Would you say: excellent, good, fair, or poor?" Figures reported are from an index created by combining negative responses (fair and poor) to these two questions.

Source: Suzanne L. Parker, Florida Annual Policy Survey, Tallahassee, FL: Survey Research Laboratory, Policy Sciences Program, Florida State University.

Note: Respondents were asked: "How would you rate the job the [President; Governor] has been doing as [president/governor]? Would you say: excellent, good, fair, or poor?" Figures reported are from an index created by combining negative responses (fair and poor) to these two questions.

Source: Suzanne L. Parker, Florida Annual Policy Survey, Tallahassee, FL: Survey Research Laboratory, Policy Sciences Program, Florida State University.

SUMMARY

Americans' opinions on foreign policy issues change more rapidly than their opinions on domestic policy issues, although the two are increasingly intertwined. Economics is often the common link. When economic problems prevail at home, foreign policy problems and solutions will generally be judged on the basis of how they affect the domestic economy. And on the home front, the more that people believe a noneconomic issue will affect them economically—such as health and crime issues for the elderly or education and employment policies for the young—the more likely they are to rank that issue as a high-priority problem to be addressed.

It is the younger middle-aged cohort (30- to 49-year-olds) that sees most problems as urgent, perhaps because they have the most interaction with and responsibility for persons at both ends of the age continuum. But this is also the group that is often the least trusting of government's ability to solve problems or to do what's right, an attitude that can be attributed, at least in part, to the time in which they came of age politically—that is, during the Civil Rights/Vietnam/Watergate era.

The opinions of older persons are less volatile than those of the younger cohorts. However, though it is true that older persons are more likely than younger ones to prefer more incremental approaches to solving societal problems, I certainly found evidence that the intensity and direction of older people's opinions can and have changed, especially with regard to race and individual rights.

Overall, the old and the young are more likely to differ in the intensity rather than the direction of their opinions on a wide array of domestic and foreign policy issues. They differ little in their identification of pressing issues facing the nation but considerably in their ratings of which issues the government should address first and which policy alternatives should be implemented. Their place in the life cycle and in history can explain many of these differences. In general, older persons are less inclined to label a problem as critical or to believe that government intervention is necessarily the best or most effective way of solving societal problems.

On domestic issues, a survey of Florida's legislators gives us a glimpse of age-group differences that we might expect to see nationally. The young are the most concerned about the economy and jobs, the old about taxes and government spending. On the noneconomic side of domestic issues, both young and old worry about crime and moral issues. The young are the most attentive to educational and environmental issues, and the old closely follow health and social welfare issues.

The two age-extreme generations differ most in their outlooks on moral, tax, social welfare, and health policy issues. But their conflicts primarily involve what to do first—perceptions that are largely guided by the degree to which a problem directly affects an individual (especially economically). For example, in the health care area, the young favor reforms that secure protection for them in the face of a job change or job loss. The older prefer reforms that address long-term health care.

When alternatives are posed as a trade-off between the protection of individual rights or of society at large, the young tend to favor individual rights, and the old favor societal rights. This schism is most evident in opinions on moral and social equality issues. The younger cohorts, especially the 30- to 49-year-olds, also are more in favor of preventive rather than reactive or punitive approaches, most notably in the health and crime areas, although the age-group differences in this respect are not dramatic. In the crime area, young and old alike are more in favor of punishment than rehabilitation.

The young are slightly more in favor of government mandates and guaranteed levels of service provision, especially in the welfare and employment policy arenas, than are the older cohorts. Older persons are more supportive of policy alternatives emphasizing the development of individual self-sufficiency and responsibility. The young lean slightly more in the direction of government guarantees (of jobs, of public assistance), reflecting their pessimism about their own economic futures. They, more than the old, see government as their safety net. Today's elderly have generally received more help in their later years from their families, friends, churches, and social organizations than from government programs.

There is a growing tendency to link social problems, especially among the young, with declining morals. The public lays much of the blame for increases in juvenile crime, teenaged pregnancies, and other social ills on television and movies. Young and old alike strongly agree that violence on television is harmful to society. They also agree that it has made Americans more fearful and desensitized the young to violence. But they disagree on the basic causes of these rising social ills. The young are more prone to attribute moral decline to economics; the old cite the decline of the traditional family structure.

On the foreign policy front, it is clear that the U.S. public's movement toward or away from protectionism and isolationism tracks closely with the condition of the economy at home. But a person's outlook on the appropriate U.S. role in foreign affairs also greatly depends on the outcome of U.S. involvement in a war, confrontation, or other crisis that occurred at the time he or she was coming of age politically. If the outcome was judged successful, that person tends to be more positive toward future U.S. involvement (the Reagan generation and its experience with the Persian Gulf War and Somalia). If not, he or she is more negative (the Civil Rights/Vietnam/Watergate generation).

In the 1990s, young and old alike rate economic and trade issues as more important U.S. foreign policy goals than promoting the spread of democracy around the world. However, as is true on the domestic front, the young are also much more inclined to rate the protection of the global environment as a high priority, even when meeting that goal involves a trade-off—that is, environmental protection versus loss of jobs. And the World War I and Depression generations are more supportive of policies closely monitoring old enemies such as North Korea, Germany, and China.

Americans of all ages remain committed to having the United States play an active role in world affairs, but most (80-some percent) prefer that the United States be no more or less active than other leading nations. However, they firmly believe that U.S. soldiers should be under the command of an American officer when our troops are part of a permanent United Nations command or any other multilateral peacekeeping or military operation.

Americans are realists and more culturally sensitive than normally portrayed. Overwhelming majorities of all age-groups acknowledge that a strict imposition of our democratic values on other countries with different value systems and cultures may not always be a desirable foreign policy goal or have a positive outcome at home. The younger cohorts are consistently more willing to do whatever is necessary to spread democratic principles across the globe, including sending U.S. troops, than the older cohorts (although less than a majority of even the young are heavily interventionist in the 1990s). Older persons are generally more cynical about the impact of foreign aid—they are much more likely to think that countries we help end up turning against us.

Americans' confidence in our government's problem-solving abilities has been declining for some time. Analyses of trend data among Floridians show, even more vividly than national data, the net decline in trust and confidence in government and the sharp increase in the public's negative performance ratings on executive and legislative leaders and institutions. The steepest decline has occurred among the youngest (Reagan) generation, which means that by the mid-1990s, the gap between young and old had almost closed. This growing cynicism among the young reflects their disillusionment with the government's handling of economic problems and their own concerns about their economic future.

If this cynicism among all age-groups about the government's ability to solve problems continues, it will make coalition-building and leadership more difficult and the reallocation of scarce resources quite bitter. The good news is that Americans remain optimistic that we can solve our problems, although they do not necessarily believe that government is always the best or the only problem-solver.

TABLE 6.1 Lawmakers' Views of Issues Followed Closely by Younger and Older Constituents and Those Where Disagreements Are Most Prevalent (in percentages)

Issue closely followed	Young (under 24)	65 and older	Age-groups have different perspective on the issue
Taxes	46.8	**93.5**	**34.4**
Government spending	16.9	**75.3**	9.7
Government growth	9.1	28.9	6.5
Economy/jobs	**75.3**	13.2	16.1
Health	28.6	**81.8**	**29.0**
Crime	**58.4**	**92.2**	8.1
Social services	13.0	59.7	**33.9**
Public assistance	9.1	23.4	11.3
Elementary/secondary education	**53.2**	15.6	22.6
Higher education	**54.5**	6.5	16.1
Environment	46.8	20.8	17.7
Discrimination	23.4	16.9	8.1
Race	18.2	9.1	4.8
Gender	14.3	5.2	4.8
Age	5.2	11.7	4.8
Sexual preference	14.3	2.6	6.5
Highways/roads	9.1	22.1	4.8
Public transportation	6.5	**36.4**	1.6
Parks & recreation	26.0	7.8	6.5
Growth management	11.7	13.0	8.1
Moral issues	**48.1**	**63.6**	**40.3**
Abortion[a]	72.7	33.3	—
School prayer[a]	30.0	16.7	66.7
Gun control[a]	50.0	83.3	66.7
Pornography[a]	10.0	8.3	33.3
Privacy[a]	10.0	8.3	—
Other	1.3	1.3	1.6

[a]Percent of those identifying moral issues as a closely followed category.

Notes: Respondents were asked: "What issues do *younger* (under 24) [*older* voters (65 or older)] in your district follow most closely? (check all applicable)" **Bold**-faced issues are the most closely watched issues.

Source: Mail survey of Florida legislators conducted January–February, 1994, by Susan A. MacManus.

TABLE 6.2 Support for Changes in a New Health Care System (in percentages)

	Age-Group			
Change would accept	**18–29**	**30–49**	**50–64**	**65+**
1993				
Slower introduction of new medical procedures and technologies into hospitals	51.3	48.1	46.1	46.6
Waiting longer for nonemergency medical and hospital care	56.2	61.4	55.9	43.5
More restrictions on your choice of doctors and hospitals	38.2	43.8	35.8	30.8
1994				
Slower introduction of new medical procedures and technologies into hospitals	48.1	42.7	43.8	41.1
Waiting longer for nonemergency medical and hospital care	47.6	49.1	45.1	36.9
More restrictions on your choice of doctors and hospitals	34.1	30.6	28.3	20.2
Paying more for your own health insurance premiums, deductibles, or co-payments	34.0	42.9	37.7	34.9
Not allowing some expensive medical procedures and technologies if they would not do much to improve or extend a patient's life	47.6	60.6	60.3	42.1

Note: Respondents were asked: "As I read from a list, please tell me which of these would you be willing to accept in a new health care system."

Sources: The Times Mirror Center for The People & The Press. Telephone survey of a nationally representative sample of 1,011 adults 18 years of age or older, conducted April 1-4, 1993; telephone survey of a nationally representative sample of 2,001 adults 18 years of age or older, conducted March 16-21, 1994. Reprinted with permission.

TABLE 6.3 Ways to Reduce Violent Crime (in percentages)

Reduction technique	Age-Group			
	18-29	30-49	50-64	65+
1993				
Longer jail terms for those convicted of violent crimes	58.0	62.4	71.3	64.7
Jobs programs for inner city areas	57.6	53.2	56.3	54.3
More police on the streets	51.2	51.7	56.6	56.1
Restrictions on the amount of violence shown on TV	35.7	45.4	57.7	64.6
Stricter gun control laws	39.2	39.6	40.0	47.2
1994				
Longer jail terms for those convicted of violent crimes	63.1	69.3	69.2	72.3
Jobs programs for inner city areas	58.3	57.4	56.3	48.3
More police on the streets	59.3	55.1	58.7	58.0
Stricter gun control laws	43.7	35.7	41.7	39.2
More prisons and less opportunity for parole	49.7	58.9	58.0	61.6
Legalizing drugs like marijuana and cocaine	15.2	12.9	10.7	10.7
Restrictions on the amount of violence shown on TV	30.9	37.9	48.0	64.1

Note: Respondents were asked: "I am going to read some things that might be done to reduce violent crime in this country. For each, tell me if you think this would reduce the amount of violent crime a lot, a little, or not at all? Do you think [technique] would reduce the amount of violent crime a lot, a little, or not at all?" Percentages reported are for "A lot."

Source: The Times Mirror Center for The People & The Press. Telephone survey of a nationally representative sample of 1,479 adults 18 years of age or older, conducted December 2–5, 1993; telephone survey of a nationally representative sample of 2,001 adults 18 years of age or older, conducted March 16–21, 1994. Reprinted with permission.

TABLE 6.4 Equal Opportunity: Early Signs of a Backlash? (in percentages)

	Age-Group			
Statement	18-29	30-49	50-64	65[a]+
Our society should do what is necessary to make sure that everyone has an equal opportunity to *succeed*				
May 1987	91.5	89.6	89.0	88.7
May 1990	94.4	91.4	85.1	91.4
We have gone too far in pushing equal rights in this country				
May 1987	34.8	40.9	44.6	49.3
May 1990	34.7	41.1	48.6	52.2
May 1993	35.6	42.3	45.4	57.9

Notes: [a]May 1987 and May 1990 age-break categories are: 18-29; 30-49; 50-59; 60 and over. Respondents were asked: "Here are some other statements on a variety of topics. Please tell me how much you agree or disagree with each of these statements: completely agree, mostly agree, mostly disagree, completely disagree, don't know?" Percentages reported are completely and mostly agree.

Sources: The Times Mirror Center for The People & The Press. Face-to-face survey of a nationally representative sample of 4,244 adults 18 years of age or older, conducted April 25-May 10, 1987; face-to-face survey of a nationally representative sample of 3,004 adults 18 years of age or older, conducted May 1-31, 1990; telephone survey of a nationally representative sample of 1,507 adults 18 years of age or older, conducted May 18-24, 1993. Reprinted with permission.

TABLE 6.5 Support for Proposals to Reform the Welfare System (in percentages)

	Age-Group			
Reform proposal that would help a lot	18–29	30–49	50–64	65+
Requiring ALL people on welfare—even mothers of young children—to do some kind of work in return for their welfare checks	58.9	60.5	68.0	63.9
New government programs to provide job training and public service jobs for people on welfare	65.7	58.4	64.4	52.2
Guaranteed health insurance so poor people without health coverage don't quit their jobs or stay on welfare to get Medicaid	48.7	46.3	50.5	33.1
Changing policy so that a woman on welfare does NOT receive a larger check when she has another child	42.9	49.7	64.8	49.7
Putting a two-year limit on how long someone can receive welfare benefits	44.9	51.2	57.9	45.5

Note: Respondents were asked: "As I read you some proposals to change the welfare system, please tell me how much you think each would improve the situation. First, what about [ ]? Would this improve things a lot, improve things a little, or only make things worse?" Percentages reported are "improve things a lot."

Source: The Times Mirror Center for The People & The Press. Telephone survey of a nationally representative sample of 992 adults 18 years of age or older, conducted March 16-21, 1994. Reprinted with permission.

TABLE 6.6 Ways to Improve the Job Situation in the United States (in percentages)

Reform proposal believe would help a lot	Age-Group			
	18–29	30–49	50–64	65+
Restricting the number of immigrants coming into the country each year	76.0	76.4	75.8	70.6
Increasing taxes on imported products	64.8	58.2	57.5	50.8
Spending more money on education	90.5	85.2	74.3	62.5
Expanding job training opportunities	93.5	91.6	86.5	81.5
Encouraging business and government to work more closely together	80.1	80.3	79.7	82.3
More free trade agreements with other countries, such as NAFTA	52.3	53.6	49.0	51.7
Changing to a four-day work week, with workers' weekly pay reduced for a shorter 32-hour schedule	22.4	19.9	25.4	26.1
Increasing the minimum wage	78.4	69.4	70.7	59.0

Note: Respondents were asked: "Thinking about job opportunities in the country as a whole, please tell me how you think each of the following measures would affect the overall job situation. First [ ] help the overall job situation a lot, help it a little, or hurt the job situation a lot?" Percentages reported are "help a lot."

Source: The Times Mirror Center for The People & The Press. Telephone survey of a nationally representative sample of 992 adults 18 years of age or older, conducted March 16–21, 1994. Reprinted with permission.

TABLE 6.7 Americans' Views on What Long-Range U.S. Foreign Policy Goals Should Have Top Priority (in percentages)

| | Age-Group | | | |
Long-range goal	18–29	30–49	50–64	65+
Preventing spread of weapons of mass destruction	67	69	75	67
Improving the global environment	64	57	54	47
Helping improve the living standards in developing nations	24	18	12	22
Insuring adequate energy supplies for the U.S.	55	61	64	61
Promoting democracy in other nations	23	19	23	27
Aiding the interests of U.S. business abroad	33	26	21	25
Protecting the jobs of American workers	89	83	83	84
Strengthening the United Nations	43	36	43	45
Reducing our trade deficit with foreign countries	54	55	59	55
Promoting and defending human rights in other countries	25	25	16	19
Protecting weaker nations against foreign aggression even if U.S. vital interests are not at stake	15	15	17	20

Note: Respondents were asked: "As I read a list of possible LONG-RANGE foreign policy goals which the United States might have, tell me if you think they should have top priority, priority but not top priority, or no priority at all." Percentages reported are "top priority."

Source: The Times Mirror Center for The People & The Press. Telephone survey of a nationally representative sample of 2,000 adults 18 years of age or older, conducted September 9–15, 1993. Reprinted with permission.

TABLE 6.8 Situations in Which Americans Would Approve Use of U.S. Forces
(in percentages)

Situation/Location	Age-Group			
	18–29	30–49	50–64	65+
September 1993				
If Russia invaded the Ukraine	27	21	18	16
If Iraq invaded Saudi Arabia	60	59	48	39
If the Mexican government were threatened by revolution or civil war	47	42	38	33
If North Korea invaded South Korea	28	31	36	27
If Arab forces invaded Israel	52	50	43	29
October 1993				
To Asian or African countries to prevent famines and mass starvation	63.4	58.4	55.0	45.2
To Latin American or Caribbean countries to restore law and order if the governments completely break down	44.7	37.3	32.4	34.3
To Asian or African countries to restore law and order if the governments completely break down	38.9	35.6	21.4	26.1

Note: Respondents were asked: "Do you approve or disapprove of the use of the U.S. forces in the following situations?" "Do you approve or disapprove of sending U.S. military forces to [ ] if [ ]."

Sources: The Times Mirror Center for The People & The Press. Telephone survey of a nationally representative sample of 2,000 adults 18 years of age or older, conducted September 9-15, 1993; telephone survey of a nationally representative sample of 1,200 adults 18 years of age or older, conducted October 21-24, 1993. Reprinted with permission.

TABLE 6.9 Favorable Overall Opinions of Institutions, Groups, and Media (in percentages)

Institution/Group/Media	Age-Group			
	18–29	30–49	50–64	65+
Political				
Republican Party	66.6	63.9	62.3	59.2
Democratic Party	58.3	60.6	66.0	63.6
Congress	53.4	52.2	54.0	51.3
U.S. Supreme Court	81.1	80.9	81.6	77.4
Professional/Business				
Military	84.6	87.2	91.0	87.1
Wall Street investors	64.2	60.7	61.3	43.8
Business corporations	71.6	68.8	68.5	70.3
Tobacco companies	27.3	23.7	24.1	17.9
Insurance companies	40.3	31.9	45.9	51.3
Interest Groups				
Women's movement	80.2	71.1	62.9	50.9
National Rifle Association (NRA)	60.2	58.0	48.9	44.4
Labor unions	67.6	51.9	59.8	55.4
Evangelical Christians	40.5	45.0	43.0	44.8
Gay Rights movement	42.3	35.1	23.2	25.0
Animal Rights movement	74.3	66.7	58.1	58.4
Media				
MTV	59.0	33.7	27.0	20.9
Network TV news	67.7	65.2	69.9	76.6

Note: Respondents were asked: "Now I'd like your opinion of some groups and organizations. (First), would you say your overall opinion of . . . is very favorable, mostly favorable, mostly unfavorable, or very unfavorable?" The percentages reported are very favorable and mostly favorable.

Source: The Times Mirror Center for The People & The Press. Telephone survey of a nationally representative sample of 3,800 adults 18 years of age or older living within the continental U.S., conducted July 12-27, 1994. Reprinted with permission.

PART IV

Projections for the Future

7

How Wide the Generational Divide? Changes over Time

Generational politics is nothing new. As recently as the 1960s, young people in the United States openly opposed their elders about the Vietnam War. In the 1990s, slow growth and a leviathan deficit could lead the generations to compete with one another over the same pot of money. Increasingly, voters and policymakers will face questions such as: Do we rob from our children's education to pay for our aging parents' health care? Do we build more nursing homes for the increasing numbers of frail elderly or more medical clinics for growing numbers of poor children?

On the other hand, certain signs indicate a narrowing in the generational divide. Young workers support many programs for the elderly, perhaps recognizing that those programs will lessen their own burdens of caring for their aging parents. In *Young v. Old,* my comprehensive, longitudinal look at generational differences in political participation and policy preferences has shown that age is often a good predictor of individual political actions and reactions. But in certain other instances, it simply isn't. It is impossible to come to a single conclusion about how wide is or will be the generational divide in the world of politics. The answer varies depending upon the specific situation in which the question is asked.

I began this book by posing five questions: (1) Do older Americans participate more in politics than their younger counterparts? (2) Do the generations differ sharply in their opinions about government, public officials, taxing, and spending? (3) Are there substantial disagreements among the generations on most public issues and policies? (4) Are there issues that tend to being the generations together? and (5) Will today's intergenerational differences and similarities persist for several decades more?

I found that age-group differences are often primarily attributable to one's place in the life cycle. The needs and priorities of the young are simply different from those of the old, especially on economic issues. But in other instances, the differences are more a product of the time in history during which each generation became socialized politically, for example, foreign and defense policy preferences. Sometimes, the attitudes and opinions of the young and the old are actually quite similar; their differences are with the *middle-aged* cohorts. The

FIGURE 7.1 What's in Store for the Future

Some future facts from the Census Bureau about:

People: The nation's population will top 275 million by the end of the century.

Kids: The under-18 crowd will increase by about 6 million by the turn of the century, then grow another 20 million by 2050. They are a fourth of the population now, but their share never again may be as great. They will make up 23 percent of the population in 2050.

Seniors: By 2050 there will be 80 million Americans over age 65. That's 1 American in 5, compared with 1 in 8 today.

Grade schools: Some 36 million pupils will crowd the classrooms by 2000, 4 million more than today. Afterward, however, the number of pupils will start to shrink through 2015.

Babies: Births are expected to decline slightly as the century ends. But 2012 may see the nation in the midst of a new baby boom, with births exceeding the 4.3-million-a-year born in the decades following World War II.

Baby boomers: The generation born between 1946 and 1964 will help push the median age from the present 32.8 years to 39.1 years in 2035. The first boomers turn 65 in 2011; the last, in 2029. Their share of the population will drop from a third now to a fourth in 2010 to a sixth in 2030.

Source: Associated Press, "Minority Population to Keep Growing," *St. Petersburg Times*, September 29, 1993, p. 1A. Reprinted with permission.

middle-aged, often called the "sandwich generation," are frequently subjected to cross-pressures from the young and the old, who are increasingly living side by side with them in the same household. This cross-pressure tends to make the middle-aged more politically active. They also see a wider range of issues and problems as critical.

Some generational participatory and policy preference gaps have narrowed as one age-extreme group has changed faster than the other. For example, among the young, the rapid change has occurred in respect to registration and voting rates, more conservative attitudes toward moral and crime issues, and less trust and confidence in government as a problem-solver. Among the old, the change has occurred in their attitudes toward certain issues of social justice and individual rights. Usually, the involvement and opinions of the young shift the most as they gain more experience and are exposed to more information about the political world. But the age projections for the next half-century put the elderly in the driver's seat in terms of sheer numbers (see Figure 7.1).

PARTICIPATION RATE GAPS: NARROWING
AND DRIVEN BY ECONOMICS

Generational contrasts of political participation have generally focused on the two most common forms of such participation—registration and voting—and to a lesser extent on certain types of campaign and contacting activities, such as wearing political buttons, contributing money to a candidate or party, writing letters, or calling elected officials. Few have focused, as I have in *Young v. Old*, on how individuals get information about a candidate or campaign, how much interest they have in national elections as opposed to state and local elections, how subject they are to voter overload and fatigue, or why they do not register or vote. In addition, not much attention has been paid to whether age matters in terms of when individuals decide whom to vote for, how often they vote the party line, the extent to which they follow various phases of an election campaign, and how they view the effectiveness of certain forms of political participation.

In *Young v. Old*, I have examined age-group differences in a wide array of participatory activities, including how often the young and old get involved in party organizational activities, enter into groups and protests, take part in litigation, sign and circulate petitions, and run for office. For the most part, the differentials in participation in each of these forms of political involvement can be explained by an individual's interest, experience, physical capacity, economic means, family and employment circumstance, technological expertise, and time available. These factors obviously differ across the age-groups as a consequece of where individuals are in the life cycle.

Registration and Voting

Without question, older persons register and vote more than the young, confirming conventional wisdom. Older people are also more consistent voters, participating in national, state, and local elections, even if they are held at different times (i.e., election overload doesn't deter them from voting). They are also more likely to complete a ballot, voting in all or most of the contests on the slate, including propositions or amendments normally placed at the end.

The registration rate and voter turnout gaps between the youngest and oldest cohorts narrowed slightly between 1988 and 1992. The participation rates of the younger generation jumped, while those of the older voters remained fairly stable. The 1992 presidential campaign was more personally relevant to younger voters than previous elections, a fact that I and others attribute to its economic focus. I also attribute the registration and turnout rate increases among the young to media mobilization efforts, most notably infotainment cable television programs and late-night comedy shows, which are targeted at them and which they use more than others do as a source of political information.

Older persons are more likely to register and vote than the young, often out of a sense of civic duty. Older voters are also more likely to feel guilty when they don't vote. Younger cohorts do not consider voting as essential or effective as their older counterparts do. However, the gap in this regard is closing. Younger cohorts today are more patriotic and more likely to see voting as a civic duty than younger cohorts even a decade or less ago. This change goes hand in hand with the narrowing of the generational gap in registration and voter turnout rates.

The young and old alike agree that the main reason they do not always vote is because they lack sufficient information about the candidates. Beyond that, the reasons Americans give for not always voting vary with their place in the life cycle. Younger voters are more apt to be cynical about the quality of the candidates (i.e., they feel that none are worth voting for) or to say they are busy (at work or school), out of town, or not registered. Registration is often more difficult or confusing for younger persons because they tend to be more mobile and thus run up against the minimum residency periods that most states have established as registration requirements.

Older persons who don't vote are more likely to attribute their nonvoting to illness, registration difficulties, a desire to stay out of politics (disengagement), or a belief that it doesn't really matter who's elected (cynicism).

The middle-aged are less likely than either the youngest or oldest cohorts to attribute their nonvoting to registration complexities, difficulty in getting to the polls, lack of interest, or insufficient information about the candidates. They are more likely than the other age-groups to give no particular reason for not voting or to say they simply weren't interested in the campaign. However, the middle-aged are generally the most politically active of any age-group, coming the closest to what some refer to as "the complete activists."

Sources of Political Information

The old and the young clearly vary on where they get their information about politics. Older voters rely on a wider variety of news sources—electronic and print media—for political information. Although television is the news source most relied upon by all age-groups, the young rely more on soft-news infotainment programs, whereas the old rely more on standard nightly news and weekly news magazine programs. Older persons also regularly rely more on the print media, especially daily newspapers, than younger individuals, who are frequent (although still not heavy) readers of personality magazines. The young are more prone to see the establishment news media as biased and having too much influence over who is nominated and elected to office. Across all age-groups, the proportion believing that the news media have too much influence declines as a campaign progresses but remains sizable to the end.

Following Campaigns from Beginning to End: What Matters Most?

Older voters are more attentive to campaigns—be they primaries or general elections at the federal, state, or local levels. However, they also get tired of the media-intense election hoopla much more quickly, often having made up their minds for whom to vote much earlier than the younger voters.

Surveys show that younger voters are more supportive of extensive television coverage of all aspects of a campaign, primarily because they rely almost exclusively on television for political information. The irony is that they still end up watching televised campaign events less than older voters. The young are also more likely to change their opinions based on television coverage of debates and conventions and even political advertising.

A majority of each age-group finds political ads helpful in learning about the candidates and their platforms, priorities, and personae, although most (three-fourths) still rate the news as a better source than ads. Younger voters are slightly more likely to attribute their candidate awareness (learning about who is running) to political ads and to find ads instrumental in their vote decisions, although a third of the electorate at large credited ads in this manner. The old are somewhat more inclined to say ads tell them something about the candidate's persona. New ad formats, such as the 1992 Ross Perot infomercials, capture the attention of young and old alike, although they don't necessarily change a person's vote choice.

Pre-election surveys consistently show that the young and old alike want more media coverage of a candidate's issue positions, less coverage of his or her personal character, and less analysis of campaign commercials. Postelection surveys reveal that after all is said and done, older voters weigh a candidate's personality, character, and experience a little more heavily in their vote decisions than do the young, who weigh leadership and issue stances more heavily. Older persons are less likely to see an issue as always being clear-cut. They are also more prone to believe that experienced candidates of strong character can tackle just about any problem placed before them.

Political Party Identification and Participation

There are age-group differences in terms of party affiliation and participation, often driven by a person's political socialization experiences (identification) and by his or her stage in the life cycle (activism). Age differences with regard to political party affiliation are sizable, although not as great as those observed in the more hands-on political experiences. Party still means the most to older voters, but the young and old alike are increasingly likely to classify themselves as independents or to vote a split ticket; an overwhelming majority of each group, however, give themselves a partisan label when asked to do so.

Higher proportions of the youngest cohort of partisans are Republicans, as compared to the elderly, who are more heavily Democratic. Each group's partisan leanings in the 1990s reflect the strength of their party in the historical period (realignment, dealignment) during which they became politically socialized. However, across all age-groups, the proportion identifying themselves as independents has risen over the past several decades, even though higher percentages of the elder group still regard their political party as important to them personally.

Generally, older persons articulate more differences and more likes or dislikes of each party than younger people, primarily because they have had more years of experience with the political party system. And younger Americans, because of their lack of experience, are somewhat more likely to shift the intensity of their opinions toward the two parties' issue-handling capacity. The generational gap on these party dimensions has remained fairly stable over the past decade or so.

A majority of each age-group believes that joining local party organizations is an effective form of political participation, although the young are slightly more positive in their assessments in this respect. Among the party activists, the young tend to be somewhat more involved in campaign-related activities—door-to-door canvassing, organizing campaign events, arranging fund-raising activities, sending mailings to voters, distributing campaign literature and posters, dealing with the media, and working with volunteers. Older party activists are more involved in registering voters, contacting voters, recruiting candidates, and organizing and attending party functions. Middle-aged party activists are the most likely to hold party leadership positions, especially at the grassroots level, often seeing them as stepping-stones to elective or appointive political offices.

Direct and Indirect Contacting of Public Officials: A Growing Form of Participation

There are quite a few differences among members of various age-groups in the type and extent of their involvement in various activities designed to let public officials know exactly what they think about issues and situations. The gap between the young and the old is fairly wide with regard to contacting a public official. Older constituents are much more likely than the young to write a letter to an elected official or to call or send a letter to the White House or a member of Congress. This gap occurs because older people are more interested in and attentive to political happenings, and they are more heavily involved in groups that send out policy alerts to their memberships along with more information on how to contact public officials.

More citizens in all age-groups are using the press as an indirect way to contact politicos—via letters to the editor, calling public affairs talk shows, and responding to newspaper, television, or interest group polls. The generational gap in the use of this form of political participation is not nearly as wide as it is in direct contacting. But neither is this type of participation used by as many people, although this will likely change rapidly as the press establishes more interactive communication networks. The young are slightly more responsive to requests from the electronic media for opinion feedback. And the greater attractiveness to the young of these alternative forms of individual contacting has the potential to reduce historically wide participation gaps between young and old in the future.

Both young and old are more prone to take part in attendance-related activities only when an issue or problem affects them very directly. Although more of the youngest cohort engaged in this form of nonvoting participation than in any other, they are still less involved than the middle-aged and older cohorts. The middle-aged are the most frequent attendees at public hearings and forums; the oldest cohorts are the most likely to speak at such a meeting since they are more experienced at public speaking and more comfortable in criticizing government officials.

Younger cohorts and the middle-aged Civil Rights/Vietnam/Watergate cohort are the most likely to actively participate in demonstrations, protests, boycotts, and civil disobedience. However, small percentages of any age-group actually get involved in willfully breaking the law. Protests and economic boycotts are seen as more effective tools; the young see them as somewhat more effective than the older cohorts. Furthermore, protests and demonstrations today are less likely to be concentrated on college campuses or to be held for exclusively liberal causes—witness the abortion protests.

Middle-aged and younger voters work more actively in signing and circulating petitions. This activity generally takes place in heavily congested public places, which often deters older persons from becoming involved. Petition-drive leaders try to convince younger, more educated persons to sign a petition by posing it as "simply a chance to let both sides be heard or to let the voters decide," rather than by emphasizing the specific issue at hand. Middle-aged persons, by virtue of their leadership positions in many civic and political organizations, are the most likely to circulate petitions, although only a small proportion actually do.

Americans also let public officials know what they want and expect via collaborative group efforts, ranging from belonging to groups to contributing money to PACs to being part of a lawsuit against a governmental entity. The number of people joining expressly political interest groups has escalated sharply in recent years, rising from 17 to 27 percent between 1987 and 1993. Today, group participation, like other forms of participation, is more interactive and less demanding of physical attendance. People can be active from their living rooms via telephone, personal computers, letters, or monetary contributions. Consequently, older persons have been slower to disengage from group activism in recent years than in the past.

The number of interest groups representing each generation has increased dramatically since 1985. However, in respect to cohesiveness and proximity to national centers of power, they differ considerably. National membership groups representing older Americans, such as the American Association of Retired Persons, are more likely to be headquartered in Washington, DC. Nearly three-fourths of such groups were founded between 1970 and 1990, reflecting the onslaught of interest groups in recent years and the aging of the U.S. population. In contrast, groups representing infants, children, youth, and young adults are older, more often oriented toward a single purpose, typically located outside Washington, and more independent vis-à-vis one another, making it difficult to compete against the more cohesive, elderly oriented groups like AARP.

The greatest increase in PAC contributors has occurred among those over 50, including those 65 and older, again reflecting both the growing power of interest groups representing older Americans and the elderly's relatively better financial position.

Individuals and groups often file lawsuits against the government when they feel they are shut out of the regular political process, and a desire to protect a group's economic interests is more likely to spark litigation than its concern with individual or civil rights. To date, litigation as a form of political participation is used most often by middle-aged and younger cohorts—those who have grown up in a more litigious society, are better educated, and in the case of the middle-aged, are often in a better financial position to engage in such activity (in the case of the young, they have the least to lose).

The number of economically based lawsuits emanating from groups representing both age extremes undoubtedly will escalate in the future. Groups representing younger Americans will likely file more suits challenging the fairness or equity of government spending patterns. Groups representing older Americans will be more inclined to litigate in situations in which older people's income (including government entitlements), retirement benefits, seniority, or job security are threatened.

Participating as an Elected Official

Americans of all ages have less and less respect for elected officials, and few believe a political career is desirable. Less than 1 percent of the population ever runs for political office. Beyond that, nearly three-fourths of all Americans (more old than young) do not want a son, daughter, or other family member to choose a political career. Although exhilarating, holding an elective office can exert a heavy toll on one's professional and personal life. Depending upon the office sought, lots of traveling and even maintaining a second home in another city or state may be required. Fears about losing one's privacy and facing an increasingly hostile press are other factors that often deter individuals from running.

Age affects a person's decision to seek elective office in a number of ways. Certain offices have minimum age requirements—for instance, the presidency, seats in the U.S. Senate and House of Representatives, and some positions at the state and local levels. Because they are seen as more prestigious and higher up in the hierarchy of political office, certain posts are sought by older persons who initially entered elective politics by winning lower or base offices—for example, a post on the city council, county commission, or school board.

Increasingly, older persons are seeking base offices with no intent to move up the political ladder. Likewise, people who initially entered base positions when fairly young with progressive ambitions are simply staying in them longer today. They have abandoned thoughts of seeking higher office, for reasons already elaborated. Thus, the age profiles of many elected bodies have gradually turned grayer. However, as more jurisdictions adopt term limits, the age profiles of elective officials may actually get younger over the next few decades.

GENERATIONAL GAPS IN TAXING AND SPENDING
POLICY PREFERENCES?

Another key question posed in *Young v. Old* is whether the generations differ sharply in their taxing and spending preferences. An offshoot question is whether there is any truth to the perception that the youngest and oldest cohorts are the most "selfish" in their fiscal priorities. Based on the data I reviewed, I conclude that some significant generational differences have arisen with respect to taxing and spending priorities and alternatives, gaps that I predict will widen, not narrow, as the nation's age profile changes. However, when it comes to taxing and spending choices, all age-groups express a preference for policies that are (or would be) most advantageous to them at that point in their lives. No one age-group holds exclusive rights to being labeled "greedy" or "self-centered."

The intergroup tensions over taxing and spending issues are projected to intensify in the future, for several reasons. First, there will be considerably more older voters than younger voters (see Figure 7.1). Second, budgeting is a zero-sum game. When economic times are tight, someone's gain, whether on the taxing side or the spending side of the budgetary ledger, is generally perceived as someone else's loss. Third, a person's economic status is greatly affected by his or her age and place in the work/life cycle. Fourth, the programmatic needs of younger and older persons vary, again largely driven by their place in the life cycle. Fifth, sharp increases in tax burdens have always prompted those most affected to become politically active. As the nation ages, the young will see their tax burdens escalate because of the greater numbers of retirees receiving government benefits such as Social Security and Medicare, with fewer people of working age available to support those entitlements.[1]

As taxing and spending preference gaps widen, political participation rates will likely narrow. The young, I think, will increasingly become more active at the ballot box and in the halls of government, contrary to what others have projected, although this may not occur as rapidly as young political activists and their advocacy groups would like. Younger cohorts will attempt to guard against tax structures that would place heavy burdens on them and to fight for a fair share of scarce resources for themselves and their children. Equity concerns will likely supplant efficiency issues in the 1990s and beyond.

Regardless of age, most Americans say their taxes are too high. At the same time, they think the taxes of many others, especially the rich, are too low. Predictably, middle-aged persons see virtually all taxes as more unfair than do younger or older persons, primarily because they typically bear a heavier tax burden than the other two age-groups. However, the youngest and oldest cohorts do differ in their perceptions of tax fairness. Over the years, older persons have rated the property tax as the least fair; younger persons cite the federal income tax. Again, this perception has to do with life cycle and burden. Younger persons are less likely to own property; older persons are less likely to be earning income in the workforce. Moreover, the young see the Social Security tax as less fair than do the old. Clearly, part of the explanation is that younger generations are far less likely than the Depression or World War II generations to believe they will get back more (or even a sum equal to) what they pay in to the Social Security system.

A majority of all age-groups believes the best way to make the tax system fairer is to require upper-income taxpayers to pay more. They prefer this method over other options such as reducing taxes on lower-income individuals, making businesses pay more even if it costs jobs, or leaving the system alone because, as some say, "it's as fair as it's gonna get." The middle-aged are the most supportive of making the rich pay more, again because their tax burdens are usually heavier.

Across all age-groups, a plurality favors closing loopholes rather than creating new taxes or raising individual income tax rates. But if taxes have to be imposed or raised, sales taxes and user fees are far more preferable to each age-group than individual income or property taxes. The old and the young differ somewhat in their reasons for opposing more property taxes. The young are more likely to see the tax as a deterrent to owning a home. The old, in contrast, more often cite its regressivity and steady rate of increase, reflecting their concern for any revenue source that appears to bite off a consistently bigger chunk of their relatively fixed incomes.

For the same reason, older persons are generally more likely to volunteer that they favor *no* new or increased taxes. However, if they face a choice of higher taxes or a service reduction, then they are more likely than other age-groups to choose taxes. This is the basis for my prediction that in the future, older generations may actually push for greater government spending while younger generations push for reductions—a reversal of past patterns.

The spending priorities of the different age-groups vary considerably but in the expected direction. Among the younger cohorts, education and social programs primarily benefiting the young but also Medicare rank as top priorities. Among the elderly, spending on programs to combat crime are a high priority, along with health, Social Security, and Medicare. These priorities were derived by asking each age-group which program cuts they would vehemently oppose.

The groups' different spending priorities often track somewhat closely with what level of government they believe is the most cost effective (i.e., gives them the most for their tax dollars). Between 1972 and 1993, a majority of the younger cohorts said either the local or the state government gave them the most for their money, compared to only a plurality of the older cohorts. And more older than younger persons consistently ranked the federal government as the most cost effective. These patterns are not surprising: A higher proportion of the old receive financial benefits from the federal government in the form of Social Security, Medicare, and other payments, and a higher proportion of the young benefit from educational, employment, and social service programs financed and delivered by state and local governments.

GENERATIONAL DIFFERENCES IN POLICY PREFERENCES?

Another of the key questions I posed at the beginning of the book was whether there are substantial disagreements among the generations on most public issues and policies or whether there are issues that tend to bring the generations together. Based on my review of the available data, I conclude that there is greater consensus among Americans of all ages about the importance of a problem than there is about *how* to address it or *when* it should be addressed relative to other problems. Mostly, the generations differ in the intensity, rather than the direction, of their opinions. I project that will change, however, when zero-sum economic-based issues move to the forefront as the nation's age profile gets grayer. In general, older persons are less inclined to label problems as "critical" or to believe that government intervention is necessarily the best or most effective way of solving societal ills—either at home or abroad.

Domestic Policy Issues

On the home economic front, the young are most concerned about the economy and jobs; the old worry about taxes and government spending. On noneconomic domestic issues, both the young and the old are concerned about crime and moral issues. The young are more attentive to educational and environmental issues, while the old closely follow health and social service issues. Legislators identify moral, tax, social service, and health issues as the ones igniting the most intense intergenerational conflicts. There are few signs that this pattern will change much over the coming decades.

Health Care Policy. As is true in most policy areas, the opinions of both the young and the old on various health care issues reflect their assessments of how problems—and reforms—will affect them personally. These judgments naturally vary with a person's place in the life cycle. For example, younger people are more concerned about losing health insurance if they change or lose jobs. Older persons see paying for long-term care in a nursing home as a more pressing problem, along with the mountains of paperwork involved in tapping into their insurance to cover medical expenses. The "sandwich generation" is quite fearful of losing health insurance, paying for long-term nursing home care (for their parents primarily), having to pay the cost of a major illness, and having to pay more for their own health care. It is the young middle-aged (30- to 49-year-olds) who more strongly support preventive care. They are often most aware of the medical histories of their children, parents, and grandparents, and they see how such an approach might have saved considerable amounts of money in the long run.

When asked trade-off questions about their willingness to settle for less health care in order to control costs and promote universal coverage, the young are more in favor of waiting longer for nonemergency medical and hospital care rather than having added restrictions placed on their choice of doctors and hospitals or slowing the introduction of new medical procedures and technologies into hospitals. A majority of those older than 65 do not prefer any of these alternatives. But of the three alternatives, the elderly are slightly more supportive of slowing the introduction of new medical procedures and technologies.

Government intervention in health-related practices that are viewed as harmful to individuals and society at large, such as smoking and alcohol abuse, does not spark the same intergenerational differences as does government involvement in health issues with a moral dimension. For example, younger cohorts are much more supportive than the older ones of government regulations and programs permitting sex education and condom distribution in the schools and promoting drug treatment rather than punishment for drug use.

The generational divide in health care policy is likely to widen in the future as health care rationing becomes necessary. When disease-specific funding and care choices are posed to the public, the generational differences will be dramatic—and each group will become more combative.

Crime and Criminal Justice Policy. The generational gap on crime and criminal justice policy has closed considerably over the past several decades. Young and old alike have grown more fearful of becoming victims of crime. Although the elderly are the most fearful of this, more young people than old are actually victims of crime. Consequently, the young have increasingly moved in the direction of favoring punishment over rehabilitation, thereby narrowing the generational gap on this policy dimension. However, the young are still somewhat more positively inclined toward rehabilitation and prevention than the old. Generational divides could emerge on crime and justice issues if the debate turns to one of education versus crime, which is most likely to occur at the state and local levels.

Moral and Social Issues. Moral and social issues used to be quite distinct, but by the 1990s they had become interlocked. Issues regarded as having strong moral *and* social overtones include abortion, gay rights, school prayer, pornography, women's and minorities' rights, and increasingly, adoption rights and medical ethics, especially with regard to procreation. Some of these moral and social issues (abortion, gay rights) evoke vastly different opinions across the generations; others (school prayer, medical ethics) do not. In general, when public policy issue alternatives are posed in terms of individual rights versus societal rights, the young tend to come down on the side of protecting individual rights; the old favor protecting society.

The generational gaps on the rights and roles of women and minorities have narrowed in some areas but widened in others. Both young and old support the notion of equal opportunity, but the old are considerably more likely to think we have gone beyond equal opportunity. They are more likely to oppose government-imposed affirmative action programs designed to achieve gender and racial balances in the workplace. However, there is a growing feeling across all generations that government mandates are widening, rather than narrowing, the racial and gender divides. And a substantial proportion of each age-group is concerned about the long-term effects of children being raised in day care centers as a consequence of mothers working.

Generational differences on social welfare and employment policies center on whether those on public assistance are exploiting the government and taxpayers. Older cohorts are more inclined to believe most recipients are taking advantage of the system, whereas younger cohorts are not. The young and young middle-aged are also less likely to favor punitive solutions that reduce payments to women who have more children while on welfare or to reduce welfare spending in general. These age-groups tend to see children as bearing the brunt of such punitive approaches.

Overwhelming majorities of each age-group favor government programs designed to promote individual self-sufficiency, especially when government resources are tight. But in recent years, support among the youngest (Reagan) generation for government guarantees of employment and a good standard of living has increased. In contrast, each of the other generations increasingly supports leaving the primary responsibility up to each individual. This is yet another indication that members of the Reagan generation are more and more pessimistic about their economic future.

Foreign and Defense Issues

Throughout U.S. history, domestic and foreign policy issues have been highly interrelated. When things at home are tough economically, Americans become less supportive of foreign and defense policies that they perceive will either drain money from the domestic economy or result in job losses at home. Generally, opinions on foreign policy fluctuate considerably more than those on domestic policy, primarily reflecting responses to the rapidly changing media coverage of world hot spots.

An individual's support for U.S. involvement in foreign affairs, especially by military troops, greatly depends upon whether such involvement during the time he or she came of age politically was judged to have been positive or negative. An individual's judgments about other countries' actions and potential threats to the United States are similarly affected. For example, a much higher proportion of persons 65 and older believe the U.S. government should closely monitor the activities of some of our old enemies, such as North Korea, Japan, Germany, and China. Older Americans are also less inclined to cut defense spending, even in the midst of a recession, than the young, reflecting their long-standing distrust of these countries and communism, as well as their years of exposure to the constant eruption of new trouble spots around the globe. The young are more likely to be suspicious of our more recent enemies, such as Iraq, and more fearful of the spread of nuclear weapons. But the young are more willing to commit U.S. troops abroad because of their positive experience with the Persian Gulf War.

By and large, all generations of Americans are somewhat more positive about sending U.S. troops abroad for humanitarian or economic reasons than simply to restore law and order in strife-torn countries. Although they believe the United States should play an active role in world affairs, they don't necessarily think it should play a *more* active role than other leading nations. They support involvement in multilateral organizations but strongly prefer that U.S. soldiers remain under the command of American officers in any conflict situation.

The young are much more likely than the old to rate environmental issues abroad and at home as quite pressing, high-priority problems to be addressed by our government. The young's strong support for cleaning up the environment, even in the face of losing jobs, reflects the emphasis the issue has received in school curricula—beginning with the energy crisis of the 1970s and heightened by intense media coverage of global warming, recycling, air and water pollution, and green peace issues during the 1980s.

The generations have few quarrels about the nation's long-term foreign policy goals. Each age-group rates economic and defense goals as more important than the promotion of democracy, human rights, or multilateral organizations. Only weak support exists in any generation for imposing our democratic values on other countries with different value systems when such an imposition might cause damage at home or abroad. However, the younger cohorts are consistently more zealous about spreading democratic principles around the globe, regardless of the consequences (although less than a majority of them would make such choices). A majority of each generation believes that most of the countries who have received U.S. aid end up resenting the United States, but this feeling is much more intense among the older cohorts.

The gap between the young and the old in respect to trust and confidence in government has narrowed in recent years, as more of the young have come to see government as an ineffective problem-solver. The middle-aged Civil Rights/ Vietnam/Watergate generation remains the most cynical (although not by much), reflecting their political socialization during a time when highly negative views of government and government leaders prevailed. Significantly, trust and confidence among the youngest (Reagan) generation has eroded the fastest in recent years, indicative of that generation's growing disillusionment with the government's handling of economic problems and an increasing concern about the economic future.

WHAT TO EXPECT FOR THE FUTURE

Regardless of whether one attributes generational differences to maturational, period, or cohort effects, it is clear that older persons have different economic needs and priorities than the young. That fact is not likely to change. What will change is how often each generation views various policy proposals as us-against-them choices. It will become a more common phenomenon as the age pyramid takes on a different shape. What in the past has shown up more as a difference in intensity will begin to emerge as a difference in direction.

We certainly know that older Americans participate more in almost all facets of politics and are generally better informed. The key question as we look to the future is whether today's higher cynicism levels among the younger cohorts will depress or stimulate their political participation rates as they age. My bet is that sheer economics will force this younger generation (and those that follow it) to get more involved in politics in spite of an earlier onset of cynicism toward government. Technological innovations will make it easier and more interesting for all age-groups to be more politically active—and not just on election day.

I anticipate more frequent opportunities for individuals to interact with the media, pollsters, interest groups, and policymakers during each stage of the policymaking process—that is, formation, adoption, implementation, and evaluation. Public opinion surveys will increasingly ask the public trade-off, or choice, policy preference questions that are cast in real-life legislative and budgetary terms. Constituents will increasingly be asked to prioritize, rank, or make either-or choices. The more this happens, the more likely that the economic dimensions of noneconomic issues will surface.

As noted, today's intergenerational differences primarily involve intensity rather than direction. The young and old differ in the magnitude of their policy preferences, but majorities or pluralities of each group tend to hold similar views. Tomorrow, we are more likely to find different generations supporting policy priorities that are diametrically opposed to each other as the nation undergoes its graying metamorphosis and the economic realities associated with it sink in. These shifts will show up first in states like Florida, where age profiles are changing at the fastest rate.

FLORIDA: EARLY SIGNS OF WHAT THE NATION'S AGING WILL MEAN POLITICALLY

When Naisbitt published *Megatrends*, he had already observed a "growing tension between the state's older and younger residents."[2] That was at the beginning of the 1980s. According to Florida's legislators, the pattern has continued into the 1990s. Nearly half (45 percent) project that intergenerational tensions will be more noticeable throughout the state over the next five years.[3] In contrast, only 10 percent see them diminishing. Lawmakers in all parts of the country will soon be making the same projections—especially as the national debates on Social Security, Medicare, the national debt, and income tax reform take center stage—and the new "age-group consciousness" transcends down to the state and local levels, as it already has in Florida.

Florida's legislators, regardless of their own age, have fairly clear perceptions about which issues are most likely to spark intergenerational conflicts in the future. They see these as moral, tax, social service, and health issues. (These are also showing up in national surveys as being the policy areas where the young and old have the most divergent preferences and priorities.)

The sheer number of older voters compared to the young, and their still higher turnout rates, especially in state and local elections, have already started to impact funding levels for programs that more directly benefit one age-group over another. Nowhere is this more obvious than in the classic funding battle between education and criminal justice. A former state university president framed the issue in this manner: "We now spend more in Florida on the 56,000 incarcerated convicts that we have in this state than the 203,000 university students we have in this state or the 300,000 community college students."[4] The proportion of

Florida's budget going to education has steadily declined,[5] while the proportion allocated to criminal justice has increased. Although I am certainly not prepared to attribute these trends exclusively to the aging profile of the electorate, they do, I believe, have something to do with it. Youth advocacy groups also lament the state's "flat" spending levels for other children's services, especially as compared to other states. At the same time, Floridians voted in 1990 to create a new state agency to represent the needs and concerns of older residents (the Department of Elder Affairs).

The growing awareness of "age politics" in Florida has already sparked more political interest among the young, even in state and local contests. The participation rate gap between the youngest and oldest cohorts has narrowed somewhat, even in off-year elections that feature state and local contests. And, in line with my theory, exit polls and postelection voting analyses conducted by some age-specific groups increasingly find it is often the *youngest* voting-aged cohorts who most oppose referenda requiring more taxes—sometimes even those earmarked for schools or children's services boards.[6] Based on Florida's experience, I predict that the younger generation's interest in state and local politics will increase as more state and local budgetary choices are perceived in age-related, "us-versus-them" terms.

Florida's experiences have also demonstrated the expertise and technical capacities of various age-specific interest groups in doing their own analyses of state and local spending patterns, as well as the state media's interest in sharing these independent analyses with the public. I predict the national media will increasingly pick up on this trend and cast more public policy debates in young-versus-old terms. Age will likely be to the next millennium what race has been to the last half of the twentieth century—a high-profile, highly divisive problem for which it will be extremely difficult to devise solutions that work.

BRIDGING THE GENERATION GAP: PREVENTIVE STRATEGIES

A number of signs indicate that ageism may replace or at least equal racism as the nation's most severe social problem in the twenty-first century. According to a recent survey by *Parade Magazine*, 88 percent of Americans think young people do not understand the elderly, and at the same time, two-thirds think the elderly do not understand young people.[7] Before the simmering misunderstandings between generations reach the boiling point, this nation needs to rethink some of its policies and priorities and begin to develop and implement preventive strategies. Torres-Gil, in *The New Aging,* stressed that "intergenerational" must become the watchword for the future. He urged the abandonment of "age-segregated policies that base eligibility on one's age, and interest-group politics that pit old age-groups against other needy constituents."[8] He also concluded that "we must determine how to prepare young people for a long life." But how can we do this?

Develop Educational Programs

U.S. experience in combating all sorts of social problems, from racial discrimination to substance abuse, has proven that education is one of the most effective tools for shaping attitudes and behavior. Thus, the development of educational materials aimed at promoting an intergenerational understanding of the special concerns, needs, and problems of different age-groups should be accelerated. The emergence of the information superhighway and various other high-tech, interactive forms of communication will provide an excellent conduit for the dissemination of this information to all age-groups.

One approach is to produce videos that illustrate why individuals of different ages have varied opinions and preferences about a wide array of public policy issues. These programs, developed by interdisciplinary and intergenerational teams of experts, should integrate audio and visual elements to explain the key events, music, pop culture, and economic and social problems that dominated the periods in which different age-groups were politically socialized.

Interactive educational computer games could allow players to predict what different generations' political preferences and forms of activism would be under various circumstances. Some games might challenge players to forecast how changes in the shape of the nation's age profile (pyramid) might affect political participation, policy preferences, and budgetary outcomes. Such games would promote a better understanding of the impact of shifts in the nation's age structure on taxing and spending demands.

At the same time, educational software programs could be developed that simulate the life-cycle economics of different generations. Ideally, many of these programs would fit a four-generation family—which many demographers predict will more likely live under the same roof in the next century.

Expand Community Programs

A number of communities have experimented successfully with programs that bring the young and the old together. On one side are programs such as Grandparents in School, which pairs elderly adult tutors (all volunteers) with preschool and school-aged children. On the other side are youth organizations such as Boys Clubs and Girls Clubs that make decorations for Meals on Wheels trays and periodically visit the elderly in nursing homes. Such programs have already been proven to promote understanding between the age extremes.

But there have been too few programs linking junior and senior high school students with persons from different generations. Some middle schools and high schools have just begun experimenting with curricula that promote community service, encouraging and rewarding students who work with different age-groups.

A number of private sector companies are doing the same with their employees, promoting and offering opportunities for them to do volunteer work with the young and the old. Responding to the need for education reform, businesses have increased their volunteer efforts in schools in recent years, particularly in such areas as mentoring and counseling students. Through Homework Hotline in St. Louis, for example, students struggling with homework assignments can obtain help from retired teachers and volunteers from McDonnell Douglas and Monsanto.[9]

But intergenerational interactions need not and should not be limited to educational settings or restricted to the public sector. And they should not be restricted to in-person interactions alone. Advances in telecommunications have made it possible for people to interact across geographical boundaries. These methods include: (1) audioconferencing, also known as telephone conference-calling; (2) videoconferencing, both the broadcast type, in which the speaker cannot see viewers but can take their phoned-in questions, and the fully interactive type, in which everyone can see and hear everyone else; and (3) computer-conferencing, which can link people via electronic mail and community bulletin boards. Communities can use these methods to promote simple communication across age-groups as well as for more specific purposes. For example, specialized interactive video networks, known as "telemedicine systems," are already operating in a number of communities to bring medical care to rural areas, which contain sizable populations of the elderly.[10] In low-demand times, these systems could connect the old and young in educational, work, and recreational contexts.

Rethink What It Means to Be Old

At the heart of these efforts is a fundamental rethinking of what it means to be old. Increasingly, many retirees do not consider themselves elderly. To a vigorous 70-year-old, "old people" are the homebound 90-year-olds that he delivers meals to every day. Experts predict that in 2011, the year the baby boomers begin to turn 65, this massive group will give entirely new meaning to their stage of life, just as they did with campus revolts in the 1960s and with yuppie lifestyles in the 1980s.

Betty Friedan, author of *The Fountain of Age*, proposed a new vision of aging, one that defines older people not in terms of deterioration and helplessness but as persons in a new period of life. Getting older "is an adventure, not a problem," she said.[11] She specifically advised against seeing the elderly as "objects of care," just as she warned in the 1960s against labeling women as sex objects. The "objects" view promotes the fear that the elderly will eat up the national wealth with their demands for health care and retirement benefits, and, more important, it distances us from our own aging. Instead of lumping together those older than 65, Friedan insisted on seeing older people as individuals, emphasizing their strengths, and supporting their independence and communal involvement as they move through this part of the natural continuum of life.

Indeed, many Americans can look forward to their "third age" as one in which they take up a new career or pursue interests they had no time for earlier. A 1987 federal law has eliminated mandatory retirement ages, with a few exceptions, and starting in the year 2000, the minimum age for receiving full Social Security benefits rises from 65 to 67 for people born after 1959. Some believe that age will be pushed to 70. Although many companies have used early retirement to cut costs during tough economic times, a few employers (notably Days Inn, McDonalds, and the Travelers Corporation) have begun to hire older workers to fill labor shortages and make use of their experience and reliability. Increasingly, we will find that mere chronological age cannot be used as a measure of ability.

Moreover, technological advances plus the shift away from defense-related industries have forced many older workers to find new employers, open their own businesses, or in some cases return to school for retraining. Though a significant number of older people have enrolled in college classes to prepare for new careers, the vast majority are going to school for the sheer joy of learning. Learning in Retirement study groups and seminars sponsored by such groups as Elderhostel give retirees the chance to choose from a rich assortment of courses—from the art of the Italian Renaissance to genetics and disease. We can also expect major changes in colleges and universities as they shift their hours and course offerings to better meet the needs of lifelong learners, including classes via video and computer links that enable older people to participate from their living rooms.

Yet aging, for all its promise of adventure, is not without peril. Although physical and psychological health varies widely among those 65 and older, it is true that bones and muscles begin to weaken, and vision and hearing begin to decline. Moreover, the risk of acquiring a variety of chronic ailments and disabilities such as arthritis, osteoporosis, diabetes, and dementia increases in later years. These conditions have raised questions about the length of life versus the quality of life, particularly in regard to policies governing health care spending and medical research. In the future, more and more Americans will confront quality-of-life issues that impact themselves and their loved ones, suggesting that a greater emphasis is needed on preventive measures and ethics in health education programs for all ages.

These are but a few of the more obvious ways to begin to educate the U.S. public about the causes and consequences of generational differences—and to transform our consciousness about the roles the young and the old play in a meaningful life together. But these can be important first steps in helping change young-versus-old scenarios into situations in which the young and old, even if they differ, at least have a better understanding of each other's choices. Based on the findings reported in this book, I believe a strong, well-integrated connection between education, technology, and the media is the key to minimizing intergenerational conflicts and promoting cross-generational understanding as our nation ages.

Notes

CHAPTER 1

1. Persons 65 and older are often classified into different age categories. Those 65 to 74 years of age are frequently labeled the *young-old*. Those 75 to 84 are referred to as the *aged*, and persons 85 and older are called the *oldest-old*. The term *frail elderly* is used to describe persons 65 and older with significant physical and cognitive health problems. These terms are primarily used for the sake of convenience and simplification, according to the U.S. Census Bureau in its report entitled *Sixty-Five Plus in America*, Current Population Reports, Series P-23, No. 178 (Washington, DC: U.S. Government Printing Office, August 1992). There is actually a great deal of variation in the usage of these terms by journalists and scholars.

2. For excellent overviews of age trends in the United States, see: U.S. Bureau of the Census, *Sixty-Five Plus in America*; U.S. Bureau of the Census, *Population Projections of the United States, by Age, Sex, Race, and Hispanic Origin: 1992 to 2050*, Current Population Reports, Series P-25, No. 1092 (Washington, DC: U.S. Government Printing Office, November 1992); and U.S. Senate Special Committee on Aging, in conjunction with the American Association of Retired Persons, *Aging America: Trends and Projections* (Washington, DC: U.S. Senate Special Committee on Aging, 1991).

3. In its 1992–2050 projections, the U.S. Census Bureau assumes that age-specific fertility rates will be constant at slightly below 1990 levels for non-Hispanic whites, non-Hispanic blacks, and the non-Hispanic American Indians, Eskimos, and Aleuts. It assumes a 10 percent increase in fertility rates after the year 2000 for the Hispanic-origin and the non-Hispanic Asian and Pacific Islander populations because the share of their fertility contributed by the foreign born is expected to decrease. Convergence of the birthrates by race and origin is not assumed. Life expectancy is expected to increase slowly from 75.8 years in 1992 to 82.1 years in 2050. No race convergence is assumed. Net immigration is expected to remain constant throughout the projection at 880,000 per year (about 1,040,000 immigrants and 160,000 emigrants). This reflects the 1990 immigration law changes and current knowledge of emigration, undocumented migration, and movement to and from Puerto Rico. See: U.S. Bureau of the Census, *Population Projections of the United States, by Age, Sex, Race, and Hispanic Origin*, p. xi.

4. U.S. Bureau of the Census, *Sixty-Five Plus in America*.

5. According to the Census Bureau, "It is because of the relatively low birth rates of these years that growth in the size of the elderly population will be steady but undramatic until after 2011 when the Baby Boom begins to reach age 65"; (see U.S. Bureau of the Census, *Sixty-Five Plus in America*, p. 2–1).

6. Technically, the term *cohort* refers to persons born in the same year. The term *cohort-group* describes persons born in a limited span of consecutive years, often five or ten years. A generation is composed of different cohorts and cohort-groups and is usually given a label based upon a significant historical event that occurred during the young adult years of the group, for example, the Depression, the 1960s, and so forth. See William Strauss and Neil Howe, *Generations: The History of America's Future, 1584 to 2089* (New York: Quill William Morrow, 1961), and Fernando M. Torres-Gil, *The New Aging: Politics and Change in America* (New York: Auburn House, 1992).

7. U.S. Bureau of the Census, *Sixty-Five Plus in America*, p. 2–1.

8. The total support ratio is actually projected to decline somewhat in the 1990s and 2000s but then increase sharply by 2010, as the baby boomers reach their elder years and the number of persons of traditional working ages declines. However, some are concerned that the elderly support ratio will actually increase in the 1990s and 2000s and that the youth support ratio will dip. The common assumption is that the relative costs of supporting the elderly exceed those of supporting the young, although there have been few empirical tests of this proposition, according to Donald J. Adamcheck and Eugene A. Friedman, "Societal Aging and Generational Dependency Relationships," *Research on Aging* 5 (September 1983), pp. 319—338. And youth advocates argue that even if this is true, society *ought* to spend far more on youth than it currently does, which would, in turn, reduce the amount that must be spent on the elderly in the long term.

9. Ken Dychtwald and Joe Flower, *Age Wave* (New York: Bantam Books, 1990).

10. Eskenazi, quoted in the *New York Times,* May 4, 1992.

11. Lee Smith, "The Tyranny of America's Old," *Fortune,* January 13, 1992.

12. U.S. Bureau of the Census, *Sixty-Five Plus in America;* Diane Crispell and William H. Frey, "American Maturity," *American Demographics* 15 (March 1993), pp. 31–42; and William Dunn, "Hanging Out with American Youth," *American Demographics* 14 (February 1992), pp. 24–35.

13. William March, "Longer Life Gives Chance to Enhance Quality of Old Age," *The Tampa Tribune,* September 29, 1992.

14. Reported in U.S. Bureau of the Census, *Sixty-Five Plus in America.*

15. Ibid.

16. Kay Mannello, quoted in Melinda Beck et al., "Attention, Willard Scott," *Newsweek,* May 4, 1992.

17. Crispell and Frey, "American Maturity," p. 32.

18. Ibid., p. 33.

19. Dunn, "Hanging Out with American Youth," pp. 24–25.

20. See James W. Button and Walter A. Rosenbaum, "Seeing Gray: School Bond Issues and the Aging in Florida," *Research on Aging* 11, no. 2 (June 1989), pp. 158–173; and Stanley K. Smith, "Population," in David A. Denslow et al., eds., *The Economy of Florida* (Gainesville: Bureau of Economic and Business Research, University of Florida, 1990), pp. 19–35.

21. John Naisbitt, *Megatrends: Ten New Directions Transforming Our Lives* (New York: Warner Books, 1982), p. 8.

22. See Walter A. Rosenbaum and James W. Button, "Is There a Gray Peril? Retirement Politics in Florida," *The Gerontologist* 29 (1989), pp. 300–306; and Charles F. Longino, Jr., "From Sunbelt to Sunspots," *American Demographics* 16 (November 1994), pp. 22–31.

23. Longino, "From Sunbelt to Sunspots."

24. For good overviews of Florida's changing political environment, see Susan A. MacManus, ed., *Reapportionment and Representation in Florida: A Historical Collection* (Tampa: Intrabay Innovation Institute, University of South Florida, 1991); and Robert Huckshorn, ed., *Florida Politics* (Gainesville: University Presses of Florida, 1991).

25. Neil E. Cutler, paraphrasing Karl Mannheim, "The Problem of Generations," in Paul K. Kecskemeti, ed., *Essays on the Sociology of Knowledge by Karl Mannheim* (London: Routledge & Paul, 1952), p. 282; see Cutler, "Aging and Generations in Politics: The Conflict of Explanations and Inference," in Allen R. Wilcox, ed., *Public Opinion and Political Attitudes* (New York: John Wiley, 1974), p. 441.

26. Strauss and Howe, *Generations,* p. 34. The authors acknowledged (p. 61) that the twenty-two-year definition is imprecise and always shifting a bit from one era to another.

27. Ibid., p. 64.

28. Ibid, p. 74.

29. Torres-Gil, *The New Aging,* pp. 12–16.

30. Ibid., pp. 13, 15.

31. Ibid., p. 15.

32. Ibid., p. 129.

33. Douglas Coupland, *Generation X* (New York: St. Martin's Press, 1991).

34. Frank Bruni, "Generation X," *The Tampa Tribune*, November 16, 1993.

35. This study lumped the voting-age population into five generations or cohorts: (1) those born before 1895, who came of voting age before or during World War I; (2) those born between 1895 and 1910, entering the electorate between the end of World War I and the Hoover-Roosevelt election of 1932; (3) those born between 1911 and 1926, who came of political age during the Roosevelt years and World War II; (4) those born between 1927 and 1942, who entered the electorate between 1948 and 1963; and (5) those born in 1943 or later, who entered the electorate no earlier than the Johnson election of 1964. See Warren E. Miller, Arthur H. Miller, and Edward J. Schneider, *American National Election Studies Data Sourcebook, 1952–1978* (Cambridge, MA: Harvard University Press, 1980), p. 8.

36. One popular college text on the U.S. government defined "political socialization" as "the process by which parents and others teach children about the values, beliefs, and attitudes of a political culture"; see James MacGregor Burns et al., *Government by the People,* 15th ed. (Englewood Cliffs, NJ: Prentice-Hall, 1993), pp. 221–222. By one's early teens, political interest is fairly high and has been influenced greatly by family, school, and peers.

37. For excellent discussions of methodologies used to test these different kinds of effects, see Erdman Palmore, "When Can Age, Period, and Cohort Be Separated?" *Social Forces* 57 (September 1978), pp. 282–295; and Cutler, "Aging and Generations in Politics."

38. Torres-Gil, *The New Aging,* p. 17.

CHAPTER 2

1. Good overviews of these common perceptions can be found in: John B. Williamson, Linda Evans, and Lawrence A. Powell, *The Politics of Aging: Power and Policy* (Springfield, IL: Charles E. Thomas Publisher, 1982); M. Margaret Conway, *Political Participation in the United States*, 2nd ed. (Washington, DC: CQ Press, 1991), chapter 2; William H. Flanigan and Nancy H. Zingale, *Political Behavior of the American Electorate*, 8th ed. (Washington, DC: CQ Press, 1994), chapter 2; Ruy A. Teixeira, *The Disappearing American Voter* (Washington, DC: Brookings Institution, 1992), chapter 1; and John M. Strate et al., "Life Span Civic Development and Voting Participation," *American Political Science Review* 83 (June 1989), pp. 443–464.

2. For excellent discussions of voter eligibility criteria and rights, see Alexander J. Bott, *Handbook of United States Election Laws and Practices: Political Rights* (Westport, CT: Greenwood Press, 1990); and Kimball W. Brace and the Staff of Election Data Services, Inc., eds., *The Election Data Book: A Statistical Portrait of Voting in America 1992* (Lanham, MD: Bernan Press, 1993).

3. Bott, *Handbook of United States Election Laws and Practices,* p. 25.

4. Ibid., p. 2.

5. The white primary prohibited blacks from voting in political party primary elections. Grandfather clauses were a way of permitting whites who failed literacy tests to register and vote. These clauses "allowed otherwise unqualified persons to vote if they met certain qualifications, such as descent from a legal voter or service in the state's Confederate militia, that blacks could not possibly meet. Other provisions allowed [white] illiterates to participate if they owned real property or if they could demonstrate 'good moral character.'" For an excellent account of these restrictions and their impact on blacks, see Steven J. Rosenstone and John Mark Hansen, *Mobilization, Participation, and Democracy in America* (New York: Macmillan, 1993), pp. 196–205. Also see V. O. Key, Jr., *Southern Politics in State and Nation* (New York: Vintage, 1949).

6. The most comprehensive discussion of the fight to make 18- to 21-year-olds eligible to vote is by Wendell W. Cultice, *Youth's Battle for the Ballot: A History of Voting Age in America* (Westport, CT: Greenwood Press, 1992).

7. Informative discussions of voter qualifications and registration requirements appear in: Thomas R. Dye, *Politics in States and Communities*, 8th ed. (Englewood Cliffs, NJ: Prentice-Hall, 1994), chapter 4; and in Raymond E. Wolfinger and Steven J. Rosenstone, *Who Votes?* (New Haven: Yale University

Press, 1980), chapter 4. *The Book of the States,* compiled and published biennially by the Council of State Governments, is a good source of state-by-state data, as are periodic reports prepared by the National Clearinghouse on Election Administration, an agency of the Federal Election Commission.

8. Bott, *Handbook of United States Election Laws and Practices,* p. 8.

9. Peverill Squire, Raymond E. Wolfinger, and David P. Glass, "Residential Mobility and Voter Turnout," *American Political Science Review* 81 (March 1987), pp. 45–65.

10. Joshua Hammer, with Adam Wolfberg, "Not Just Hit Videos Anymore: MTV Energizes a Young—and Powerful—Electorate," *Newsweek,* November 2, 1992, p. 93.

11. See Frances Fox Piven and Richard A. Cloward, *Why Americans Don't Vote* (New York: Pantheon Books, 1988); Wolfinger and Rosenstone, *Who Votes?;* and Jonathan Nagler, "The Effect of Registration Laws and Education on U.S. Voter Turnout," *American Political Science Review* 85 (December 1991), pp. 1393–1405. For a different viewpoint, see Teixeira, *The Disappearing American Voter.*

12. Wolfinger and Rosenstone, *Who Votes?* p. 61.

13. Robert Montjoy, "Implementation and Impact of Voter Registration Outreach Programs in the United States," paper presented at the annual meeting of the Southern Political Science Association, Savannah, GA, November 4–6, 1993.

14. Ellen Weir, "The Road to Motor Voter," *National Voter* 43 (September-October 1993), pp. 4–5.

15. Robert S. Montjoy, *Motor Vehicle Registration Programs* (Washington, DC: Federal Election Commission, September 1992).

16. Times Mirror Center for The People & The Press telephone survey of a nationally representative sample of 3,517 adults 18 years of age or older, conducted May 28–June 10, 1992.

17. Williamson, Evans, and Powell, *The Politics of Aging.*

18. Bruce C. Straits, "The Social Context of Voter Turnout," *Public Opinion Quarterly* 54, no. 1 (1990), pp. 64–73.

19. A 1992 survey by the Times Mirror Center for The People & The Press found that when asked whether they agree that "it is a citizen's duty to always vote," 94.6 percent of those 65 and over agreed, compared to 84.2 percent of those 18 to 24 years of age. In response to the question of whether they "feel guilty when they don't get a chance to vote," 67.1 percent of those 65 and over answered in the affirmative, compared to just 59.6 percent of the 18- to 24-year-olds. This was a telephone survey of a nationally representative sample of 3,517 adults 18 or older, conducted May 28–June 10, 1992.

20. Times Mirror Center for the People & the Press, *The People, the Press, & Politics, Campaign '92: "The Generations Divide,"* (Washington, DC: Times Mirror Center for The People & The Press, 1992), p. 42; based on a nationally representative random telephone survey of those 18 and older, conducted May 28–June 10, 1992.

21. See Thomas R. Palfrey and Keith T. Poole, "The Relationship Between Information, Ideology, and Voting Behavior," *American Journal of Political Science* 31 (August 1987), pp. 511–530.

22. See Michael X. Delli Carpini and Scott Keeter, "Measuring Political Knowledge: Putting First Things First," *American Journal of Political Science* 37 (November 1993), pp. 1179–1206; and Robert C. Luskin, "Measuring Political Sophistication," *American Journal of Political Science* 31 (November 1987), pp. 856–899.

23. For a good summary of this argument, see Stephen Earl Bennett and David Resnick, "The Implications of Nonvoting for Democracy in the United States," *American Journal of Political Science* 34 (August 1990), pp. 771–802.

24. Hammer, with Wolfberg, "Not Just Hit Videos Anymore."

25. For a good argument of this thesis, see Kurt Shirkey and Sue Tolleson-Rinehart, "The Political Mobilization of Generation X, 1980–1992," paper presented at the annual meeting of the Southern Political Science Association, Atlanta, GA, November 2–5, 1994.

26. For an excellent review of this literature, see William Crotty, ed., *Political Participation and American Democracy* (Westport, CT: Greenwood Press, 1991).

27. Jerry T. Jennings, *Voting and Registration in the Election of November 1992,* Current Population Reports, Population Characteristics, P20-466 (Washington, DC: Bureau of the Census, U.S. Department of Commerce, April 1993), p. VIII.

28. Register Once Coalition and Lead . . . or Leave, *Register Once: The National Campaign for Student Voting Rights, The Register Once Legislative Guide* (Washington, DC: Register Once Coalition and Lead . . . or Leave, 1994).

29. Walter Dean Burnham, "The Turnout Problem," in A. James Reichley, ed., *Elections American Style* (Washington, DC: Brookings Institution, 1987), p. 98.

30. Gregory A. Caldeira, Samuel C. Patterson, and Gregory A. Markko, "The Mobilization of Voters in Congressional Elections," *Journal of Politics* 47 (May 1985), pp. 490–509.

31. See Stanley Kelley, Jr., Richard E. Ayres, and William G. Bowen, "Registration and Voting: Putting First Things First," *American Political Science Review* 61 (June 1967), pp. 359–379; Robert Blank, "State Electoral Structure," *Journal of Politics* 35 (November 1973), pp. 988–994; Jae On Kim, John R. Petrocik, and Stephen N. Enokson, "Voter Turnout in the American States," *American Political Science Review* 69 (March 1975), pp. 107–123; Steven J. Rosenstone and Raymond E. Wolfinger, "The Effect of Registration Laws on Voter Turnout," *American Political Science Review* 72 (March 1978), pp. 22–45; Wolfinger and Rosenstone, *Who Votes?*; Paul Kleppner, *Who Voted?* (New York: Praeger, 1982); Caldeira, Patterson, and Markko, "The Mobilization of Voters in Congressional Elections"; Gary W. Cox and Michael C. Munger, "Closeness, Expenditures, and Turnout in the 1982 House Elections," *American Political Science Review* 83 (March 1989), pp. 217–231; Robert W. Jackman, "Political Institutions and Voter Turnout in the Industrial Democracies," *American Political Science Review* 81 (June 1987), pp. 405–423; Jonathan Nagler, "The Effect of Registration Laws and Education on U.S. Voter Turnout"; and Kim Quaile Hill and Jan E. Leighley, "Party Ideology, Organization, and Competitiveness as Mobilizing Forces in Gubernatorial Elections," *American Journal of Political Science* 37 (November 1993), pp. 1158–1178. Also see Farley Peters, Sandra Martin, and Beth Kyle, eds., *Voter Registration and the States: Effective Policy Approaches to Increasing Participation* (Washington, DC: National Center for Policy Alternatives, 1986); Peverill Squire, Raymond E. Wolfinger, and David P. Glass, "Residential Mobility and Turnout," *American Political Science Review* 81 (March 1987), pp. 45–65; and Piven and Cloward, *Why Americans Don't Vote.*

32. Rosenstone and Hansen, *Mobilization, Participation, and Democracy in America,* pp. 208–209.

33. See Edward D. Feigenbaum and James A. Palmer, *Absentee Voting: Issues and Options* (Washington, DC: National Clearinghouse of Election Administration, Federal Election Commission, Autumn 1987). For an intriguing look at the liberal absentee voting law in Texas, see Robert M. Stein and Patricia A. Garcia, "Voting Early, But Not Often," paper presented at the annual meeting of the Southern Political Science Association, Savannah, GA, November 4–6, 1993. Any Texas voter can vote early, in person, up to seventeen days prior to election day (an unusual form of absentee voting). In addition to the added number of days, hours, and sites at which voters could cast their ballots, the early voting locations in the 1992 presidential election included familiar and more frequented venues than traditional election-day sites. The result was a slightly higher turnout overall but especially among newly registered voters, who traditionally have turned out at lower rates than longtime registrants.

34. A dozen states now permit mail ballots—Alaska, Arizona, California, Colorado, Florida, Kansas, Minnesota, Missouri, Montana, New Mexico, Oregon, and Washington. For an excellent overview of the pros and cons of mail ballots, see Paul E. Parker and James T. Przybylski, "'It's in the Mail'—Present Use and Future Prospects of Mail Elections," *State and Local Government Review* 25 (Spring 1993), pp. 97–106. As of 1993, only one county in the nation conducts its elections entirely by mail (Stanislaus County, CA). In the county's first mail election held, turnout was estimated to be 35 to 40 percent higher than usual. The drawback was that it took longer to determine who won. See *New York Times,* November 4, 1993, p. A11.

35. For an excellent discussion of the election frequency hypothesis, see Richard W. Boyd, "Election Calendars and Voter Turnout," *American Politics Quarterly* 14 (January 1986), pp. 89–104; and Richard W. Boyd, "The Effects of Primaries and Statewide Races on Voter Turnout," *Journal of Politics* 51 (August 1989), pp. 730–739.

36. For state-by-state figures on drop-off, or roll-off, see Brace et al., *The Election Data Book 1992.*

37. Ricardo Korman, "Chronopolitics: What Time Do People Vote?" *Public Opinion Quarterly* 14, no. 2 (1976), pp. 182–193.

38. Jennings, *Voting and Registration in the Election of November 1992.*

39. Ibid.

40. Lead . . . or Leave, *50 State Ranking of Student Voting Rights* (Washington, DC: Lead . . . or Leave, 1994). Also see "Make Them Students of Democracy," *Atlanta Journal/Constitution,* October 30, 1994.

41. Even the earliest voting studies found linkages between socioeconomic factors, especially education, and turnout. See, for example, Bernard Berelson, Paul Lazarsfeld, and William McPhee, *Voting* (Chicago: University of Chicago Press, 1954); Robert Lane, *Political Life: Why People Get Involved in Politics* (Glencoe, IL: Free Press, 1959); Angus Campbell et al., *The American Voter* (New York: Wiley, 1960); Seymour Lipset, *Political Man* (New York: Doubleday, 1960); Gabriel Almond and Sidney Verba, *The Civic Culture* (Boston: Little, Brown, 1963); Sidney Verba and Norman Nie, *Participation in America* (New York: Harper & Row, 1972); Norman H. Nie, Sidney Verba, and John Petrocik, *The Changing American Voter* (Cambridge, MA: Harvard University Press, 1976); and Lester W. Milbrath and M. L. Goel, *Political Participation: How and Why Do People Get Involved in Politics?* (Chicago: Rand McNally, 1977).

42. Straits, "The Social Context of Voter Turnout."

43. See, for example, Lawrence Bobo and Franklin D. Gilliam, Jr., "Race, Sociopolitical Participation and Black Empowerment," *American Political Science Review* 84 (June 1990), pp. 377–386; and Carole Jean Uhlaner, "Political Participation and Discrimination: A Comparative Analysis of Asians, Blacks, and Latinos," in William Crotty, ed., *Political Participation and American Democracy* (Westport, CT: Greenwood Press, 1991), pp. 138–170.

44. See, for example, Uhlaner, "Political Participation and Discrimination," and Rodney E. Hero, *Latinos and the U.S. Political System* (Philadelphia: Temple University Press, 1992).

45. Optimally, multivariate analytic approaches help separate out the relative weight of age from various other socioeconomic, legal, and political variables. It is often quite difficult to consistently use such approaches. The problem is that many public opinion surveys vary in the specific individual-level information elicited from survey respondents from one survey to another. Even the format and categories of information may change from one survey to another, often constrained by the question at hand, the time frame in which the survey is completed, and the money available to conduct the survey. Socioeconomic data are generally more available than legal or political data. In addition, researchers who use public opinion data generated by private entities (many national polling firms) are limited in their access to these databases. This explains why most multivariate studies attempting to sort out the independent effects of age are based on databases with easy and inexpensive *public* access (e.g., the National Election Studies conducted by the University of Michigan but funded with public money). These studies, as noted throughout the text, invariably show that age matters in explaining both political participation and policy preferences. This increases my confidence that where sizable age-group differences are found, age is likely to be an important variable that would show up as statistically significant if submitted to a multivariate analysis.

46. Rosenstone and Hansen, *Mobilization, Participation, and Democracy in America,* p. 215. Another study that found a strong relationship between age and voter turnout is Lee Sigelman et al., "Voting and Nonvoting: A Multi-Election Perspective," *American Journal of Political Science* 29 (November 1985), pp. 749–765.

47. See Stein and Garcia, "Voting Early, But Not Often"; Teixeira, *The Disappearing American Voter;* and Rosenstone and Hansen, *Mobilization, Participation, and Democracy in America.*

48. Many studies have linked sociopsychological attributes to voting behavior, some more strongly than others. See Campbell et al., *The American Voter;* Almond and Verba, *The Civic Culture;* Verba and Nie, *Participation in America;* Milbrath and Goel, *Political Participation;* Stephen D. Shaffer, "A Multivariate Explanation of Decreasing Turnout in Presidential Elections, 1960–1970," *American Journal of Political Science* 25 (February 1981), pp. 68–95; Paul R. Abramson and John H. Aldrich, "The Decline of Participation in America," *American Political Science Review* 76 (September 1982), pp. 502–521; Orley Ashenfelter and Stanley Kelley, Jr., "Determinants of Participation in Presidential Elections," *Journal of Law and Economics* 18 (December 1976), pp. 695–731; Paul R. Abramson,

Political Attitudes in America (San Francisco: W. H. Freeman, 1983); Steven E. Finkel, "Reciprocal Effects of Participation and Political Efficacy: A Panel Analysis," *American Journal of Political Science* 29 (November 1985), pp. 891–913; Jan Leighley, "Participation as a Stimulus of Political Conceptualization," *Journal of Politics* 53 (February 1991), pp. 198–211; and Walter Dean Burnham, *The Current Crisis in American Politics* (New York: Oxford University Press, 1982).

49. Caldeira, Patterson, and Markko, "The Mobilization of Voters in Congressional Elections," p. 506.

50. There have been only a few studies using social-psychological variables to explain voter turnout. The most prominent studies in this area are by political scientist Warren Miller, who used the concept of "political generation" to explain differences between the young and old in voter turnout and party identification. His definitions of generations were based upon political events that occurred during the youthful days of various age-groups when they were being politically socialized. See Warren E. Miller, "The Puzzle Transformed: Explaining Declining Turnout," *Political Behavior* 14 (1992), pp. 1–43; and "Generational Changes and Party Identification," *Political Behavior* 14 (1992), pp. 335–352.

51. See Note 19.

52. See Campbell et al., *The American Voter;* Verba and Nie, *Participation in America;* Milbrath and Goel, *Political Participation;* Steven E. Finkel and Karl-Dieter Opp, "Party Identification and Participation in Collective Action," *Journal of Politics* 53 (May 1991), pp. 339–371; Shaffer, "A Multivariate Explanation"; Carol A. Cassel and David B. Hill, "Explanations of Voter Turnout Decline: A Multivariate Test," *American Politics Quarterly* 9 (April 1981), pp. 181–195; Burnham, *The Current Crisis;* Abramson and Aldrich, "The Decline of Participation"; Ashenfelter and Kelley, "Determinants of Participation"; and Rosenstone and Hansen, *Mobilization, Participation, and Democracy in America.*

53. Rosenstone and Hansen, *Mobilization, Participation, and Democracy in America,* pp. 155–156.

54. See, for example, Stephen Earl Bennett, "Left Behind: Exploring Declining Turnout Among Noncollege Young Whites, 1964–1988," *Social Science Quarterly* 72 (June 1991), pp. 314–333; Flanigan and Zingale, *Political Behavior of the American Electorate,* chapter 4.

55. Surveys by the Times Mirror Center for The People & The Press have asked respondents these questions: (1) "Generally speaking would you say that you personally care a good deal which party wins the [1992] presidential election or don't you care that much?" and "Generally speaking would you say that you personally care a good deal who wins the [1992] presidential election or that you don't care very much?" For the 1992 election, the results showed that 49 percent of the 18- to 29-year-olds and 63 percent of those 50 and older cared which party won; comparable figures for who won were 64 percent versus 74 percent, respectively. These results were based on a telephone survey of a nationally representative sample of 1,211 adults 18 years of age and older, conducted October 3–6, 1991.

56. For a study of this phenomenon among the elderly, see Wilma L.B. Rule, "Political Alienation and Voting Attitudes Among the Elderly Generation," *The Gerontologist* 17, no. 5 (1977), pp. 400–404; and Williamson, Evans, and Powell, *The Politics of Aging,* pp. 125–128.

57. Williamson, Evans, and Powell, *The Politics of Aging,* p. 126.

58. For an excellent review of this linkage, see Edward Tufte, *Political Control of the Economy* (Princeton, NJ: Princeton University Press, 1978). Also see Caldeira, Patterson, and Markko, "The Mobilization of Voters in Congressional Elections."

59. All quotes are from Caldeira, Patterson, and Markko, "The Mobilization of Voters in Congressional Elections."

60. For a good summary of this viewpoint, see Frank Luntz and Ron Dermer, "A Farewell to the American Dream?" *The Public Perspective* 5 (September-October 1994), pp. 12–14. However, there are those who disagree with this interpretation. One study has found that younger persons historically are more optimistic about their economic future than those in older generations because "young persons are at the beginning of their career and their earning potential when everything seems possible and attainable"; see Janie S. Steckenrider, "Consumer Sentiment: A Generational Approach," paper presented at the annual meeting of the American Political Science Association, Chicago, September 3–6, 1992. Recent studies by Everett C. Ladd concluded that there are few generational differences regarding one's

economic outlook. See Everett C. Ladd, "Generation Gap? What Generation Gap?" *Wall Street Journal,* December 9, 1994, p. A16. These differences are generally explained by the way questions on the economic future are worded.

61. See Rosenstone and Hansen, *Mobilization, Participation, and Democracy in America,* for an excellent review of this literature. Also see Larry J. Sabato, *Campaigns and Elections* (Glenview, IL: Scott, Foresman/Little Brown, 1989); Gary C. Jacobson, *The Politics of Congressional Elections,* 3rd ed. (New York: HarperCollins, 1992); John Kessel, *Presidential Campaign Politics,* 4th ed. (Belmont, CA: Brooks Cole, 1992); Nelson W. Polsby and Aaron Wildavsky, *Presidential Elections: Contemporary Strategies of American Politics,* 8th ed. (New York: Free Press, 1991); Samuel L. Popkin, *The Reasoning Voter: Communication and Persuasion in Presidential Campaigns* (Chicago: University of Chicago Press, 1991); Frank J. Sorauf, *Inside Campaign Finance: Myths and Realities* (New Haven: Yale University Press, 1992); Stephen J. Wayne, *The Road to the White House, 1992: The Politics of Presidential Elections,* 4th ed. (New York: St. Martin's Press, 1992); and Stephen Ansolabehere, Roy Behr, and Shanto Iyengar, *The Media Game: American Politics in the Television Age* (New York: Macmillan, 1993).

62. For an excellent review of this research, see John F. Zipp, "Perceived Representativeness and Voting: An Assessment of the Impact of 'Choices' vs. 'Echoes,'" *American Political Science Review* 79 (March 1985), pp. 50–61; Conway, *Political Participation in the United States;* and Caldeira, Patterson, and Markko, "The Mobilization of Voters in Congressional Elections."

63. Volumes of studies have found that party competition stimulates voter turnout at all levels—national, state, and local. See Key, *Southern Politics in State and Nation;* Elmer E. Schattschneider, *The Semisovereign People* (New York: Holt, Rinehart and Winston, 1960); Sarah M. Morehouse, *State Politics, Parties, and Policy* (New York: Holt, Rinehart and Winston, 1981); Samuel C. Patterson and Gregory A. Caldeira, "Getting Out the Vote: Participation in Gubernatorial Elections," *American Political Science Review* 77 (September 1983), pp. 675–689; Franklin D. Gilliam, "Influences on Voter Turnout for U.S. House Elections in Non-Presidential Years," *Legislative Studies Quarterly* 10 (August 1985), pp. 339–351; Milbrath and Goel, *Political Participation;* and Gary W. Cox, "Closeness and Turnout: A Methodological Note," *Journal of Politics* 50 (August 1988), pp. 768–775.

64. See Rosenstone and Hansen, *Mobilization, Participation, and Democracy in America,* for an excellent review of this literature. Also see Anthony Downs, *An Economic Theory of Democracy* (New York: Harper & Row, 1957); William H. Riker and Peter C. Ordeshook, *An Introduction to Positive Political Theory* (Englewood Cliffs, NJ: Prentice-Hall, 1973); and John Ferejohn and Morris Fiorina, "Closeness Counts Only in Horseshoes and Dancing," *American Political Science Review* 69 (September 1975), pp. 920–925.

65. Lyn Ragsdale and Jerrold G. Rusk, "Who Are Nonvoters? Profiles from the 1990 Senate Elections," *American Journal of Political Science* 37 (August 1993), p. 724.

66. Ibid., p. 721.

67. Williamson, Evans, and Powell, *The Politics of Aging,* p 115.

68. For an enlightening discussion of the intricacies of calculating voter turnout rates, see Brace et al., *The Election Data Book,* pp. XIII–XVII.

69. Ibid., p. xv.

70. Ibid., p. xvi.

71. Times Mirror Center for The People & The Press, *The People, The Press, & Politics, Campaign '92,* pp. 40–42.

72. For an informative discussion of turnout differences in presidential and midterm elections, see James E. Campbell, "The Presidential Surge and Its Midterm Decline in Congressional Elections, 1868–1988," *Journal of Politics* 53 (May 1991), pp. 477–487.

73. Times Mirror Center for The People & The Press, telephone survey of a nationally representative sample of 2,000 adults 18 years of age and older, conducted November 3–5, 1994.

74. Wendy Bounds and Erle Norton, "Disaffected Youth Are Truant from Polls," *Wall Street Journal,* November 16, 1994.

75. Times Mirror Center for The People & The Press, *The People, The Press, & Politics, Campaign '92,* p. 42.

76. Times Mirror Center for The People & The Press, survey conducted after the 1988 presidential election, November 1988.

CHAPTER 3

1. This expression is attributed to George Wallace, who ran for president in 1968 as a third-party candidate (the American Independent Party).

2. Martin P. Wattenberg, *The Decline of American Political Parties 1952–1988* (Cambridge, MA: Harvard University Press, 1990).

3. Quoted in Vern McLellan, *A Collection of Political Humor* (Hong Kong: Great Quotations, 1992), p. 25.

4. Stephen Ansolabehere, Roy Behr, and Shanto Iyengar, *The Media Game: American Politics in the Television Age* (New York: Macmillan, 1993), p. 131. For in-depth studies of political socialization, see Fred I. Greenstein, *Children and Politics* (New Haven: Yale University Press, 1965); Richard Dawson, Kenneth Prewitt, and Karen S. Dawson, *Political Socialization,* 2nd ed. (Boston: Little, Brown, 1977); Robert Hess and Judith Torney, *The Development of Political Attitudes in Children* (Chicago: Aldine, 1967); M. Kent Jennings and Richard G. Niemi, "The Transmission of Political Values from Parent to Child," *American Political Science Review* 62 (March 1968), pp. 169–184; David Easton and Jack Dennis, *Children in the Political System* (New York: McGraw-Hill, 1969); Charles F. Andrain, *Children and Civic Awareness* (Columbus, OH: Charles E. Merrill, 1971); M. Kent Jennings and Richard G. Niemi, *The Political Character of Adolescence: The Influence of Families and Schools* (Princeton, NJ: Princeton University Press, 1974); and M. Kent Jennings and Richard G. Niemi, *Generations and Politics: A Panel Study of Young Adults and Their Parents* (Princeton: Princeton University Press, 1981).

5. Studies have found that "normally, more than two-thirds of the electorate identify with their parents' party if both parents had the same party identification." However, parental influence "diminishes as the child comes into contact with other political and social influences during the teenage years"; see William H. Flanigan and Nancy H. Zingale, *Political Behavior of the American Electorate,* 8th ed. (Washington, DC: CQ Press, 1994), p. 85.

6. John M. Strate et al., "Life Span Civic Development and Voting Participation," *American Political Science Review* 83 (June 1989), pp. 443–464.

7. James MacGregor Burns et al., *Government by the People,* 15th ed. (Englewood Cliffs, NJ: Prentice-Hall, 1993), p. 300.

8. A critical election is "an electoral earthquake: the ground shakes beneath the parties; fissures appear, in each party's coalition, and they begin to fracture; new issues appear, dividing the electorate. A new coalition is formed for each party—one that endures for years. A critical election period may require more than one election before change is apparent, but in the end, the party system will be transformed [realigned]." This definition is from Robert L. Lineberry, George C. Edwards III, and Martin P. Wattenberg, *Government in America: People, Politics, and Policy,* 6th ed. (New York: HarperCollins College Publishers, 1994), p. 238. V. O. Key first coined the term in "A Theory of Critical Elections," *Journal of Politics* 17 (February 1955), pp. 3–18. An excellent analysis of critical elections is Walter Dean Burnham, *Critical Elections and the Mainsprings of American Politics* (New York: Norton, 1970).

9. For excellent reviews and discussion of the realignment issue, see Byron E. Shafer, *The End of Realignment: Interpreting American Electoral Eras* (Madison: University of Wisconsin Press, 1991); James Sundquist, *Dynamics of the Party System: Alignment and Realignment of Political Parties in the United States,* rev. ed. (Washington, DC: Brookings Institution, 1983); Jerome M. Clubb, William H. Flanigan, and Nancy H. Zingale, *Partisan Realignment* (Beverly Hills, CA: Sage Publications, 1980); Alan R. Gitelson, M. Margaret Conway, and Frank B. Feigert, *American Political Parties: Stability and Change* (Boston: Houghton Mifflin, 1984); and Bruce A. Campbell and Richard J. Trilling, eds., *Realignment in American Politics: Toward a Theory* (Austin: University of Texas Press, 1980). For a critique of the realignment concept, see Everett Carll Ladd, Jr., "Like Waiting for Godot: The Uselessness

of *Realignment* for Understanding Change in Contemporary Politics," *Polity* 22 (Spring 1990), pp. 511–525.

10. This theory is attributed to Paul Allen Beck, "A Socialization Theory of Partisan Realignment," in Richard G. Niemi, ed., *The Politics of Future Citizens: New Dimensions in the Political Socialization of Children* (San Francisco: Jossey-Bass, 1974), pp. 199–219. The quoted summary is from Wattenberg, *The Decline of American Political Parties 1952–1988,* pp. 121–122. Wattenberg faulted Beck's theory by pointing out that split-ticket voting has increased even among the older generations.

11. Burns et al., *Government by the People,* p. 301.

12. See Everett Carll Ladd, Jr., and Charles D. Hadley, Jr., *Transformations of the American Party System* (New York: Norton, 1975); and Frank Sorauf, *Party Politics in America,* 4th ed. (Boston: Little, Brown, 1980). But for a counterview, see Wattenberg, *The Decline of American Political Parties 1952–1988.*

13. For good discussions on the rise of the independent voter, see Hedrick Smith, *The Power Game: How Washington Works* (New York: Random House, 1988), and Bruce E. Keith et al., *The Myth of the Independent Voter* (Berkeley: University of California Press, 1992). Excellent studies showing links between age or generation, weakening party identification, and split-ticket voting include Warren E. Miller, "Generational Changes and Party Identification," *Political Behavior* 14 (1992), pp. 335–352; and Richard A. Brody, David W. Brady, and Valerie Heitshusen, "Accounting for Divided Government: Generational Effects on Party and Split-Ticket Voting," in M. Kent Jennings and Thomas E. Mann, eds., *Elections at Home and Abroad* (Ann Arbor: University of Michigan Press, 1994), pp. 157–177.

14. Larry Sabato, *The Party's Just Begun: Shaping Political Parties for America's Future* (Glenview, IL: Scott, Foresman/Little, Brown, 1988), p. 117.

15. Burns et al., *Government by the People,* p. 288.

16. Ansolabehere, Behr, and Iyengar, *The Media Game,* p. 134. For other observations about the role of the media in creating candidate-centered (rather than partisan-centered) politics, see Tom Rosenstiel, Strange Bedfellows: How Television and the Presidential Candidates Changed American Politics, 1992 (New York: Hyperion, 1993); and Thomas E. Patterson, *Out of Order* (New York: Knopf, 1993).

17. A. James Reichley, *The Life of the Parties: A History of American Political Parties* (New York: Free Press, 1992), p. 10.

18. Excellent sources on the history and structure of U.S. political parties include: Reichley, *The Life of the Parties;* Paul Allen Beck and Frank J. Sorauf, *Party Politics in America,* 7th ed. (New York: HarperCollins, 1992); Leon Epstein, *Political Parties in the American Mold* (Madison: University of Wisconsin Press, 1986); Sandy L. Maisel, ed., *The Parties Respond: Changes in the American Party System* (Boulder: Westview Press, 1990); John F. Bibby, *Politics, Parties and Elections in America* (Chicago: Nelson-Hall, 1992); William J. Keefe, *Parties, Politics, and Public Policy in America, 6th ed.* (Washington, DC: CQ Press, 1991); Wattenberg, *The Decline of American Political Parties 1952–1988;* Michael Barone, *Our Country: The Shaping of America from Roosevelt to Reagan* (New York: Free Press, 1990); Gerald M. Pomper, ed., *Party Organizations in American Politics* (New York: Praeger, 1984); David E. Price, *Bringing Back the Parties* (Washington, DC: CQ Press, 1984); Sabato, *The Party's Just Begun;* David S. Broder, *The Party's Over* (New York: Harper & Row, 1971); Nelson W. Polsby, *Consequences of Party Reform* (New York: Oxford University Press, 1983); Sidney M. Milkis, *The President and the Parties: The Transformation of the American Party System Since the New Deal* (New York: Oxford University Press, 1993); and Joel H. Silbey, "The Rise and Fall of American Political Parties, 1970–1990," in Sandy L. Maisel, ed., *The Parties Respond: Changes in the American Party System* (Boulder: Westview Press, 1990), pp. 3–17.

19. E. E. Schattschneider, *Party Government* (New York: Holt, Rinehart and Winston, 1942), p. 1.

20. Burns et al., *Government by the People,* p. 307.

21. This fourfold classification comes from James Q. Wilson, *American Institutions and Politics,* 5th ed. (Lexington, MA: D. C. Heath, 1992), p. 161. Some distinguish between third and minor parties. Third parties are "temporary parties that often arise during presidential campaigns," whereas minor

parties "are more persistent and generally composed of ideologues," according to Burns et al., Government by the People, p. 283.

22. For excellent discussions of third parties in U.S. history, see Steven J. Rosenstone, Roy L. Behr, and Edward H. Lazarus, *Third Parties in America: Citizen Response to Major Party Failure* (Princeton: Princeton University Press, 1984); Howard R. Penniman, "Presidential Third Parties and the Modern American Two-Party System," in William J. Crotty, ed., *The Party Symbol* (Salt Lake City: W. H. Freeman, 1980), pp. 101–117; and Xandra Kayden and Eddie Mahe, Jr., *The Party Goes On: The Persistence of the Two-Party System in the United States* (New York: Basic Books, 1985).

23. Nonpartisan elections, in which candidates run without a party label, are most common at the city level. Nearly three-fourths of all U.S. cities have nonpartisan elections, according to Charles R. Adrian, "Forms of City Government in American History," in International City Management Association, ed., *The Municipal Year Book 1988*, (Washington, DC: ICMA, 1988), pp. 3–11. Nonpartisan elections were a key component of the Progressive reform movement, which sought to make municipal governments run more efficiently and economically by getting rid of patronage. For an excellent history of this movement, see Richard J. Hofstadter, *The Age of Reform* (New York: Knopf, 1961).

24. Warren E. Miller and Santa A. Traugott, *American National Election Studies Data Sourcebook, 1952–1986* (Cambridge, MA: Harvard College, 1989), p. 79.

25. Sabato, *The Party's Just Begun*, p. 111.

26. Flanigan and Zingale, *Political Behavior of the American Electorate, p. 81.*

27. Morris Fiorina, *Divided Government* (New York: Macmillan, 1992); Gary W. Cox and Samuel Kernell, eds., *The Politics of Divided Government* (Boulder: Westview Press, 1991); Gary Jacobson, *The Electoral Origins of Divided Government* (Boulder: Westview Press, 1990); and James Thurber, *Divided Democracy* (Washington, DC: CQ Press, 1991).

28. Fiorina, *Divided Government*, p. 6.

29. For state-by-state details on which party held the governorship and the majority of the seats in each legislative chamber in the early 1990s, see Kimball W. Brace and the staff of Election Data Services, Inc., eds., *The Election Data Book: A Statistical Portrait of Voting in America 1992* (Lanham, MD: Bernan Press, 1993). For historical trackings of the incidence of divided control among the states, see Fiorina, *Divided Government.*

30. Walter Dean Burnham, "The Reagan Heritage," in Gerald M. Pomper, ed., *The Election of 1988* (Chatham, NJ: Chatham House Publishers, 1989), pp. 1–32.

31. Steven J. Rosenstone and John Mark Hansen, *Mobilization, Participation, and Democracy in America* (New York: Macmillan, 1993), p. 174.

32. Harold W. Stanley and Richard G. Niemi, *Vital Statistics on American* Politics, 4th ed. (Washington, DC: CQ Press, 1994), p. 133.

33. Times Mirror Center for The People & The Press, *The New Political Landscape* (Washington, DC: Times Mirror, October 1994). Based on a July 1994 survey, the study found that 26.6 percent of those 65 and over saw "a great deal of difference in what the Democratic and Republican Parties stand for," compared to 20 percent of those 18 to 29, 22.9 percent of those 30 to 49, and 24.4 percent of those 50 to 64. But a greater proportion of those over 65 also saw "hardly any difference" (30 percent, compared to 21.7 percent of those 18 to 29, 21.2 percent of those 30 to 49, and 29.1 percent of those 50 to 64).

34. Sabato, *The Party's Just Begun*, pp. 134–138.

35. Phillip E. Converse, "Of Time and Partisan Stability," in Giuseppe DiPalma, ed., *Mass Politics in Industrial Societies* (Chicago: Markham, 1972), pp. 64–95.

36. Summary of Converse study in Strate et al., "Life Span Civic Development and Voting Participation," p. 453.

37. See Note 33.

38. In the 1992 National Election Study, respondents were asked, "What [do] you think are the good and bad points about the two national parties? Is there anything in particular you like/dislike about the Democratic/Republican Party? What is it? Anything else you like about the Demo-

cratic/Republican Party?" In terms of likes for the Democratic Party, the breakdown for the responses given by the youngest cohort (born in 1959 or later) was: group attributes (15 percent), government programs (9 percent), economics (4 percent), and ideology (1 percent). The breakdown for the responses of the oldest cohort (born before 1885) was: group attributes (21 percent), government programs (8 percent), economics (4 percent), and ideology (2 percent). In terms of dislikes, the youngest cohort reported: economics (8.5 percent), group attributes (4 percent), government programs (4 percent), and ideology (4 percent). For the oldest, it was: economics (14 percent), group attributes (4 percent), ideology (3 percent), and government programs (3 percent).

39. The 1992 National Election Survey found that among the youngest cohort (born in 1959 or later), 29 percent liked the Republican Party's ideology, but just 3 percent cited its economics, 2 percent its stances on government programs, and 1 percent its group representation dimensions. In contrast, among the oldest cohort (born before 1895), only 9.5 percent cited the party's ideology as a like, although it still ranked ahead of any of the others, which were cited by less than 2 percent of these respondents.

40. According to the 1992 National Election Survey, 14 percent of those born between 1927 and 1942 disliked the Republican Party's economic stances, compared to 10 percent of the youngest cohort and 7 percent of the oldest cohort. However, only the group born between 1943 and 1958 disliked something more about the Republican Party than its economics; 11 percent disliked its group representation attributes even more than its economics (10 percent).

41. Among Republicans, 44.5 percent of those 18 to 24 said their party wasn't very important to them, compared to just 34 percent of those 60 and over. Among Democrats, the comparable responses were 42.9 percent and 36 percent. Among Republicans, 61.3 percent of those 18 to 24 usually supported their party's candidates but sometimes supported Democrats, compared to 79.9 percent of those 60 and over. Among Democrats, comparable figures were 58.8 percent and 71.9 percent. These results were based on a face-to-face survey of a nationally representative sample of 4,244 adults 18 years of age or older, conducted April 25–May 10, 1987, by the Times Mirror Center for The People & The Press (unpublished data).

42. For an overview of these statistics for the population at large, see Times Mirror Center for The People & The Press, *The New Political Landscape,* p. 158.

43. John R. Petrocik, "Divided Government: Is It All in the Campaigns?" in Gary W. Cox and Samuel Kernell, eds., *The Politics of Divided Government,* (Boulder: Westview Press, 1991), p. 18.

44. For an excellent tabular presentation of the constituency bases of each major party during the 1992 presidential election year, see Stanley and Niemi, *Vital Statistics on American Politics,* p. 161.

45. A descriptive account of the linkage between religious preference, frequency of church attendance, and party identification can be found in David C. Leege and Lyman A. Kellstedt, eds., *Rediscovering the Religious Factor in American Politics* (Armonk, NY: M. E. Sharpe, 1993). They argued that religion has become a powerful predictor of both political partisanship and ideology, particularly among white voters. Among white voters, the Republican Party is increasingly becoming the home of regular churchgoers who hold strong religious beliefs. White voters who attend church irregularly or identify themselves as having no religious preference are more likely to be Democrats.

46. Petrocik, "Divided Government," p. 19.

47. Ibid., pp. 20–21.

48. Times Mirror Center for The People & The Press, telephone survey of a nationally representative sample of 3,800 adults 18 and over living in the continental United States, conducted July 12–27, 1994 (unpublished data).

49. Benjamin I. Page and Robert Shapiro, *The Rational Public: Fifty Years of Trends in Americans' Policy Preferences* (Chicago: University of Chicago Press, 1992).

50. Rosenstone and Hansen, *Mobilization, Participation, and Democracy in America,* pp. 218–219.

51. Ibid., p. 170.

52. Ann Beaudry and Bob Schaeffer, *Winning Local and State Elections: Guide to Organizing Your Campaign* (New York: Free Press, 1986), p. 19.

53. Rosenstone and Hansen, *Mobilization, Participation, and Democracy in America,* p. 168, found that "in presidential years, political parties are 22.1 percent more likely to contact the most experienced voters, those age sixty-five or older, than the least experienced voters, those eighteen years old." Another study that found contacting effective is Peter W. Wielhouwer and Brad Lockerbie, "Party Contacting and Political Participation, 1952–90," *American Journal of Political Science* 38 (February 1994), pp. 211–229.

54. Beaudry and Shaeffer, *Winning Local and State Elections.*

55. For excellent discussions of the polls and their influence on voters, see Thomas E. Mann and Gary R. Orren, eds., *Media Polls in American Politics* (Washington, DC: Brookings Institution, 1993); Herbert Asher, *Polling and the Public: What Every Citizen Should Know,* 2nd ed. (Washington, DC: CQ Press, 1992); and Albert H. Cantril, *Opinion Connection: Polling, Politics, and the Press* (Washington, DC: CQ Press, 1991). A January 1988 Times Mirror survey found that 38 percent of all Americans believed "advertising consultants and pollsters have too much influence on which candidates become presidential nominees." The age breakdowns were: 18 to 29 (33.6 percent); 30 to 49 (40.7 percent); and 50 and older (38.7 percent).

56. For detailed discussions of party primaries, see Larry M. Bartels, *Presidential Primaries and the Dynamics of Public Choice* (Princeton: Princeton University Press, 1988); James W. Davis, *Presidential Primaries,* rev. ed. (Westport, CT: Greenwood Press, 1984); Emmett H. Buell, Jr., and Lee Sigelman, eds., *Nominating the President* (Knoxville: University of Tennessee Press, 1991); William Crotty and John S. Jackson III, *Presidential Primaries and Nominations* (Washington, DC: CQ Press, 1985); and John G. Greer, *Nominating Presidents: An Evaluation of Voters and Primaries* (New York: Greenwood Press, 1989). For a detailed discussion of delegate selection in 1992, see Stephen J. Wayne, *The Road to the White House 1992: The Politics of Presidential Elections* (New York: St. Martin's Press, 1992).

57. Judith S. Trent and Robert V. Friedenberg, *Political Campaign Communication,* 2nd ed. (New York: Praeger, 1991), p. 28.

58. Bartels, *Presidential Primaries and the Dynamics of Public Choice,* p. 5.

59. Ibid., p. 6.

60. For discussions of the importance of media coverage of the Iowa caucus and New Hampshire primary, see David S. Castle, "Media Coverage of Presidential Primaries," *American Politics Quarterly* 19 (January 1991), pp. 33–42; Hugh Winebrenner, *The Iowa Precinct Caucuses: The Making of a Media Event* (Ames: Iowa State University Press, 1987); and Gary R. Orren and Nelson W. Polsby, eds., *Media and Momentum* (Chatham, NJ: Chatham House, 1987).

61. Center for Media and Public Affairs content analysis of the ABC, CBS, and NBC evening news, as reported in Stanley and Niemi, *Vital Statistics on American Politics,* pp. 60–62.

62. Karen O' Connor and Larry J. Sabato, *American Government: Roots and Reform* (New York: Macmillan, 1993), p. 431.

63. "A New York Surprise: Front-Loading the '96 Primary Calendar," *Washington Post,* January 9, 1994, p. A17.

64. Mark Shields, "High-Stakes Presidential Poker," *Washington Post,* February 6, 1994, p. C7.

65. Ansolabehere, Behr, and Iyengar, *The Media Game,* p. 168.

66. Anthony Downs, *An Economic Theory of Democracy* (New York: Harper & Row, 1957). Economist Downs (and other public choice theorists) argue that nonvoting is perfectly rational behavior if a potential voter perceives that his or her vote will make little difference in the outcome.

67. The Democratic and Republican conventions of 1952 were the last in which the presidential nomination hung in balance until the party convened; see Byron E. Shafer, *Bifurcated Politics: Evolution and Reform in the National Party Convention* (Cambridge, MA: Harvard University Press, 1988).

68. Ansolabehere, Behr, and Iyengar, *The Media Game,* p. 165.

69. Shafer, Bifurcated Politics, p. 290.

70. Ansolabehere, Behr, and Iyengar, *The Media Game,* p. 165.

71. Wayne, *The Road to the White House 1992,* p. 227.

72. Ibid., pp. 228–229.

73. Beaudry and Schaeffer, *Winning Local and State Elections*, p. 111.

74. Wayne, *The Road to the White House*, p. 229.

75. Ansolabehere, Behr, and Iyengar, *The Media Game*, p. 1.

76. Larry Sabato, *Feeding Frenzy: How Attack Journalism Has Transformed American Politics* (New York: Free Press, 1991), p. 6.

77. Patterson, *Out of Order*, p. 137.

78. Kathleen Hall Jamieson, *Dirty Politics: Deception, Distraction, and Democracy* (New York: Oxford University Press, 1992), p. 266.

79. Rosenstiel, *Strange Bedfellows*, p. 168.

80. Sabato, *Feeding Frenzy*, p. 129.

81. Trent and Friedenberg, *Political Campaign Communication*, p. 268.

82. Ansolabehere, Behr, and Iyengar, *The Media Game*, p. 97.

83. For an excellent discussion of the consequences of negative advertising on voters, see Jamieson, *Dirty Politics*; and West, *Air Wars: Television Advertising in Election Campaigns, 1952–1992* (Washington, DC: Congressional Quarterly, Inc., 1993).

84. West, *Air Wars*, p. 146.

85. James M. Perry, "Young Guns: A Second Generation of Political Handlers Outduels Forebears," *Wall Street Journal*, January 10, 1994, p. A1.

86. Rosenstone and Hansen, *Mobilization, Participation, and Democracy in America*, pp. 140–141.

87. For concise discussions of state and local party organizations, see Beck and Sorauf, *Party Politics in America*; Malcolm Jewell and David Olson, *Political Parties and Elections in American States* (Homewood, IL: Dorsey, 1982); Malcolm Jewell, *Parties and Primaries: Nominating State Governors* (New York: Praeger, 1984); John F. Bibby et al., "Parties in State Politics," in Virginia Gray, Herbert Jacob, and Robert Albritton, eds., *Politics in the American States*, 5th ed. (Glenview, IL: Scott, Foresman, 1990), pp. 85–112; Timothy Bledsoe and Susan Welch, "Patterns of Political Party Activity Among U.S. Cities," *Urban Affairs Quarterly* 23 (December 1987), pp. 249–269; David. R. Mayhew, *Placing Parties in American Politics* (Princeton: Princeton University Press, 1986); John P. Frendreis, James L. Gibson, and Laura L. Vertz, "The Electoral Relevance of Local Party Organizations," *American Political Science Review* 84 (March 1990), pp. 225–235; and Cornelius Cotter et al., *Party Organizations in American Politics* (New York: Praeger, 1984).

88. Stephen D. Shaffer and David Breaux, "Generational Differences Among Southern Grassroots Party Workers," paper presented at the annual meeting of the American Political Science Association, Chicago: September 3–6, 1992, p. 9.

89. Charles E. Hadley and Lewis Bowman, eds., *Southern Party Activists and Organizations* (New York: Praeger, 1994); age breakdowns contributed by Charles Hadley from unpublished data.

90. For good reviews of the emergence of two-party competition in Florida, see Susan A. MacManus, ed., *Reapportionment & Representation in Florida: A Historical Collection* (Tampa: Intrabay Innovation Institute, University of South Florida, 1991); Suzanne L. Parker, "Are Party Loyalties Shifting in Florida?" *Florida Public Opinion* 1 (1985), pp. 16–20; Suzanne L. Parker, "Shifting Party Tides in Florida: Where Have All the Democrats Gone?" in Robert H. Swansbrough and David M. Brodsky, eds., *The South's New Politics: Realignment and Dealignment* (Columbia: University of South Carolina Press, 1988), pp. 22–37; and William E. Hulbary, Anne E. Kelley, and Lewis Bowman, "Florida: The Republican Surge Continues," in Laurence W. Moreland, Robert P. Steed, and Tod Baker, eds., *The 1988 Presidential Election in the South* (Westport, CT: Praeger, 1991).

91. Paul Allen Beck, "Realignment Begins? The Republican Surge in Florida," *American Politics Quarterly* 10 (October 1982), pp. 421–438.

92. This was also the conclusion of Anne Kelley, in "Party Images in Florida: A Comparative Analysis of Three Organizational Levels," *Governing Florida* 3 (Spring-Summer 1993), pp. 9–17.

93. Excellent analyses of the profiles of party activists in Florida can be found in William E. Hulbary, Anne E. Kelley, and Lewis Bowman, "Florida: From Freebooting to Real Parties," in Charles E.

Hadley and Lewis Bowman, eds., *Southern Party Activists and Organizations* (New York: Praeger, 1994), chapter 7.

CHAPTER 4

1. M. Margaret Conway, *Political Participation in the United States,* 2nd ed. (Washington, DC: CQ Press, 1991), pp. 129–130.

2. Sidney Verba and Norman I. Nie, *Participation in America: Political Democracy and Social Equality* (New York: Harper & Row, 1972). These peak periods were identified after controls were made for a person's socioeconomic status (education, income) and length of residence in the community.

3. Paul L. Hain, "Age, Ambitions, and Political Careers: The Middle-Age Crisis," in Angus McIntyre, ed., *Aging and Political Leadership* (Albany: State University of New York Press, 1988), pp. 64–77.

4. Verba and Nie, *Participation in America,* p. 139.

5. Ibid. Other excellent studies of citizen contacting include Elaine Sharp, *Citizen Demand Making in the Urban Context* (Tuscaloosa: University of Alabama Press, 1986); and Philip B. Coulter, *Political Voice: Citizen Demand for Urban Services* (Tuscaloosa: University of Alabama Press, 1988).

6. A National Election Survey, reported in Conway, *Political Participation in the United States,* p. 134.

7. Times Mirror Center for The People & The Press, *The Vocal Minority in American Politics* (Washington, DC: Times Mirror Center for The People & The Press, July 16, 1993). By 1994, 42 percent answered yes when asked, "Have you ever called or sent or faxed a letter to your Congressional representative or Senator to express your opinion on any issue?"; the age-group breakdowns were: 18 to 29, 27.3 percent; 30 to 49, 43 percent; 50 to 64, 54.9 percent; and 65 and older, 42.8 percent. Results were based on a Times Mirror Center for The People & The Press telephone survey of a nationally representative sample of 1,513 adults 18 and older, conducted October 6–9, 1994.

8. M. Kent Jennings and Gregory B. Markus, "Political Involvement in the Later Years: A Longitudinal Survey," *American Journal of Political Science* 32 (May 1988), p. 312.

9. Ibid.; and Christine L. Day, *What Older Americans Think* (Princeton: Princeton University Press, 1990).

10. Times Mirror Center for The People & The Press telephone survey of a nationally representative sample of 1,207 adults 18 and over, conducted January 1994.

11. Richard Davis, *The Press and American Politics: The New Mediator* (New York: Longman, 1992).

12. Leo Bogart, "The State of the Industry," in Philip S. Cook, Douglas Gomery, and Lawrence W. Lichty, eds., *The Future of News: Television-Newspapers-Wire Services-Newsmagazines* (Washington, DC: Woodrow Wilson Center Press, 1992), pp. 85–103. Also see Marilyn Ross, *National Survey of Newspaper "Op-Ed" Pages* (Saguache, CO: Communication Creativity, 1986).

13. Thomas B. Rosenstiel, "Talk-Show Journalism," in Philip S. Cook, Douglas Gomery, and Lawrence W. Lichty, eds., *The Future of News: Television-Newspapers-Wire Services-Newsmagazines* (Washington, DC: Woodrow Wilson Center Press, 1992), pp. 73–82.

14. Cf. Albert H. Cantril, *The Opinion Connection: Polling, Politics, and the Press* (Washington, DC: CQ Press, 1991); Herbert Asher, *Polling and the Public: What Every Citizen Should Know,* 2nd ed. (Washington, DC: CQ Press, 1992); and Thomas E. Mann and Gary R. Orren, eds., *Media Polls in American Politics* (Washington, DC: Brookings Institution, 1992).

15. Times Mirror Center for The People & The Press telephone survey of a nationally representative sample of 1,207 adults 18 and over, conducted January 1994.

16. Conway, *Political Participation in the United States.*

17. One study found that older persons are more likely to attend meetings devoted exclusively to the problems of the elderly; see Jennings and Markus, "Political Involvement in the Later Years".

18. See Jeffrey B. Abramson, F. Christopher Arterton, and Gary R. Orren, *The Electronic Commonwealth: The Impact of New Media Technologies on Democratic Politics* (New York: Basic Books,

1988); and Ted Wachtel, *The Electronic Congress: A Blueprint for Participatory Democracy* (Pipersville, PA: Piper's Press, 1992).

19. Times Mirror Center for The People & The Press, *The Vocal Minority in American Politics* (Washington, DC: Times Mirror Center for The People & The Press, July 16, 1993).

20. For example, among those 18 to 29, it jumped from 20.8 percent to 26.3 percent. Among those 30 to 49, it jumped from 28.1 to 38.3 percent. Jumps similar to those observed among the 30 to 49 age-group characterized the older cohorts.

21. A 1987 survey found that only 5.6 percent reported having spoken at a public hearing. The percentage breakdowns by age-group are: 18–29 (2.6 percent); 30–49 (7.5 percent); 50–59 (7.2 percent); and 60 and over (10.4 percent). Results were based on a Times Mirror Center for The People & The Press face-to-face survey of a nationally representative sample of 4,244 adults 18 and over, conducted in May-June 1987.

22. Cf. Neal E. Cutler and Vern L. Bengston, "Age and Political Alienation: Maturation, Generation, and Period Effects," *Annals of the American Academy of Political and Social Sciences* 415 (1974), pp. 160–175.

23. For good histories of protest movements in the United States, see Madeleine Adamson, Seth Borgos, and Paul Kegan, *This Mighty Dream: Social Protest Movements in the United States* (Boston: Routledge, 1984); Michael Useem, *Protest Movements in America* (Indianapolis: Bobbs-Merrill, 1975); Sidney Lens, *Vietnam: A War on Two Fronts* (New York: Lodestar Books, 1990); Richard G. Braungart, "Historical Generations and Youth Movements: A Theoretical Perspective," in Richard F. Ratcliff, ed., *Research in Social Movements, Conflict, and Change* (Greenwich, CT: JAI Press, 1984); Aldon D. Morris, *The Origins of the Civil Rights Movement: Black Communities Organizing for Change* (New York: Free Press, 1984); Jo Freeman, *The Politics of Women's Liberation* (New York: David McKay, 1975); Charles Tilley, *From Mobilization to Revolution* (New York: Random House, 1978); William A Gamson, *The Strategy of Social Protest* (Homewood, IL: Dorsey, 1975); Gary Delgado, *Organizing the Movement: The Roots and Growth of Acorn* (Philadelphia: Temple University Press, 1986); Nancy E. McGlen and Karen O'Connor, *Women's Rights: The Struggle for Equality in the Nineteeth and Twentieth Centuries* (New York: Praeger, 1983); Frances Fox Piven and Richard A. Cloward, *Poor People's Movements: Why They Succeed, How They Fail* (New York: Vintage Books, 1977); and Saul Alinksy, *Rules for Radicals: A Pragmatic Primer for Realistic Radicals* (New York: Vintage Books, 1971).

24. William H. Flanigan and Nancy H. Zingale, *Political Behavior of the American Electorate,* 7th ed. (Washington, DC: CQ Press, 1991), p. 184.

25. Douglas M. McLeod and James K. Hertog, "The Manufacture of 'Public Opinion' by Reporters: Informal Cues for Public Perceptions of Protest Groups," in Doris A. Graber, ed., *Media Power in Politics,* 3rd ed. (Washington, DC: CQ Press 1994), pp. 296–310.

26. For good discussions of the role of civil disobedience, see Paul F. Power, "Civil Disobedience as Functional Opposition," *Journal of Politics* 34 (February 1972), pp. 37–55; Peter K. Eisenger, "The Conditions of Protest Behavior in American Cities," *American Political Science Review* 67 (March 1973), pp. 11–29; Michael Lipsky, *Protest in City Politics* (Chicago: Rand McNally, 1970); and Paul D. Schumaker, "Policy Responsiveness to Protest Group Demands," *Journal of Politics* 37 (May 1975), pp. 488–521.

27. Thomas R. Dye, *Politics in States and Communities,* 8th ed. (Englewood Cliffs, NJ: Prentice-Hall, 1994), p. 119.

28. Reported in Conway, *Political Participation in the United States,* p. 134.

29. A similar conclusion was reached by M. Kent Jennings, "Residues of a Movement: The Aging of the American Protest Generation," *American Political Science Review* 81 (June 1987), pp. 367–382. But Jennings found that protesters of that generation have become more conservative than might have been expected.

30. David D. Schmidt, *Citizen Lawmakers: The Ballot Initiative Revolution* (Philadelphia: Temple University Press, 1989), p. 30.

31. Ibid., p. 202.

32. This is different from a referendum where state law requires that certain types of legislative proposals (such as constitutional amendments and bonds) automatically be submitted to the voters for their approval or situations in which the legislature places a proposed statute on the ballot for voter approval. In neither of these instances are petitions the impetus for the issue being submitted directly to the voters for approval. Thomas E. Cronin, *Direct Democracy: The Politics of Initiative, Referendum, and Recall* (Cambridge, MA: Harvard University Press, 1989), noted, "There is confusion about the difference between the initiative and referendum because [the term] *referendum* is frequently used in a casual or generic way to describe all ballot measures" (p. 2).

33. Ibid.

34. Ibid., pp. 2–3.

35. Recall efforts getting a lot of attention in recent years have been those directed at elected judges. For some intriguing case study discussions of how such efforts work, see Laura R. Woliver, *From Outrage to Action: The Politics of Grass-Roots Dissent* (Urbana: University of Illinois Press, 1993).

36. For excellent, in-depth discussions of the types of citizen initiatives, the frequency of their use, and their pros and cons, see Schmidt, *Citizen Lawmakers;* Cronin, *Direct Democracy;* Joseph F. Zimmerman, *Participatory Democracy: Populism Revived* (New York: Praeger, 1986); Harlan Hahn and Sheldon Kamieniecki, *Referendum Voting: Social Status and Policy Preferences* (Westport, CT: Greenwood Press, 1987); Wachtel, *The Electronic Congress;* David Magleby, *Direct Legislation: Voting on Ballot Propositions in the United States,* (Baltimore, MD: Johns Hopkins University Press, 1984); David Butler and Austin Ranney, eds., *Referendums: A Comparative Study of Practice and Theory* (Washington, DC: American Enterprise Institute for Public Policy Research, 1978); Betty H. Zisk, *Money, Media, and the Grass Roots: State Ballot Issues and the Electoral Process* (Newbury Park, CA: Sage, 1987); Alexander J. Bott, *Handbook of United States Election Laws and Practices: Political Rights* (Westport, CT: Greenwood Press, 1990); Edward A. Jaksha, *Of the People: Democracy and the Petition Process* (Omaha: Simmons-Boardman Books, 1988); John M. Allswang, *California Initiatives and Referendums, 1912–1990: A Survey and Guide to Research* (Los Angeles: Edmund G. "Pat" Brown Institute of Public Affairs, California State University, 1991); Mary Kay Falconer, *Initiatives and Referenda: Issues in Citizen Lawmaking* (Tallahassee: Florida Advisory Council on Intergovernmental Relations, 1986); and Daniel F. Ritsche, *Let the People Decide: Initiative and Referendum in Wisconsin and Other States* (Madison: State of Wisconsin Legislative Reference Bureau, 1990).

37. Wachtel, *The Electronic Congress,* pp. 50–51.

38. Schmidt, *Citizen Lawmakers,* p. 29.

39. For a good discussion of voter fatigue, see Shaun Bowler, Todd Donovan, and Trudi Happ, "Ballot Propositions and Information Costs: Direct Democracy and the Fatigued Voter," *Western Political Quarterly* 45 (June 1992), pp. 559–568. For discussions of the role of money in referenda outcomes, see Zisk, *Money, Media, and the Grass Roots;* Cronin, *Direct Democracy;* John R. Owens and Larry L. Wade, "Campaign Spending on California Ballot Propositions," *Western Political Quarterly* 39 (December 1986), pp. 675–689; David Hadwiger, "Money, Turnout, and Ballot Measure Success in California Cities," *Western Political Quarterly* 45 (June 1992), pp. 539–547; and Schmidt, *Citizen Lawmakers.*

40. Tom Fiedler, "Petition Drives Have Potential to Harm State," *The Tampa Tribune,* February 8, 1994.

41. Paid petition circulators are used most in the states with the largest signature requirements: California, Ohio, and Florida.

42. Schmidt, *Citizen Lawmakers,* p. 37.

43. A Times Mirror Center for The People & The Press telephone survey of a nationally representative sample of 3,517 adults 18 years of age or older, conducted May 28–June 10, 1992, asked the respondent whether he or she had "signed or circulated a petition in the past year to express your opinions on issues that concern you." Those responding affirmatively by age-group were: 18- to 29-year-olds, 51.7 percent; 30- to 49-year-olds, 61 percent; 50- to 64-year-olds, 52.4 percent; and those 65 and over, 34.3 percent.

44. Cronin, *Direct Democracy,* p. 64.

45. Peggy Kneffel Daniels and Carol A. Schwartz, eds., *Encyclopedia of Associations 1994*, 28th ed. (Detroit, MI: Gale Research 1994,).

46. For excellent discussions of why people join (or do not join) groups, see Mancur Olson, *The Logic of Collective Action* (Cambridge, MA: Harvard University Press, 1965); E. E. Schattschneider, *The Semisovereign People*. (New York: Holt, Rinehart and Winston, 1960); Robert H. Salisbury, "An Exchange Theory of Interest Groups," *Midwest Journal of Political Science* 13 (February 1969), pp. 1–32; James Q. Wilson, *Political Organizations* (New York: Basic Books, 1973); Terry M. Moe, *The Organization of Interests* (Chicago: University of Chicago Press, 1980); and Paul A. Sabatier, "Interest Group Membership and Organization: Multiple Theories," in Mark P. Petracca, ed., *The Politics of Interests: Interest Groups Transformed* (Boulder: Westview Press, 1992), pp. 99–129.

47. Jeffrey M. Berry, *The Interest Group Society*, 2nd ed. (Boston: Little, Brown, 1989), p. 6.

48. Cf. Salisbury, "An Exchange Theory of Interest Groups"; and Albert O. Hirschman, *Exit, Voice and Loyalty: Responses to Decline in Firms, Organizations, and States* (Cambridge, MA: Harvard University Press, 1970).

49. David Truman, in *The Governmental Process* (New York: Knopf, 1951), argued convincingly that "people in society who share an interest, but are as yet unorganized, are brought together when they are adversely affected by a 'disturbance'—some identifiable event or series of events that alter the 'equilibrium' in some sector of society," as articulated in Berry, *The Interest Group Society*, p. 45.

50. Berry, *The Interest Group Society*, p. 4.

51. Cf. Burdett A. Loomis and Allan J. Cigler, "Introduction: The Changing Nature of *Interest Group Politics*," in Allan J. Cigler and Burdett A. Loomis, eds., *Interest Group Politics*, 3rd ed. (Washington, DC: CQ Press, 1991), pp. 1–32; Philip A. Mundo, *Interest Groups: Cases and Characteristics* (Chicago: Nelson-Hall Publishers, 1992); Jack L. Walker, *Mobilizing Interest Groups in America: Patrons, Professions, and Social Movements* (Ann Arbor: University of Michigan Press, 1991); Kay L. Schlotzman and John T. Tierney, *Organized Interests in American Democracy* (New York: Harper & Row, 1986); H. R. Mahood, *Interest Group Politics in America: A New Intensity* (Englewood Cliffs, NJ: Prentice-Hall, 1990); Ronald J. Hrebenar and Ruth K. Scott, *Interest Group Politics in America* (Englewood Cliffs, NJ: Prentice-Hall, 1990); Graham K. Wilson, *Interest Groups* (Cambridge, MA: Blackwell, 1990); Graham Wootton, *Interests Groups: Policy and Politics in America* (Englewood Cliffs, NJ: Prentice-Hall, 1985); and R. Kenneth Godwin, *One Billion Dollars of Influence: The Direct Marketing of Politics* (Chatham, NJ: Chatham House, 1988).

52. A face-to-face Times Mirror Center for The People & The Press Survey of a nationally representative sample of 4,244 adults 18 and over, conducted in May 1987, and a Times Mirror Center for The People & The Press telephone survey of a nationally representative sample of 3,517 adults 18 and over, conducted in June 1992.

53. Schlotzman and Tierney, *Organized Interests in American Democracy*, pp. 61–63.

54. For a good discussion of these techniques, see R. Kenneth Godwin, "Money, Technology, and Political Interests: The Direct Marketing of Politics," in Mark P. Petracca, ed., *The Politics of Interests: Interest Groups Transformed* (Boulder: Westview Press, 1992), pp. 308–325.

55. Christine L. Day, "Older Americans, Interest Groups, and the Medicare Catastrophic Coverage Act of 1988," paper presented at the annual meeting of the Southern Political Science Association, Atlanta, GA, November 1990, pp. 7–8; also see Day, "Older Americans' Attitudes Toward the Medicare Catastrophic Coverage Act of 1988," *Journal of Politics* 55 (February 1993), pp. 167–177.

56. Day, *What Older Americans Think*, p. 3.

57. The growth in senior citizen interest groups is attributed to four factors: "(1) the growing sense of common needs and interests among older people, (2) the leadership of organizational 'entrepreneurs,' (3) the variety of incentives offered to members, and (4) patronage by government agencies and private foundations"; see Day, *What Older Americans Think*, p. 30.

58. Cf. Day, *What Older Americans Think*; David VanTassel and Jimmy Elaine Wilkonson Meyers, eds., *U.S. Aging Policy Interest Groups: Institutional Profiles* (New York: Greenwood Press, 1992); Henry J. Pratt, *The Gray Lobby* (Chicago: University of Chicago Press, 1976); Douglas Dobson and Douglas St. Angelo, *Politics and Senior Citizens: Advocacy and Policy Formation in a Local Context* (DeKalb:

Center for Governmental Studies, Northern Illinois University, 1980); Michael K. Carlie, "The Politics of Age: Interest Group or Social Movement?" *Gerontologist 9*, no. 2 (1969), pp. 259–263; Paul C. Light, *Artful Work: The Politics of Social Security Reform* (New York: Random House, 1985); and Jill Quadagno, "Interest-Group Politics and the Future of U.S. Social Security," in John Myles and Jill Quadagno, eds., *States, Labor Markets, and the Future of Old-Age Policy* (Philadelphia: Temple University Press, 1991), pp. 36–58.

59. Day, *What Older Americans Think*, p. 25.

60. Linkley H. Clark, Jr., "How the Biggest Lobby Grew," *Wall Street Journal*, January 27, 1994, p. A14.

61. Ibid.

62. For another look at the growing diversity of groups representing older citizens, see Henry J. Pratt, "Seniors Organizations and Group Maintenance: Patronage Reconsidered," paper presented at the annual meeting of the American Political Science Association, New York, September 1–4, 1994. Pratt concluded: "Even though united in their opposition to threatened reductions in existing aging benefits, such groups' non-crisis behavior is now perhaps less reflective of the commonalitites, and more of the disparities in policy outlooks, and political aspirations" (p. 17). Other excellent sources covering the growing conflicts within the ranks of the elderly include Day, "Older Americans' Attitudes Toward the Medicare Catastropic Coverage Act," and Richard B. McKenzie, "Senior Power: Has the Power of the Elderly Peaked?" *The American Enterprise 4* (May-June 1993), pp. 74–80.

63. George de Lama, "Baby Boomer Bonanza Looms: AARP Licking Its Chops as Nation's Largest Group Nears 50," *Chicago Tribune* article, as reported in the *Houston Chronicle*, March 6, 1994, p. 10A.

64. Daniels and Schwartz, eds., *Encyclopedia of Associations 1994*, p. 1233.

65. See Victoria Jueds, "From Statistics to Soup Kitchens: Youth as Resources in the 1990s," *National Civic Review 83* (Spring-Summer 1994), pp. 120–125; and Michael Hancock, "Collaboration for Youth Development: Youth Action Programming," *National Civic Review* 83 (Spring-Summer 1994), pp. 139–145.

66. Berry, *The Interest Group Society*, identified "organizational egos" as the major difficulty in holding coalitions together. "The more resources an interest group devotes to coalition activities, the less it has for doing things in its own name. Interest group leaders and lobbyists have a personal stake in working to enhance their own reputation and that of their organizations. The broader and more lasting a prospective coalition is, the more difficult it becomes for the organizers to overcome this problem" (p. 202). An excellent case study describing the special difficulties of sustaining a citywide senior coalition is Donald C. Reitzes and Dietrich C. Reitzes, "Metro Seniors in Action: A Case Study of a Citywide Senior Organization," *The Gerontologist* 31, no. 2 (1991), pp. 256–262.

67. Jill Quadagno, "Generational Equity and the Politics of the Welfare State," *Politics & Society* 17, no. 3 (1987), pp. 323–376.

68. Gary Blonston, "New Generation Takes Aim at Lawmakers," Knight-Ridder Newspapers article, reported in *The Tampa Tribune*, February 20, 1993, Nation/World, p. 11.

69. Quoted in Michele Kay, "Retirees, Boomers, Twentysomethings Clash Over Lean Social Security Coffers," *Austin American-Statesman*, May 8, 1994.

70. Quoted in "Politics of a Generation," *The Tampa Tribune*, March 23, 1993, Baylife, p. 4.

71. Mike Tapp, "Leading a New Generation," *St. Petersburg Times*, November 3, 1994, p. 5B.

72. For good discussions of the nature and scope of interest groups at the state and local levels, see Virginia Gray and David Lowery, "Stability and Change in State Interest Group Systems, 1975–1990," *State and Local Government Review* 25 (Spring 1993), pp. 87–96; Virginia Gray and David Lowery, "The Diversity of State Interest Group Systems," *Political Research Quarterly* 46, no. 1 (1993), pp. 81–97; Kennith G. Hunter, Laura Ann Wilson, and Gregory W. Brunk, "Societal Complexity and Interest Group Lobbying in the American States," *Journal of Politics* 53, no. 2 (1991), pp. 488–503; L. Harmon Ziegler, "Interest Groups in the States," in Virginia Gray, Herbert Jacob, and Kenneth Vines, eds., *Politics in the American States*, 4th ed. (Boston: Little, Brown, 1983), pp. 97–132; Ronald J. Hrebenar and Clive S. Thomas, eds., *Interest Group Politics in the Southern States* (Tuscaloosa: University of Alabama Press, 1992); Virginia Gray and David Lowery, "Interest Group Politics and

Economic Growth in the American States," *American Political Science Review* 82 (March 1988), pp. 109–131; and David C. Nice, "Interest Groups and Policymaking in the American States, *Political Behavior* 6, no. 2 (1984), pp. 183–196.

73. Anne E. Kelley and Ella L. Taylor, "Florida: The Changing Patterns of Power," in Ronald J. Hrebenar and Clive S. Thomas, eds., *Interest Group Politics in the Southern States* (Tuscaloosa: University of Alabama Press, 1992), pp. 125–151.

74. James MacGregor Burns, et al., *Government by the People,* 15th ed. (Englewood Cliffs, NJ: Prentice-Hall, 1993), p. 268.

75. For insightful overviews of campaign finance and PACs, see Frank J. Sorauf, *Inside Campaign Finance: Myths and Realities* (New Haven: Yale University Press, 1992); David B. Magleby and Candice J. Nelson, *The Money Chase: Congressional Campaign Finance Reform* (Washington, DC: Brookings Institution, 1990); Larry J. Sabato, *PAC Power: Inside the World of Political Action Committees* (New York: Norton, 1985); and Anthony Corrado, *Creative Campaigning: PACs and the Presidential Selection Process* (Boulder: Westview Press, 1992).

76. Harold W. Stanley and Richard G. Niemi, *Vital Statistics on American Politics,* 4th ed. (Washington, DC: CQ Press, 1994), p. 175.

77. Ibid., p. 134.

78. Sorauf, *Inside Campaign Finance,* pp. 98–99.

79. M. Margaret Conway, "PACs in the Political Process," in Allan J. Cigler and J. Burdett Loomis, eds., *Interest Group Politics,* 3rd ed. (Washington, DC: CQ Press, 1991), pp. 199–216; Larry Makinson, *The Price of Admission: Campaign Spending in the 1990 Elections* (Washington, DC: Center for Responsive Politics, 1991); Philip Stern, *The Best Congress Money Can Buy* (New York: Pantheon Books, 1988); Margaret L. Nugent and John R. Johannes, eds., *Money, Elections, and Democracy: Reforming Congressional Campaign Finance* (Boulder: Westview Press, 1990); Theodore J. Eismeier and Philip H. Pollack III, *Business, Money, and the Rise of Corporate PACs in American Elections* (New York: Quorum Books, 1988); Michael Malbin, *Money and Politics in the United States* (Chatham, NJ: Chatham House, 1984); Larry Makinson, *Open Secrets: The Dollar Power of PACs in Congress* (Washington, DC: CQ Press, 1990); Richard L. Hall and Frank W. Wayman, "Buying Time: Moneyed Interests and the Mobilization of Bias in Congressional Committees," *American Political Science Review* 84 (September 1990), pp. 797–820; and Brooks Jackson, *Honest Graft: Big Money and the American Political Process* (New York: Knopf, 1988).

80. In "Organized Interests and the Search for Certainty," the concluding chapter to their edited volume *Interest Group Politics,* Cigler and Loomis pointed out, "Perhaps nowhere in political science is impact harder to assess than in judging the role played by organized interests. . . . Statistical associations between PAC contributions and legislative behavior tell us little about causal relationships. For example, PACs and public officials insist that money ordinarily follows votes rather than determines them. In any event, legislative decisions are usually complex, with an official's constituency, party, ideology, peer influence, and independent judgment all potentially important" (pp. 387–388). Also see Janet M. Grenzke, "PACs and the Congressional Supermarket: The Currency Is Complex," *American Journal of Political Science* 33 (February 1989), pp. 1–24.

81. Jeffrey M. Berry, *The Interest Group Society,* (Boston: Little, Brown, 1984), p. 196.

82. See Walter K. Olson, *The Litigation Explosion: What Happened When America Unleashed the Lawsuit* (New York: Truman Talley Books, 1991); Susan A. MacManus, "Litigation: A Real Budget Buster for Many U.S. Municipalities," *Government Finance Review* 10 (February 1994), pp. 27–41.

83. See Karen O'Connor and Lee Epstein, "The Rise of Conservative Interest Group Litigation," *Journal of Politics* 45 (1983), pp. 479–489; Lee Epstein, *Conservatives in Court* (Knoxville: University of Tennessee Press, 1986); and Karen O'Connor and Bryant Scott McFall, "Conservative Interest Group Litigation in the Reagan Era and Beyond," in Mark P. Petracca, ed., *The Politics of Interests: Interest Groups Transformed* (Boulder: Westview Press, 1992), pp. 263–281.

84. Kim Lane Scheppele and Jack L. Walker, Jr., "The Litigation Strategies of Interest Groups," in Jack L. Walker, Jr., ed., *Mobilizing Interest Groups in America: Patrons, Professions, and Social Movements* (Ann Arbor: University of Michigan Press, 1991), p. 158.

85. Ibid., p. 167.

86. *A* group must have legal standing to go to court. That is, it must be an appropriate party to the suit. As noted by Berry, *The Interest Group Society* (1984 ed.), "The courts' traditional test is that plaintiffs must show some direct injury to have standing," although the courts have expanded their rules for standing somewhat in recent years (p. 199).

87. Ibid., pp. 181–182.

88. Walker, *Mobilizing Interest Groups in America*, p. 182.

89. Susan Gluck Mezey, "Constitutional Adjudication of Children's Rights Claims in the United States Supreme Court, 1953–92," Special Symposium Issues on the Rights of Children, *Family Law Quarterly* 27 (Fall 1993), pp. 307–325; and Donald J. Hernandez, *America's Children: Resources from Family, Government, and the Economy* (New York: Russell Sage Foundation, 1993).

90. Henry J. Pratt, *Gray Agendas: Interest Groups and Public Pensions in Canada, Britain, and the United States* (Ann Arbor: University of Michigan Press, 1993); Alicia H. Munnell, ed., *Retirement and Public Policy* (Dubuque, IA: Kendall/Hunt Publishing, 1991); and Miles and Quadagno, *States, Labor Markets, and the Future of Old-Age Policy.*

91. According to the U.S. Equal Employment Opportunity Commission, age-related cases increased from 19,271 in 1992 to 19,884 in 1993. Age-related cases are already the third most frequent category of job-bias claims, ranking behind only race and gender, as reported in the *Wall Street Journal*, April 1, 1994, p. B3.

92. Times Mirror Center for The People & The Press face-to-face survey of a nationally representative sample of 4,244 adults 18 years of age or older, conducted April 25–May 10, 1987.

93. For a good discussion of why people don't run, see Timothy Bledsoe, *Careers in City Politics* (Pittsburgh: University of Pittsburgh Press, 1993), pp. 62–64.

94. Alan Ehrenhalt, *The United States of Ambition: Politicians, Power, and the Pursuit of Office* (New York: Times Books, 1991), p. 273.

95. Joseph A. Schlesinger, *Ambition and Politics: Political Careers in the United States* (Chicago: Rand McNally, 1966).

96. For excellent discussions of why people run (or don't run), see Schlesinger, *Ambition and Politics*; Bledsoe, *Careers in City Politics*; Kenneth Prewitt, *The Recruitment of Political Leaders: A Study of Citizen Politicians* (Indianapolis: Bobbs-Merrill, 1970); Kenneth Prewitt and William Nowlin, "Political Ambitions and the Behavior of Incumbent Politicians," *Western Political Quarterly* 22 (June 1969), pp. 298–308; David W. Rohde, "Risk-Bearing and Progressive Ambition: The Case of Members of the United States House of Representatives," *American Journal of Political Science* 23 (February 1979), pp. 1–26; James David Barber, *The Lawmakers: Recruitment and Adaptation to Legislative Life* (New Haven: Yale University Press, 1965); Gordon S. Black, "A Theory of Political Ambition: Career Choices and the Role of Structural Incentives," *American Political Science Review* 66 (March 1972), pp. 144–159; Jeff Fishel, *Party and Opposition: Congressional Challengers in American Politics* (New York: David McKay, 1973); Linda L. Fowler and Robert D. McClure, *Political Ambition: Who Decides to Run for Congress* (New Haven: Yale University Press, 1989); John R. Hibbing, *Congressional Careers: Contours of Life in the U.S. House of Representatives* (Chapel Hill: University of North Carolina Press, 1991); D. Roderick Kiewiet and Langche Zeng, "An Analysis of Congressional Career Decisions, 1947–1986," *American Political Science Review* 87 (December 1993), pp. 928–941; Paul Brace, "Progressive Ambition in the House: A Probabilistic Approach," *Journal of Politics* 46 (1984), pp. 556–569; Peverill Squire, "Member Career Opportunities and the Internal Organization of Legislatures," *Journal of Politics* 50 (1988), pp. 726–744; David T. Canon, "Sacrificial Lambs or Strategic Politicians? Political Amateurs in U.S. House Elections," *American Journal of Political Science* 37 (November 1993), pp. 1119–1141; Peverill Squire, "Challengers in U.S. Senate Elections," *Legislative Studies Quarterly* 14 (November 1989), pp. 531–547; Jon R. Bond, Cary Covington, and Richard Fleisher, "Explaining Challenger Quality in Congressional Elections," *Journal of Politics* 47 (1985), pp. 511–529; Jonathan S. Krasno and Donald Philip Green, "Preempting Quality Challengers in House Elections," *Journal of Politics* 50 (1988), pp. 920–936; Paul R. Abramson, John H. Aldrich, and David

W. Rohde, "Progressive Ambition Among United States Senators: 1972–1988," *Journal of Politics* 49 (1987), pp. 3–35; Timothy Bledsoe and Mary Herring, "Victims of Circumstances: Women in Pursuit of Political Office," *American Political Science Review* 84 (March 1990), pp. 213–223; Gary C. Jacobson, "Strategic Politicians and the Dynamics of U.S. House Elections, 1946–86," *American Political Science Review* 83 (1989), pp. 773–793; Jeffrey S. Banks and D. Roderick Kiewiet, "Explaining Patterns of Competition in Congressional Elections," *American Journal of Political Science* 33 (1989), pp. 997–1015; David T. Canon, *Actors, Athletes, and Astronauts: Political Amateurs in the United States Congress* (Chicago: University of Chicago Press, 1990); William T. Bianco, "Strategic Decisions on Candidacy in U.S. Congressional Districts," *Legislative Studies Quarterly 9 (1984), pp. 351–364; Sandy L. Maisel, From Obscurity to Oblivion: Running in the Congressional Primary,* rev. ed. (Knoxville: University of Tennessee Press, 1986); Charles Stewart, "A Sequential Model of U.S. Senate Elections," *Legislative Studies Quarterly* 14 (1989), pp. 567–601; Gary F. Moncrief and Joel A. Thompson, eds., *Changing Patterns in State Legislative Careers* (Ann Arbor: University of Michigan Press, 1992); and Linda L. Fowler, *Candidates, Congress, and the American Democracy* (Ann Arbor: University of Michigan Press, 1993).

97. Ehrenhalt, *The United States of Ambition*, p. 273.

98. U.S. Bureau of the Census, *Statistical Abstract of the United States 1993* (Washington, DC: U.S. Government Printing Office, 1993), p. 291.

99. For up-to-date lists of elective offices in each state, see Council of State Governments, *Book of the States*, published biennially in Lexington, KY, by the Council of State Governments.

100. Ehrenhalt, *The United States of Ambition*, p. 15.

101. Alexander J. Bott, *Handbook of United States Election Laws and Practices* (Westport, CT: Greenwood Press, 1990), p. 58.

102. George C. Kiser, "Are Senior Citizens Too Old for the Vice Presidency? A Look at the Record," *Presidential Studies Quarterly* 24 (Fall 1994), pp. 809–821.

103. Bledsoe, *Careers in City Politics*, p. 50.

104. Susan A. MacManus, "It's Never Too Late to Run—And Win! The Graying of Women in Local Politics," *National Civic Review* 80 (Summer 1991), pp. 294–310. A 1986 survey found that over half of Florida's city council members were over 50 years of age; 29 percent were over 60. Seventeen cities, mostly coastal retirement communities, had four or more council members over 60 years of age; see Susan A. MacManus, "Representation at the Local Level in Florida: County Commissions, School Boards, and City Councils," in Susan A. MacManus, ed., *Reapportionment & Representation in Florida: A Historical Collection* (Tampa: Intrabay Innovation Institute, University of South Florida, 1991), pp. 493–538.

105. Respondents were asked: "How strongly do you agree or disagree with the idea that both Clinton and Gore are young candidates?" The age-group breakdowns (percent agreeing with this idea) were: 18- to 29-year-olds, 67.9 percent; 65 and over, 68.9 percent; 30- to 49-year-olds, 60.8 percent; and 50- to 64-year-olds, 60.9 percent. Times Mirror Center for The People & The Press telephone survey of a nationally representative sample of registered voters, conducted October 20–22, 1992.

106. Schlesinger, *Ambition and Politics;* Hain, "Age, Ambitions, and Political Careers"; Prewitt and Nowlin, "Political Ambitions and the Behavior of Incumbent Politicians"; and Black, "A Theory of Political Ambition."

107. Fowler and McClure, *Political Ambition*, p. 134.

108. Kenneth J. Cooper, "3 in House Announce Retirement," *Washington Post,* January 5, 1993, p. A13.

109. Bledsoe, *Careers in City Politics*, p. 49.

110. National School Boards Association, mimeo, 1993.

111. Susan A. MacManus, "Governing Boards, Partisanship, and Elections," in Donald C. Menzel, ed., *The American County* (forthcoming, University of Alabama Press, 1996). Results are based on a mail survey of large U.S. counties, conducted December 1992–January 1993; data reported are as of January 1993.

112. The reasons for early retirement may be strictly personal. But some politicians may also retire because they face serious electoral challenges due to partisan shifts in their home states, national economic conditions, or personal scandal. For a good discussion of the research on retirement, see Kiewiet and Zeng, "An Analysis of Congressional Career Desions."

113. A mail survey conducted by Susan A. MacManus, January-February 1994. The response rate was 51 percent.

114. Susan A. MacManus, "Women in Elective Office: Age, Ambition, and Perceptions of Generational Gaps in Policy Preferences," paper presented at the annual meeting of the Urban Affairs Association, New Orleans, LA, March 3–5, 1994.

115. These activities were: written a letter to any elected official; written a letter to the editor of a newspaper; contributed money to a political action group or committee sponsored by a union, business, or other issue group that supported a candidate in an election; attended a public hearing; dialed a 1-800 or 1-900 number to register an opinion on some issue of public concern; contributed money to a candidate running for public office; joined an organization in support of a particular cause; called in or sent in a response to a question or issue put up for discussion by a newspaper or TV station; called or sent a letter to the White House; called or sent a letter to a congress member; called a television station or a cable company with some complaint about a program; participated in an opinion poll sent by some interest group or a group one belongs to; participated in a "town meeting" or public affairs discussion group; attended a city or town council meeting in the community where one lives; or gave money to or joined Ross Perot's organization, United We Stand. Results are from a Times Mirror Center for The People & The Press telephone survey of a nationally representative sample of 1,507 adults 18 years of age or older, conducted May 18–24, 1993.

CHAPTER 5

1. Fernando M. Torres-Gil, *The New Aging: Politics and Change in America* (New York: Auburn House, 1992), p. 103.

2. Ibid., p. 113. Also see Phillip Longman, *Born to Pay: The New Politics of Aging* (Boston: Houghton Mifflin, 1987).

3. James Q. Wilson and Edward C. Banfield, "Public Regardingness as a Value Premise in Voting Behavior," *American Political Science Review* 58 (December 1964), pp. 876–887; James Q. Wilson and Edward C. Banfield, "Political Ethos Revisited," *American Political Science Review* 65 (December 1971), pp. 1048–1062; and Raymond E. Wolfinger and John Field, "Political Ethos and the Structure of City Government," *American Political Science Review* 60 (June 1966), pp. 306–326.

4. John L. Palmer, Timothy Smeeding, and Barbara Boyle Torrey, eds., *The Vulnerable* (Washington, DC: Urban Institute Press, 1988), p. 1.

5. Neil Howe and Bill Strauss, *13th Generation: Abort, Retry, Ignore, Fail?* (New York: Vintage Books, 1993), p. 220.

6. Written in a letter to Jean-Baptiste Leroy, November 13, 1789; from Gorton Carruth and Eugene Ehrlich, *American Quotations* (Avenel, NJ: Wings Books, 1992), p. 543.

7. Written in a Supreme Court opinion, *Compania de Tabacos* v. *Collector,* 1904; from Carruth and Ehrlich, *American Quotations,* p. 543.

8. Joseph A. Pechman, *Federal Tax Policy,* 5th ed. (Washington, DC: Brookings Institution, 1987), p. 5. Other good sources detailing the history and purposes of taxation in the United States are: B. Guy Peters, *The Politics of Taxation* (Cambridge, MA: Blackwell, 1991); C. Eugene Steuerle, *The Tax Decade* (Washington, DC: Urban Institute Press, 1992); and John L. Mikesell, *Fiscal Administration,* 4th ed. (Pacific Grove, CA: Brooks/Cole, 1995).

9. *Merriam-Webster's Collegiate Dictionary,* 10th ed. (Springfield, MA: Merriam-Webster, 1993), p. 1208.

10. These states without income taxes as of 1992 were Alaska, Florida, Nevada, South Dakota, Texas, Washington, and Wyoming.

11. See John H. Bowman and John L. Mikesell, *Local Government Tax Authority and Use* (Washington, DC: National League of Cities, 1987); Susan A. MacManus, "State Government: The Overseer of Municipal Finance," in Alberta M. Sbragia, ed., *The Municipal Money Chase: The Politics of Local Government Finance* (Boulder: Westview Press, 1983), pp. 145–183; and Advisory Commission on Intergovernmental Relations, *Significant Features of Fiscal Federalism* (Washington, DC: ACIR, published annually).

12. For overviews of nontax revenue use, see Pechman, *Federal Tax Policy*; J. Richard Aronson and Eli Schwartz, eds., *Management Policies in Local Government Finance* (Washington, DC: International City Management Association, 1987); Robert L. Bland, *A Revenue Guide for Local Government* (Washington, DC: International City Management Association, 1989); Academy for State and Local Government, *Where Will the Money Come From? Finding Reliable Revenue for State and Local Government in a Changing Economy,* vol. 1, *Summary of the Fiscal Futures Study* (Washington, DC: Academy for State and Local Government, 1986); Susan A. MacManus, "Financing Federal, State, and Local Governments in the 1990s," *Annals of the American Academy of Political and Social Science* 509 (May 1990), pp. 22–35; John E. Petersen and Dennis R. Strachota, eds., *Local Government Finance* (Chicago: Government Finance Officers Association, 1991).

13. For good overviews of the history and the pros and cons of public lotteries in the United States, see Tim J. Watts, *State-Run Lotteries: A Bibliography* (Monticello, IL: Vance Bibliographies, 1991); Mary O. Borg, *The Economic Consequences of State Lotteries* (New York: Praeger, 1991); Ann E. Weiss, *Lotteries: Who Wins, Who Loses?* (Hillside, NJ: Enslow Publishers, 1991); Charles T. Clotfelter, *Selling Hope: State Lotteries in America* (Cambridge, MA: Harvard University Press, 1989); and Alan J. Karcher, *Lotteries* (New Brunswick, NJ: Transaction Books, 1989).

14. Impact fees, also known as financial exactions, have become quite popular, although they remain controversial. Governments "mandate that real estate developers, as a condition for receiving permits, expend resources for the provision of public facilities or services. . . . Governments having reasonably determined that certain public needs are 'attributable' to new development, may require that their costs be 'internalized' as part of the development process"; see Alan A. Altschuler and Jose A. Gomez-Ibanez, *Regulation for Revenue: The Political Economy of Land Use Exactions* (Washington, DC: Brookings Institution, 1993), pp. 3–4. Before 1960, about 10 percent of U.S. localities imposed such fees. By the mid-1980s, the figure had reached 90 percent or so.

15. Borrowing is often preferable to elected officials and taxpayers alike because it allows them to pass the payment problem on to future generations of officeholders. See Elaine B. Sharp, "The Politics and Economics of the New City Debt," *American Political Science Review* 80 (December 1986), pp. 1271–1288, and Susan A. MacManus, "Budget Battles: Strategies of Local Government Officers During Recession," *Journal of Urban Affairs* 15, no. 3 (1993), pp. 293–307.

16. Pechman, *Federal Tax Policy*; John W. Ellwood, ed., *Reductions in U.S. Domestic Spending: How They Affect State and Local Governments* (New Brunswick, NJ: Transaction Books, 1982); Helen F. Ladd and J. Yinger, *America's Ailing Cities: Fiscal Health and the Design of Urban Policy* (Baltimore, MD: Johns Hopkins University Press, 1989); William J. Pammer, Jr., *Managing Fiscal Stress in Major American Cities* (New York: Greenwood Press, 1990); D. J. Watson and T. Vocino, "Changing Intergovernmental Fiscal Relationships: Impact of the 1985 Tax Reform Act on State and Local Governments," *Public Administration Review* 50 (July-August 1990), pp. 427–434.

17. For excellent analyses of the tax revolts of the 1970s and 1980s, see David Lowery and Lee Sigelman, "Understanding the Tax Revolt: Eight Explanations," *American Political Science Review* 75 (December 1981), pp. 963–974; James M. Buchanan, "The Potential for Taxpayers Revolt in American Democracy," *Social Science Quarterly* 59 (March 1979), pp. 691–696; Paul Allen Beck and Thomas R. Dye, "Sources of Public Opinion on Taxes," *Journal of Politics* 44 (February 1982), pp. 172–182; Carl Ladd, "The Polls: Taxing and Spending," *Public Opinion Quarterly* 43 (Spring 1979), pp. 126–135; Susan Hansen, *The Politics of Taxation* (New York: Praeger, 1983); and David O. Sears and Jack Citrin, *Tax Revolt: Something for Nothing in California* (Cambridge, MA: Harvard University Press, 1985).

18. Two other methods that could be used to amend the U.S. Constitution are (1) passage of a proposal by a two-thirds vote in both houses of Congress and ratification by conventions in three-fourths

of the states, or (2) a proposal drafted by a national constitutional convention called by Congress at the request of two-thirds of the state legislatures, which then must be ratified by conventions in three-fourths of the states.

19. Thomas R. Dye, *Politics in States and Communities,* 8th ed. (Englewood Cliffs, NJ: Prentice-Hall, 1994), pp. 516–517.

20. Susan A. MacManus, "Tricking Taxpayers with 'Earmarking,'" *USA Today,* June 28, 1993, p. 13A.

21. For a good review of this literature, see James Button and Walter Rosenbaum, "Gray Power, Gray Peril, or Gray Myth? The Political Impact of the Aging in Local Sunbelt Politics," *Social Science Quarterly* 71 (March 1990), pp. 25–38.

22. For an excellent review of this literature, see Bruce Jacobs, "Aging and Politics," in Robert H. Binstock and Linda K. George, eds., *Handbook of Aging and the Social Sciences,* 3rd ed. (New York: Academic Press, 1990), pp. 349–361; Christine L. Day, "Older Americans' Attitudes Toward the Medicare Catastrophic Coverage Act of 1988," *Journal of Politics* 55 (February 1993), pp. 166–177; Laurie A. Rhodebeck, "The Politics of Greed? Political Preferences Among the Elderly," *Journal of Politics* 55 (May 1993), pp. 342–364; Christine L. Day, *What Older Americans Think* (Princeton: Princeton University Press, 1990); Button and Rosenbaum, "Gray Power, Gray Peril, or Gray Myth?"

23. Benjamin I. Page and Robert Y. Shapiro, *The Rational Public: Fifty Years of Trends in Americans' Policy Preferences* (Chicago: University of Chicago Press, 1992), p. 160. Also see William G. Mayer, *The Changing American Mind: How and Why American Public Opinion Changed Between 1960 and 1988* (Ann Arbor: University of Michigan Press, 1992).

24. See annual surveys by the U.S. Advisory Commission on Intergovernmental Relations, *Changing Public Attitudes on Governments and Taxes* (Washington, DC: ACIR, published annually).

25. Beginning in 1987, Social Security payments became taxable if a person's income exceeded $25,000 or if a couple's income exceeded $32,000. In 1993, the figures were raised (see Note 29). Mayer, *The Changing American Mind,* p. 175.

26. Some would argue that property taxes are also highly regressive. That was a more accurate characterization in the past, before most states adopted property tax circuit-breaker programs designed to give relief to poorer homeowners.

27. Pechman, *Federal Tax Policy,* p. 260.

28. In two years, 1990 and 1992, the question asked was not worded in the same manner, making it invalid to compare those years with the others.

29. The deficit reduction plan passed by Congress in August 1993 increased the taxable portion of Social Security benefits from 50 to 85 percent for individuals whose income exceeds $34,000 and couples with incomes above $44,000. For a good discussion of this fight, see John H. Makin and Norman J. Ornstein, *Debt and Taxes* (New York: Times Books, 1994), chapter 11.

30. For a review of these polls, see Page and Shapiro, *The Rational Public,* pp. 118–121.

31. Results reported in *The Public Perspective* 5 (May-June 1994), p. 33.

32. Warren E. Miller et al., *American National Election Study: 1990–1991 Panel Study of the Political Consequences of War/1991 Pilot Study* (Ann Arbor: University of Michigan Center for Political Studies, 1991), as reported in Day, "Public Opinion Toward Costs and Benefits of Social Security and Medicare," *Research on Aging* 15 (September 1993), pp. 279–298.

33. Personal interview survey of a probability sample of 1,517 men and women 18 years of age or older living in private households in the United States, conducted April 29–May 2, 1983, by the Gallup Personal Omnibus national interviewing staff for the ACIR.

34. Ibid.

35. A. Regulat Herzog and Willard L. Rodgers, "Interviewing Older Adults: Mode Comparison Using Data from a Face-to-Face Survey and a Telephone Resurvey," *Public Opinion Quarterly* 52 (Spring 1988), pp. 84–99.

36. Reported in U.S. Advisory Commssion on Intergovernmental Relations, *Changing Public Attitudes on Governments and Taxes 1987.*

37. Personal interview survey of a nationally representative sample of 1,044 adults 18 years of age or older living in private households in the United States, conducted June 6–14, 1987, by the Gallup Personal Omnibus national interviewing staff.

38. U.S. Advisory Commission on Intergovernmental Relations, *Changing Public Attitudes on Governments and Taxes 1987*, p. 27.

39. Ibid.

40. For example, the support among 18- to 24-year-olds for higher local sales taxes was 21 percent, compared to 16 percent of those 65 and over; support for increased user fees was 37 percent among the youngest cohort and 31 percent among the oldest. The key exception was a local income tax increase, favored by more elderly (11 percent) than very young (6 percent) but generally not very popular in either group.

41. Just 4 percent of those 65 and over favored an increase in property tax rates to raise additional local revenue, compared to 11 percent of those 18 to 24.

42. The two surveys were conducted in 1974 and 1980 by ACIR. See U.S. Advisory Commission on Intergovernmental Relations, *Changing Public Attitudes on Governments and Taxes 1980*, p. 24.

43. The 1980 survey data showed that 34 percent of those 60 and over cited regressivity, versus 26 percent of those 18- to 29 years of age. Differences were minimal regarding the rate of increase of the property tax, cited by 15 percent of those 60 and over, compared to 13 percent of the 18- to 29-year-olds. Of the two traits, the property tax's regressivity was the most common complaint of both age-groups.

44. Fourteen percent of those 18 to 29 years of age cited the property tax as a deterrent to home-ownership, compared to just 6 percent of those 60 and over.

45. For a good discussion of the inequity issue, see Jonathan Kozol, *Savage Inequalities: Children in America's Schools* (New York: Crown, 1991), and Gregory G. Rocha and Robert H. Webking, *Politics and Public Education: Edgewood v. Kirby and the Reform of Public School Financing in Texas* (Minneapolis: West Publishing, 1992).

46. U.S. Advisory Commission on Intergovernmental Relations, *Changing Public Attitudes on Governments and Taxes 1993*, p. 22.

47. The new plan cut residential property taxes by 33 percent, dropping a $1,000 bill to $667. The general sales tax rate rose from 4 to 6 percent. The selective sales tax on cigarettes went from $.25 to $.75 per pack. Selective sales taxes on alcohol and other items also rose. A modest statewide property tax was adopted to replace the local property tax. The new state property tax rate is much lower than the old local ones it replaced. The formula through which the state money is passed on to local school districts was designed to set a standard minimum per pupil spending level for each school district ($4,200 per pupil by 1995, $5,000 by 1997). Local taxpayers are still able to use their property taxes as a supplement to maintain spending at the 1993 level. But future increases in the wealthy districts are sharply limited in order to achieve more equal spending per pupil across the state. See Mary Jordan, "Michigan School Taxes Herald National Change," *Washington Post*, March 17, 1994, p. A1; "Michigan's Bold Move," editorial, *Washington Post*, March 18, 1994, p. A28.

48. Quoted in the *Tuscola County Advertiser* (Caro, MI), March 9, 1994, p. A5.

49. For a detailed list of these questions, see Mayer, *The Changing American Mind*, pp. 451–457.

50. See Page and Shapiro, *The Rational Public*; and Mayer, *The Changing American Mind*.

51. Page and Shapiro, *The Rational Public*, p.118.

52. Walter A. Rosenbaum and James W. Button, "Is There a Gray Peril? Retirement Politics in Florida," *The Gerontologist* 29, no. 3 (1989), p. 301.

53. Dan Mullins and Mark S. Rosentraub, "Fiscal Pressure? The Impact of Elder Recruitment on Local Expenditures," *Urban Affairs Quarterly* 28 (December 1992), pp. 337–354; and Button and Rosenbaum, "Gray Power, Gray Peril, or Gray Myth?" Caution is in order when examining these studies. Both are based on aggregate community-level data, not individual survey data.

54. See references cited in Note 22; also see Day, *What Older Americans Think;* and Robert B. Hudson and John Strate, "Aging and Political Systems," in Robert H. Binstock and Ethel Shanas, eds., *The Handbook of Aging and the Social Sciences,* 2nd ed. (New York: Van Nostrand Reinhold, 1985), pp. 554–588.

55. Michael Ponza et al., "The Guns of Autumn: Age Differences in Support for Income Transfers to the Young and Old," *Public Opinion Quarterly* 52 (Winter 1988), pp. 441–466; Button and Rosenbaum, "Gray Power"; Mullins and Rosentraub, "Fiscal Pressure?"; and David W. Rasmussen and Allen R.

Zeman, "Self-Interest vs. the 'Public Good': Who Is Willing to Pay for Education in Florida?" *Florida Public Opinion* 4 (Winter 1989), pp. 12–17.

56. Philip K. Piele and John Stuart Hall, in *Budgets, Bonds, and Ballots: Voting Behavior in School Financial Elections* (Lexington, MA: Lexington Books, 1973), concluded that older voters are the most likely to vote against school bonds. James W. Button and Walter A. Rosenbaum, in "Seeing Gray: School Bond Issues and the Aging in Florida," *Research on Aging* 11 (June 1989), pp. 158–173, found that is not always true. They concluded that "the presence of an organized, relatively affluent, and educated aging population can lead to increased support for local educational referenda." Both of these studies were based on aggregate, not individual-level, data.

57. Day, *What Older Americans Think*, p. 48.

58. Mayer, *The Changing American Mind*, chapter 7.

59. A factor analysis of the eleven program areas in 1981, 1983, 1985, 1987, 1989, 1991, and 1993 revealed these four clusters were significant in each time period. Two other policy areas (environment, highways and roads) did not consistently load on the same factors over time.

60. An index was constructed for each of the four policy areas by counting the number of programs on which the respondent supported funding increases. For all but the social services area, the index ranged from 0 to 2; for social services, it was from 0 to 3 because there were three programs included in that broad policy area.

61. See Robert H. Binstock, "The Politics and Economics of Aging and Diversity," in Scott A. Bass, Elizabeth A. Kutza, and Fernando M. Torres-Gil, eds., *Diversity in Aging* (Glenview, IL: Scott, Foresman, 1990), pp. 73–99; and Jacobs, "Aging and Politics."

62. Suzanne L. Parker, *The Florida Annual Policy Survey: Policy Preferences and Priorities of the Florida Public, 1992* (Tallahassee: Survey Research Laboratory, Policy Sciences Program, Florida State University, 1992).

63. Typical of the many works on the rising federal debt and deficit are: James D. Savage, *Balanced Budgets and American Politics* (Ithaca: Cornell University Press, 1988); Robert Eisner, *How Real Is the Federal Deficit?* (New York: Free Press, 1986); David P. Calleo, *The Bankrupting of America: How the Federal Budget Is Impoverishing the Nation* (New York: William Morrow, 1992); Peter G. Peterson, *Facing Up: How to Rescue the Economy from Crushing Debt & Restore the American Dream* (New York: Simon & Schuster, 1993); Makin and Ornstein, *Debt and Taxes.*

64. Among those 65 and over, 26 percent indicated a preference for raising taxes, compared to just 18 percent of those 18 to 34 years of age. With regard to cutting spending, 82 percent of the 18- to 34-year-olds preferred that approach, compared to 75 percent of those 65 and over. Results were reported in Christine Day, "Older Americans, Interests Groups, and the Medicare Catastrophic Coverage Act of 1988," paper presented at the annual meeting of the Southern Political Science Association, Atlanta, GA, November 1990.

65. The precise wording of the question was: "There are a number of ways to reduce the federal budget deficit, if the government decides to. Some people say we can reduce the deficit simply by cutting spending. Others say a combination of spending cuts and tax increases is required. Which of these views comes closer to your own?" Results are from a Times Mirror Center for The People & The Press face-to-face survey of a nationally representative sample of 3,021 adults 18 years of age or older, conducted May 13–22, 1988.

66. The age-group breakdowns of those who expressed the view that cutting spending was the best way to reduce the federal deficit were: 18- to 24-year-olds, 46.5 percent; 25- to 29-year-olds, 4.8 percent; 30- to 39-year-olds, 43.4 percent; 40- to 49-year-olds, 47.6 percent; 50- to 59-year-olds, 50.8 percent; 60- to 69-year-olds, 51.5 percent; and those 70 and older, 47.3 percent.

67. Percentages indicating support for higher taxes on alcoholic beverages and increasing income taxes on the wealthy hovered around the two-thirds mark across all age-groups. Differences between the youngest and oldest cohorts were in the range of 2 to 3 percent, with the young slightly more supportive of taxes on alcoholic beverages and higher income taxes on the wealthy. Age-extreme group differences on specific spending cut approaches also hovered in the range of 2 to 3 percent. However,

when respondents were asked whether government should "freeze all federal spending at current levels until the budget is balanced" to reduce the federal deficit, more dramatic age-group differences emerged. The breakdowns of those in favor of spending freezes were: 18- to 24-year-olds, 33.7 percent; 25–29, 31.6 percent; 30–39, 35.1 percent; 40–49, 36 percent; 50–59, 32.6 percent; 60–69, 40.3 percent; and 70 and over, 42.3 percent. There was only weak support across all age-groups for privatizing either the federal prisons or the U.S. Postal Service. Working-aged adults were most in favor of these approaches (approximately one-third). The youngest and oldest cohorts disagreed most about which service to privatize, although their support for privatization was weak. Among those 70 and older, there was strongest support for privatizing the U.S. Postal Service (26.9 percent versus 16.8 percent in favor of privatizing federal prisons). Comparable figures for those 18 to 24 years of age were 14.1 percent for the U.S. Postal Service and 26.6 percent for the prisons. Results were based on a face-to-face Times Mirror Center for The People & The Press survey of a nationally representative sample of 3,021 adults 18 years of age or older, conducted May 13–22, 1988.

68. Entitlements are "any public-sector payments, received by a person or household, that do not represent contractual compensation for goods or services." At the federal level, they include Social Security, Medicare, Medicaid, food stamps, federal pensions, unemployment compensation, veterans' benefits, and farm aid, to name the most prominent; see Peterson, *Facing Up*, pp. 99–100.

69. Warren B. Rudman and Paul E. Tsongas, "Foreword," in Peterson, *Facing Up*, p. 15–16.

70. Beck and Dye, "Source of Public Opinion on Taxes."

71. Mayer, *The Changing American Mind*. The strong link between ideology and economics was also the focus of Sidney Plotkin and William E. Scheuerman, *Private Interest, Public Spending: Balanced-Budget Conservatism and the Fiscal Crisis* (Boston: South End Press, 1994); Paul Krugman, *Peddling Prosperity: Economic Sense and Nonsense in the Age of Diminished Expectations* (New York: W. W. Norton, 1994).

72. Quotes in this paragraph are from Mayer, *The Changing American Mind*, p. 75.

73. James MacGregor Burns et al., *Government by the People*, 15th ed. (Englewood Cliffs, NJ: Prentice-Hall, 1993), p. 196.

74. William S. Maddox and Stuart A. Lilie, *Beyond Liberal and Conservative: Reassessing the Political Spectrum* (Washington, DC: Cato Institute, 1984), p. 4.

75. Times Mirror Center for The People & The Press, *The People, The Press, and Politics* (Reading, MA: Addison-Wesley, 1988).

76. Maddox and Lilie, *Beyond Liberal and Conservative*, p. 4.

77. Burns et al., *Government by the People*, p. 203.

78. For good historical overviews of U.S. political ideologies, see Maddox and Lilie, *Beyond Liberal and Conservative;* Robert E. Lane, *Political Ideology* (New York: Free Press, 1962); Leon P. Baradat, *Political Ideologies: Their Origins and Impact*, 4th ed. (Englewood Cliffs, NJ: Prentice-Hall, 1991); Kenneth M. Dolbeare, *American Ideologies Today* (New York: Random House, 1988); Louis Hartz, *The Liberal Tradition in America* (New York: Harcourt Brace, 1955); George H. Nash, *The Conservative Intellectual Movement in America Since 1945* (New York: Basic Books, 1976); Peter Seinfels, *The Neoconservatives* (New York: Simon and Schuster, 1979); Irving Howe, *Socialism and America* (New York: Harcourt, 1985); Michael Harrington, *Socialism: Past and Future* (New York: Arcade, 1989); Lloyd Free and Hadley Cantril, *The Political Belief of Americans* (New York: Simon and Schuster, 1968); E. J. Dionne, *Why Americans Hate Politics* (New York: Simon and Schuster, 1991); Linda L.M. Bennett and Stephen Earl Bennett, *Living with Leviathan* (Lawrence: University of Kansas Press, 1990); and Theodore J. Lowi, *The End of Liberalism*, 2nd ed. (New York: W. W. Norton, 1979).

79. For a concise overview of this debate, see John P. Robinson and John A. Fleischman, "The Polls: Ideological Identification—Trends and Interpretations of the Liberal-Conservative Balance," *Public Opinion Quarterly* 52 (Spring 1988), pp. 134–145. Works forming the basis for the debate include Philip E. Converse, "The Nature of Belief Systems in Mass Publics," in David Apter, ed., *Ideology and Discontent* (New York: Free Press, 1964), pp. 202–261; Pamela C. Conover and Stanley Feldman, "The Origin and Meaning of Liberal/Conservative Self-Identification," *American Journal of Political Science*

25 (November 1981), pp. 617–645; Angus Campbell et al., *The American Voter* (New York: John Wiley, 1960); Norman H. Nie, Sidney Verba, and John R. Petrocik, *The Changing American Voter* (Cambridge, MA: Harvard University Press, 1976); John L. Sullivan, James E. Pierson, and George E. Marcus, "Ideological Constraint in the Mass Public: A Methodological Critique and Some New Findings," *American Journal of Political Science* 22 (May 1978), pp. 233–249; Eric R.A.N. Smith, *The Unchanging American Voter* (Berkeley: University of California Press, 1989); Thomas R. Palfrey and Keith T. Poole, "The Relationship Between Information, Ideology, and Voting Behavior," *American Journal of Political Science* 31 (August 1987), pp. 511–530; Kim Quaile Hill and Jan Leighley, "Party Ideology, Organization, and Competitiveness as Mobilizing Forces in Gubernatorial Elections," *American Journal of Political Science* 37 (November 1993), pp. 1158–1178; Norman R. Luttbeg and Michael M. Gant, "The Failure of Liberal/Conservative Ideology as a Cognitive Structure," *Public Opinion Quarterly* 49 (Spring 1985), pp. 80–93; Ruth C. Hamill and Milton Lodge, "Cognitive Consequences of Political Sophistication," in Richard R. Lau and David O. Sears, eds., *Political Cognition* (Hillsdale, NJ: Lawrence Erlbaum, 1986), pp. 69–93; John D. Holm and John P. Robinson, "Ideological Identification and the American Voter," *Public Opinion Quarterly* 42 (Summer 1978), pp. 235–246; William G. Jacoby, "Levels of Conceptualization and Reliance on the Liberal-Conservative Continuum," *Journal of Politics* 48 (May 1986), pp. 423–432; William G. Jacoby, "Ideological Identification and Issue Attitudes," *American Journal of Political Science* 35 (February 1991), pp. 178–205; Robert C. Luskin, "Measuring Political Sophistication," *American Journal of Political Science* 31 (November 1987), pp. 856–899; W. Russell Neuman, *The Paradox of Mass Politics: Knowledge and Opinion in the American Electorate* (Cambridge, MA: Harvard University Press, 1986); Carol A. Cassel, "Issues in Measurement: The 'Levels of Conceptualization' Index of Ideological Sophistication," *American Journal of Political Science* 28 (May 1984), pp. 418–429; Paul R. Hagner and John C. Pierce, "Correlative Characteristics of the Levels of Conceptualization in the American Public, 1956–1976," *Journal of Politics* 44 (August 1982), pp. 779–807; James A. Stimson, "Belief Systems: Constraint, Complexity, and the 1972 Election," *American Journal of Political Science* 19 (August 1975), pp. 393–417; and Mikel L. Wyckoff, "Issues of Measuring Ideological Sophistication: Level of Conceptualization, Attitudinal Consistency, and Attitudinal Stability," *Political Behavior* 9, no. 3 (1987), pp. 193–224.

80. The term *ideologue* is from Burns et al., *Government by the People*.

81. A July 1994 survey by the Times Mirror Center for The People & The Press showed that more Americans labeled themselves as moderates (or nonideologues) than as conservatives or liberals. Higher proportions of the youngest cohorts continued to label themselves as moderates (42.2 percent), whereas higher proportions of those 65 and older labeled themselves as conservatives (44.8 percent). Among those who labeled themselves moderates, the age-group breakdowns were: 18 to 29, 42.2 percent; 30 to 49, 40.9 percent; 50 to 64, 35.9 percent; and 65 and over, 35.3 percent. The age-group breakdowns for those who labeled themselves conservative were: 18 to 29, 28.1 percent; 30 to 49, 38.6 percent; 50 to 64, 47.8 percent; and 65 and over, 44.8 percent. Among those who identified themselves as liberals, the age breaks were: 18 to 29, 28.3 percent; 30 to 49, 18.5 percent; 50 to 64, 14.2 percent; and 65 and over, 14.8 percent. Results were based on a telephone survey of a nationally representative sample of 3,800 adults 18 and older living within the continental United States, conducted July 12–27, 1994.

82. Jacobs, "Aging and Politics," p. 358.

83. See Hudson and Strate, "Aging and Political Systems," in Binstock and Shanas, eds., *Handbook of Aging and the Social Sciences*, pp. 554–585; Jacobs, "Aging and Politics"; John B. Williamson, Linda Evans, and Lawrence A. Powell, *The Politics of Aging: Power and Policy* (Springfield, IL: Charles C. Thomas Publisher, 1982), chapter 5.

84. Williamson, Evans, and Powell, *The Politics of Aging*, pp. 106–107.

85. Michael Corbett, "Trends Among the Young: Political Issues and Identification, 1972–1991," *Southeastern Political Review* 22, no. 2 (June 1994), pp. 223–242.

86. The age-group breakdowns of respondents agreeing that a candidate's ideology is not very important to them were: 18- to 29-year-olds, 64.6 percent; 30- to 49-year-olds, 64.5 percent; 50- to 64-year-olds, 59.2 percent; and 65 and older, 62.3 percent. Based on a Times Mirror Center for The People & The Press telephone survey of a nationally representative sample of 3,004 adults, conducted May 1–31, 1990.

87. Burns et al., *Government by the People,* p. 206.

88. R. Steven Daniels, "Aging, Ideological Identification, and Issue Consistency," paper presented at the annual meeting of the American Political Science Association, Chicago, September 3–6, 1992.

89. For an excellent study of Americans' opinions toward big government, see Bennett and Bennett, *Living with Leviathan.*

90. U.S. Advisory Commission on Intergovernmental Relations, *Changing Public Attitudes on Governments and Taxes 1989,* p. 24.

91. The age-extreme groups differ most on how much more power should be given to local governments. Among the 18- to 24-year-olds, 41 percent think local governments are the most in need of more power, compared to 25 percent of those 65 and over. In general, more of those 65 and over favor giving *no* level of government more power (30 percent) than do the 18- to 24-year-olds, (14 percent).

CHAPTER 6

1. Benjamin I. Page and Robert Y. Shapiro, *The Rational Public: Fifty Years of Trends in Americans' Policy Preferences* (Chicago: University of Chicago Press, 1992). For excellent longitudinal looks at shifts in U.S. public opinion, see also William G. Mayer, *The Changing American Mind: How and Why American Public Opinion Changed Between 1960 and 1988* (Ann Arbor: The University of Michigan Press, 1992), and Tom W. Smith, "The Polls: America's Most Important Problems—Part I—National and International," *Public Opinion Quarterly* 49 (Summer 1985), pp. 264–274.

2. Smith, "The Polls: America's Most Important Problems," pp. 265–266.

3. Page and Shapiro, *The Rational Public,* p. 40.

4. Times Mirror Center for The People & The Press, *America's Place in the World: An Investigation of the Attitudes of American Opinion Leaders and the American Public About International Affairs* (Washington, DC: Times Mirror, November 1993).

5. Ken Dychtwald, quoted in "The Baby Boomers' Dilemma," *St. Petersburg Times,* March 30, 1993.

6. Donald Fowles, U.S. Administration on Aging, quoted in "Elderly Become Force for Change in America," *St. Petersburg Times,* January 15, 1992.

7. Christine L. Day, *What Older Americans Think* (Princeton: Princeton University Press, 1990), p. 41.

8. James A. Michener, "After the War: The Victories at Home," *Newsweek,* January 11, 1993.

9. Michael Corbett, *American Public Opinion* (New York: Longman, 1990), p. 252.

10. Ibid., pp. 255–256.

11. Michael Corbett, "Trends Among the Young: Political Issues and Identifications, 1972–1991," *Southeastern Political Review* 22, no. 2 (June 1994), pp. 223–242.

12. Robert Lukefahr, quoted in "Oh, Grow Up," *The Economist,* December 16, 1992–January 8, 1993.

13. Ian Williams, "Trash That Baby Boom," *Washington Post Magazine,* January 2, 1994.

14. Page and Shapiro, *The Rational Public,* pp. 129–131.

15. For those believing the major responsibility for health care insurance lies with individuals and their families, the age-group breakdowns were: 18 to 29, 20.9 percent; 30 to 49, 28.8 percent; 50 to 59, 35.9 percent; and 60 and over, 42.1 percent. Among those believing government has the major responsibility, the breaks were: 18 to 29, 43.5 percent; 30 to 49, 36.2 percent; 50 to 59, 35.1 percent; and 60 and over, 24. 3 percent. Results based on a Times Mirror Center for The People & The Press telephone survey of a nationally representative sample of 1,012 adults 18 years of age or older, conducted March 16–21, 1994.

16. Allen Schick, "Health Policy: Spending More and Protecting Less," in Marion Ein Lewin and Sean Sullivan, eds., *The Care of Tomorrow's Elderly* (Washington, DC: American Enterprise Institute for Public Policy Research, 1989), pp. 29–52.

17. Times Mirror Center for The People & The Press telephone survey of a nationally representative sample of 1,011 adults 18 years of age or older, conducted April 1–4, 1993.

18. Ibid.

19. Lawrence R. Jacobs and Robert Y. Shapiro, "The Conventional Wisdom That Portrays Americans as Narrow Individualists Is Myopic," *The Public Perspective* 4 (May-June 1993), p. 22.

20. Times Mirror Center for The People & The Press telephone survey of a nationally representative sample of 1,011 adults 18 and over, conducted April 1–4, 1993.

21. Ibid. The specific percentages for each problem among this age-group were: "the possibility of paying the cost of long-term care in a nursing home for you or a member of your family," 70.3 percent; "the possibility you might lose your insurance if you change jobs," 68.9 percent; "paying the cost of a major illness," 67 percent; and "the possibility your employer may cut back on your health care benefits and/or make you pay a larger share of the costs," 61.4 percent.

22. See Carroll L. Estes, James H. Swan, and Associates, *The Long Term Care Crisis: Elders Trapped in the No-Care Zone* (Newbury Park, CA: Sage 1993).

23. Patricia Braus, "When Mom Needs Help," *American Demographics* 16 (March 1994), pp. 38–47.

24. Times Mirror Center for The People & The Press telephone survey of a nationally representative sample of 1,012 adults 18 years of age or older, conducted March 16–21, 1994, and a sample of 1,011 adults 18 years of age or older, conducted April 1–4, 1993. On the issue of reducing the paperwork the age-group breaks of those favoring were: 18 to 29, 37.9 percent; 30 to 49, 55 percent; 50 to 64, 65.3 percent; and 65 and over, 63.4 percent—1993 survey. On the issue of making long-term nursing care more affordable, the age-group breaks were: 18 to 29, 42.4 percent; 30 to 49, 50.2 percent; 50 to 64, 59.3 percent; and 65 and over, 55.2 percent—1994 data. There was more consensus on the universal care issue. Among those favoring that as a top priority issue, the age-group breaks were: 18 to 29, 55.2 percent; 30 to 49, 48.2 percent; 50 to 64, 50.6 percent; and 65 and over, 53 percent—1994 survey.

25. Ibid. The age-group breaks on the preventive care priority were: 18 to 29, 49.1 percent; 30 to 49, 64.7 percent; 50 to 64, 59.3 percent; and 65 and over, 57.3 percent—April 1993 survey.

26. Jacobs and Shapiro, "The Conventional Wisdom That Portrays Americans as Narrow Individualists Is Myopic," p. 25.

27. Times Mirror Center for The People & The Press, *The Public, Their Doctors, and Health Care Reform* (Washington, DC: Times Mirror, April 14, 1993).

28. Times Mirror Center for The People & The Press, *Times Mirror News Interest Index, January 1994* (Washington, DC: Times Mirror, 1994); survey conducted January 27–30, 1994, of a nationally representative sample of 1,207 adults 18 years of age and older.

29. Times Mirror Center for The People & The Press telephone survey of a nationally representative sample of 1,011 adults 18 and over, conducted April 1–4, 1993.

30. *The American Enterprise* 5 (March-April 1994), p. 84.

31. The age-group breakdowns on this "government" response were: 18 to 29, 65.9 percent; 30 to 49, 69 percent; 50 to 64, 64.9 percent; and 65 and over, 55.4 percent. Results based on a Times Mirror Center for The People & The Press telephone survey of a nationally representative sample of 1,529 adults 18 years of age or older, conducted September 24–27, 1993.

32. The elderly are somewhat more opposed to anti–substance abuse government intervention programs than the other age-groups.

33. For an excellent analysis of trends in teenage smoking, see J. Howard Beales, "Teenage Smoking: Fact and Fiction," *The American Enterprise* 5 (March-April 1994), pp. 20–25.

34. An April 14–19, 1993, survey conducted by Marttila & Kiley for the American Cancer Society asked: "I am going to mention some arguments that have been raised against the proposal to increase the federal tax on cigarettes by two dollars. Please listen to each statement I read and tell me whether you consider it to be a very convincing, somewhat convincing, not very convincing, or not at all convincing argument against increasing the cigarette tax." Fifty-nine percent identified the following statement as a convincing argument: "The government should not interfere with the right of individuals to make their own choices, and that includes the choice of smokers to use tobacco. We should not penalize people for making these choices"; *The American Enterprise* 5 (March-April 1994), p. 84.

35. This skepticism is particularly evident with regard to drug abuse treatment programs. See Robert Apsler, "Is Drug Abuse Treatment Effective?" *The American Enterprise* 5 (March-April 1994), pp. 46–53.

36. Corbett, *American Public Opinion*, p. 169. For a good review of the legal dimensions of this issue, see Henry R. Glick, "The Impact of Permissive Judicial Policy: The U.S. Supreme Court and the Right to Die," *Political Research Quarterly* 47 (March 1994), pp. 207–222.

37. *The American Enterprise* 5 (March-April 1994), p. 84.

38. Jack A. Meyer and Marilyn Moon, "Health Care Spending on Children and the Elderly," in John L. Palmer, Timothy Smeeding, and Barbara Boyle Torrey, eds., *The Vulnerable* (Washington, DC: Urban Institute Press, 1988), pp. 171–200.

39. Times Mirror Center for The People & The Press survey of a nationally representative sample of 3,021 adults 18 years of age or older, conducted May 13–22, 1988.

40. Ron Faucheux, "The Politics of Crime," *Campaigns & Elections* 15 (March 1994), pp. 30–34.

41. Mayer, *The Changing American Mind*, p. 263.

42. Page and Shapiro, *The Rational Public*, p. 91.

43. Ibid.

44. Times Mirror Center for The People & The Press surveys of a nationally representative sample of adults 18 years of age and older, conducted April 25–May 10, 1987 (n = 4,244), and May 1–31, 1990 (n = 3,004).

45. Ibid., 1987 survey.

46. Times Mirror Center for The People & The Press telephone survey of a nationally representative sample of 1,516 adults 18 years of age or older, conducted February 20–23, 1993. The age breakdowns of those who said TV violence bothered them a considerable amount were: 18 to 29, 34.7 percent; 30 to 49, 47.5 percent; 50 to 64, 52.3 percent; and 65 and over, 55 percent. The age-group breakdowns of those who feel TV movie violence is a major cause of the breakdown of law and order were: 18 to 29, 26.7 percent; 30 to 49, 34.6 percent; 50 to 64, 50.1 percent; and 65 and over, 57.6 percent.

47. Ibid.

48. Seventy-four percent of those younger than 30 are in the heavy consuming category, compared to 50 percent of the 30- to 49-year-olds and only 20 percent of those 50 and older; see Times Mirror Center for The People & The Press, *TV Violence: More Objectionable in Entertainment Than in Newscasts* (Washington, DC: Times Mirror, March 24, 1993).

49. U.S. Department of Commerce, *Statistical Abstract of the United States 1993* (Washington, DC: U.S. Government Printing Office, 1993), p. 199.

50. The age breakdowns of those willing to accept more limits on their right to own guns for sport or personal protection were: 18 to 29, 65 percent; 30 to 49, 55.1 percent; 50 to 64, 40.1 percent; and 65 and over, 39.8 percent. Results based on a Times Mirror Center for The People & The Press telephone survey of a nationally representative sample of 992 adults 18 years of age or older, conducted March 16–21, 1994.

51. Page and Shapiro, *The Rational Public*, p. 94.

52. Among those 65 and over, 48.6 percent said that controlling guns is more important than protecting Americans' right to own guns; 35.1 percent felt the opposite, and the remainder weren't sure. Results based on a Times Mirror Center for The People & The Press telephone survey of a nationally representative sample of 1,479 adults 18 years of age or older, conducted December 2–5, 1993.

53. Ibid. The age breakdowns of those who opposed a law banning the sale of handguns were: 18 to 29, 57.4 percent; 30 to 49, 57.6 percent; 50 to 64, 59.6 percent; and 65 and over, 45 percent.

54. Gerald F. Seib, "Americans Feel Families and Values Are Eroding but They Disagree over the Causes and the Solutions," *Wall Street Journal*, June 11, 1993, p. A12.

55. Ibid.

56. Ibid.

57. Page and Shapiro, *The Rational Public*, p. 105.

58. Survey by Voter/Consumer Research for the Family Research Council, September 1993, reported in *The American Enterprise* 5 (March-April 1994), p. 84.

59. Corbett, *American Public Opinion*, p. 165.

60. Mayer, *The Changing American Mind*, p. 165.

61. *Wall Street Journal*, June 11, 1993, p. A12.

62. Times Mirror Center for The People & The Press telephone survey of a nationally representative sample of 1,507 adults 18 years or age or older, conducted May 18–24, 1993.

63. Times Mirror Center for The People & The Press telephone survey of a nationally representative sample of 3,517 adults 18 years of age or older, conducted May 25–June 10, 1992. Comparable figures for those 30 to 49 years of age were 31.1 percent; for those 50 to 64, 41.8 percent.

64. Page and Shapiro, *The Rational Public,* pp. 99–100.

65. For example, on the question of whether "school boards ought to have the right to fire teachers who are known homosexuals," the age-group breakdowns of those who agreed were: 18 to 29, 31.4 percent; 30 to 49, 37 percent; 50 to 64, 47 percent; and 65 and over, 49.3 percent. Results based on Times Mirror Center for The People & The Press telephone survey of a nationally representative sample of 3,517 adults 18 years of age or older, conducted May 25–June 10, 1992.

66. The age-group breakdowns of those expressing support for President Clinton's decision to ease the ban on homosexuals in the armed forces were: 18 to 29, 46.9 percent; 30 to 49, 37.2 percent; 50 to 64, 29.8 percent; and 65 and over, 17.1 percent. Results based on a Times Mirror Center for The People & The Press telephone survey of a nationally representative sample of 1,507 adults 18 or over, conducted May 18–24, 1993.

67. For an excellent overview of this topic, see David C. Leege and Lyman A. Kellstedt, eds., *Rediscovering the Religious Factor in American Politics* (Armonk, NY: M. E. Sharpe, 1993); Benton Johnson, "The Denominations: The Changing Map of Religious America," *The Public Perspective* 4 (March-April 1993), pp. 3–6; "Religious Ties and Partisan Preference," *The Public Perspective* 4 (March-April 1993), pp. 8–9; Ted Jelen and Clyde Wilcox, "The Christian Right in the 1990s," *The Public Perspective* 4 (March-April 1993), pp. 10–12; and Geoff Garin, "The Religious Factor in American Politics," *The Public Perspective* 5 (September-October 1994), pp. 17–18.

68. The age-group breakdowns of those saying "prayer is an important part of my daily life" were: 18 to 29, 69.2 percent; 30 to 49, 76.4 percent; 50 to 64, 79.5 percent; and 65 and over, 85.9 percent. Results based on a Times Mirror Center for The People & The Press face-to-face survey of a nationally representative sample of 3,004 adults 18 years of age or older, conducted May 1–31, 1990. According to that survey, support for the other religious attitudes exceeded 75 percent and varied little across age-groups.

69. William Booth, "Longing for Values Drives School Prayer Crusade," *Washington Post,* April 1, 1994, pp. A1, A4.

70. Ibid.

71. Ibid.

72. A survey of those who favor a constitutional amendment to permit prayer in the public schools showed that the idea was favored by 61.7 percent of those 18 to 29, 66.7 percent of those 30 to 49, 79 percent of those 50 to 64, and 74.2 percent of those 65 and over. Results based on a Times Mirror Center for The People & The Press telephone survey of a nationally representative sample of 1,507 adults 18 years of age or older, conducted May 18–24, 1993.

73. Corbett, *American Public Opinion,* p. 168.

74. Times Mirror Center for The People & The Press telephone survey of a nationally representative sample of 1,516 adults 18 years of age or older, conducted February 20–23, 1993. The age-group breakdowns of those who said the amount of sex on TV bothers them more than the amount of violence were: 18 to 29, 32.5 percent; 30 to 49, 26.7 percent; 50 to 64, 33.9 percent; and 65 and over, 30.9 percent.

75. *Wall Street Journal,* June 11, 1993, p. A12.

76. Times Mirror Center for The People & The Press face-to-face survey of a nationally representative sample of 3,004 adults 18 years of age or older, conducted May 1–31, 1990.

77. The age-group breakdowns of those who agreed that "too many children are being raised in day care centers these days" were: 18 to 29, 23.5 percent; 30 to 49, 26.9 percent; 50 to 64, 31.2 percent; and 65 and over, 45.8 percent. Results based on a Times Mirror Center for The People & The Press face-to-face survey of a nationally representative sample of 3,004 adults 18 years of age or older, conducted May 1–31, 1990.

78. *Wall Street Journal,* June 11, 1993, p. A12.

79. Corbett, *American Public Opinion*, p. 175.

80. Excellent historical overviews of these surveys can be found in Page and Shapiro, *The Rational Public;* Mayer, *The Changing American Mind;* and Corbett, *American Public Opinion.*

81. Page and Shapiro, *The Rational Public,* p. 68.

82. The comparable breakdown for those 30 to 49 was 15 percent; for those 50 to 64, 21 percent. Results based on a Times Mirror Center for The People & The Press telephone survey of a nationally representative sample of 1,507 adults 18 years of age or older, conducted May 18–24, 1993.

83. Mayer, *The Changing American Mind,* p. 24.

84. For an excellent discussion of this perspective, see Paul M. Sniderman and Thomas Piazza, *The Scar of Race* (Cambridge, MA: Belknap Press of Harvard University Press, 1993).

85. *The American Enterprise* 5 (March-April, 1994), p. 84.

86. Various surveys by the Times Mirror Center for The People & The Press, conducted between 1987 and 1993. It should be noted that the support for this position eroded across all age-groups between 1987 and 1993 but most notably among those 30 and older (a drop in the 10 to 15 percent range). The 1993 age-group breakdowns of those who agreed that it is the "responsibility of government to take care of people who can't take care of themselves" were: 18 to 29, 69.8 percent; 30 to 49, 59.3 percent; 50 to 64, 58.9 percent; and 65 and over, 60.6 percent. The 1992 age-group breakdowns of those who believed "government should guarantee every citizen enough to eat and a place to sleep" were: 18 to 29, 71.5 percent; 30 to 49, 67.8 percent; 50 to 64, 58.4 percent; and 65 and over, 60.3 percent.

87. Corbett, *American Public Opinion*, p. 154.

88. For a detailed description of federal social welfare programs targeted at the elderly, see Bennett M. Rich and Martha Baum, *The Aging: A Guide to Public Policy* (Pittsburgh: University of Pittsburgh Press, 1984); and Sheila R. Zedlewski et al., *The Needs of the Elderly in the 21st Century* (Washington, DC: Urban Institute Press, 1990).

89. Corbett, *American Public Opinion*, p. 154.

90. The percent declined from 71.8 percent in May 1987 to 69.8 percent in 1993. In contrast, the drop among those 65 and over was from 73.4 percent to 60.6 percent, according to surveys by the Times Mirror Center for The People & The Press.

91. By 1993, the age-group breakdowns of those who agreed that "the government should help more needy people even if it means going deeper in debt" were: 18 to 29, 54 percent; 30 to 49, 39.7 percent; 50 to 64, 42.1 percent; and 65 and over, 37.6 percent. Results based on a Times Mirror Center for The People & The Press telephone survey of a nationally representative sample of 1,507 adults 18 years of age or older, conducted May 18–24, 1993.

92. The age-group breakdowns for those who thought the "current welfare system makes able-bodied people too dependent on government aid" were: 18 to 29, 74.9 percent; 30 to 49, 73.4 percent; 50 to 64, 75.9 percent; and 65 and over, 79 percent. Results based on a Times Mirror Center for The People & The Press telephone survey of a nationally representative sample of 992 adults 18 years of age or older, conducted March 16–21, 1994.

93. Survey by Yankelovich Clancy Shulman for *Time* and CNN, conducted May 13–14, 1992.

94. Ibid.

95. For an excellent account of the difficulties of implementing workfare, see Richard P. Nathan, *Turning Promises into Performance: The Management Challenge of Implementing Workfare* (New York: Columbia University Press, 1993).

96. For a good analysis of the child care problem, see Sandra L. Hofferth et al., *National Child Care Survey 1990* (Washington, DC: Urban Institute Press, 1991).

97. All responses were reported in *The American Enterprise* 4 (September-October 1993), pp. 86–87.

98. Harold W. Stanley and Richard G. Niemi, *Vital Statistics on American Politics*, 4th ed. (Washington, DC: CQ Press, 1994), p. 343.

99. Mayer, *The Changing American Mind,* p. 64.

100. Page and Shapiro, *The Rational Public,* pp. 54–56.

101. Times Mirror Center for The People & The Press, *America's Place in the New World: An Investigation of the Attitudes of American Influentials and the American Public on International Policies* (Washington, DC: Times Mirror, November, 1993), p. 4. The study was based on a telephone survey of a nationally representative sample of 2,000 adults 18 years or older, conducted September 9–15, 1993.

102. A July 1994 survey showed nearly two-thirds of all age-groups agreed that "immigrants today are a burden on our country because they take our jobs, housing, and health care": 18 to 29, 60.8 percent; 30 to 49, 63.1 percent; 50 to 64, 66.3 percent; and 65 and over, 62.6 percent. Results based on a Times Mirror Center for The People & The Press telephone survey of a nationally representative sample of 3,800 adults 18 years of age or older living in the continental United States, conducted July 12–27, 1994.

103. Times Mirror Center for The People & The Press telephone survey of a nationally representative sample of 2,000 adults 18 years of age or older, conducted September 9–15, 1993.

104. Ibid. The age-group breakdowns on this question were: 18 to 29, 75 percent; 30 to 49, 64 percent; 50 to 64, 57 percent; and 65 and older, 55 percent.

105. By 1993, the age-group breakdowns of those who said environmental control should be increased even at the expense of jobs were: 18 to 29, 53.9 percent; 30 to 49, 50 percent; 50 to 64, 40.7 percent; and 65 and over, 39.8 percent. Results based on a Times Mirror Center for The People & The Press telephone survey of a nationally representative sample of 1,507 adults 18 and older, conducted May 18–24, 1993. A survey by the Gallup organization for *Newsweek,* conducted July 29–30, 1993, found that 62 percent of those polled believed "immigrants take the jobs of U.S. workers"; 59 percent believed "many immigrants wind up on welfare and raise taxes for Americans." However, the same survey found that 78 percent acknowledged that "many immigrants work hard—often taking jobs that Americans don't want." And 60 percent agreed that "immigrants help improve our country with their different cultures and talents"; reported in *The American Enterprise* 5 (January-February 1994), p. 98.

106. It dropped from 52.4 percent in May 1990 to 39.8 percent in 1993.

107. Times Mirror Center for The People & The Press telephone survey of a nationally representative sample of 2,000 adults 18 years of age or older, conducted September 9–15, 1993.

108. Reported in Corbett, *American Public Opinion,* p. 178.

109. Times Mirror Center for The People & The Press face-to-face survey of a nationally representative sample of 3,004 adults 18 years of age or older, conducted May 1–31, 1990.

110. Times Mirror Center for The People & The Press, *America's Place in the New World,* p. 4. The study was based on a telephone survey of a nationally representative sample of 2,000 adults 18 years or older, conducted September 9–15, 1993.

111. Ibid. The age-group breakdowns were: 18 to 29, 52 percent; 30 to 49, 49 percent; 50 to 64, 47 percent; and 65 and over, 39 percent.

112. Ibid. The age-group breakdowns were: 18 to 29, 44 percent; 30 to 49, 51 percent; 50 to 64, 44 percent; and 65 and over, 36 percent.

113. Ibid. The age-group breakdowns were: 18 to 29, 51 percent; 30 to 49, 39 percent; 50 to 64, 30 percent; and 65 and over, 31 percent.

114. Ibid. The age-group breakdowns were: 18 to 29, 20 percent; 30 to 49, 15 percent; 50 to 64, 25 percent; and 65 and over, 26 percent.

115. Ibid. The age-group breakdowns were: 18 to 29, 14 percent; 30 to 49, 23 percent; 50 to 64, 25 percent; and 65 and over, 27 percent.

116. When asked, "Do you think the United States plays a more important and powerful role as a world leader today compared to 10 years ago, or about as important a role as it did 10 years ago?" the age-group breakdowns for those who said ("a more powerful role") were: 18 to 29, 47 percent; 30 to 49, 37 percent; 50 to 64, 32 percent; and 65 and over, 30 percent. Results based on a Times Mirror Center for The People & The Press telephone survey of a nationally representative sample of 2,000 adults 18 and over, conducted September 9–15, 1993.

117. Ibid. The age-group breakdowns on this response were: 18 to 29, 52 percent; 30 to 49, 54 percent; 50 to 64, 51 percent; and 65 and over, 45 percent.

118. Times Mirror Center for The People & The Press telephone survey of a nationally representative sample of 2,000 adults 18 and over, conducted September 9–15, 1993.

119. For an overview, see Timothy J. Conlan, "Federal, State, or Local? Trends in The Public's Judgment," *The Public Perspective* 4 (January-February 1993), pp. 3–5.

120. Surveys by ABC News/Washington Post, 1984 and February 1993; reported in *The American Enterprise* 4 (March-April 1993), p. 90.

121. Times Mirror Center for The People & The Press telephone survey of a nationally representative sample of 1,507 adults 18 years of age and older, conducted May 18–24, 1993. The survey found that 74 percent of those 18 to 29 favored congressional term limits, as did 77 percent of those 30 to 49, 78 percent of those 50 to 64, and 73 percent of those 65 or older.

122. Seymour Martin Lipset and William Schneider, *The Confidence Gap: Business, Labor, and Government in the Public Mind* (New York: Free Press, 1983); Paul A. Abramson, *Political Attitudes in America: Formation and Change* (San Francisco, W. H. Freeman, 1983), chapter 13, pp. 225–238; Suzanne Lee Parker, *The Dynamics of Changing System Support: 1964–1980,* Ph.D. diss., Florida State University, 1986.

123. Corbett, *American Public Opinion,* p. 114, referencing Gabriel A. Almond and Sidney Verba, *The Civic Culture* (Princeton: Princeton University Press, 1963); Donald J. Devine, *The Political Culture of the United States* (Boston: Little, Brown, 1972); William Gamson, *Power and Discontent* (Homewood, IL: Dorsey Press, 1968); and Arthur H. Miller, "Political Issues and Trust in Government: 1960–1970," *American Political Science Review* 68 (September 1974), pp. 951–972.

124. Jack Citrin, "The Political Relevance of Trust in Government," *American Political Science Review* 68 (September 1974), pp. 973–1001.

125. Larry J. Sabato, *Feeding Frenzy* (New York: Free Press, 1991), p. 200.

126. *The American Enterprise* 4 (November-December 1993), p. 95.

127. An index of legislative performance was created by counting the number of "good" or "excellent" evaluations given to the performance of the U.S. Congress and the Florida state legislature. The values of the measure ranged from 0 (no "good"or "excellent" evaluation of either legislative entity) to 2 (a "good" or "excellent" evaluation for both legislative entities). The same technique was used to create an index of executive performance (based on "good" and "excellent" evaluations of the president and governor).

128. Richard F. Fenno, Jr., "If, as Ralph Nader Says, 'Congress Is the Broken Branch,' How Come We Love Our Congressmen So Much?" in Norman Ornstein, ed., *Congress in Change: Evolution and Reform* (New York: Praeger, 1977), pp. 277–287; and Glenn R. Parker, "Why Do Americans Love Their Congressman So Much More Than Their Congress?" *Legislative Studies Quarterly* 4 (February 1979), pp. 53–61.

129. Gamson, *Power and Discontent,* p. 43.

CHAPTER 7

1. One study has concluded that the average tax rate (total taxes paid minus government benefits received) has increased from about 22 percent of income for the generation born in 1900 to about 26 percent for those born in 1920, who are today's elderly. The average tax rate for those born in 1950 has risen to about 31 percent, and for those born since 1970, it is approaching 34 percent. Future generations, it is estimated, will make a 111 percent larger net payment to the government, on average, than those born in 1991 unless there are major changes in government policy. See David Wessel, "Budget Office Using Unlikely Script, Estimates Tax Bite for Yet-to-be-Born," *Wall Street Journal,* January 7, 1993.

2. John Naisbitt, *Megatrends: Ten New Directions Transforming Our Lives* (New York: Times Warner Books, 1982), p. 2.

3. Survey of Florida legislators, which conducted January–February, 1994.

4. Marshall Criser, quoted in Sabrina Miller, "Prevention Better Than Prisons, Group Says," *St. Petersburg Times,* January 10, 1995, p. 4B.

5. For example, the Department of Education's share of appropriated funds (all funds) dropped from 38.8 percent in fiscal year 1985 to 29.06 percent in fiscal year 1994. The Department of Corrections share increased from 2.62 percent to 3.31 percent during the same time period. (Corrections is just one dimension of the program area labeled "criminal justice," which in fiscal year 1995 made up 5.38 percent of all funds in the general appropriations act compared to education's 28.27 percent.) Sources for this information are: Executive Office of the Governor, *Florida's Final Budget Report and Ten-Year Summary of Appropriations Data 1984–85 Through 1993–1994* (Tallahassee: Office of Planning and Budgeting, October 1, 1993), p. 12, and Florida Legislature, *1994 Summary of General Legislation* (Tallahassee: Florida Legislature, June 1994), p. 34.

6. Telephone interview with the executive director of a statewide youth advocacy group, January 17, 1995.

7. Mark Clements, "What We Say About Aging," *Parade Magazine,* December 12, 1993.

8. Fernando M. Torres-Gil, *The New Aging: Politics and Change in America* (New York: Auburn House, 1992), p. 143.

9. For a look at how a hundred or more companies are contributing to education, see Nancy J. Perry, "School Reform," *Fortune,* November 29, 1993.

10. For a brief history of telemedicine efforts in the United States, along with a how-to look at starting a telemedicine system, see Jane Preston, M.D., *The Telemedicine Handbook* (Austin, Texas: Telemedical Interactive Consultative Services, 1993).

11. Quoted in Elliott Carlson and Susan L. Crowley, "The Friedan Mystique," AARP *Bulletin* 33 (September 1992), p. 20.

About the Book and Author

Richard Reeves calls it "the modern American screwing of the young." Others speak in terms of protecting the elders. On Capitol Hill, it's a matter of entitlements and the deficit. In Florida, it's a way of life. But no matter who you are or how you look at it, there is an intergenerational war brewing; this book tells us why.

Young v. Old is the first book to paint a comprehensive picture of the "aging of America" and what that will mean for politics and for policy questions regarding such issues as Social Security, health care, crime, jobs, social welfare, defense, and foreign affairs. Differences between older and younger citizens are examined in light of voting and registration patterns, ideological and party preferences, and varieties of political activism. Contemporary media and new technologies are highlighted both as sources of disparities and as bridges between the generations—how they "watch politics," how they prefer to solve social problems, and how intergenerational understanding could be improved through communication and education.

Throughout the book, Florida is viewed as a microcosm of America's future—there, the ratio between young and old already resembles the probable makeup of the nation if current age trends continue through the year 2000. These changes may have powerful effects on gender and multicultural politics. Replete with original data, Times Mirror Center For The People & The Press poll results, tables, figures, and extensive notes, *Young v. Old* will become the standard source of information about intergenerational politics in a time of transition.

Susan A. MacManus is professor of public administration and political science and past chair of the Department of Government and International Affairs at the University of South Florida–Tampa.

Index